The Moral, Social and Political
Philosophy of the British Idealists

The Moral, Social and Political Philosophy of the British Idealists

Edited by
William Sweet

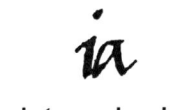

imprint-academic.com

Copyright © Imprint Academic, 2009

The moral rights of the contributors have been asserted.
No part of this publication may be reproduced in any form
without permission, except for the quotation of brief passages
in criticism and discussion.

Published in the UK by Imprint Academic
PO Box 200, Exeter EX5 5YX, UK

Published in the USA by Imprint Academic
Philosophy Documentation Center
PO Box 7147, Charlottesville, VA 22906-7147, USA

ISBN 9 780907 845676

A CIP catalogue record for this book is available from the
British Library and US Library of Congress

Contents

Contributors vii

Preface xi
   William Sweet
     Introduction:
     Idealism, Ethics, and Social and Political Thought 1

1. Avital Simhony
   A Liberal Commitment to the Common Good:
   T.H. Green's Social & Political Morality 31

2. Philip MacEwen
   The Moral and Social Philosophy of Edward Caird. 51

3. Darin R. Nesbitt
   D.G. Ritchie's Ethics. 65

4. Carol A. Keene
   The Interplay of Bradley's Social and Moral Philosophy. 87

5. Stamatoula Panagakou
   The Religious Character of Bosanquet's Moral and Social
   Philosophy 111

6. David Boucher
   Henry Jones: Idealism as a Practical Creed 137

7. Leslie Armour
   Metaphysics, Morals, and Politics:
   McTaggart's Theory of the Good and the Good Life 153

8. Jan Olof Bengtsson
   The Moral, Social, and Political Philosophy of British
   Personal Idealism 175

9. Thom Brooks
   Muirhead, Hetherington, and Mackenzie. 209

10. James Connelly
    Collingwood's Moral Philosophy:
    Character, Duty and Historical Consciousness. 233

11. Efraim Podoksik
    Without Purpose or Unity:
    Moral and Social Life in the Thought of Michael Oakeshott . . 251
12. Elizabeth Trott
    John Watson and the Foundation and Applications of
    Moral Philosophy 269
13. William Sweet
    British Idealism and Ethical Thought in South Africa
    and India 289

Index. 333

Contributors

William Sweet is Professor of Philosophy at St Francis Xavier University (Nova Scotia, Canada). Among his books are *Idealism and Rights* (1997) and *Responses to the Enlightenment: An Exchange on Foundations, Faith, and Community* (with H. Hart, 2009), and he is the editor of several collections of scholarly essays, including *Bernard Bosanquet and the Legacy of British Idealism* (2007), *The Philosophy of History: a re-examination* (2004), *Philosophical Theory and the Universal Declaration of Human Rights* (2003), *Philosophy, Culture and Pluralism* (2002), and *Idealism, Metaphysics, and Community* (2001). He has also published an edition of philosophical lectures and remains of the Anglo-South African idealist, Arthur Ritchie Lord (3 vols., 2006, with Errol E. Harris), an edition of *The Philosophical Theory of the State and Related Essays by Bernard Bosanquet* (with Gerald F. Gaus, 2001), and edited *The Collected Works of Bernard Bosanquet*, 20 volumes (1999) and *Bernard Bosanquet: Essays in Philosophy and Social Policy (1883–1922)*, 3 vols. (2003).

Leslie Armour is Research Professor of Philosophy at the Dominican College of Philosophy and Theology (Ottawa), and Professor Emeritus of Philosophy at the University of Ottawa. He is author of *"Infini Rien": Pascal's Wager and the Human Paradox* (1993), *Being and Idea: Developments of Some Themes in Spinoza and Hegel* (1992); *The Idea of Canada and the Crisis of Community* (1981), *The Faces of Reason: an essay on philosophy and culture in English Canada, 1850-1950* (1981, with Elizabeth Trott), *The Conceptualization of the Inner Life* (1980, with Edward T. Bartlett), *Logic and Reality: an Investigation into the Idea of a Dialectical System* (1972), *The Concept of Truth* (1969), and *The Rational and the Real: an Essay in Metaphysics* (1962). He is a Fellow of the Royal Society of Canada.

Jan Olof Bengtsson teaches history of ideas at Lund University, Sweden. He received his D.Phil. from the University of Oxford in 2003 and is the author of *The Worldview of Personalism: Origins and Early Development* (2006). His work focuses in studies related to personalism in a broad intellectual, cultural, and historical context. He has published a Swedish translation, with an introduction, of Eric Voegelin's *Wissenschaft, Politik und Gnosis*, and articles in Swedish, British, and American journals.

David Boucher is Professorial Fellow and Acting Head of School at the Cardiff School of European Studies at Cardiff University, and adjunct professor of international relations at the University of the Sunshine Coast, Australia. The author of *The Social and Political Thought of R. G. Collingwood* (1989), as well as *A Radical Hegelian: The Political Thought of Henry Jones* (1993) and *British Idealism and Political Theory* (2000) (with Andrew Vincent), he is Director of the Collingwood and British Idealism Centre, Cardiff University, and Executive Editor of *Collingwood and British Idealism Studies*.

Thomas Brooks is Reader in Political and Legal Philosophy at the University of Newcastle, and the Founding Editor of *Journal of Moral Philosophy*, an international journal of moral, political, and legal philosophy. He is the editor of *Rousseau and Law* (2005), *The Legacy of John Rawls* (2005, with Fabian Freyenhagen), and author of articles in the *Journal of Applied Philosophy*, the *Journal of Social Philosophy*, *History of Political Thought*, *Utilitas*, and other journals.

James Connelly is Professor of Politics and Director of the Institute of Applied Ethics at the University of Hull, UK. He has authored several studies, including *Metaphysics, Method and Politics: The Political Philosophy of R.G. Collingwood* (2003), and edited a number of volumes, on the philosophy of R.G. Collingwood (e.g., *An Essay on Philosophical Method by R.G. Collingwood*, (second edition, 2005, with Giuseppina D'Oro) and *Interdisciplinary Perspectives on R. G. Collingwood*, 1996, with David Boucher and Tariq Modood), British idealism (*Aspects of Idealism*, 2009, with S. Panagakou), environmental politics (*Politics and the Environment: from theory to practice*, 1999, with Graham Smith), and on social policy (*Citizens, charters and consumers*, 1993). He serves on the Board of Directors of the Collingwood Society.

Carol A. Keene is Professor Emerita at Southern Illinois University Edwardsville, and a former Dean of its School of Humanities. She is editor of the five volume *F. H. Bradley: Miscellaneous Writings* (1999) and a co-editor of *Responses to F.H. Bradley, A.S. Pringle-Pattison and J.M.E. McTaggart* (2004, with William Sweet).

Philip MacEwen is a graduate of the Royal Conservatory of Music in cello and the University of Toronto in philosophy. He has done graduate studies in religious studies at Westminster Theological Seminary, in philosophy at York University, and in music at the University of London. Currently, he teaches philosophy and humanities at York University and is president of a music company, *Simply Strings*. He has published in the areas of environmental ethics, philosophy of religion, and the history of modern philosophy. He is the editor of E*thics, Metaphysics and Religion in the Thought of F. H. Bradley* (1996).

Darin Nesbitt lectures in Political Science at Douglas College, New Westminster, British Columbia, Canada. He has published in *Polity* and *Paideusis*, and his PhD thesis was entitled "A Liberal Theory of Virtue and the Good: the moral and political thought of T.H. Green" (1997). His principal research interests are on late nineteenth-century British idealism, and examine topics such as individual rights, property rights, ethics, and democracy and education.

Stamatoula Panagakou is Visiting Assistant Professor in the Department of Social and Political Sciences at the University of Cyprus, and has taught at the Universities of York, Durham, Newcastle, and Manchester. She has published in a number of journals, including *The British Journal of Politics & International Relations*, *Collingwood and British Idealism Studies*, the *British Journal for the History of Philosophy*, and *Bradley Studies*, and has co-edited (with James Connelly) a collection of essays on British Idealism, entitled *Aspects of Idealism* (2009). She is a founding member of the British Idealism Specialist Group of the Political Studies Association of the United Kingdom.

Efraim Podoksik is a Lecturer in Political Science at the Hebrew University of Jerusalem. He is the author of *In Defence of Modernity: Vision and Philosophy in Michael Oakeshott* (2003) and has published in the *Journal of the History of Ideas*.

Avital Simhony is Associate Professor in the Department of Political Science at the Arizona State University. She is co-editor of *The New Liberalism: reconciling liberty and community* (2001, with D. Weinstein), and has contributed articles to *History of Political Thought*, *Political Studies*, *Political Theory* and *Utilitas*. Currently, she is completing a book on T.H. Green's liberalism. Her research interests focus on the New Liberalism of T.H. Green and, more broadly, the liberal philosophical tradition with emphasis on the relationship between liberalism and the ideas of positive freedom, self-realization and the common good as well as liberalism and individualism.

Elizabeth Trott is Professor of Philosophy at the Ryerson University in Toronto, Canada. She is co-author (with Leslie Armour) of *The Faces of Reason: An Essay on Philosophy and Culture in English Canada, 1850-1950* (1981), co-editor (with Leslie Armour) of *The Industrial Kingdom Of God* by John Clark Murray (1981), and has published in *The Journal of Aesthetics and Education* and in *Dialogue*, as well as in collections on *Philosophy and Culture* and *Philosophy after F.H. Bradley* (1996) and *The Canadian Encyclopedia*.

Preface

Despite the renewal of scholarly interest in late 19th and early 20th century British idealism, little has been written on its moral philosophy, and nothing at all that covers the range of approaches to moral, social and political philosophy exemplified in the work of that school's major figures. The present volume provides both an introduction to and a survey of work that is not only valuable in its own right, but increasingly relevant to contemporary debates in ethics and political thought.

I would like to record my thanks to a number of individuals, without whom this volume would have been much less than it is. Peter Nicholson, whose scholarly breadth and depth and meticulous attention to detail have long been an example to those working on British idealism, has been an invaluable source of suggestions and support throughout. I would also like to thank the Publisher of Imprint Academic, Keith Sutherland, and the Managing Editor, Anthony Freeman for their interest in, and patience through, what proved to be a very challenging project. I am grateful for the help of Marlo Burks and Heather Carson, who assisted in the copy-editing and in the preparation of the index. I wish to acknowledge as well a number of friends and colleagues for their continuing support and advice — among them, Leslie Armour, David Boucher, James Connelly, Louis Groarke, Paul Groarke, Errol Harris, Bill Mander, Stamatoula Panagakou, and Colin Tyler.

Finally, I wish to express my gratitude to Cambridge University Press for permitting Avital Simhony to contribute, in revised form, her essay, "T.H. Green's Complex Common Good: between liberalism and communitarianism," initially published in Avital Simhony and David Weinstein (eds.), *The New Liberalism: Reconciling Liberty and Community* (Cambridge: Cambridge University Press, 2001), pp. 69–91.

William Sweet
July 31, 2009

William Sweet

Introduction
Idealism, Ethics, and Social and
Political Thought

The British idealists of the late 19th and early 20th centuries are known for their work in metaphysics and logic and, to a significant extent, for their social and political philosophy. Yet there has been relatively little extended study of their moral philosophy.[1] And while idealist moral philosophy had a place alongside utilitarianism, Kantian deontology, and natural rights based ethics in the late 19th century, unlike these latter theories, there is little trace of it in contemporary philosophy.[2]

It has been suggested by some critics that British idealist ethics had little to contribute; W.H. Walsh writes, for example, that even a figure as reputed as F.H. Bradley lacked the "breadth of historical knowledge and depth of historical insight" which Hegel had (Walsh, 1969, p. 73). Some have also suggested that the idealists themselves — particularly Bradley — had, through their analyses of ethics, put an end to ethical theorizing; certainly few wrote much on moral philosophy. And given the character of the debates among some of the British idealists, one might surmise that there is little chance of finding a general constructive ethical view. There are critics who have dismissed the idealist movement as a whole, regard-

---

[1] There are studies of some individual figures—principally Green and, to a lesser extent, Bradley—but there is little on others, and virtually nothing on the movement as a whole. For relatively recent studies on Green's ethics, see, for example, Prichard (1968), Kemp (1972), Wollheim (1975), Thomas (1987), Tyler (1997), Dimova-Cookson (2001), Carter (2003), and Brink (2003); on Bradley, see, for example, MacNiven (1987), MacEwan (1993), Crossley (1996), and Sweet (2000). The few studies on the moral philosophy of other authors in the British idealist tradition, or on related themes in the movement as a whole, include Hodgson (1901-2), Muirhead (1928), Stocks et al. (1928), Pucelle (1955), Milne (1962), LeChevalier (1963), Walsh (1969), Crossley (1977), Hemingway (1979), and Nicholson (1990).

[2] There has been some discussion recently of the theory of "moral perfectionism", and several of the British idealists (along with a number of authors, stretching back to Plato) have been described as "perfectionists" (though in a way that is rather critical of idealism as a whole). See, for example, Hurka (1996) and Brink (2003). Whether this captures a sufficient range of idealist thinking on ethics is not clear, and this "perfectionism" does not have a central or secure place in contemporary moral philosophy.

ing it as an aberrant stage in the history of British philosophy.[3] For these and other reasons, some may conclude that little can or need be said in favour of the moral — and, by extension, the social and political — philosophy of British idealism.

There is, however, reason to be sceptical of at least some of these claims. There was a strong and consistent interest in ethics among the idealists, from Green's *Prolegomena to Ethics*, through Bradley's *Ethical Studies* and Bosanquet's *Some Suggestions in Ethics*, and the various textbooks on ethics by James Seth, J.H. Muirhead and J.S. Mackenzie, to the work of later figures in Britain and beyond — such as John Watson in Canada, R.F.A. Hoernlé in South Africa, and Sarvepalli Radhakrishnan in India. It is also clear that many idealists made significant contributions to social and public policy as well as politics in Britain and much of its empire.

This volume provides a re-examination of the work of some of the major British idealists and those influenced by them in order to see the place and contribution of not only their moral and social philosophy, but the political philosophy that follows from it. It also raises the issue whether, despite the differences among them, one can speak of *a* generic British idealist moral and social philosophy. Such a discussion may also allow one to reflect on the question of why it is that a theory which, in large part, attempted to provide an alternative to ethical theories that remain dominant today, should have become virtually unknown in the late twentieth and twenty-first centuries — and on whether it could, nevertheless, have a bearing on contemporary moral philosophy.

I. The British Idealists

Indebted to Kant and Hegel, but also to a rich heritage of thought rooted in Plato and Aristotle, British idealism seems to stand apart from the major currents of Anglo-American philosophy. The British idealists held the metaphysical view that reality is spiritual or mental, and that ultimately only mind (or "Mind") and its contents are real. Though they held that mind in some way "makes" nature, they denied the view that reality was simply a product of human minds or perceptions, that reality was structured only by (or is simply the sum of the perceptions of) human consciousness, and that we could not know things as independent of consciousness.

Frequently, British idealism has been divided into "absolute" and "personal" idealism. The Absolute idealists insisted that what was real was something they called "the Absolute" — an all-inclusive, comprehensive and coherent unity or whole that was above all categories, free of all

---

[3] See Hill (1975), p. 324: "There is a tendency to look on British idealism as a sort of contradiction, as if idealism was somehow not British. From this point of view, the fifty years or so during which idealism predominated in British philosophy can only be dismissed with regret as an interlude within the more typical empiricist tradition."

dualisms or contradiction, and the *only* thing that was entirely "real" or (to be more precise) entirely "actual". Human consciousness is dependent upon this "whole", and human "realisation" or development is part of the realisation of the Absolute. Absolute idealism is also sometimes described as "objective idealism", as distinct from Berkeleyan subjective idealism. Personal idealists, on the other hand, emphasized the numerical and qualitative distinctness and uniqueness of each person, and held that each self was ultimately independent of every other, never losing its distinctiveness, even when it is assumed into the Absolute (e.g., after death). Many of the personal idealists also argued for the existence of a personal Deity.

Though it has faint antecedents in the Cambridge Platonists of the 1600s, British idealism is a product of the mid-nineteenth century. The early idealists—Benjamin Jowett, but particularly T.H. Green and Edward Caird—sought to respond to the empiricist legacy of David Hume, including the empiricism and the associationism of Jeremy Bentham and J.S. Mill, and reflected in the views of Alexander Bain, George Lewes, and Herbert Spencer. In the generation that followed, which included F.H. Bradley, Bernard Bosanquet, William Wallace, and R.L. Nettleship, but also Henry Jones, D.G. Ritchie, A.S. Pringle-Pattison, John Watson, R.B. Haldane, J.M.E. McTaggart, J.S. Mackenzie, and J.H. Muirhead, one finds a broadening and a deepening of philosophical analysis, but also an increasing diversity in views. By the early twentieth century, one can plausibly speak of a third generation of idealism—of figures such as R.G. Collingwood, A.R. Lord, C.C.J. Webb, H.J.W. Hetherington, and G.R.G. Mure—who, in varying degrees, were greatly influenced by the earlier idealism, but who generally did not consider themselves constrained by it, who sometimes even sought to avoid being labelled as such, and whose emphasis was not to defend the idealism of their predecessors but to engage new views, such as logical empiricism and, later, ordinary language philosophy, and to challenge various versions of individualism. It is particularly in this third generation that disciples of the major thinkers of the second generation moved from Britain to teach and sometimes to preach in the outreaches of the British Empire. Throughout their work, theory was never far from practice, and frequently they wrote on applied ethics, political issues, and social and public policy.

This diversity, both in the evolution of British idealism as a whole and in its various species, attests to its breadth, but also is a sign of the number of challenges to it. How are these challenges reflected in, and how do they bear on, British idealist moral, social, and political philosophy? The authors of the essays in this volume present the moral, social, and political philosophy of the principal figures of the movement, provide a context for the then-contemporary debates, but also serve to identify a number of distinctive themes in idealist ethics and how this ethics may be understood today.

1.1 The first generation

In the first chapter in this volume, Avital Simhony considers one of the principal figures of the "first generation" of British idealism—one who may also be regarded as a precursor of Absolute Idealism—T.H. Green (1836–82). For Green, central to ethics is the common good, and while he never gives a full account of this good, it is what he calls "self-realisation"[4]—the perfection of human character. This common good, Simhony points out, has a complex nature: it is universal, but also distributive (as distinct from collective). Here, Simhony argues, Green is clearly influenced by Kant—exhibiting Kant's conception of the self as an absolute end, but at the same time insisting that this be related to something universal, namely "law". Green, however, blends this Kantianism together with an Aristotelianism and an Hegelianism, so that the self is seen to be mediated through others, that the community (*qua* kingdom of ends) is necessary to the realisation of the self, and that this kingdom of ends is reflected in existing institutions. Thus, the common good involves a "joint realisability"—that is, it is a good realized in individuals and yet is dependent upon others. While there is a common form of the good, i.e., self-realisation or the good life, there is not a single path to this life, and whichever path one chooses requires effort. Simhony concludes that, in Green, there is no fundamental conflict between the social and the individual. In Green's ethics we have, then, a hybrid of deontology and teleology, but his view is not evolutionary, not hedonistic or historicist, and certainly not quietistic.

The other central figure of the first generation of British idealists is Edward Caird (1835–1908). Caird's influence is particularly strong—perhaps in part because he outlived Green by some 25 years. In Chapter 2, Philip MacEwen argues that Caird's moral philosophy is largely a consequence of his "Absolute idealism"—he was influenced by Jowett and his own reading of Kant, Hegel, and the classical Greek philosophers—but also by the work of Auguste Comte. Caird never published a book devoted exclusively to ethics, but MacEwen finds his accounts of religion and epistemology to provide us with indications of his moral theory.[5] To begin with, ethics is the practical side of epistemology, in the sense that the process of knowledge—and hence of ethical knowledge—is one whereby an object is brought "more and more within the net of its own categories, until

---

[4] According to Laurence S. Lockridge, "The OED gives the first use [of the term 'self-realization'] to FH Bradley in 1876"; Lockridge argues that the word was coined by Coleridge, see Lockridge (1977), p. 149. The term is found infrequently in Green—notably, in his *Prolegomena to Ethics* (Green, 1906) § 182, and in an essay "The Word is Nigh Thee", in (Green, 1997, Vol. III, p. 224). Green does, however, talk of the end as the "realisation of human capabilities", see (Green, 1906) § 263, § 337.

[5] Some of Caird's views on moral philosophy may be found in texts published in Tyler, 2008.

it has been made one with the thought that apprehends it."[6] Caird's ethics, then, reflects a principle of coherence. Moreover, Caird understands human beings to be essentially social; the "pure" individual is a false abstraction. Here we see the influence of Comte. But what is central to and distinctive of Caird's account of ethics is that ethics is broadly evolutionary; human consciousness, religion, and morality are all given a developmental account.[7] On what MacEwen calls Caird's "organic view of morality", the moral life is the product of a long odyssey — from understanding the good as external to consciousness, to the good as internalized in subjective consciousness (as in the categorical imperative), to a third stage, where morality is seen from a "religious" point of view, whereby the self attempts to realize the best self. MacEwen concludes that, for Caird, full moral consciousness is religious consciousness, where religion is whatever it is that ultimately sustains the individual.

1.2 The second generation

The "second generation" of British idealists were those who were students in the 1870s and 1880s, once idealism had begun to become established in the universities. In most cases, these men had studied at Oxford, Glasgow, or Edinburgh, and had fallen under the influence of Green or Caird — though others, like J.M.E. McTaggart, came to idealism via a different route.

Perhaps one of the best known — though not necessarily best understood — accounts of idealist ethics is that of F.H. Bradley (1846–1924), and his work had a significant influence on a number of his contemporaries. In Chapter 3, Carol Keene notes that, while most readers focus on Bradley's early *Ethical Studies* — and it was through this work that he had his greatest impact on idealist ethical thought — Bradley's views underwent changes over his lifetime.

According to Keene, for Bradley, moral philosophy is speculative (i.e., seeks to understand what is), and not practical (i.e., seeks how to determine right and wrong). In *Ethical Studies*, Bradley's aim was not, however, to articulate a system or grand theory of ethics; rather, it was to explore the bases of ethics and raise a number of challenges to leading ethical theories. Nevertheless, *Ethical Studies* does provide a statement of Bradley's positive views. Drawing on Green, but also on Aristotle, Bradley holds that an adequate ethics must have three features: a true conception of the self, a moral psychology, and an appreciation of teleology. First, then, much like Green, Bradley sees the end of morality as self-realisation[8] — and this self is not just the self of one's private wishes and wills, but a social self. Some have concluded that this self can be realized only within the community —

---

6   See MacEwen, this volume, p. 54.
7   See, for example, Caird, 1893.
8   See note 4 above on 'self-realisation.'

i.e., in what Bradley describes as a morality of "my station and its duties" — but Keene emphasizes that this is not Bradley's ultimate view. The self "as a whole" is "the ideal self" — a concrete universal — which is rooted in, but extends beyond, the social. A second key feature of Bradley's ethics, according to Keene's reading, is that it has a moral psychology, specifically one that focuses on the role of the will, and which recognises how morality depends on the tension between "is" and "ought". The will is important for Bradley, for "whatever comes under the will is in the moral sphere."[9] The will to realize the self is one that involves a struggle against one's own desires and, possibly, even one's society. Finally, Keene points out, there is a teleology in Bradley's ethics — a quest for a harmonious realisation of the self. Such a process of realisation, by its very nature, supersedes the tensions within morality between "is" and "ought" as well as the demands of "one's station", to move one to "ideal morality" and, eventually, to what Bradley calls "religion".

Bradley is conscious of the historical character of human nature and its development, and the essential place of society in moral growth. He also recognises that ethics be open to experience and change. It is the *phronimos* — not merely the person of experience, but the philosopher — who can discern the moral thing to do when duties or principles conflict. But despite this awareness of contingency in ethics, Bradley would insist that his position is not ultimately historicist or relativistic.

D.G. Ritchie (1853–1903) was one of Bradley's younger contemporaries. After studies in Edinburgh, Ritchie came to Balliol, Oxford, where he studied under Jowett and, principally, Green. But as Darren Nesbitt points out in Chapter 4, Ritchie's views went beyond those of his teachers. Ritchie saw ethics as a science[10] — as descriptive, historical, systematized, and explanatory knowledge. It was the science of human conduct in society. Ritchie attempted, then, to bring together utilitarianism (with its emphasis on social well-being), evolutionary theory (because, unlike Green, he thought it provided a scientific and rigorous account of human progress), social organicism (which he thought best expressed the relations between part and whole), and an account of the social nature of the self and of the role of social institutions (inspired by Green and, more generally, Plato and Aristotle). The result was an ethical theory that Nesbitt calls "an individualized ethical collectivism."[11]

For Ritchie, the ethical end or common good is self-development or self-realisation. It is a self-realisation, however, that operates with a

---

9   "Whatever has been brought under the control of the will, it is not too much to say, has been brought into the sphere of morality" Bradley (1927), p. 217.
10 See Ritchie, (1905), p. 282: "Ethics is the science of man as capable of realizing an ideal in conduct." This was unlike Green who saw science as naturalistic and, as such, reducing human beings to animals. See Green, (1906), § 5.
11 Nesbitt, this volume, p. 67.

"large" conception of the self—both the eternal self, which serves as an ideal, but also the communal self, as the self living in community and which requires the active involvement of each with others. Fundamental to Ritchie's ethics, then, is his understanding of society as "a community of self-interpretation",[12] whose members are moral agents seeking a self-realisation that is possible only in society. Nesbitt notes that Ritchie had a utilitarian conception of the good, but his ethics retained a Kantian influence that emphasized the importance of motive. And while Ritchie had an evolutionary account of self-development, the evolution of the self is not automatic; it requires individual effort. As a result, Nesbitt argues, in Ritchie's ethics we find a strong sense of self, a balance between the social and the individual, but also a teleology of self-realisation.

Another leading figure of the second generation of British idealists, equal in stature to Bradley, is Bernard Bosanquet (1848–1923). One of the most prolific authors of the idealist movement, Bosanquet had a lifelong interest in what we would today call applied ethics and social policy, and (like Henry Jones) much of his writing addressed issues on moral practice and moral education. In Chapter 5, Stamatoula Panagakou reviews Bosanquet's moral and social philosophy, placing it in the context of his account of religion.

Bosanquet wrote little on ethical theory, partly because Bradley's critique of existing moral theories seemed—at least initially—to leave in doubt the possibility of any constructive ethical theorizing,[13] but principally because moral philosophy was unable to provide a complete set of principles for practice.[14] Bosanquet recognized that the fundamental concern of ethics was the development of the individual, and this could be accomplished only through practical moral education and training. Almost all of Bosanquet's moral and social philosophy, as well as his writings on social and public policy, had this practical aim as its focus.

Nevertheless, this applied philosophy had to have a foundation. Panagakou argues that the root and impetus of Bosanquet's social ethics lie in its "spiritual" character. Many of the sources for Bosanquet's moral and social philosophy, Panagakou notes, are texts dealing primarily with religion or metaphysics. This being said, however, Bosanquet did not appeal to an "otherworldly" foundation for ethics, and Panagakou fre-

---

12 See Nesbitt, this volume, p. 74; cf. Ritchie, (1905), p. 249.
13 Bosanquet writes: "At first on reading Bradley's book [*Ethical Studies*] I felt as if blown to the winds" (Muirhead 1935, p. 37). But see Green's letter of 8 July 1876, in which Green wrote that while he "thought some of Bradley's essays" on ethics were "excellent", there was "no reason why [Bosanquet] should not write on the subject, too" (Green, 1997, Vol. 5, pp. 464–5).
14 As William Sweet has argued; see Sweet (1999). Some important work by Bosanquet here is "The Civilization of Christendom," "The Communication of Moral Ideas as a Function of an Ethical Society", "The Antithesis between Individualism and Socialism Philosophically Considered", and "Liberty and Legislation", in Bosanquet (1893); "Character in its Bearing on Social Causation", "Socialism and Natural Selection", and "The Principle of Private Property", in Bosanquet (2003); Bosanquet (1895); and Bosanquet (1919).

quently reminds us that we should not be misled by Bosanquet's use of theological terminology. For example, by the "spiritual", Bosanquet was referring, not to something mystical, but to the relation of one's finite will to one's real will, and the "spiritual world", the world of truth, beauty and goodness, is "the Kingdom of God *on earth*". Yet this does not deny the strong metaphysical character of his ethics. All of reality has a "nisus" to totality or completion, i.e., a distinct teleological character, and moral development involves coherence as well, specifically between a person's self-interested desires and private will and what Bosanquet calls one's real will or "the general will". This development is not, however, automatic. Bosanquet recognizes that finite individuals must take an active role in this process, and that, since it deals with life in the world, ethics needs to be open to the diversity of experience. The end or goal of ethics is self-realisation — the perfection of human personality — but this end is possible only in conjunction with others. Like the idealists before him, then, Bosanquet's concept of the person or self is "social". But he emphasises that relations among consciousnesses — and, hence, society — lie at the "spiritual" level. Understood in this way, according to Panagakou, we see that the key to Bosanquet's moral and social philosophy is what he calls "religion". And so, Bosanquet's conception of the moral end is, more precisely, that of self-*transcendence*, and not simply self-*realisation*.

Though he does not explicitly refer to Bradley, Bosanquet is sympathetic to Bradley's conclusions on the limitations of rule-following in morality; Bosanquet's own view is that the watchword in ethics is "to be adequate to the situation".[15] At the same time, however, he seems more doubtful than Bradley about the capacity of ethical agents, and in the vast majority of cases he would seem to be willing to see morality as simply carrying out one's "station and its duties".

A student of Edward Caird at Glasgow and Caird's successor there as Professor of Moral Philosophy, Henry Jones (1852–1922) was perhaps one of the British idealists most strongly influenced by Hegel. Nevertheless, as David Boucher points out in Chapter 6, Jones spent much of his career concerned with the practical side of ethics. In texts such as *The Working Faith of a Social Reformer* (1910), Jones rejects any dualism between knowledge and reality, and presents a moral and a social philosophy that brings together theory and the practical life. Jones emphasized the value of character and (against strict evolutionists) the importance of self-development, and he insisted, therefore, on the centrality of individual freedom to moral agency. Nevertheless, the moral agent — and, hence, ethics — is "social". Each self "mediates" the social world and, at the same time, is united in consciousness with all free individuals in what Jones calls a "social organism". This "rational unity" is ultimately the Absolute. The resulting ethical

---

15 See Bosanquet, (1919), p. 146.

theory, then, is one that, Boucher says, reflects the one *in* the many. Jones's view, however, is that such a unity does not obliterate, but transcends, difference, and thus there is no fundamental conflict between the individual and the community. Because this unity exists at a "spiritual" level, Jones saw his idealism as religious, though—like Bosanquet—in a sense far from that of orthodox religion. Moreover, because ethics is rooted in experience, it cannot be a closed system. Jones therefore offers, Boucher claims, a moral and social philosophy that is open to novelty and change.

Many of the leading figures in British idealism, such as Bradley, Bosanquet, and Jones, were "absolute idealists"; J.M.E. McTaggart (1866-1925), however, is often considered to be a 'personal idealist'—though many would regard him as holding a view that is rather *sui generis*.[16] McTaggart is certainly among the best known of the idealists, largely for his discussion of time, but little has been written about his moral and social philosophy. In Chapter 7, Leslie Armour points out that McTaggart's ethics is rooted in his understanding of the nature of reality, and that this ethics has a number of distinctive features. Like other idealists, for McTaggart, ethics is practical; it focuses on how to act and participate in the community, but also on how one is to organize one's life. Moreover, the possibility of morality and moral responsibility requires the existence of individual moral agents—and McTaggart was consistently concerned that individuality be recognised and valued. According to Armour, for McTaggart, the universe contains an infinity of substances, each becoming more determinate by entering into relations with other substances. Since each thing is capable of an infinity of relations, is thereby united to others, and is richer for it, so each conscious being is capable of this, is united to others, and is richer as well. McTaggart holds that value lies in consciousness and in the expressed conscious states of sentient beings. The most valuable of conscious states is a "perfect sharing" with all other sentient beings—this is what McTaggart calls "love". On McTaggart's view, the capacity of all for such a perfect sharing shows that all persons are fundamentally equal, but also that moral growth and development require community; there is no basic tension between the community and the individual. Armour concludes, then, that for McTaggart we all share the same reality, we are all equal in value, and we all need to work together in community—and love is the principle that binds us all together. Thus, ethics rests on the existence of a community of an infinite number of sentient beings united by love.

Aside from McTaggart, there were a number of other personal idealists—notably, Andrew Seth Pringle-Pattison (1856-1931), his brother

---

16 Unlike many of the other leading British idealists, McTaggart studied neither at the Scottish universities nor at Oxford. His teacher, James Ward, similarly had no direct connection to Oxford or to the Scottish schools.

James Seth (1860-1924), and Clement C.J. Webb (1865-1954).[17] Though one finds differences in emphasis, focus, and scope in their respective views, Jan Olof Bengtsson argues in Chapter 8 that their positions are also highly complementary, and he holds that one can construct a fairly comprehensive account of the ethics of personal idealism by drawing on all three.

The personal idealists took a strong interest in moral and social thought, emphasizing an ethics of self-realisation. Unlike Green and some of the absolute idealists, the personal idealists saw ethics as a science — a "moral science" — distinct from speculative metaphysics,[18] and the approach they took to ethics was different as well. Responding to enlightenment individualism, they were also deeply concerned by the putative monism of absolute idealism. As Bengtsson points out, personal idealists believed that such views not only undermined the nature and value of individual personality, but the ethics and axiological views associated with them. The personal idealists argued that to see individuals as "adjectival" to what is real, rather than as substantial, was to overlook their significance, to ignore the importance of human freedom, and to undermine divine personality. Ethics, then, had to be not just an ethics of self-realisation, but (in Seth's terminology) "an ethics of personality".[19]

The influence of Kant is strong here, but the personalist idealists emphasized — in a way in which Bengtsson says Kant did not — the distinction between personality and individuality. While individuality has an ontological primacy, to be a person is more than being an individual; persons are social beings as well. The realisation of one's "true self", then, requires activity in the community, without losing sight of one's distinctness and distinctiveness as a person. Since the moral life and self-realisation involve a social context, Pringle-Pattison, for example, reminds us of the importance of service to country. Despite its emphasis on the uniqueness of personality, there is a fundamental compatibility of the individual and the community in personal idealism, and Bengtsson quotes James Seth that "The individual and the social are in reality... two aspects of the one undivided life of virtue, and their unity is discovered with their reduction to the common principle of personality" (Seth, 1921, p. 276). A personal idealist moral and social philosophy, unlike that of Absolute idealism, holds, however, that this common principle or ultimate ground of persons is an Absolute person. Still, what this Absolute person is, and whether its role goes much further than simply to preserve 'persons' against the adjectival account attributed to Absolute idealism, are not clear. For some critics,

---

17 Other personal idealists include William Ritchie Sorley, Hastings Rashdall, and J.R. Illingworth.
18 See Seth, (1921), p. 25. Seth sees ethics as both a natural, descriptive science and a normative science in which ethical judgments are organized into a rational system.
19 Seth describes his view as "Eudaimonism or the ethics of personality" (Seth, 1921, p. 82); cf. Bengtsson (2006), p. 256.

then, other than to insist on retaining the ontological status and value of persons, the ethics of personal idealism does not seem to be all that far from the principles of an Absolute idealism.

Idealist moral, social, and political philosophy had a place in the public realm as well as in the scholarly. Many of the British idealists were engaged in discussions of social and public policy, in the arts and letters, in political affairs, in adult education, and the like. One area in which they had a particular impact—though it has been little discussed—is within universities, through university organization and governance but particularly in the curriculum. In Chapter 9, Thom Brooks reviews the contributions to idealist moral and social philosophy of John Henry Muirhead (1855–1940), John Stuart Mackenzie (1860–1935), and Sir Hector James Wright Hetherington (1888–1965). While all engaged in scholarly work, Hetherington spent most of his career as a university administrator, and Muirhead and Mackenzie wrote influential textbooks in ethics and social philosophy.

Like many of their predecessors, but perhaps more than most, these men were concerned with practical matters. Their public talks and university textbooks reached beyond the academy, and what we find in their work is an ethics and social philosophy that bears on the concerns of a broad audience. While they regarded ethics as a science (i.e., in the sense of being concerned with practical needs and explaining how to act, or as explaining moral judgements within a coherent system), its scope was limited: in Muirhead, for example, ethics deals with standards of right and wrong, and not right and wrong in themselves. While these men differed with one another on certain aspects of their ethics, the substance of their accounts was quite similar. All recognized that ethics requires a foundation, though they held different views on what exactly that foundation was. Moreover, Muirhead (unlike Mackenzie, but also unlike Green) saw ethics as fundamentally distinct from metaphysics. Nevertheless, all were strongly influenced by the Kantian idea of humanity as an end, and also by the duty to develop the self. The "self-realisation" that they advocated reflected the view that individuals are embedded in social contexts and that they can be understood only when seen as members of a community and participating in a common good. All agreed that self-realisation requires the development of all members of the community, and that this involves a coherence of all individual interests according to rational principles. Self-realisation in this sense is, again, key. In the words of J.S. Mackenzie, self-realisation is "the realization of a rational universe" (Mackenzie 1901, p. 295)—and this is fundamental. As Mackenzie adds elsewhere, "To realize a complete humanity, so far as that is at any moment possible, is our only ultimate right and duty" (Mackenzie 1896, p. 431).

Brooks points out that Muirhead, Mackenzie, and Hetherington recognized the particular importance of social institutions in self-realisation.

For Hetherington, individuals contribute to the development of humanity as members of social institutions, and Mackenzie recognized that law gives expression to a moral standard in community, and thereby enables human flourishing. While the precise impact of their views on moral and social philosophy is difficult to gauge, it is worth noting that the texts of Muirhead and Mackenzie remained in print through much of the twentieth century — Mackenzie's going into six different editions — and they long figured on the syllabi of ethics courses in Britain and its dominions.[20]

1.3 A third generation

Idealism in Britain was in decline by the end of the second decade of the twentieth century. The later writings of many of the idealists of the second generation came under sustained criticism not only from within philosophy, but from sociology, psychology, and those involved with social and public policy. Yet the idealist movement did not disappear — it continues to this day[21] — and it had a legacy in a third generation of philosophers, for example, R.G. Collingwood (1889-1943), C.E.M. Joad (1891-1953), A.C. Ewing (1899-1973), G.R.G. Mure (1893-1979), C.A. Campbell (1897-1974), Michael Oakeshott (1901-90), and Dorothy Emmet (1904-2000). Some — such as Joad, Mure, and Campbell — were unapologetic in their idealism, but found themselves isolated in varying degrees. Others, like Emmet, moved beyond it. Collingwood and Oakeshott, however, simply did not wish to be identified with idealism — though it is present through much of their work.

R.G. Collingwood is known best for his philosophy of history and aesthetics, and — to an extent — his political philosophy and metaphysics, but he also wrote extensively on moral philosophy, which influenced both his political philosophy and his views on philosophical method. In Chapter 10, drawing on Collingwood's many — and still unpublished — series of lectures on moral philosophy, James Connelly presents Collingwood's "agent centred ethics of character" and his emphasis on apprehending the specifics of cases — his "particularism". Collingwood's ethics is independent of many of the explicitly metaphysical elements of idealist moral and social philosophy. Nevertheless, a number of characteristics associated with idealism remain. In Collingwood's moral philosophy, there is clearly a Kantian element — with an emphasis on duty and on the will (which is the locus of the goodness of a dutiful act) — but also a teleological element, for the fundamental ethical issue is how one can achieve the end of becom-

---

20 Mackenzie's *A Manual of Ethics* went through six editions, from 1893 to 1929, and was often reprinted, including in 1997 in India. Muirhead's *Elements of Ethics* went through at least four different editions from 1892 to 1932. Another frequently used text was James Seth's *A Study of Ethical Principles*, which reached its 17th edition in 1926.

21 For example, in the work of Errol E. Harris, Nicholas Rescher, Leslie Armour, Timothy Sprigge, and their students.

ing a particular "kind of person".[22] (While Collingwood's ethics contains a general conception of the good, it is simply "what is worthy to be desired" or chosen.) Connelly points out that, for Collingwood, doing one's duty is more than rule following, though it certainly involves this. There is no rigid method, for novelty and change may oblige one to think and rethink what one ought to do; such an ethics, therefore, is "open". What is important is for the moral agent to have a "trained eye" to see the particularities of the situation, to judge, and to act. Ethical action, then, is to respond—thoughtfully—"to the individual features of the situation".[23] (We see here the consequence of his agent centred and particularist views). Responding appropriately may not be an easy matter, and Collingwood acknowledges that moral effort is required in determining how to act accordingly, but this is unavoidable in ethical action.

Although trained as an historian at Cambridge (where he attended lectures by J.M.E. McTaggart), and while best known today as a political thinker, throughout his life Michael Oakeshott was interested in philosophical questions that lay at the root of history and politics. In Chapter 11, Efraim Podoksik introduces Oakeshott's views on moral and social philosophy—particularly his account of the development of individual character and human excellence, and of the importance of leading a good life. Podoksik notes that while Oakeshott's views changed during his lifetime, for much of it—Podoksik believes, well into the 1950s—one finds a strong strain of idealism in his moral and social thought.

In Oakeshott's early writings, Podoksik points out, moral conduct and social action are understood in purposive terms. The purpose of morality is "to lead a good life" which, he holds, is a "unified" life or an "integrated state of mind". Institutions and associations are evaluated in terms of how they serve this purpose. This "good life", then, is the common good, and it brings together—or, better said, shows the fundamental relation of—the individual and society. Podoksik holds that, according to Oakeshott—though this is a view that can be traced back at least to Bosanquet—the individual and society are two sides of the same unity, and this unity exists fundamentally in the state. What is necessary for an understanding of human purpose then, is the recognition that individuality and the state (i.e., society as manifested in institutions[24]) are not funda-

---

22 Collingwood develops this in *The New Leviathan*, where the issue is presented as "what kind of man you intend to be" (Collingwood, 1999, 16.72).
23 See Connelly, this volume, p. 246. There seems to be an echo of Bosanquet here. See also Collingwood, (1989), p. 154: "The consciousness of duty is thus the agent's consciousness of his action as a unique individual action relevant to a unique individual situation." It is not enough, of course, merely to note the details; "The historian will not do very much to help us in our moral and political difficulties if he only makes us see the features of the situation and does not also provide us with rules for acting in that situation" (Collingwood, 1978, p. 100).
24 Oakeshott writes, in the unpublished "A Discussion of Some Matters Preliminary to the Study of Political Philosophy" (1925): "the self is the State, the State is the self." Cited in Franco (2005, p. 119).

mentally independent of one another. This teleology towards the good life, and this holist view of the self and the state, Podoksik notes, clearly indicate the idealist character of Oakeshott's early views. But, as Podoksik goes on to describe, Oakeshott moved from this idealist view, through a middle period where teleology was still seen as important to morality but holism less so, to a final period where he held that the development of character and human excellence required abandoning all talk of 'ends' — be it of civil association, of institutions, or of human excellence itself. The strong metaphysical character of Oakeshott's early work is also absent from these later writings. Podoksik suggests that the reason for this is that Oakeshott's insistence on pluralism, openness, and spontaneity could not be accommodated within a teleological model, and that this led him to abandon teleology and, by extension, idealism.

1.4 Idealism beyond Britain

British Idealism had a significant impact in philosophy far beyond the British Isles — in Canada (with John Watson [1847–1939], T.B. Kilpatrick [1857–1930], and S.W. Dyde [1862–1947]), Australia (with W.R. Boyce-Gibson [1869–1935] and Sir William Mitchell [1861–1962]), in South Africa (with R.F.A. Hoernlé [1880–1943], Arthur Ritchie Lord [1880–1941], Andrew Howson Murray [1905–97], and Jan Christian Smuts [1870–1950]), and in India (with Sarvepalli Radhakrishnan [1888–1975], J.C.P. d'Andrade [1888–1949], and P.T. Raju [1904–92]). There was an influence as well, albeit more indirect, on philosophers in the United States (e.g., George Holmes Howison [1834–1917], Josiah Royce [1855–1916], Evander Bradley McGilvary [1864–1953], W.E. Hocking [1873–1966], Elijah Jordan [1875–1953], Gustavus Watts Cunningham [1881–1968], and Brand Blanshard [1892–1987]), and beyond. While the conclusions of these authors often became less and less homogeneous with those of their predecessors, their principal concerns (such as the rejection of naturalism, materialism, individualism, and various forms of reductionism, and the insistence on a greater recognition of the community and the role of 'mind' in the understanding of social and political reality) remained fairly constant.

In the final two chapters of this volume, the authors look at the moral and social philosophy of representative thinkers from Canada, South Africa, and India — philosophers from Britain or who had a longstanding connexion with it, but who spent most of their philosophical careers abroad. In these chapters, one will note how idealist moral and social philosophy responded to contemporary critiques but also how it developed. These examples also raise the question of whether the difference in social and political environment had any effect on the way in this British idealism was expressed or applied.

A prime example of British idealist moral, social, and political philosophy outside of Britain is found in the writings of John Watson. A student of Edward Caird, and regarded by Caird as one of his best students, Watson left his home in Scotland to spend his professorial career in Canada, at Queen's University in Kingston. In Chapter 12, Elizabeth Trott reconstructs and reviews Watson's moral philosophy — Watson wrote no major text on ethics — placing it in context with his political philosophy and his views on religion.

According to Trott, the key to Watson's moral philosophy lies his account of the self and the community. For Watson, the ethical end is self-realisation. Personal identity and individuality require a relation to others; the community serves as a "set of shared meanings in terms of which one acts, responds and gradually individuates oneself."[25] In a sense, the community gives rise to individuals. But, Trott asserts, Watson resists what he takes to be Green's view that human beings are simply "expressions of a universal mind." Watson also rejects the claim that evolution can explain morality, because morality requires free choice. Hedonistic utilitarianism fails, as well, because it ultimately has to appeal to non-hedonistic principles in order to explain moral preferences.

Trott argues that there is a strong pluralism in Watson's moral philosophy. Nevertheless, there are certain constants. Because of the emphasis on self-realisation or self-determination, there must be freedom — though Watson rejects the notion that individuals have a natural right to this freedom. Moreover, the good must be rationally consistent; it is not simply to be based on individual preferences. Finally, political community is required for the good life. The role of the state, therefore, is to serve as the condition for not only individual self determination, but that of communities; "its job was to make provisions for many expressions of reason."[26] Trott maintains, then, that Watson did not think that there was one, fundamental ethical theory, but that, because there is a rational order in community, over time, as individuals engage with their communities, they will gradually discover appropriate moral principles.

Trott notes that, in his moral, social, and political philosophy, Watson adverts to the concept of God — what he called the Absolute. This God is not the unchanging and impassive God of the scholastics, but the God of a "rational religion". God exists, Watson holds, through each conscious mind — i.e., in individuals, and not transcending them. Thus, when Watson talks about "carrying God" within the person, Watson is not appealing to a principle that lies outside the world, and he sees the community as the set of the various expressions of God in the world.

---

25 See Trott, this volume, p. 271.
26 See Trott, this volume, pp. 276–7.

There are many other examples of British idealist moral, social, and political philosophy finding a home outside of its country of origin, and in the final chapter, William Sweet presents the moral philosophy of two of the better known: R.F.A. Hoernlé in South Africa and Sarvepalli Radhakrishnan in India. Neither was born in Britain and both spent most of their careers far from it, yet both were products of a British curriculum, were British subjects, and counted the leading British idealists among their major interlocutors and colleagues.

Hoernlé's philosophical views were greatly influenced by Bernard Bosanquet, though his moral, social, and political thought was not developed until after he became Professor at Witwatersrand in Johannesburg in 1923. Like many of the idealists, Hoernlé's interests were primarily practical; in his case, they focused largely on questions of liberty and equality in a multiethnic and multicultural society. Sweet notes that Hoernlé was suspicious of importing theories *ad hoc* to address local issues, and that Hoernlé's synoptic method—recognizing that the truth has many sides and that every point of view has some contribution to make—and his practice of identifying with "the life around me, to enter into it and share it from the inside", led him to articulate an "ethics of liberty" that was attentive to the South African context. Such an ethics was rooted in the concrete conditions of culture and of community, and yet, at the same time, recognised the inherent value of human beings, the importance of self-realisation, the fact that a "life worth living" had to be in community, and that the proper ethical response may sometimes be to go beyond culture and convention. The common good is "rational", in the sense that it seeks to eliminate inconsistency and incoherence, but it is also pluralistic. This ethics of liberty, then, aimed at allowing individuals to lead a "life worth living" and to realise their particular capacities within a broad cultural unity. Hoernlé's South African experience confirmed the importance of pluralism but also, presumably, his confidence that, in spite of the many differences of culture, a common good was still achievable.

The influence of British idealism on Radhakrishnan was less direct; he was a student of students of personal idealists who came to India to staff many of the colleges and early universities. Still, not only was Radhakrishnan schooled in the major writings of the British idealists, but he found, in Bradley and others, a certain resonance, and his philosophical career was greatly enhanced through the support of idealist philosophers from Britain. By drawing on British idealism together with Hindu Advaita Vedanta, Radhakrishnan articulated an ethics that had, as its end, the duty to seek universal spiritual emancipation. Radhakrishnan's aim, however, was not simply to apply this ethics to practical issues, but also to attempt to express clearly its metaphysical underpinnings. Radhakrishnan saw ethics as social—indeed, transgenerational (for he held to the existence of karma)—yet he also recognised the importance of the development of individual character and liberation. Such an ethics, he believed, is dependent upon a theory of the Absolute, which he saw as exemplifying rational principle. Self-realisation and the "rationality" of the Absolute demanded, he believed, that such an ethics be open and pluralistic. But because the Absolute is comprehensive and, therefore, "social", it also carried ethical responsibilities to the community. In general, then, in bringing western idealist and Vedanta philosophy into contact at the metaphysical level, Radhakrishnan not only continued, but built on, a number of key features of the British idealist traditions.

1.5 Summary

The authors of the chapters in this volume, then, provide the context, and identify some of the principal themes and contributions, of the moral and social, but also the political philosophy of the British idealists. With an emphasis on moral practice and life in community, the recognition of the value of culture and social institutions, the centrality of self-realisation and human flourishing, and an openness to new experience, one can see how the varieties of idealist moral and social philosophy spoke to concerns of the late nineteenth and early twentieth centuries, but also how it might bear on current issues. It is, no doubt, for this reason that there has been a renewal of interest in British idealism today. We may, however, also ask whether, despite the differences among them, one can speak of *a* generic British idealist moral and social philosophy, and, more specifically, whether such an ethics might have something to offer us today. How do these authors bear on contemporary thought?

II. Reconstructing a British Idealist Moral, Social and Political Philosophy

2.1 Some general features of an idealist moral philosophy

Is it possible to speak of *a* British idealist moral philosophy? From what we have seen, the focus of an idealist ethics is on practice, not theory. This, plausibly, reflects both elements of the Platonic and Aristotelian traditions, mediated through Hegel, which emphasized practice and conduct over moral theorizing,[27] as well as the evangelical Protestant home life of many of the early idealists, which focused on moral conduct rather than dogma and doctrine.

For the British idealists, ethics is focused on the community. People have basic duties to their communities and, indeed, individual identity or the self is based in community. Even for those Brithish idealists who

---

[27] See, for example, Aristotle's comment about theory as subordinate to practice: "the account of particular cases is yet more lacking in exactness; for they do not fall under any art or precept but the agents themselves must in each case consider what is appropriate to the occasion, as happens also in the art of medicine or of navigation." See *Nicomachean Ethics* (tr. W. D. Ross), Bk II, ii, 1103b26–1104a10.

believed in God or a spiritual order, the ethical community was not a supernatural or a transcendent one, but in "the here and now" — what Bosanquet sometimes referred to as "the Kingdom of God *on earth*." An idealist moral (and, for that matter, social and political) philosophy, then, does not propose a community beyond the natural order, although it does not foreclose on the possibility of one either.

At the same time, idealist moral and social philosophy is attentive to particulars: the ethical subject is the individual agent, there is an emphasis on individual responsibility and personal morality, the ethical analysis of a situation and judgements must take account of the specific (social, cultural, and political) situation, and the moralizing force within society is the individual will or self. Many idealists also note the value of individual moral effort and struggle in the development of moral character, and that there can be a range of legitimate moral practices and moral discourses. While the true individual is, for many of the idealists, what they called the concrete universal, there is no inconsistency here; this "universal" is simply a unity or whole that reflects, but also is reflected in, each particular being. British idealist ethics acknowledges as well, however, the importance and value of individual agents as objects of ethical development. In short, for the British idealists, the individual is both the subject and the object of moral activity.

There must be something that brings the 'social' and the 'individual' dimensions together, and in the essays in this volume, one sees repeatedly that what does this is the presence of an end of moral action in general — a *common* good. For the British idealists, this is central to the relation of the individual and the community. This common good is a *rational* end (in the sense of bringing a plethora of experiences together into coherence),[28] and reflects the view that individuals have capacities and potentialities that, broadly speaking, *must* be developed — and preferably developed by themselves — so that they will thrive and flourish. This common good is also sometimes seen as a higher self; satisfying one's moral obligations largely involves bringing one's ordinary or lower self into accord with this higher self. This process is generally called 'self-realisation'; as we develop our capacities and potential, we come to be who we are, and we come to know who we are. (Thus, a British idealist ethics supposes that individual human beings as human beings have natures, functions, and ends.) This

---

28 By 'rational', here, many of the British idealists had in mind, not just a formal deductive process, but something that reflects or produces coherence. Thus, feeling — including pleasure — is a relevant datum in the description of that end. Caird writes: "if, in order that reason may rule, all such impulses have to be driven out, reason will rule in an empty house." See Caird (1904), Vol. 2, p. 125. See also A.R. Lord: "By 'reason' here I mean new rationalism which, instead of eliminating differences, was to justify them and include them as movements or aspects in a more concretely conceived Universal — hence, comes the new *conception* of the philosophic reason: of which indeed the whole work of Hegel is an exposition" Lord, (2006), p. 262.

flourishing and thriving, then, is *the* human end—i.e., it is, in a broad sense, the "same" end for all, and it is one where the welfare of the individual and of the community coincides. It is more than a natural good (such as pleasure is, in hedonism), and it has an objective value. This flourishing shows the importance of the community. And since one's relation to that community is established at the mental or psychological level, community is sometimes referred to as objective mind.[29] Because of the relation of individuals to the community, individuals are called to build that community. Thus, moral action involves a real solidarity and moral community. But the condition for this flourishing and thriving is a positive freedom.

The Scylla and Charybdis of such a moral philosophy would seem to be, on the one hand, an ethical homogeneity that is blind to cultural or local difference and, on the other hand, an emphasis on the individual will and self-realisation that makes any social unity unstable. Yet while the notion of a common good indicates the teleological character of this moral philosophy, and while there is a recognition of an ultimate human end (at least, in a broad sense), this notion does not dictate a particular model of human flourishing. It does not exclude particular goods or practices in advance, it does not claim that any particular good or practice is "the last word", it recognizes that different particular situations give rise to different understandings of the good, and that all understandings of the good are incomplete—and it would challenge any theory that claimed that it was 'the last word'. Consequently, as many of the British idealists insist, although teleological, idealist ethics are not closed theories. Moreover, while idealist moral philosophy recognizes the importance of the individual will, it is not voluntaristic; it does not identify or base "the good" on will but on reason. Since achieving one's end requires carrying out certain responsibilities (i.e., duties) and developing certain capacities (i.e., character or virtues), and because similar or the same duties and virtues are required of others, as noted above, one's "end" or good is the same for all. Thus, the means to one's good and to the common good is the development of character and the performance of duty. (Which particular virtues or what aspects of character need to be developed are determined based on this good, in the context and circumstances of daily life.) Thus, a British idealist moral philosophy can have a teleological character—which is consistent with those idealists who held that there was a teleological character to reality—while avoiding the charge of entailing ethical uniformity. Indeed, such a teleology requires that ethics be open to new experience and change.

---

29 See Walsh, (1969), p. 19.

2.2 Definition of 'the good'

It is not insignificant — both to its success in Britain in the late nineteenth and early twentieth centuries, and as it spread over the English-speaking world, and beyond — that, rather than being a theory focussing on a conception of the good, or on the specific features of an action or a person that one should look at in making moral judgements, or even on the standards one should adopt, idealist ethics is primarily concerned with conduct. For the British idealists, then, the central question is: How is one to lead a good life? or, what is the same: How can one lead a truly human life, given one's individual capacities and will, and given one's relations to others? For this, however, one needs to know what the good is.

The understanding of good and evil that we find in the British idealists is, generally, that evil is, broadly, what is contradictory, inconsistent, and incomplete; good is what is complete, unified, and rational. Some idealists identified "good" with "the Absolute" or with "human perfection" or with the perfection of human personality as a whole, but the effort of trying to determine in advance what specifically "the good" is would have seemed to many to be a sterile and relatively unimportant exercise. Thus, when they look at, and make moral judgements concerning, the acts or behaviour of human individuals, their focus was on the will or intention and on the consequences for the community, but particularly on character — both one's own and others. How one is to assess something as good, however, was not something that could be determined in the abstract, but required an account of the relations among individuals and to the community as a whole — and neither this, nor the good that this reflects, can be given in detail in advance.

2.3 What the idealist account is not

British idealist ethics has had its critics, and it is important therefore not only to be careful in identifying the views that the British idealists had in common, but also to indicate what such a theory does not, or need not, hold.

A critic might object that this ethics does not offer any substantive moral guidance because its concept of the common good is vague. What several of the authors in this volume will show, however, is that its openness (which is not the same as "vagueness") is an advantage. Idealist ethics need not, and indeed cannot, give an exhaustive account of a common good. Idealists recognize that no conception of the common good in this world is complete, and that any particular common good (or principle or value) will inevitably be less than it could be. There is, in any case, little point in providing a general model when we need to address concrete, individual cases.

Again, a critic might argue that, because an idealist ethics reflects a teleological conception of reality and of the good, it is quietistic. The assumption here seems to be that, since the attainment of the good is inevitable, struggle and effort are simply not necessary — and that there is no need to challenge the *status quo* (either because it reflects the best that we can have presently, or because "the good" will be achieved eventually by itself). But while an idealist ethics recognises the value of social institutions, it does not follow that it reflects only the *status quo* — i.e., is committed to defending existing institutions. The development of one's character inevitably involves moral struggle. And, as the authors here show, proponents of idealist ethics challenged a number of social and political policies and institutions. They recognized that no society or set of institutions can ever be fully consistent and, therefore, stand beyond criticism.

Is an idealist ethics an evolutionary ethics?[30] It is certainly true that some, like David Ritchie, tried explicitly to bring the theories of Darwin and Hegel into closer contact.[31] And, more broadly, if, by evolution, one means that there is a dynamic character to reality, i.e., a nisus, at both the physical and mental levels — that there is a development of body and mind which is broadly progressive, and that through human activity there are increasingly realized capacities and a development of a conception of 'humanity,' so that the contradictions between oneself and the world around one are decreased — then we can speak of evolution. If, however, one sees evolution as a process that is purely naturalistic and involves change as the result of arbitrary natural selection, with no particular direction, improvement, increased coherence, or normative character, then it is inconsistent with the kinds of ethics described by the British idealists. So while it is true that idealist ethics was influenced by evolutionary theory, it is not necessarily an evolutionary ethics (i.e., in the latter sense, above). One might better say — and as, for example, Oakeshott did say — that it is an ethics that is integrative, moving from part to whole.

Does British idealism offer a hedonistic ethics? Certainly, many idealists — though perhaps not all[32] — explicitly reject such a view. So, here, there may be a division of opinion. Nevertheless, there is clearly a place for pleasure in such an ethics. While idealism does not identify pleasure as the

---

30 See Caird (1893). See also Muirhead (1892), pp. 133–148, attacking evolutionary hedonism. Green thought that evolutionary theory led to naturalism (Green, 1906, §4). Bradley seems to have been somewhat open on the matter. John Watson saw "a tendency in man to seek the good of others as well as himself", but this is far from inevitable, and Watson insisted that each person "must be capable not only of abstracting from his own immediate impulses, but of putting himself at the point of view of others" — which can even lead to self-sacrifice (Watson, 1898, pp. 148-9)

31 See, for example, Neill (2003).

32 Some idealists, such as McTaggart, seem to have an openness towards hedonism. In his 1903 two-part essay, "Hedonism Among Idealists", Bernard Bosanquet challenges what he sees as a nascent hedonism in McTaggart's *Studies in Hegelian Cosmology*. According to Bosanquet, while McTaggart says that pleasure is not "the good", he does allow that the criterion of morality is "hedonic" (Bosanquet, 1903, pp. 203-4). Bosanquet, then, defends what he takes to be T.H. Green's position against McTaggart.

ultimate human end, it does acknowledge that it is important[33] and that, *ceteris paribus*, right action and the development of character, for example, have corresponding pleasures.

Do the idealist ethics described in this volume reflect a historicist view — that historical circumstance so permeates culture and ideas that there can be no universal standards or principles — so that all that can be said is that there is a multiplicity of ethical systems, and no one of them is better or worse or final or correct? This is a much more difficult question, and it has been a matter of lengthy debate.[34] One would be mistaken, however, if one thought that idealist ethics were not historically informed. While it is true that there is relatively little explicit interest in many of the idealists in a philosophy of history — Bradley and Collingwood being exceptions — or in the history of philosophy as such, not only does the role of history have an important place in idealist thought, but it can plausibly be said to have a particular relevance to ethics. J.H. Muirhead, for example, thought it important that it be seen "how moral ideas have a history",[35] and a similar view is held by Bradley and Bosanquet as well.[36] Certainly, given that one's "station and its duties" are described and ascribed within a particular historical and cultural context, and so far as they reflect a person's specific qualities and aptitudes and bear on particular goods to be achieved, there is no doubt that there is a historical character to that person's rights and obligations. It does not follow from this, however, that such an ethics is purely culturally determined or subjective.

Some critics may be concerned — as indeed some were — that British idealist ethics is ultimately a disguised religious ethics.[37] But as the chapters

---

33 For Bradley's views, see his *Ethical Studies* (1927).
34 See for example Strauss (1952) and Mink (1987).
35 Muirhead, (1892), p. 134.
36 Bradley introduced the question of history and historical knowledge in his *The Presuppositions of Critical History* (1874) — a lengthy essay written just two years prior to the publication of *Ethical Studies* (1876) — and it seems plausible that his treatment of this issue can cast some light on his account of ethics. Just as history or historical fact was not something 'out in the world' to be collected by the historian, ethical principle (or 'the good' or 'the Absolute') was not something 'out in the world' either. The philosopher of critical history recognises that historical testimony must be evaluated from the perspective of the historian, and that history is an activity that must be engaged in 'critically' — i.e., with an awareness of the presuppositions of the historian — and that events must be understood within their context. We can, then, properly speak of historical fact, but it is something that must be interpreted, and this interpretation must take account of the presuppositions of the historian and the specific questions the historian is interested in. By extension, it seems that this approach can be used to examine the conditions and presuppositions of ethics — of any ethics. And just as it is left to the historian to engage the particular phenomena critically in arriving at history, so moral theorists must critically engage the phenomena in terms of the problems they are faced with and the questions that they are interested in addressing. Consequently, in determining what one ought to do in a particular situation, or how one ought to conduct oneself morally, it would not be inappropriate to take into account, at the very least, one's "stations and duties" in society — even if one were to have to move beyond what they required.
37 See Stove (1991). This was also raised by some early Japanese commentators on T.H. Green (see Atsuko, 1979).

on Caird, Bosanquet, Watson, among others, illustrate, while their ethics were often presented or discussed using metaphors or allusions to religion, these authors did not rely in their arguments on orthodox religious doctrine. Admittedly, self-realisation as an ethical view fits with the metaphysical view of self-consciousness understood as a process whereby the self "takes" more and more of the "outside" into itself, or brings objects "into oneness with thought" — but this is not religion. The references to religion in the writings of many of the idealists focus on its function and not its content, and their arguments do not depend on dogmas or creeds. Indeed, as indicated earlier in this Introduction, for some, ethics was a science and not dependent even on a "thick" metaphysical theory, and several of the British idealists had well-developed ethical views long before providing an explicit or complete statement of their metaphysics.

Does British idealist ethics reflect a kind of pragmatism? There is a lengthy correspondence on this between William James and F.H. Bradley,[38] and some would note, for example, that the emphasis on starting with and focussing on ethical activity rather than theory would be consistent with pragmatism. But idealist ethics, as described in the present volume, is broadly teleological, and reflects a theory of self-realisation and a common good, which most pragmatists would eschew.

Finally, one might ask whether British idealist ethics reflects a hybrid of deontology and teleology that is incoherent[39] — attempting to combine a Kantian emphasis on the individual (as an autonomous agent with an inherent dignity who is focussed on the development of a "good will") with a Hegelian emphasis on the *telos* and the social (where ethics is characteristic of "a corporate life lived in a community"[40]). While one would be right to note both influences in idealist ethics, in many of the authors discussed in this volume, these were seen as complementary rather than as in tension, and some scholars would hold — influenced, perhaps, by Kant's discussion in the *Metaphysical Principles of Justice* — that the positions of Kant and Hegel are closer on this issue than has generally been thought.[41]

2.4 Implications for social and political philosophy

In the essays in this volume, we see that idealist moral philosophy is fundamentally social, and the questions of social philosophy — "philosophical questions about social relations"[42] — almost invariably refer back to morality, ethics, and moral practice. As we see, the key issue for an idealist ethics is not the analysis of terms or articulating the criteria for moral judgement, but moral conduct — i.e., the pursuit of a moral end in social life.

---

38 For a discussion, see Sprigge 1993.
39 See Vincent (1982), especially pp. 165–6.
40 Walsh, (1969), p. 77.
41 See Sweet (2004).
42 See, for example, Feinberg, 1973.

Social philosophy, in most of the western philosophical traditions, is focussed on the question of freedom, particularly freedom from constraint. But social philosophy could just as well be focussed on duties to others and to the community as a whole, or on justice (e.g., as a formal and material principle). This is where, within the history of Anglo-American philosophy, British idealist ethics has been recognized as having made a contribution — i.e., in its critical response to individualism, in its account of fundamental moral obligations to others in society and in its account of a positive liberty that includes but also goes beyond 'freedom from'.

In British idealism, then, moral philosophy is inseparable from a social philosophy, and *vice versa* — and the idealists took the 'social' implication of ethics seriously.[43] This is not always so with ethical theories. This concern for social obligations, and social philosophy, is not only very unlike what is found in some individualistic ethical theories, but is arguably different even from some putatively 'social' ethics, such as utilitarianism.[44]

Ethical conduct requires engagement by an individual in social life and, therefore, in the realisation of a common good. On an idealist view, however, persons are already 'socially engaged' by having a number of functions and roles in the family, the neighbourhood, the workplace, and so on. A person has rights — and obligations — rooted in that social dimension.

Idealist moral and social philosophy, in turn, led — and leads — to political philosophy. The character of the political philosophy, one will note in the chapters that follow, can vary, but one can say that, in general, the idealists saw the purpose of political institutions as primarily to hinder hindrances to the development of human personality. Both law and morality have the common good as their end, and resort to legal and political sanctions was to be made only once certain moral criteria were satisfied. An idealist would hold that, given that no society was without inconsistency, there could often be conflict between morality and the political, but there is no opposition in principle. Indeed, for the British idealists, political and legal institutions are not neutral with regard to conceptions of the good,

---

43 For example, Green was an assistant commissioner on the Schools Enquiry Commission (1865-6), and served on the Oxford School Board and the Oxford town council; Caird was similarly active in local politics in Glasgow; Haldane was a member of Parliament from 1885, and served as Secretary of State for War (1905-12) and Lord Chancellor (1912-15; 1924); Henry Jones was called on by the parliamentary recruitment committee in late 1915 to undertake a number of public meetings throughout Wales to defend the Asquith government and encourage recruitment into the armed forces; Bosanquet was a long time chair and advisor to the Charity Organization Society (which followed and applied the British Government's Poor Law in the late nineteenth century) and active in adult education, the university extension programme, and the London School of Social Philosophy. The students of these men went on, after their studies, to be active in University Settlement houses and in the work of the Charity Organisation Society and, later, in public life, politics, social reform, and the church. The list is extensive.
44 The associationist character of the psychological theories of Mill and Bentham, and the formulation of a 'greatest good' based on the preferences of individuals suggest such a basic individualism.

and they maintained that such institutions must reflect, and be subject to, morality.

2.5 Summary

As this volume shows, there are many, sometimes significant, differences among the British idealists. Nevertheless, given the number of recurring themes, similar critiques of existing theories, and common proposals in their work—it seems plausible to speak of *a* generic British idealist moral and social philosophy.

Is it possible to state a moral rule or principle that captures the fundamental character of idealist ethics? If Kantianism is reflected in the categorical imperative and utilitarianism in the greatest happiness principle, what would the "dictum" for idealism be? Is there any way in which we might express, in an encapsulated form, the basic principle of idealist ethics? How might one put into a few words the key insight of its moral philosophy? Three possibilities come to mind.

The first (and the most commonly given) is to identify British idealist ethics with the moral notion of 'my station and its duties,' popularised by Bradley, but also found in Green and Bosanquet.[45] Such a moral standard is based on the roles or functions one has in social life. But a close look at the British idealists shows that they saw ethics as something more than this. With Bradley, at least, 'my station and its duties' is not the standard of ethical behaviour, but a stage in moral development.[46] Moreover, for this morality to be even possible, there must be something which establishes and grounds each person's station and, thereby, the corresponding duties—i.e.,"the supreme values that can guide desire aright, and keep patriotism clean and sweet" (Bosanquet, 2001, p. 46). And so in Bradley, and arguably in Bosanquet, idealist ethics goes beyond a morality of 'my station.'

A second option suggested by many of the authors in this volume is that the basic moral injunction is "to realise the self". The self to be realised is, as we have seen, a 'social' self, by which the idealists meant each individual's 'true self', which is not simply the product of one's wants and wishes, but of one's reason in the light of as much information as possible. Whether it is meaningful to speak of such a self, whether it is *one's* self in any meaningful sense, and whether this leaves any place for the value of the individual, are, however, far from clear to many critics. Moreover, it is not obvious what such a self-realisation involves. Some—for example, Caird and Bosanquet—refer to the notion of "dying to the self", derived from St Paul and from Goethe's phrase "stirb und werde" ("die to live"). But what such self sacrifice—or alternatively, as Bosanquet suggests,

---

[45] This approach to ethics is articulated by Bosanquet in Bosanquet, (1889), and, indirectly, in Bosanquet, (1893).
[46] See MacNiven (1987).

self-transcendence—means is itself the subject of much debate. If idealist ethics is reflected in the notion of self-realisation, it clearly rests on a rather rich metaphysics. But, more to the point, it would seem to be vague and problematic, and to impose a rather rigorous standard.

A third possibility of how to express the basic principle of idealist ethics is expressed in Bosanquet's later work: one must "Be adequate to the situation." A similar view is found in Collingwood, and is reflected in his particularism, where he sees moral action as involving how to respond to the individual features of the situation.[47] Thus, as Bosanquet writes in *Some Suggestions in Ethics* (1918), "'To respond adequately to the situation' is not a bad formula if you want to put the rules of moral guidance in six words."[48] This is, admittedly, no less vague than the notion of self-realisation, but the standard certainly seems more practicable, and the underlying metaphysics more modest.

Whether any of these articulations is sufficiently helpful or satisfactory as an encapsulation or dictum of the standard of idealist ethics may, perhaps, be best left to further discussion.

III. Building on British Idealism

The essays in this volume invite a number of questions. Why did British idealist moral, social, and political philosophy largely disappear from philosophical discussion? Could a reconsideration of it have a bearing on ethical theory today? As noted at the beginning of this Introduction, by the early twentieth century, there were a number of challenges to this idealism—from philosophers, such as William James, L.T. Hobhouse, and Harold Laski; from sociologists such as R.M. MacIver, Morris Ginsberg, and others for whom the critique of idealism was a "rite of passage";[49] from those involved in social and public policy, such as Sidney and Beatrice Webb and John Hobson; and from others besides.[50] There is little doubt that, for some time, such challenges were taken to be conclusive.

In the pages that follow, however, one will find that there are several features in idealist moral, social, and political philosophy which are particularly relevant today to the quest for an ethics that can engage contem-

---

47 See Connelly, this volume, p. 246.
48 Bosanquet (1919), p. 146. See also p. 150 and Bosanquet's review of John Dewey's *Studies in Logical Theory*: "To be 'equal to the situation' is at once the inmost nature of thought, and its law as a principle of adaptation. It is not a mechanical adaptation; that is quite true. But, after all, conclusions follow from premisses, i.e. from a situation, though not in the same way as effects from causes. I cannot see how thought should exhibit its nature, if not by adjustment within situations; nor how it should prove equal to situations (the definition—I take it both of truth and morality) unless it was 'its nature to'" (Bosanquet, 1911, p. 435).
49 Stefan Collini writes that, until the 1920s, "[a]n attack on the neo-Hegelian theory of the state became almost a *rite de passage* for the budding social scientist." Collini, (1978), p. 27, n. 27.
50 For a survey of some of the reasons for these criticisms, see James Bradley (1979, especially pp. 169–82) and the Editorial Introduction to Bosanquet (2001), pp. xxxi–xxxii.

porary ethical and political issues, and which can, arguably, provide an alternative theory.

For the British idealists, human flourishing was key at both the individual level and at the level of the community, and they insisted that there was no inherent conflict between the two. The welfare of the individual and the community go together. This idealism focused on practice and on community life. It recognised the importance of social action—of being involved in the "here and now"—as well as the "ethical activism" of the individual and, to that extent, it provided an explanation of rights. But these rights were not independent of duties, and therefore not absolute and inalienable.

This idealism recognised that moral agents are social beings with a history and context that is rooted in a network of natural and social relations. The British idealists appealed to virtue and to character, determined in view of the fundamental good or goods of the community, and which included a recognition of civic responsibilities, and so this view was suited—and is, arguably, suitable—to the lived experience of many cultures. In general, British idealism respected tradition, although it did not see any existing institution as a 'finished story' and complete, and so it was not essentially conservative.

Such an ethics, then, acknowledged the existing interrelations among individuals, but also between them and the world. It recognised something valuable in the environment, but also in laws and institutions as manifestations of human spirit and activity.

Importantly for today, this ethics professed to be open to new experience. Its assumption was that reality is rational (in a broad sense), that different minds could uncover it, and that different people did and can uncover it in different ways. Because no particular expression of the good is automatically privileged, it saw itself as pluralistic, without being subjectivistic. While idealistic ethics was open to religion and the transcendent, it did not require either and it eschewed religious dogma. It was, then, immanentist. Yet it did not preclude the spiritual.

Such characteristics are, clearly, of central interest to those engaged in contemporary ethical theory and, at the very least, are elements which can serve as points for the discussion of related moral, social, and political issues.

The essays in this volume, then, describe ways in which British idealist moral, social, and political philosophy addressed some of the dominant views of the period, but also signal features of that view which may serve in the contemporary world as a shared ground or basis for dialogue concerning ethics, within and across traditions and cultures. Such an approach may, therefore, provide a starting point for the articulation of an idealist ethical theory today.

References

Aristotle (1908), *Nicomachean Ethics*, tr. W. D. Ross (Oxford: Clarendon Press).

Atsuko, Hirai (1979), "Self-Realization and Common Good: T.H. Green in Meiji Ethical Thought", *Journal of Japanese Studies*, 5 (1979), pp. 107-36.

Bengtsson, Jan Olof (2006), *The Worldview of Personalism: origins and early development* (Oxford: Oxford University Press).

Bosanquet, Bernard (1889), "The Kingdom of God on Earth", in *Essays and Addresses* (London: Macmillan), pp. 108-30.

Bosanquet, Bernard (1897-8), "Review of Henry Sidgwick's *Practical Ethics*", *International Journal of Ethics*, 7, pp. 390-4.

Bosanquet, Bernard (1893), *The Civilization of Christendom and Other Studies* (London: Macmillan).

Bosanquet, Bernard (1903), "Hedonism Among Idealists" (I) and (II), *Mind*, 12, pp. 202-24; 303-16.

Bosanquet, Bernard (1911), "Review of John Dewey, et al, *Studies in Logical Theory*", *Mind*, 20, p. 435.

Bosanquet, Bernard (1919) *Some Suggestions in Ethics*, 2nd ed. (London: Macmillan).

Bosanquet, Bernard (1927), "On the Practical Value of Moral Philosophy. Inaugural Address Delivered October 21, 1903 [at the University of St. Andrews]", in *Science and Philosophy and Other Essays by the Late Bernard Bosanquet*, ed J. H. Muirhead and R. C. Bosanquet (London: Allen and Unwin).

Bosanquet, Bernard (2001) *The Philosophical Theory of the State and Related Essays*, ed. W. Sweet, and G.F. Gaus (South Bend, IN: St Augustine's Press).

Bosanquet, Bernard (2003) *Essays on Aspects of the Social Problem and Social Policy*, Vol. 3, *Essays on Philosophy and Social Policy 1883-1922*, ed. William Sweet (Bristol: Thoemmes).

Boucher, David and Andrew Vincent (2000), *British Idealism and Political Theory* (Edinburgh: Edinburgh University Press).

Bradley, F.H. (1874), *The Presuppositions of Critical History* (Oxford: J. Parker & Co.).

Bradley, F.H. (1927), Ethical Studies, 2nd ed (London: Oxford University Press).

Bradley, James (1979), "Hegel in Britain: A Brief History of British Commentary and Attitudes" (1) and (2)," *The Heythrop Journal*, 20, pp. 1- 24; 163-82.

Brink, David Owen (2003), *Perfectionism and the Common Good: themes in the philosophy of T.H. Green* (Oxford: Oxford University Press).

Caird, Edward (1893), *The Evolution of Religion*, 2 vols. (Glasgow: James Maclehose).

Caird, Edward (1904), *The Evolution of Theology in the Greek Philosophers*, 2 vols. (Glasgow: J. Maclehose).

Carter, Matt (2003), *T.H. Green and the Development of Ethical Socialism* (Exeter: Imprint Academic).

Collini, S. (1978), "Sociology and Idealism in Britain: 1880-1920", *Archives européennes de sociologie*, 19, pp. 3-50.

Collingwood, R.G. (1978), *An Autobiography*, intro. Stephen Toulmin (Oxford: Clarendon Press).

Collingwood, R.G. (1989), *Essays in Political Philosophy*, ed. David Boucher (Oxford: Clarendon Press).

Collingwood, R.G. (1999), *The New Leviathan: Or Man, Society, Civilization and Barbarism*, 2nd ed., ed. David Boucher (Oxford: Oxford University Press).

Crossley, D.J. (1977), "Holism, Individuation, and Internal Relations", *Journal of the History of Philosophy*, 15, pp. 183-94.

Crossley, D.J. (1996), "Feeling in Bradley's *Ethical Studies*," in P. MacEwen (ed.), *Metaphysics and Religion in the Thought of F.H. Bradley* (Lewiston: Mellen), pp. 154-178.

Dimova-Cookson, Maria (2001), *T.H. Green's Moral and Political Philosophy: A Phenomenological Perspective* (Basingstoke: Palgrave Macmillan).

Dimova-Cookson, Maria and W.J. Mander (eds) (2006), *T.H. Green: ethics, metaphysics, and political philosophy* (Oxford: Oxford University Press).

Feinberg, Joel (1973), *Social Philosophy* (Englewood Cliffs, NJ: Prentice-Hall).

Franco, Paul (2005), "Oakeshott's Relationship to Hegel", in Corey Abel and Timothy Fuller (eds), *The Intellectual Legacy of Michael Oakeshott* (Exeter: Imprint Academic), pp. 117–31.
Green, T.H. (1906), *Prolegomena to Ethics*, 5th. ed. (Oxford: Clarendon Press).
Green, T.H. (1997), *Collected Works of T.H. Green*, ed. Peter P. Nicholson, 5 vols. (Bristol: Thoemmes Press).
Hemingway, John Luther (1979), *The Emergence of an Ethical Liberalism: A Study in Idealist Liberalism from Thomas Hill Green to the Present*. Ph.D. thesis in political science. University of Iowa.
Hetherington, H.J.W. (1953), *The Social Function of the University* (London: Lindsey Press).
Hodgson, S.H. (1901–2), "Bernard Bosanquet's Recent Criticism of Green's Ethics", *Proceedings of the Aristotelian Society*, 2, pp. 66–71.
Hill, John (1975), "Moore: Idealist or Realist?," *New Scholasticism*, 49, pp. 321–30.
Hurka, Thomas (1996), *Perfectionism* (Oxford: Oxford University Press).
Kemp, J. (1972), "T.H. Green and the Ethics of Self-Realization," in *Reason and Reality* [Royal Institute of Philosophy Lectures], 5, pp. 222–40.
Lamont, W.D. (1946), *The Principles of Moral Judgement* (Oxford: Clarendon Press).
LeChevalier, Charles (1963), *La pensée morale de Bernard Bosanquet (1848–1923): Etude sur l'univers moral de l'idéalisme anglais au 19e siècle*. (Thèse complémentaire pour le doctorat ès lettres) Paris, Vrin. (Republished under the title *Ethique et idéalisme: le courant néo-hegelien en Angleterre, Bernard Bosanquet et ses amis* [Paris, Vrin]).
Lockridge, Laurence S. (1977), *Coleridge the moralist* (Ithaca: Cornell University Press).
Lord, A.R. (2006), *The History of Philosophy from Descartes to Hegel*, ed. William Sweet and E.E. Harris (Lewiston: Mellen).
MacEwen, P. (ed.) (1993), *Ethics, Metaphysics and Religion in the Thought of F.H. Bradley* (Lewiston: Mellen).
Mackenzie, John Stuart (1896), "Rights and Duties", *International Journal of Ethics*, 6, pp. 425–41.
Mackenzie, John Stuart (1901), *A Manual of Ethics*, 4th ed (London: W.B. Clive).
MacNiven, D. (1987) *Bradley's Moral Psychology* (Lewiston: Mellen).
Manser, Anthony Richards and Guy Stock (eds) (1984), *The Philosophy of F.H. Bradley* (Oxford: Clarendon Press).
Mink, Louis O. (1987), "Collingwood's Historicism: A Dialectic of Process", and "Collingwood's Dialectic of History", in Louis O. Mink, *Historical Understanding*, ed. Brian Fay, Eugene O. Golob, and Richard T. Vann (Ithaca: Cornell University Press), pp. 223–45, 246–85.
Morefield, Jeanne (2005), *Covenants Without Swords: Idealist Liberalism and the Spirit of Empire* (Princeton: Princeton University Press).
Muirhead, J.H. (1892), *Elements of Ethics* (London: John Murray).
Muirhead, J.H. (1928), "Is there a Moral End?," *Mind*, 37, pp. 485–8.
Muirhead, J.H. (ed.) (1935), *Bernard Bosanquet and His Friends. Letters Illustrating the Sources and the development of his Philosophical Opinions* (London: Allen and Unwin; reprinted in *The Collected Works of Bernard Bosanquet*, ed. William Sweet [Bristol, UK: Thoemmes, 1999], Vol. 20).
Neill, E. (2003), "Evolutionary theory and British idealism: the case of David George Ritchie," *History of European Ideas*, 29, pp. 313–38.
Nicholson, Peter P. (1990), *The Political Philosophy of the British Idealists: Selected Studies* (Cambridge: Cambridge University Press).
Prichard, H.A. (1968), *Moral Obligation and Duty and Interest: essays and lectures*, intro. J.O. Urmson (London: Oxford University Press).
Pucelle, Jean (1955), *L' idéalisme en Angleterre de Coleridge à Bradley* (Neuchâtel: Éditions de la Baconnière).
Ritchie, D.G. (1905), *Philosophical Studies*, ed. Robert Latta (London: Macmillan).
Seth, James (1926), *A Study of Ethical Principles*, 17th ed. (New York: C. Scribner's).
Sidgwick, Henry (1902), *Lectures on the Ethics of T.H. Green, Mr. Herbert Spencer, and J. Martineau* (London: Macmillan).
Sprigge, Timothy L.S. (1988), *The Rational Foundations of Ethics* (London: Routledge & Kegan Paul).

Sprigge, Timothy L.S. (1993), *James and Bradley: American Truth and British Reality* (Chicago: Open Court).
Stocks, J.L., W. G. DeBurgh and W. D. Ross (1928), "Is there a Moral End?", *Proceedings of the Aristotelian Society*, n.s. supp. vol. 7, pp. 62–98.
Stove, D.C. (1991), *The Plato Cult and Other Philosophical Follies* (Oxford: Blackwell).
Strauss, Leo (1952), "On Collingwood's Philosophy of History", *Review of Metaphysics*, 5, pp. 559–86.
Sweet, William (1999), "Social Policy and Bosanquet's Moral Philosophy", *Collingwood Studies*, 6, pp. 127–46.
Sweet, William (2000), "Bosanquet and Bradley: some recent discussions", *Bradley Studies*, 6, pp. 63–91.
Sweet, William (2004), "Kant, Rights, and the General Will," *Indian Philosophical Quarterly*, 31, pp. 333–58.
Thomas, Geoffrey (1987), *The Moral Philosophy of T.H. Green* (Oxford: Clarendon Press).
Tyler, Colin (1997), *Thomas Hill Green (1836–1882) and the Philosophical Foundations of Politics: An internal critique* (Lewiston: Edwin Mellen).
Tyler, Colin (ed.) (2008), *Unpublished Manuscripts in British Idealism: Political Philosophy, Theology and Social Theory*, 2 vols. (Exeter: Imprint Academic).
Vincent, Andrew (1982), "The Individual in Hegelian Thought," *Idealistic Studies*, 12, pp. 156–68.
Vincent, Andrew and Raymond Plant (1984), *Philosophy, Politics and Citizenship: The Life and Thought of the British Idealists* (Oxford: Blackwell).
Walsh, W.H. (1969), *Hegelian Ethics* (London: Macmillan).
Watson, John (1898), *An Outline of Philosophy*, 2nd ed. (Glasgow, Maclehose).
Wilde, Norman (1924), *The Ethical Basis of the State* (Princeton, NJ: Princeton University Press).
Wollheim, R. (1969), *F.H. Bradley*, 2nd ed. (Harmondsworth: Penguin).
Wollheim, Richard (1975), "The Good Self and the Bad Self: The Moral Psychology of British Idealism and the English School of Psychoanalysis Compared", *Proceedings of the British Academy*, 61, pp. 373–98.

Avital Simhony

A Liberal Commitment to the Common Good
T.H. Green's Social & Political Morality

Introduction

The central feature of Thomas Hill Green's moral and social philosophy is his account of the common good, and it is with Green that this idea entered modern liberal political thought. The connexion between the moral, social, and the political is, not surprisingly therefore, profound; one would be hard pressed to delineate the role of the common good in Green's thought without recognizing its relation to his account of "the good society". Green's advocacy of the common good, then, is not simply a matter of moral and social philosophy; it reflects his deliberate effort to rid liberalism of its earlier association with the morality and politics of a self-centred individualism.

Green's common good has its intellectual roots in Hegel and Aristotle, as well as in Kant, all of whose resources he integrates, and which accounts for his view of the complex nature of this good. Its complex nature reveals Green's attempt to forge a third way which escapes the dualism between what is called by Michael Sandel the liberal "politics of rights" and the communitarian/republican "politics of the common good". Thus, it bears on a debate which is as significant today as it was in Green's own time.

Liberal politics of rights, so the argument goes, is premised on the Kantian insistence on the primacy of the right. Call it rightness-common good.[1] Taylor makes a similar claim; that because "[t]he ethic central to a

---

[1] Both liberals and critics of liberalism lend support to the claim that liberalism embraces only rightness-common good. In a vigorous response to communitarian criticism Holmes argues that liberals hold "an emphatic conception of the common good". Because they are pluralists, liberals, he holds, do not provide a definition of "the good life" as opposed to "the bad life"; but they do provide an obligatory distinction between "right action" and "wrong action": "Rightness ... defines the liberal conception of the common good" (Holmes, 1993: 200, 237–40).

liberal society is an ethic of the right, rather than the good", "procedural liberalism" cannot recognize "a socially endorsed conception of the good." But he adds that liberalism can and does endorse a conception of common good in terms of the right (Taylor, 1989: 164, 165, 172). Questioning that primacy of the right, Sandel grounds the politics of the common good in a conception of the good life, and claims Hegel and Aristotle as its intellectual fountainhead. Call it goodness-common good.

The complex nature of Green's common good defies and transcends this rightness-common good and goodness-common good dualism. Yet to appreciate how it does so, requires us to see how, for Green, though the right (as rights and justice) is derivative from the good (which is primary), the right is, nevertheless, constitutive of the good and is necessary for its realization. I do this in the next five sections.

Section I introduces the common good as the good society which is grounded in an ethics of joint self-realization. I then proceed, in the following three sections, to explore the Kantian, Hegelian and Aristotelian resources which give form and content to the common good conception of the good society. The final section focuses on justice and citizenship as the positive expressions of the complexity of the common good. The essay concludes with briefly diffusing liberal anxieties about the "commonness" of the good.

I: Introducing the Common Good

There is no doubt that the idea of the common good is the central concept of Green's thought. Doubts, however, abound as to the nature and role of that concept. What is necessary, then, is to reconstruct the common good from within Green's own thought. Though he nowhere provides a full account of the common good, that concept does not float free of the context of his ethical writings. The result of my reconstruction is an understanding of the common good as an ethics of joint realizability, which is an ethics of a certain kind of social life: co-operative individual-developing social life or harmonious individual-realizing sociability. The common good emerges as an ideal of the good society: a community of mutually developing individuals, the moral requiredeness of which justifies the construction of social order in terms of both justice and citizenship. My reconstruction of the common good is twofold: analyzing the two components of "common good", and seeing how the latter transcends the dichotomy of egoism and altruism.

I shall first analyze the two components in "common good". The "good" in "common good" is self-realization, self-development, abiding self-satisfaction, or perfecting human character. By self-realization Green means,

Though made pronounced in response to communitarian criticism, that liberal conception of the common good is not entirely new (Benn and Peters, 1959: 318–21; Diggs, 1972–3: 283–93)

in Aristotelian fashion, exercising one's human capacities. The "common" good, then, is "common" self-realization. But how is self-realization common? What does "common" in "common good" mean? I suggest three related senses of "common", without appreciation of which Green's common good cannot be fully apprehended: "mutual", "universal" and "distributive".

The primary sense of "common" is, I believe, "mutual", or "joint" as opposed to "separate" or "private".[2] It can be gleaned from the contrast, foundational to Green's common good project, between common and private good (Green, 1906a: §§107–8, 118, 123; see Green, 1906b: §§16–18, 21–24, and Green, 1911a). Enjoying private good consists in "separating ... instead of uniting" (Green, 1906a: §118), and may be described as "separate satisfiability" in that the end (good) one pursues is logically independent of the ends of other individuals and hence can be enjoyed without other individuals. Each person desires and pursues it as one's *own-good* and not as good.

Self-realization, by contrast, is mutual good: no one can achieve self-realization in separation from and independent of others; one's development is dependent on and is reciprocal with others. As Hobhouse puts it, "The development that each man can achieve is conditioned in kind and degree by the development of others" (Hobhouse, 1921: 90). This claim presupposes a view of shared social life: "In thinking of ultimate good he thinks of it indeed necessarily as perfection for himself ... But he cannot think of himself as satisfied in any life other than a social life ... in which ... all men, shall participate" (Green, 1907: §§288, 370). "All" alludes to the inclusive and distributive nature of the common good.

"Common" is also "universal" as opposed to "particular" or "exclusive". The good as self-realization equally relates to all human beings in virtue of "unfulfilled possibilities of the rational nature common to all men", and "not merely ... [of] the members of a particular community" (Green, 1907: §207). Importantly, therefore, the good society is premised on the moral equality of individuals, which renders it an inclusive rather than exclusionary ideal. It is also distributive.

"Common" in "common good" is, finally, "distributive" as opposed to "collective". "Common" may mean two things here: either the good in question pertains to society as a whole (collective sense), or to each of its members individually (distributive sense) (Scruton, 1982: 77; Gewirth, 1996: 94). The good society is "common" in the distributive sense, such that justice, as we shall see, is constitutive of it. The distributive nature of the common good may be seen in two ways. For Green, the good does pertain to society as a whole which is, strictly speaking, the collective sense; but he employs "society as a whole" distributively, meaning each and

---

2   What I describe as mutual good Philip Pettit (1994: 176–204) describes as "interactive good".

every member of society individually, though jointly and not separately (Green, 1986a: §§132, 142; Green, 1986b: 199). Alternatively, Green insists, "Our ultimate standard of worth is an ideal of *personal* worth. All other values are relative to value for, of, or in a person" (Green, 1907: §184; Green, 1986c: §6; Green, 1986a: §§23, 25). The good, then, pertains to each member of society individually though not separately: "It is only in the *inter*course of men ... that the capacity [for self-realization] is actualised and that we really live as persons" (Green, 1907: §§183 [italics added], 184, 288; Simhony, 1991).

The second element in my reconstruction of the common good is that, as a mutual good or ethic of joint self-realizability, Green intends the common good to escape the dualism of egoism and altruism, self-love and benevolence. Instead, the common good ethic forges a non-dichotomous moral framework which aims to occupy a moral terrain of human connectedness where one's good and the good of others are intertwined, and where one's fundamental interest in one's development is not pitted against one's interest in the development of others. Such social connectedness does not give rise to rival egoist and altruist interests, but rather to social interest which escapes that rivalry. Social interest is central to the common good in a way in which selfish (egoist) interest is essential to private good. That contrast may be best appreciated as that between two conceptions of social life: communal society vs. private society. Green's common good aims at rejecting private society as the ethical basis of liberalism.

According to the idea of private society, individuals enter into social relations only to meet their egoistic needs. Individuals have interests in others, but only as a means to the satisfaction of these narrowly self-centered needs. It is in this way that, for Green, private good is inextricably bound up with selfishness: "Selfishness ... [is] the direction of a man's dominant interests to an object private to himself, a good in which others cannot share" (Green, 1906a: §123). To be selfish or egoistic is, as Bradley holds, to think only of oneself. As Rawls explains, "An egoist is someone committed to the point of view of his own interests. His final ends are related to himself" (1971: 568). For Rawls, the problem with the egoist is that he lacks the settled desire to take up the standpoint of justice. Without forcing any comparison with Rawls,[3] Green may be said to have a similar complaint taken from the common good vantage point: the egoist lacks the settled desire to take up the standpoint of the common good society (which embraces the standpoint of justice but also of citizenship), without which its justification and viability are put in jeopardy. The problem of private society, therefore, is the problem of egoism (or selfish interest). Insofar as egoist interest is the primary basis of judgment and action, ego-

---

3 A comparison, however, is likely to be intriguing; see Gaus (1983); Simhony (2006: 259-61).

ism cannot be the basis of common society because it cannot be the basis of individual-developing sociability. Being an egoist is inconsistent with the reasons and motivation that the standpoint of sociability requires. Social interest is. "The man cannot contemplate himself as in a better state … without contemplating others, not merely as a means to that better state, but as sharing it with him" (Green, 1907: §199; see also §§234–6, 239, 242–3, 253; 1986a: §248). This is what Green describes as "distinctive social interest" (Green, 1907: §200). "Distinctive" means that to have social interest is to have intrinsic rather than instrumental interest in others. It means that social relations with others are not simply of derivative interest, as means to egoistic gratification, but of direct interest to us. Such interest is premised on seeing others as our "alter ego" (Green, 1907: §§191, 200) and, therefore, internal to our own life. Hence, "distinctive social interest" also means interest which is neither merely selfish nor purely altruistic, but mutual:[4] it is other-regarding without being self-forgetfulness or selfless.

Two points follow. Nicholson is quite right to insist on keeping apart Green's idea of the common good and the idea of public interest (Nicholson, 1990: 62–4). This claim, however, is fully consistent with my insistence that the common good and social interest are inextricably bound up. For social interest is not public interest. Green rids the idea of interest of its selfish, competitive, materialist and maximizing associations (all connected with public interest), much as he rids the idea of rights of its atomist connection. That he does not abandon the language of interests situates him firmly within modern liberal tradition. In particular, his idea of social interest ought to be appreciated against a sustained attempt of modern liberals to rid liberalism of its association with self-centered individualism.

The second point concerns communitarian and republican criticism of liberalism. Communitarians and republicans object to the way, as they allege, liberals see society as nothing more than a cooperative venture for the pursuit of individual advantage, as an essential private association formed by individuals whose essential interests are defined independently of, and in a sense prior to, the community of which they are members. Green's common good ethics of joint realizability aims at rejecting just such an idea of private society as the ethical core of liberalism. Kant, I suggest, is essential to such a project, but it is not immediately obvious how since, whereas Green defends goodness-common good, Kant defends rightness-common good; hence, the reversal argument to which I now turn.

II: The Reversal Argument: The Relevance of Kant

The reversal argument reverses the relationship between the good and the right such that the good precedes the right but the right, though derivative

---

4 Compare Green's interchangeable use of social and mutual recognition to explain rights (e.g., Green, 1986a: §§25–26, 136, 139).

of the good, is internal to it and is essential to its realization. This is how Kantian rightness-common good is essential to Green's goodness-common good: Kantian rightness (common good) is constitutive of and is essential to the realization of Green's goodness-common good. I proceed, then, in two steps. First, I look at the reversal itself which, I claim, Green pursues from within Kant's own resources. The second step is to show how, once the right-good relationship is reversed, the right is, nevertheless, essential to the common good project.

First step: the primacy of the good

A typical statement of the reversal argument is found in Green's revision of "Kant's statement, 'everything in nature works according to laws; *the distinction of a rational being is the faculty of acting according to the consciousness of laws the distinction of a rational, or free, being, is that he acts*, not so as to yield certain results, but from consciousness of ends in attaining which he may satisfy himself, *out of which arises the consciousness of laws according to which they are to be attained*" (Green, 1906: §84; italics added). This revision rests on Green's claim that "[a]ction according to the consciousness of laws clearly presupposes the consciousness of ends to be attained by conformity to these laws" (Green, 1906: §84). Thus, consciousness of ends precedes consciousness of laws, conformity to which realizes the end. Consciousness of laws (right) arises out of consciousness of ends (good), but adhering to those laws (right) is essential to attaining the ends (good).

Green's reversal argument is employed from Kant's own resources. In particular, he makes use of the teleological nature of Kant's philosophy. To the standard Hegelian-communitarian criticism that Kant's notion of "duty for duty's sake" reduces itself to a duty to do nothing, Green answers:

> [W]hen Kant excludes all reference to an object, of which the reality is desired, from the law of which the mere idea determines the *good will*, he means all reference to an object *other than* that of which the presentation ipso facto constitutes the moral law. That in that law, the willing obedience to which characterises a *good will*, there is implied some relation to an object, and that this object moves the will in the right sort of obedience to the law, appears from his account of man as an absolute end, on which he founds the second statement of the categorical imperative (Green, 1906a: §111; italics added).

Green's answer, then, is that Kantian duty is inseparable from realizing the "self as an absolute end" for "man in his rational nature is an absolute end" (Green, 1906a: §§118, 112), which, in turn, is bound up with the idea of the good will. The good will is "desire determined not merely by ... *any* kind of conception of self as an absolute end, but by a *true* conception of self as an absolute end" (Green, 1906a: §115); thus, consciousness of "absolute good" — the good will — "carries with it the idea of a law", that is, "as having a claim on me …" In other words, conforming to "a universally binding law of conduct … the rule of conduct … upon which the good man acts … bears an authority derived from an ideal of absolute good" (Green, 1906a: §§111, 125). The problem with Kant, therefore, is not that he lacks a view of the end or good; the problem is that his view of the end is lacking. Mending that lack is the concern of the complementary argument, to which I shall turn once the second step of the reversal argument is completed.

Second step: the constitutive role of the right

The reversal of good-right relationship understood, the task now is to appreciate the constitutive role Kantian rightness-common good plays in Green's goodness-common good. The essential text for that purpose is that which supports Green's claim that Kantian reason "gives us the idea of a common good" (Green, 1906a: §107). How does reason give us the idea of a common good? Negatively, because non-egoistic reason rejects the idea of private society; positively, that rejection presupposes a positive ideal of moral community which lies at the heart of the common good society, society which is realizable through Kantian rightness.

Kantian reason rejects the idea of private society. Recall that the common good may be seen as a view of social life in contradistinction to egoism-based private society. Egoism cannot justify common good society because the egoist's desires are for things for him. For Kant, however, "the moral faculty is a faculty of 'categorical' imperative, namely pure practical reason, which is not egoistic but universalizing" (Frankena, 1991: 191); hence, "[s]uch conformity [to universal law] on the part of everyone else I must desire in desiring it for myself, and everyone else in desiring it for himself must desire it for me" (Green, 1906a: §107 [italics added]). Universalizing reason is non-egoist in that it guides one's actions such that they are not concerned only with oneself. "My own reason" is not personal, "but is, to speak metaphorically, an inlet which the general will of humanity can enter and enable the individual to control personal needs and desires" (Acton, 1970: 41). Hence: "It is in *my own person* that I seek to realise it [the end] but in so doing I am realising it for the *benefit of everyone else* …" (Green, 1906a: §107). Universalizing reason, in its reciprocal capability, rules out egoism. This is in form Green's idea of the common good as mutual good and this is how reason "unites us".

Rejecting egoism-based private society presupposes a positive ideal of a community (viz., a kingdom of ends) of mutually respecting persons, each recognizing the others as equal members of one community. That ideal of community is both constitutive of Green's common good society and is essential to its realization. It is constitutive of Green's common good society in that the latter is a "society of equals" in which each member respects and is respected by all other members. This is what Greek ethics did not recognize, that is, the universality of "the principle that humanity in the person of every one is to be treated always as an end, never merely as a means ..." (Green, 1907: §§267, 280).

Kantian moral community is essential to the realization of the common good society. To see this is to see how justice-as-fairness is internal to the common good project. In the Kantian ideal community no one would be required to do anything which he would not think it reasonable for everyone to do. Thus, Kant holds that "no one is bound to refrain from encroaching upon the possession of another man if the latter does not in equal measure guarantee that the same kind of restraint will be exercised with regard to him" (Qtd. in Murphy, 1970: 115). This is moral rightness which, according to Stephen Holmes, is "the ethical center of liberalism" (Holmes, 1993: 238). This ethical center generates, for Kant, the obligation of reciprocity (Murphy, 1970: 121). And some such obligation justifies the structural requirement, grounded in the common good ethic, for mutually assured self-realization without which the common good project cannot be realized. How so?

That Kant's community of ends structures the common good society has consequences for the sort of claims that members of the common good society can make on one another. Of particular importance is the claim for self-realization. Since self-realization consists in exercising distinctive human capacities, and since the common good society is concerned with the self-realization of all its members, members can expect their society to enable and maintain the exercise of such capacities. But since the basis of the claim to self-realization is the claim to status as an equal member in the community, to claim self-realization for oneself is to recognize the perfectly reciprocal and equally legitimate claims to self-realization by others. Accordingly, the good society is a "social union, in which the claims of all are acknowledged by the loyal citizen as the measure of what he may claim for himself ...", and therefore, rests on "[the] recognition of reciprocal claims" (Green, 1907: §§283, 216).

Now, since self-realization is an exercise-conception, one's claim to self-realization for oneself is a claim to be secured by the conditions for self-realization, among which rights are of particular importance; hence "on the part of every person ... the claim ... to rights on his own part is co-ordinate with his recognition of rights on the part of others", that is 'mutual recognition' (Green, 1986a: §§26, 139). These, we shall see, embrace justice as impartial maintenance of a system of rights as well as distributive justice, with regard to which Green goes beyond Kant, who regarded the state as a just protector of rights (Murphy, 1970: 124–5; 125, fn. 26). The point to stress now is that Kantian rightness is essential to realizing the common good society.

III: The Complementary Argument

Now that the reversal of the relations between the good and the right has been accomplished, the complementary argument comes into play. Why so? Because, as we have just seen, Kant's ideal of moral community structures the common good society; hence, Green does not seek to displace, but rather to mend the Kantian argument by complementing it. A useful entry into the complementary argument is Norman's claim that Kant fails to refute egoism. I said that Kant's ruling out egoism structures Green's common good society by rejecting private society and justifying the kingdom of ends as a positive ideal of community of equals. Norman's criticism might jeopardize Green's reliance on Kant. Seeing how it does not is doubly helpful: it helps explain how Green's common good is liberal in a complex way. Also, since Norman's criticism is of a communitarian nature, the complementary argument shows how Green's Kant is immune to such criticism while essential to Green's liberalism.

Richard Norman claims that Kant fails to provide a refutation of egoism because his universalizing reason is consistent with justifying a world of self-respecting egoists (Norman, 1983: 119). Without a shift from universality as impersonality to universality as impartiality Kant cannot refute egoism. That shift, however, cannot be achieved as long as the universalizability principle is grounded in purely formal rationality. Rather, "we have to start ... with the idea of the individual as a social being involved in relations which carry with them commitments to others" (Norman, 1983: 156). Norman's criticism recalls the communitarian claim that Kant conceives rationality in purely procedural terms and considers the agent in abstraction from any concrete historical, social or political context.

My response to Norman's criticism is that Kant's problem is not a problem for Green's Kant. It is not, because much like Norman, Green starts "with the idea of the individual as a social being". The self, Green insists, "is not an abstract or empty self" (Green, 1907: §199), but "a determinate self" (Green, 1906a: §§118, 124), namely the social self. Norman's understanding of the social self as relational is based on Bradley. Unlike Norman, though, Green may be said to take two routes to the social individual: the "relational self" route, which is not surprising given the Bradley connection, and the self as a "subject of interests" route, which is surprising unless we appreciate the role of the language of interest in Green's common good argument, as I claim we should. The essential point, however, is that both routes aim to achieve that which Norman's single route does: the appreciation of the social nature of the individual provides a refutation of egoism by "revealing the inadequacy of the dichotomy between egoism and altruism" (Norman, 1983: 156–7). Further, both routes reveal, respectively, the Hegelian and Aristotelian complementing of Kant. I shall address the Hegelian route first.

The complementary argument: the Hegelian route

Green, like Bradley, holds that the self is not "an abstract empty self" since it "is from the first" a self "existing in manifold relations to nature and other persons" and "these relations form the reality of the self" (Green, 1906a: §124). Intriguingly, however, this account of the relational self is, for Green, "the germ of what Kant calls ... 'kingdom of ends'" (Green, 1906a: §124). It becomes less intriguing, however, if we give that claim a Hegelian twist as Green does. The Hegelian twist complements Kant in two ways: one, Kant's community of ends is grounded in the Hegelian community of mutual recognition; two, the Kantian ideal is socially situated.

Green grounds the Kantian community of rights (mutual respect for persons) in the Hegelian-inspired community of mutual recognition (Green, 1986c: 312). In such a community, each person finds his identity as a free individual through relations with others. Similarly, Green holds that such a community of mutual recognition is essential to sustain a Kantian community of reciprocal respect, for "it is only in the intercourse of men, each recognised by each as an end, not merely a means, and thus having reciprocal claims, that the capacity is actualised and that we really live as persons"; hence, the relation of mutual recognition is the sphere of the individual's "*realised* possibility" (Green, 1907: §183).[5] This sphere, therefore, "must be a social life, in which all men freely and consciously co-operate, since otherwise the possibilities of their nature, as agents who are ends to themselves, could not be realized in it" (Green, 1907: §288).

Membership in shared co-operative social life is, to borrow from Joseph Raz's relevant anti-individualist argument, a "collective good" (Raz, 1986: 189–90, 203–7), namely it is constitutive of the very possibility of individuals becoming self-realizing persons. In other words, such membership is one and the same normative source of both one's pursuit of valuable goals and one's obligation to others and service to one's community. This non-confrontational view of morality which propels Green's common good calls into question the whole opposition between the individual and community in a way that transcends the terms of debate between liberals and communitarians/republicans.

This is abundantly clear from the way Green revises the link forged by Kant between respect for persons and the separateness of individuals. Whereas Kantian subjects are conceived of as selves equal by virtue of exclusion of difference, for Hegel each self is for the other a means through which each mediates itself with itself. In this reciprocal process subjects

---

5 Italics in original; see also §288.

recognize themselves as mutually recognizing one another. This process produces a subject which is relational at its core. This is, Green believes, how moral philosophy regards the individual, that is "as related to himself in relation to others—as through relation to others gaining realization of the relation to himself, which is otherwise merely formal" (Green, 1986c: 310).[6] Relational social ontology informs the common good society, which is not just a collection of individuals, but neither is it a mere collectivity above and beyond individuals.

The second Hegelian complementing of Kant is the appreciation of how the Kantian kingdom of ends is taking shape in actual social institutions. This Hegelian argument is important to Green's interpretation of Kant:

> The mistake of those who deny the *a priori* character of such 'intuitions' of the conscience as that represented by Kant's formula [i.e. respect for persons], does not lie in a history of the intuitions, but in ignoring the immanent operation of ideas of the reason in the process of social organisation, upon which the intuitions as in the individual depend. (Green, 1907: §215)

For Green, then, the Kantian principle of humanity takes shape in concrete social institutions because they "are, so to speak, the form and body of reason, as practical in men" (Green, 1907: §205).[7] Hence, the social practices which embody "reciprocal rights and obligations" educate individuals such that "we are conscious of ourselves and others as ourselves", and hence treat others as an "alter ego" (Green, 1907: §§204, 200).[8] Though the "articulation, and application to the particulars of life, of that principle of an absolute value in the human person as such, of a like claim to consideration in all men, which is implied in the law and conventional morality is in fact partial and inconsistent", it nevertheless is essential in establishing "practice of justice" (Green, 1907: §215) which is, in turn, essential to the realization of the common good society. Essential also is the practice of virtue which connects Kant with Aristotle.

The complementary argument: the Aristotelian route

Recall that the result of the reversal argument was to show that the problem with Kant was not that he lacks a view of the good (for the good consists of the good will), but that his view of the good is lacking. This is because the good will "may be taken to mean a will presented by some abstract idea of goodness or of moral law" (Green, 1907: §247).[9] The charge of abstraction, recall, propels Norman's claim that Kant fails to refute ego-

---

6 See also Green (1986a, §138; 1907, §216; 1911b: 60–71; 1911a: 112–3, 116–20, 123–4). For the Hegelian twist of Kant to which Green clearly subscribes, see Caird (1893: 328–50, 554–66, 570–53).
7 See also Green, 1907: §§204, 216–7.
8 See also Green, 1907: §201.
9 See also Green, 1907: §266.

ism. "But it is not thus that we understand the good will" (Green, 1907: §247), Green would retort.

How, then, does he understand the good will? "When we speak of the formation of such will [the good will] ... we understand it, not as determined merely by an abstract idea of law, but as implying (what in fact it must imply) a whole world of beneficent social activities ..." (Green, 1907: §288).[10] The reference to beneficence is significant not only because it overcomes Kantian abstract reason by connecting the good will with social activities, but because that connection is distinctively Aristotelian. The capacity of beneficence is one of Aristotle's definitions of virtue as Green well recognizes when he states: "Virtue was ... a faculty of beneficence" (Green, 1907: §248), citing Aristotle's definition of virtue in his *Rhetoric*. The beneficence definition of virtue exposes the connection of virtue with fine action.

Fine activity contrasts with "acting for the sake of either expedience or extrinsic pleasure. It is the end of virtue, but an immanent end ..." (Sherman, 1989: 114). Fine activity, then, cannot be selfish activity as T.H. Irwin establishes by reference to Aristotle's beneficence definition of virtue. All virtues aim at the fine; "the fine is both intrinsically good and praiseworthy ... hence concern for the fine is contrasted with narrow and exclusive concern for one's own interest"; therefore, "actions displaying great virtues [which are for the sake of the fine] insofar as they especially benefit others" (Irwin, 1991: 296). The connection between virtue and fine activity reveals the distinctive nature of virtuous activity as mutually beneficial. Green intends the practice of virtue to occupy the ethical terrain of shared social relations which the dualism between self-love and benevolence squeezes out of consideration. Such dualism is invalidated by the Aristotelian account of self-love: "correct self-love does not allow selfishness" (Irwin, 1988: §208, p. 390). If "correct self-love" is in the first place unselfish, then the dualism of self-love and benevolence is excluded: "The Aristotelian self-lover does not suffer from the kind of self-love we normally condemn: He does not suffer from excessive self-concern or think himself better than others" (Homiak, 1981: 639). Such self-centered self-love may characterize Hobbes' idea of self-love but not Aristotle's.

This reading of Aristotle should be seen as a resource for Green's revision and retention of the language of interest as essential, rather than hostile, to the language of the common good. Recall that the problem with the good will is Kant's "too abstract view of the *interest* on which he held that goodness must depend". Green employs a similar language of interest with regard to Aristotle who, Green claims, "[o]nce and for all ... conceived and expressed the conception of a free or pure morality, as resting on ... *disinterested interest in the good*" (Green, 1907: §253; emphasis added).

---

10 See also §247, where Green connects the good will with virtues explicitly.

That claim—having an "interest in the development of our faculties" (Green, 1907: §234)[11]—is foundational to the common good project. For Aristotle to complement Kant is, therefore, to give content to the abstract interest in the good. This Aristotelian virtues do since, following Aristotle, Green regards "the several virtues as so many applications of that interest to the main relations of life" (Green, 1907: §253). And virtues do so not as external means to the good of self-realization; rather, following Aristotle again, Green views "the good itself not as anything external to the capacities virtuously exercised in its own pursuit but as their full realisation" (Green, 1907: §253). Because the human good, for Aristotle, consists in virtuous activity, this closes the gap between what is in one's interest and the life of virtue. Green views such an "interest in the development of our faculties" as "a governing interest", which is "not in abstraction from other interests, but as an organising influence upon and among them" (Green, 1907: §247),[12] but "must be active in every character" (Green, 1907: §247) which pursues perfection, thereby giving reality to the Kantian "true conception of self as an absolute end" (Green, 1906a: §115). It is, therefore, appropriate to describe that self as a "subject of interests" (Green, 1906b: §4), which Green does. It is in this way that the language of interest is not hostile, but indeed essential to the language of the common good.

Let me conclude with that claim by drawing attention to two points. One point is that to make this claim is to go against the standard view that pits the idea of the common good against the idea of self-interest. This is a version of the dualism of morality and self-interest. For Green, the common good is itself a resolution of such dualism. From the point of view of the common good, the tension is not between common good and interest as such, but between common good and selfish interest. The second point is that the connection between social interest and the common good gains special importance if we are to be able properly to situate Green in the liberal tradition. Here's why: not appreciating the importance of social interest to the common good runs the risk of excluding Green as a fully paid-up liberal. For one thing, the idea of the goodness-common good has not played a central role in liberal thinking; indeed, it has been associated with non-liberal and even antiliberal trends of thought (Holmes, 1993: 198–9). For another, the language of interest is essential to liberalism. Michael Freeden claims that the idea of general interest is one of the core concepts of liberalism, and that the full core is essential to the identity of any liberal tradition. "Remove one [concept of the core] and we are looking at a borderline case" (Freeden, 1996: 16). Seeing how Green employs "general interest" in terms of "social interest" rather than "public interest" shows

---

11 See also Green, 1907: §§247, 255.
12 See also Green, 1907: §§252, 255.

that he is not. It also shows Green's contribution to the modern liberal's effort to revise liberalism's link with the idea of self-interest.

A final word. For Green to speak of an Aristotelian Kant is equally to speak of a Kantian Aristotle. D.G. Ritchie put the point well: "If we are to connect him [Green] with any particular names of philosophers, it would be least misleading to say that he corrected Kant by Aristotle and Aristotle by Kant" (Ritchie, 1891: 139). Perhaps the main Kantian correction of Aristotle concerns universality. Whereas Green finds room in Kantian ethic of rules for Aristotelian idea of character, the Kantian claim that all moral agents are ends-in-themselves creates the possibility of universality of character.[13] Though there are some current attempts to reconcile Kantian and Aristotelian ethics in a similar vein,[14] it is, nevertheless, the case that contemporary moral and political discourse views them as rival dualistic perspectives, as the liberal-communitarian debate amply shows. Green's refusal to subscribe to that dualism reveals the complexity of his common good. This is the focus of the final section.

IV: Complex Common Good: Justice and Citizenship

That Green's project of the common good draws both on Kantian and Aristotelian (and Hegelian) resources reveals its complexity and is the source of our inability to place the common good neatly in the classification of either liberal or communitarian/republican. That classification is grounded in the divide between rightness- and goodness-common good, ethics of right vs. ethics of good, and politics of rights vs. politics of common good. Green's common good defies and transcends these dualisms. This is how the complexity of the common good reveals itself negatively. But how does it reveal itself positively? It does in the ideas of justice and citizenship as normatively interdependent implementations of the good society. This is the focus of the final section. I shall conclude by looking briefly at liberal anxieties about the "commonness" of the good, which I shall find to be unfounded, and a brief comment on Green's extending liberal concerns, the locus of which, I hold, lies in the ethic of the common good.

Justice and citizenship

The claim that justice and citizenship are mutually supportive and essential for a viable good community reveals the complexity of the common good positively. The essential point is this: the common good as ethics of joint self-realization requires that both justice and citizenship will structure the social order. Both, that is, are justified by, and are derivative of, one ethical foundation of individual-developing sociability.

---

13 See, e.g., Green (1907: §267).
14 See Crisp (1996).

Citizenship, for Green, is captured by the idea of "rendering service to the state" (Green, 1907: §263), where the state is understood widely as the entire political community or scheme of social relations (Green, 1907: §264). To render service to the state is to act as a member: "He [Aristotle] regards the state … as a society of which life is maintained by what its members do for the sake of maintaining it" (Green, 1986a: §38). It is, unsurprisingly, on this Aristotelian ground that Green's common good meets communitarian/republican common good.

This is especially evident in relation to Taylor's 1989 discussion of the communitarian/republican common good. Green, like Taylor, views the relation of the individual member and political community in terms of identification which is properly understood neither in terms of enlightened self-interest nor abstract altruism (Taylor, 1989: 160–70). This is Green's point—that Aristotle's view of the state has "[n]o need to dwell on benevolence as a balance of selfishness" (Qtd. by Irwin, 1991: 309–10, fn.33). For the state is not viewed instrumentally, but as a system of institutions and arrangements which are expressive and enhancing of joint realizability of individuals as a common enterprise, and which is, therefore, intrinsically valuable. Further, Taylor's distinction between two models of citizens' dignity highlights Green's own understanding of citizenship. Taylor distinguishes between the liberal model of equal rights and treatment and the republican model of participatory self-rule as well as his claim that the viability of liberal rightness-common good is put in jeopardy insofar as it adopts the former model (Taylor, 1989: 178–79). In a similar vein Green insists on "active interest in the service of the state … [which] can hardly arise while the individual's relation to the state is that of a passive recipient of protection in the exercise of his rights of person and property" (Green, 1986a: §122), which he, much like Taylor, describes as (intelligent) patriotism.

Against this basic accord, two points of difference are important. One point is that Green's "active service in the interest of the state" is not the same as Taylor's participatory self-rule account of citizenship insofar as the latter is the same as participating in political decision-making (Taylor, 1989: 170). To be sure, Green recognizes the need of the active citizen "to have a share, direct or indirect, by himself as a member or by voting for the members of supreme or provincial assemblies, in making and maintaining the laws which he obeys" (Green, 1986a: §122). But the activity of Green's citizen is not as strictly political as that; rather, it embraces activities of "mutual helpfulness" in the "maintenance and furtherance of a free society" (Green, 1986a: §248),[15] which may be described as "obligation of support". Moreover, it is telling that Green concedes "a lowering of civil

---

15 This wider understanding of citizenship probably applies to Taylor's citizen too, but he is insufficiently clear on that issue.

vitality" in the modern state, but endorses "the price of having recognised the claim to citizenship as the claim of *all* men" (Green, 1986a: §119, italics added. See also §258). This tells that Green would refuse to see Taylor's two models of citizen dignity as two rival and mutually exclusive perspectives. Hence, my second point.

The second point is that the requiredness of citizenship is justified only in a just state: "It is the fault of the state if this conception [of a common good maintained by law] fails to make him a loyal citizen, if not an intelligent patriot. It is a sign that the state is not a true state; that it is not fulfilling its primary function of maintaining law equally in the interest of all ..." (Green, 1986a: §121). Setting aside for a moment the important point regarding the "primary function" of the state, the essential point is that rendering service to the state, though required by the common good, is inseparable from and is reciprocal with, the state rendering service to its members: "the function of society being the development of persons, the realisation of the human spirit in society can only be attained according to the measure in which that function is fulfilled" (Green, 1907: §191).[16] But how is that function to be fulfilled? By establishing and maintaining "a society of men really free ... ('really free', in the sense of being enabled to make the most of their capabilities)" (Green, 1986a: §248). The obligation of supporting a free society depends on the obligation of society to enable freedom for all. Consequently, as the above quotation suggests, the "primary function" of the state is that of "maintaining law equally in the interest of all". Therefore, the "active interest in the service of the state" on the side of its members is normatively inseparable from and is reciprocal with the state acting "equally in the interest of all" (Green, 1986a: §§121–2). Because the state fulfills its "primary function", and hence service to its members, individual members come to value it for itself and not as a mere instrument. They can identify themselves with their society because it embodies the ideal of joint self-realization whose value and requiredness they support. The individual comes to identify with his political community "as the condition of the maintenance of those rights and interests, common to himself with his neighbours, which he understands" (Green, 1986a: §121).

The "primary function" of the state, then, may be described as justice, and is twofold. One function is that of maintaining law equally in the interest of all by upholding "equal rights" (Green, 1907: §258): "maintaining the rights of its members as a whole or a system, in such a way that none gains at the expense of another (no one has any power guaranteed to him through another's being deprived of that power)" (Green, 1986a: §132). The second aspect is distributive justice, the importance of which is clearly implicit in Green's claim that "[t]he justice of punishment depends on the

---

16 See also Green (1907: §184).

justice of the general system of rights ... on the question whether the social organization in which a criminal has lived and acted has given him a fair chance of not being a criminal" (Green, 1986a: §189).[17] The point is that the state's "primary function" embraces the fact that it secures its members a "real opportunity of self-development" with a special emphasis on "the less favoured members of society" (Green, 1907: §245).

Justice is constitutive of the very possibility of realizing the common good and, indeed, may be best understood as giving effect to the "distributive" sense of "common", without which the "joint" sense of "common" remains unfulfilled. Securing a real opportunity for self-development for all with a special emphasis on the worse-off members of society illustrates that the good of the common good society is understood in terms of benefit to each and every member of society, not separately but jointly. As Hobhouse puts it relevantly, "the good of society is bound up with the recognition of the rights of its members" (Hobhouse, 1922: 40, fn.). And the good of the common good society is joint or mutual good, such that no member (or group of members) can enjoy a good at the expense or loss of others' real opportunity. This imbalance, Green holds, is just what utilitarianism is consistent with; hence, from the standpoint of the common good, it is not only the utilitarian hedonist good which is unacceptable, but also the utilitarian principle of moral rightness (Green, 1907: §214).[18] It is in this way that rightness (as twofold justice), though it is derivative of the good which precedes it, is nevertheless internal to the common good project such that justice is essential to the realization of the common good society.

Normative reciprocity of justice and citizenship as ethical requiredness of the common good creates a distinctive justificatory sequence of twofold significance. First, this justificatory sequence suggests that communitarians who tend to emphasize one-sidedly the obligation of support run the risk of endorsing unjust communities as worthy of support.[19] The point cannot be overstated that the just society is internal to the common good society which is unrealizable without justice. Second, the obligation of support is an obligation of reciprocity (or of mutual service). Insofar as the just state maintains a system of law and rights equally in the interest of all, and secures a real opportunity of self-development with emphasis on the worse-off, then supporting the state is mutual support: supporting oneself and others at the same time. Put differently, rendering service to the just state is mutual service to oneself and others because a just state serves everyone.

---

17 On Green's idea of positive right not to starve, see Simhony (2006: 254–5).
18 For Green's relationship to utilitarianism, see Simhony (1995) and Simhony (forthcoming).
19 Gewirth (1996: 86–7) makes this criticism explicit. See also Dagger (1997: 114–5).

Liberal anxieties and extending liberal concerns

Certain issues never go away. Liberal anxieties about Green's liberalism is a case in point. Space does not allow discussing them in detail, nor is there a pressing need, since many of the criticisms have been sufficiently shown to be groundless.[20] I shall, therefore, focus on liberal anxiety that the "commonness" of the (common) good is exclusionary and suppressive of diversity and difference. The commonness of Green's common good is, I claim, immune to this liberal charge. For one thing, "common" is not collective, but distributive, as is evident from the centrality of justice to the common good project; for another, Green does not believe that there is one single correct path to the good life. The good as self-realization is multi-pathed. Since the former point ought to be clear by now, I shall focus briefly on the latter.

Two points need attention. First, what is single is the form, not the substance of self-realization (Green, 1907: §283; 1906a: §118). The form is realizing one's capacities. To do that one pursues "dominant interests" (or lifeplans) which give effect to one's conception of oneself; "dominant interests" are the substance of self-realization, of which there is a "great variety" (Green, 1906a: §123).[21] Personal pursuits of dominant interests depend on the available stock of social forms, and therefore there are as many possible pursuits as one's society may offer. To be sure, not all pursuits are self-realizing. For one thing, like Raz (1986: 378–81), Green holds that self-realization obtains only in valuable pursuits of which, however, there is a "great variety", as I have just explained, and there is certainly no single path. What valuable pursuits clearly exclude is habitual pleasure-seekers: the voluptuary is not self-realizing. Further, no one can achieve self-realization by exploiting, oppressing or degrading others. Thus, though both constraints restrict self-realization, they do not reduce it to a single-path good.

The second point is that the good is *self*-realization; it can be achieved only by one's own effort. As Green famously claims: "No one can convey a good character to another. Everyone must make his character for himself. All that one man can do to make another better is to remove obstacles, and supply conditions favourable to the formation of a good character" (1907: §332). Though he is indebted to Aristotle's understanding of self-realization, Green parts ways inasmuch as he denies that it is the role of the state to legislate self-realization. This is abundantly clear from his view of punishment (1986a: §§204–6).[22] Though the ultimate end of the state is moral, its primary goal in punishing is maintenance of rights. Thus, "… it is the business of the state, not indeed directly to promote moral goodness … but

---

20 See Nicholson (1990: 83–95).
21 See also Green (1907: §§283, 234).
22 See also Green (1907: §232; 1986b:202).

to maintain the conditions without which a free exercise of the human faculties is impossible" (1986b: 202). This is how justice is internal to the common good project.

V. Conclusion

A final point. Freeden claims that "Green's importance lies in his input into modern liberal thinking about rights" (Freeden, 1991: 22). Specifically: "Rights were ... moral claims for self-development but extended the concerns of liberal theory by their equal emphasis on the development of others" (Freeden, 1991: 21). It is extending the concerns of liberal theory that I wish to comment on, and this is not by rejecting Freeden's claim; rather, I suggest that to fully appreciate his claim is to appreciate the common good ethics of joint self-development as the proper locus of that extension. Recall my claim regarding "mutually assured self-realization": one's claim for self-realization for oneself is reciprocal with the equally legitimate claim of others for self-realization. The normative requiredenss of this claim is grounded in the ethic of mutual or joint self-realization. This is the ethic of the common good in which, therefore, we should, ultimately, locate Green's extension of liberal political theory, and of Green's moral, social, and political philosophy, overall.

References

Acton, H. (1970) *Kant's Moral Philosophy* (London: Macmillan).
Benn, S. and Peters, R. (1959) *The Principles of Political Thought* (New York: The Free Press).
Brink, David O. (2003), *Perfectionism and the Common Good: Themes in the Philosophy of T. H. Green* (Oxford: Clarendon Press).
Caird, E. (1893) *The Critical Philosophy of Immanuel Kant*, 2nd edn. (Glasgow: James Maclehose & Sons).
Crisp, R. (ed.) (1996) *How Should One Live? Essays on Virtues* (Oxford: Clarendon Press).
Dagger, R. (1997) *Civic Virtues: Rights, Citizenship and Republican Liberalism* (Oxford: Oxford University Press).
Diggs, B. (1972–3) "The Common Good as Reason for Action", *Ethics*, 83, pp. 283–93.
Dimova-Cookson, M. and W.J. Mander, eds. (2006), *T.H. Green: Ethics, Metaphysics, and Political Philosophy* (Oxford: Clarendon Press), pp. 236-261.
Frankena, W. (1991) "Sidgwick and the History of Ethical Dualism", in B. Schultz (ed.), *Essays on Henry Sidgwick*, pp. 175–98 (Cambridge: Cambridge University Press).
Freeden, M. (1991) *Rights* (Minneapolis: University of Minnesota Press).
Freeden, M. (1996) "The family of liberalisms: a morphological analysis", in J. Meadowcroft (ed.), *The Liberal Political Tradition: Contemporary Reappraisals*, pp. 14–39 (Cheltenham: Edward Elgar).
Gaus, G. (1983) *Modern Liberal Theory of Man* (London: Croom Helm).
Gewirth, A. (1996) *The Community of Rights* (Chicago: Chicago University Press).
Green, T.H. (1906a) "Lectures on the Philosophy of Kant, II. The Metaphysic of Ethics" in R.L. Nettleship (ed.), *Works of Thomas Hill Green*, Vol. 2 (London: Longmans, Green).
Green, T.H. (1906b) "Introduction to the Moral Part of Hume's 'Treatise'", in R.L. Nettleship (ed.), *Works of Thomas Hill Green*, Vol. 1 (London: Longmans, Green).
Green, T.H. (1911a) "Popular Philosophy and Its Relation to Life", in R.L. Nettleship (ed.), *Works of Thomas Hill Green*, Vol. 3 (London: Longmans, Green).

Green, T.H. (1911b) "The Philosophy of Aristotle", in R.L. Nettleship (ed.), *Works of Thomas Hill Green*, vol. 3 (London: Longmans, Green).
Green, T.H. (1907) *Prolegomena to Ethics by the Late Thomas Hill Green*, ed. A.C. Bradley, 5th edn. (Oxford: Clarendon Press).
Green, T.H. (1986a) "Lectures on the Principles of Political Obligation", in P. Harris and J. Morrow (eds.), *T.H. Green: Lectures on the Principles of Political Obligation and Other Writings* (Cambridge: Cambridge University Press).
Green, T.H. (1986b) "Lecture on Liberal Legislation and the Freedom of Contract", in P. Harris and J. Morrow (eds.), *T.H. Green: Lectures on the Principles of Political Obligation and Other Writings* (Cambridge: Cambridge University Press).
Green, T.H. (1986c) "On Different Senses of 'Freedom' as Applied to Will and to Moral Progress of Man", in P. Harris and J. Morrow (eds.), *T.H. Green: Lectures on the Principles of Political Obligation and Other Writings* (Cambridge: Cambridge University Press).
Hobhouse, L. (1921) *The Rational Good* (London: George Allen & Unwin).
Hobhouse, L. (1922) *The Elements of Social Justice* (London: George Allen & Unwin).
Holmes, S. (1993) *The Anatomy of Antiliberalism* (Cambridge, MA: Harvard University Press).
Homiak, M. (1981) "Virtue and Self-Love in Aristotle's Ethics", *Canadian Journal of Philosophy*, 11/4 (December), pp. 633–51.
Irwin, T. (1988) *Aristotle's First Principles* (Oxford: Oxford University Press).
Irwin, T. (1991) "Eminent Victorians and Greek Ethics. Green, Sidgwick and Aristotle's Ethics", in B. Schultz (ed.), *Essays on Henry Sidgwick*, pp. 279–310 (Cambridge: Cambridge University Press).
Murphy, G. (1970) *Kant: The Philosophy of Right* (Macon, Georgia: Mercer University Press).
Nicholson, P. (1990) *The Political Philosophy of the British Idealists* (Cambridge: Cambridge University Press).
Norman, R. (1983) *The Moral Philosophers. An Introduction to Ethics* (Oxford: Oxford University Press).
Pettit, P. (1994) "Liberal/Communitarian: MacIntyre's mesmeric dichotomy", in J. Horton and S. Mendus (eds.), *After MacIntyre*, pp. 176–204 (Cambridge: Polity Press).
Rawls, J. (1971) *A Theory of Justice* (Cambridge, MA: Harvard University Press).
Raz, J. (1986) *The Morality of Freedom* (Oxford: Clarendon Press).
Ritchie, D. (1891) *The Principle of State Interference: Four Essays on the Political Philosophy of Mr. Herbert Spencer, J.S. Mill, and T.H. Green* (London: Sonnenschein).
Scruton, R. (1982) "Common good", in *Dictionary of Political Thought* (London & Basingstoke: Macmillan).
Sherman, N. (1989) *The Fabric of Character* (Oxford: Clarendon Press).
Simhony, A. (1991) "Idealist Organicism: Beyond Holism and Individualism", *History of Political Thought*, 12/3 (Autumn), pp. 514–35.
Simhony, A. (1995) "Was T.H. Green a Utilitarian?" *Utilitas*, 7/1 (May), pp. 122–44.
Simhony, A. (2006), "Rights that Bind: T.H. Green on Rights and Community", in M. Dimova-Cookson and W.J. Mander, eds. *T.H. Green: Ethics, Metaphysics, and Political Philosophy* (Oxford: Clarendon Press), pp. 236-261.
Simhony, A. (forthcoming), "T.H. Green: Beyond Deontological and Consequentialist Liberalism", *Collingwood and British Idealism Studies*.
Skorupski, J. (2006), "Green and the Idealist Conception of a Person's Good", in M. Dimova-Cookson and W.J. Mander, eds. *T.H. Green: Ethics, Metaphysics, and Political Philosophy* (Oxford: Clarendon Press), pp. 47-75.
Taylor, C. (1989) "Cross-Purposes: The Liberal-Communitarian Debate", in N. Rosenblum (ed.), *Liberalism and the Good Life*, pp. 159–82 (Cambridge, MA: Harvard University Press).
Tyler, Colin (2006), *Idealist Political Philosophy: Pluralism and Conflict in the Absolute Idealist Tradition* (New York: Continuum).

Philip MacEwen

The Moral and Social Philosophy of Edward Caird

> While ... knowledge is a process which, in its first aspect, seems to involve the negation of intellectual activity, and the absolute surrender of the mind to an indifferent and external object, it is really a process in which the mind is continually bringing that object more and more within the net of its categories and changing its aspect, till all its strangeness has disappeared, and it has been made one with the thought that apprehends it. ... Thus the perfect revelation of what the object is, is also the return of intelligence into itself, or rather the discovery that in all its travels, it has never really gone beyond itself. The highest fruit of knowledge is the deepening of self-consciousness (Caird, 1883: 186–7).

The above passage is not only a summary of the Hegelian logic; it is a summary of Caird's whole philosophy, both as it had developed to that point and as it was to develop thereafter. In 1883, Caird was Professor of Moral Philosophy at the University of Glasgow, a position he held for almost thirty years (1866–93). The years at Glasgow were prolific ones for Caird, marking both his development as a scholar and his emergence as a Gifford Lecturer. During this time, he wrote two books on Kant, a book on Comte, and the aforementioned book on Hegel. The first work on Kant, entitled *A Critical Account of the Philosophy of Kant with an Historical Introduction* (1877), was an examination of Kant's *Critique of Pure Reason* and the historical background leading up to it, especially the thought of Descartes, Locke, and Leibniz. The second work on Kant, entitled *The Critical Philosophy of Immanuel Kant* (2 vols., 1889), was an extensive examination of Kant's larger philosophy, including the pre-Critical period, the three *Critiques*, *Religion within the Limits of Reason Alone*, and the *Metaphysics of Morals*. To this day, it remains the longest and most comprehensive English commentary written on Kant. Caird's work on Comte, entitled *The Social Philosophy and Religion of Comte* (1885), was based on a series of four articles which were published in the *Contemporary Review* in 1879. It is the shortest of Caird's books (210 pages), but provides an interesting example both of Comte's importance to nineteenth-century thought and Comte's influence on Caird's own social philosophy.

Caird's Glasgow period concluded with his first set of Gifford Lectures. These lectures, entitled *The Evolution of Religion*, were delivered at the University of St. Andrews in Sessions 1890-1 and 1891-2, and subsequently published, with additions, in 1893.[1] Reviewing Caird's second book on Kant shortly beforehand, Andrew Seth had encouraged Caird to try the Gifford route:

> ... [N]ow that Prof. Caird has fully unburdened himself on Kant, let him give us that 'complete treatise on Natural Theology' which he says in one place [*The Critical Philosophy of Immanuel Kant*, 2:128] would be required to develop the argument summarised in a few of his paragraphs. There are Gifford Lectureships enough in Scotland to furnish the appropriate occasion, and they could not be put to better use (Seth, 1890: 279).

While "natural theology" is hardly the rubric under which Caird's first set of Gifford Lectures seems to fall, this classification is actually quite apt. With Darwin's account of evolution taking the intellectual world by storm, there was an increasing tendency during the late nineteenth-century to see not only the biological, but also the cultural world as operating within the domain of evolution. Thus construed, nature and culture were not binary opposites, for the same principle of development was working itself out in both. Seen in this light, natural theology would be the study by reflective consciousness of how human beings gradually appropriate the knowledge that God, through the common evolutionary principle in nature and the various forms of religion, is working out all things "according to his riches in glory" (Phil. 4:19).

In Caird's hands, natural theology is religion brought to self-consciousness. Natural theology can be conducted as the reflective study of religious consciousness by someone who, if not outside this process, is sufficiently late in its development to give as comprehensive, i.e., self-conscious, an account of it as the process permits to date. Alternatively, natural theology can be conducted as the reflective study of the development of religious consciousness by someone who is, in a sense, still inside that religious situation. Plato and Aristotle examining Greek religion are examples. In *The Evolution of Religion*, Caird is doing natural theology in the first sense. His major work on natural theology in the second sense came later, after he left Glasgow to become Master of Balliol College at Oxford.

In 1893, Benjamin Jowett, the long-time Master of Balliol College, passed away. Edward Caird, who belonged to the Balliol class of 1865, was chosen as his successor. Caird remained in this position until 1907, one year before his death. Despite the administrative duties which came with the office, Caird was able to maintain his productivity throughout this period. His

---

1   Caird added two lectures (Lectures Six and Twelve) to the First Course (Volume 1) in preparing *The Evolution of Religion* for publication. See Caird (1893b: 1.vii).

most important work was his second set of Gifford Lectures, entitled *The Evolution of Theology in the Greek Philosophers*. These Lectures were delivered before the University of Glasgow in sessions 1900–1 and 1901–2 and published, with revisions and additions, in 1904.[2] They are a continuation of the first set but focus on the evolution of theology in the thought of some of the major Greek philosophers as these figures became more self-conscious of the specific form of religious life which they themselves, in a sense, still represented.[3]

I want to examine Caird's moral and social philosophy by looking at some of the major works I have cited. Caird's philosophy is best understood as a working out of the process described at the beginning of this chapter. Looking first at his social philosophy, such as it is, reveals that Caird derived it largely from his study of Auguste Comte's positivism, while his moral philosophy is the practical side of his epistemology. I shall conclude with a few observations about how Caird's social and moral philosophy may be of help in contemporary social and moral theory.

Caird's social philosophy is an Hegelian response to the premier sociologist of the nineteenth century, Auguste Comte. Comte's significance to his own time may be lost on many students today because, for much of the twentieth century, Comte studies went through a deep freeze from which they have emerged only relatively recently. If one were raised in this environment, it would be difficult to understand why John Stuart Mill, for example, praised Comte as the equal of Descartes and Leibniz,[4] the two thinkers Comte regarded as his principal precursors. Yet in recognizing Comte's importance to philosophy, Mill was simply expressing the consensus of his time. If one wanted to be on the cutting edge of intellectual history in the latter half of the nineteenth century, knowing Comte's philosophy was *de rigueur*.

Unlike Mill, Caird was too young to initiate a correspondence with Comte since he would have been only in his teens when Comte died.[5] Even

---

2   Caird rewrote most of this set of Lectures and added three lectures on material he was originally unable to discuss to his satisfaction. See Caird (1904: 1.vii).
3   For other notable publications by Caird during his period as Master at Balliol College, see Caird (1898, 1899, 1907).
4   "We think M. Comte as great as either of these philosophers [Descartes and Leibniz]" (Mill, 1969: 368). In addition to writing about Comte, John Stuart Mill carried on an extensive correspondence with him from 1841 to 1847. The correspondence consists of eighty-nine letters, all of them in French. They have been translated into English by Oscar A. Haac (1995).
5   Mill both initiated and terminated his correspondence with Comte. He initiated it to express "the great intellectual debt" he owed to Comte and to articulate his sympathy with, and support for, Comte's positive philosophy (Haac, 1995: 35). He terminated it, not by refusing to answer Comte's letters, but by rejecting the religion of humanity, later detailed by Comte in his *Système de Politique Positive* (1851–4), and, symbolically, by rejecting any continuation of the financial support that Mill and his friends had extended to the struggling Comte, commencing in 1844, through decrying the poor law which England had devised at the time for dealing with the problem of unemployment among the peasants in Ireland! (see Haac, 1995: esp. letter 89, pp. 382–4).

if such an opportunity had existed, however, Caird would not have availed himself of it. Caird admired Comte, not in the sense of being a supporter of the positive philosophy—as Mill who, for all his subsequent reservations, continued to be—but in the sense that Comte's philosophy was a particularly salient—albeit ultimately unsuccessful—example of the earlier claim that knowledge is a process of the mind continually bringing the object more and more within the net of its own categories until it has been made one with the thought that apprehends it. Specifically, Comte failed to achieve an ultimate synthesis in his philosophy because he ended by retracting all the negations with which he began. If we can determine what Caird meant by this criticism, we shall understand both his Hegelian critique of Comte and a good deal of Caird's own social philosophy as well.

Caird identified two central thoughts in Comte's philosophy which are the sources of most of its peculiarities: the law of the three stages of social development and the subordination of science to man's social being—or, as Comte put it, of the intellect to the heart. The first functions as Comte's criterion of knowledge and the second is the principle by which he seeks to systematize knowledge and to estimate the relative value of its parts. These two central thoughts are virtually tailor-made to contradict each other, though it will take some analysis to sort this out.

According to the first, societies and, indeed, human intelligence as a whole, necessarily pass through three stages: the theological or fictitious, the metaphysical or abstract, and the scientific or positive. While it is not the case that every later event in this process is better than every earlier event, the overall effect of change up through the stages is progressive. In the theological or fictitious stage, people believe that more or less numerous supernatural agents control phenomena by direct and continuous action which explains all the apparent anomalies of the world. Knowledge at this stage thus aims at an absolute account of phenomena in terms of their first and final causes. As an initial stage, there is nothing wrong with the theological way of looking at things—in fact Comte regarded it as a necessary part of human growth—but it is immature in the sense that it fails to recognize both the actual laws which control phenomena and the limits of our knowledge about them, discoveries which are not made until the third stage. In the metaphysical or abstract stage, which Comte insisted was only a modification of the first stage and a transitional phase between the first and last stages, the more or less supernatural agents of the first stage are replaced by abstract forces, real entities, or personified abstractions inherent in the different beings in the world, and these are used to give a complete account of all phenomena, each phenomenon being assigned to its corresponding force, entity, or abstraction. In the scientific or positive stage, which Comte saw himself as originating and abetting, the quest for absolute truth is given up as impossible and, with it, the search for the origin and final causes of the universe. The focus is now on discovering, through the use of reasoning within the limits of empirical observation, the invariable laws of resemblance, coexistence, and succession which control phenomena. Reduced to its real terms, the explanations of facts consist only in connecting particular phenomena with the general laws that explain them, the number of which, Comte thought, would diminish with the progress of science.[6]

According to Comte's second central thought, science must be subordinated to human social being or, as he often put it, the intellect to the heart. This is not an insight one is likely to take away from the *Cours*, which proceeds to work out a synoptic account of the development of the sciences *vis-à-vis* the law of the three stages. On the other hand, it is not contrary to the *Cours,* which always insists on viewing the human mind "as a whole." In his principal works after the *Cours,* therefore, Comte focussed on presenting positivism as a philosophy which includes all aspects of human life and integrating the three kinds of phenomena of which our lives consist: feelings, thought, and actions.[7] Of the three, the one which preponderates in every human being is the first, since it gives stimulus and direction to the other two. Without feelings, thought would waste its energy in ill-conceived or useless study, and action would be barren or even dangerous.

In each of the three stages of society, one of these phenomena is the basis of the other two. In the theological stage, it is feelings or our affective nature. While this might seem to be the way things should have been, giving Comte's ranking, theology was not adequate to feelings since it exercised no real control over thought or actions. Theology asserted all phenomena to be under the dominion of more or less supernatural agents, whereas, both in their intellectual and practical lives, people were led more and more clearly to the conclusion that phenomena were controlled by invariable laws. In the metaphysical stage, thought predominated, but its abstract forces, real entities, and personified abstractions could provide no avenue for fulfilling the needs of feelings through actions, or the practical side of human life. In the scientific stage, actions come to the fore since

---

6 Comte's presentation of the states of social development appears in the first two chapters of the first volume of his six-volume *Cours de philosophie positive* (1830–42). For a handy edition of these chapters, see (Comte, 1988).

7 One of the great merits of Caird's interpretation of Comte is that, unlike many of Comte's interpreters such as Émile Littré (1863) and Mill, he recognized the continuity of thought between the *Cours* and *Système de Politique Positive*. "I have not attempted to deal with the detailed discussion of the nature and methods of the sciences in Comte's [*Cours de*] *Philosophie Positive*, except in so far as is necessary for the understanding of the [*Système de*] *Politique Positive*, in which the social and religious aims of his philosophy are for the first time explicitly stated. Not, indeed, that there is any very marked division between his earlier and his later treatises. The changes observable in the latter do not show, as has sometimes been represented, a sudden revolution of opinion; they are only the last result of tendencies which had been gaining ground in Comte's mind as his work advanced ..." (Caird, 1893a: xi–xii).

this stage renounces the useless quest for absolute knowledge and focuses on discovering, through the use of thought within the limits of empirical observation, the invariable laws which control phenomena. The knowledge derived thereby is to be used for improving the conditions of human life and finding proper satisfaction for our needs as these are suggested to thought by the heart.

Thus presented, it is not obvious that the scientific stage is dominated by feelings at all. While thought may be the handmaiden of feelings, in the sense that thought is to find proper satisfaction for human needs as suggested to it by the heart, feelings can only do so within the parameters of invariable laws which have been discovered by thought. Thought, furthermore, is the servant of actions since its knowledge is to be used for improving human life. How can feelings claim their proper place under these conditions? Comte recognized this difficulty and addressed it in his later writings, especially by developing the religion of Humanity. The religion of Humanity is the culmination of Comte's *politique positive* or consideration of the agencies by which the propagation of positivist philosophy, as outlined in the *Cours,* was to be effected. The point towards which feelings, thought, and actions converge is Humanity because feelings are the felt needs of human beings which thought tries to fulfill, subject to the invariable laws of phenomena, through appropriate actions. More precisely, the subjective principle (or the subordination of the intellect to the heart) working in tandem with the objective principle (or the order of phenomena by which humanity and everything else is regulated) produce love, since the economy of the external world checks the power of the selfish instincts of human beings and calls our social instincts into constant exercise. Paradoxically, were it not for the harsh realities of life, our social sympathies would be squashed by self-love. Since love of Humanity is itself a feeling, the synthesis of the two principles yields love which, in turn, is the basis for actions. Thus, love underlies actions in the scientific stage.

Using the love of Humanity as the point at which feelings, thought, and actions converge, Comte developed his new religion. Humanity takes the place of God, science takes the place of theology as the means by which we come to know the nature and conditions of the "Great Being", the philosophers of positivism become the priests of Humanity, festivals or holidays are set aside for the worship of Humanity, poetry and the other arts, which turn impersonal nature into a friend, are deployed in the worship of Humanity, and the new religion is to take the place of the old religion, Christianity, which failed to attend to anything but the feelings of human beings.[8]

---

[8] The best introduction to Comte's religion of humanity may be found in Chapter VI of *Discours sur l'ensemble de positivisme*. For an English translation, see Bridges (1909). Comte intended the *Discours* to function as the introduction to *Système de Politique Positive*.

We are now in a position to see why Caird said that Comte ended by retracting all the negations with which he began. The law of the three stages of development describes a process in which an immature and, indeed, fictitious, view of the world is gradually replaced by a mature and correct view of the world. This view is mature because it comes at the end of a long process of development; it is correct because it describes objects the way they are within the limits of human understanding. The truth is that we are controlled by impersonal and invariable laws over which we, in turn, have no control, though we can reap certain benefits from knowing what these laws are and putting that knowledge to use for human benefit. In terms of Caird's summary of the Hegelian logic, the third state of development features a pronounced dualism between knowing and being, since knowledge involves the absolute surrender of the mind to an indifferent and external object. Comte shrank from this dualism because he realized that it had no room for the subjective principle. How can feelings be foundational in a stage such as this?

Comte's response was to try to bring the objective world within the categories of the mind, so that its strangeness disappeared and it became one with the consciousness that apprehended it, by developing the religion of Humanity. In so doing, however, he had to retract all the negations with which he began. On the side of knowing, the point at which feelings, thought, and actions converge is not the objective world of impersonal and invariable laws; in fact, that is the world from which they recoil. The point of convergence is man, and knowledge becomes worship. On the side of being, the world of impersonal and invariable laws is no longer the objective world but the world of Humanity as the object of love. This is not a duplication of the theological stage but, in its religious interpretation of the world and consequent estrangement from the "truth" of the world, it is eerily similar.

Despite his rejection of Comte's "subjective synthesis", Caird thought there was much in Comte's social philosophy worth preserving. In particular, Comte was correct in maintaining that human being is inevitably social:

> Our consciousness of ourselves is essentially social, and the individualistic point of view is the result of a false abstraction, which can never be more than a partial abstraction. For, strive as we will, we cannot in thought any more than in reality, isolate the individual from society, without at the same time taking from him all that characterises him even as an individual. To speak, therefore, of knowing man, except as a member of the family, of the nation, of the race, is irrational. The science of man would be impossible if we were not able to get beyond our individuality, and to look at it, as well as at all other individualities, from the point of view of humanity. (Caird, 1893a: 121–2)

What Comte failed to see is that if we extend social life to the race, there is no reason why we should not go on and consider the relation of humanity to the world. "If the relativity of man to man makes it impossible to know him except from the point of view of humanity, the relativity of man to the world makes it impossible to know humanity except from the point of view of the unity of the whole" (Caird, 1893a: 123). This is an insight which Caird was later to use with great success in his two sets of Gifford Lectures. Had Comte taken one step further and realized the metaphysical implications of his social philosophy, he would have achieved the synthesis of the objective and subjective principles which he was seeking. The world would not be an impersonal order of invariable laws which controls us and is impermeable to feelings, but an order through which we come to know ourselves as feeling, thinking, and acting beings. In so doing, we humanize the world or change it from its otherness into a reflection of ourselves. We find ourselves in the world and the world finds itself in us. "[T]he perfect revelation of what the object is, is also the return of intelligence into itself, or rather the discovery that in all its travels, [intelligence] has never really gone beyond itself. The highest fruit of knowledge is the deepening of self-consciousness" (Caird, 1883: 187).

Turning now to Caird's moral philosophy, like many of the British Idealists, Caird did not write a work on ethics *per se*. The reason for this is that ethics was just the practical side of his epistemology which, in turn, endorsed the view that "… neither the subject nor the object can be known for what it really is, until their reciprocal correlation is taken into account, and until this correlation is itself seen in the light of the unity which it presupposes" (Caird, 1903–04: 108). What we do (descriptive ethics), or a reasonable expectation of what we ought to do (prescriptive ethics), has to be referenced to where we are at in the epistemological odyssey from consciousness to self-consciousness. Like Odysseus, we are all travelling from Troy to Ithaca. Some have just left Troy, others are at various stops along the way, and some have arrived at Ithaca to claim, with a greatly deepened and expanded sense of consciousness, what they knew imperfectly to be theirs in the first place. Accordingly, the best way to understand Caird's moral philosophy is to take his most complete version of the human odyssey, *The Evolution of Religion*, and correlate the main stages of the evolution of religion with the main stages of the evolution of morality. This can be done at the level of personal morality, social morality, or even global morality, though I will concentrate on the nature of the consciousness which characterizes each of these stages, summarized so succinctly by Caird in the citation from *Hegel*, and how it can be used to describe a correlative stage of morality.

In language that is reminiscent of Comte, though it owes its origin to Hegel's *Lectures on the Philosophy of Religion*, Caird identifies three stages of religious consciousness: the objective, the subjective, and the absolute or universal.[9] Before describing each of these stages, Caird insists that all of them already have the idea of unity which they are seeking, especially the unity of the self and not-self and inner and outer experience. If this were not the case, they could not evolve self-consciously from one stage to the next. While they have the idea of unity, however, the first two stages do not have it in a form which is *adequate* to the idea. The first stage thinks of it in a purely objective way—as an object out there in the world—while the second stage thinks of it in a purely subjective way—as an inner feeling or experience. Only in the third stage does consciousness attain the concept of the idea as that which unites the self and the not-self, the inner and the outer, in an overarching whole.

In objective religion, consciousness relates to objects *qua* objects. "Man at first looks outward, and not inward: he can form no idea of anything to which he cannot give a 'local habitation and a name,' which he cannot body forth as an existence in space and time" (Caird, 1893b: 1.189). There is no idea here that objects are related to a consciousness, nor how this changes both the object and the subject for whom objects exist. Even the self is posited as an object among other objects since the self is one's physical body. Spiritual realities are objectified too as forces or powers "…before which man trembles with a sense of weakness" (Caird, 1893b: 1.189–90). What we have here, as Caird put it so eloquently in his book on Hegel, is "the absolute surrender of the mind to an indifferent and external object" (Caird, 1883: 186).

The kind of morality this stage implies identifies the good as something which is external to consciousness and an object in the world. In the *Enuma Elish*, the Babylonian hymn of creation, for example, man is created to do the work that the gods hate doing themselves—cleaning canals, building dams, irrigating fields, harvesting crops, and so on. Work is something good for man, since the gods ordained it, but both it and they are external to him as objects in the world. Man is even external to himself for he is the one who must do the work imposed upon him or else face the harsh justice meted out by Marduk. This is an early precursor, in many ways, of Marx's

---

9 In his 1827 *Lectures*, Hegel identified three stages of religious consciousness: nature religion, religion which elevates the spiritual above the natural, and consummate religion (see Hegel, 1988). Hegel gave four sets of lectures on the philosophy of religion at the University of Berlin in 1821, 1824, 1827, and 1831 respectively. Each of the subsequent sets was substantially revised, though the editions generally in use today are based on the 1827 lectures. Caird used the 1840 edition of Hegel's *Werke*, edited by Bruno Bauer, but published under the name of Philipp Marheineke who edited the first edition (1832). Bauer used a number of sources, including the 1821 lectures, which Marheineke had not used and which are very different from the later lectures. However, this did not affect the main divisions of Hegel's *Lectures*—the Concept of Religion, Determinate Religion, and Consummate Religion—or the three stages of religion indicated above.

critique of alienated labour under capitalism.[10] In general, any morality which locates the good or the right in an external state of affairs and presents itself to consciousness as the good or the right, independently of the latter's own determinations, can be identified as an objective morality. This cuts a pretty wide swath in moral and legal consciousness. Traffic laws, the violation of which is a strict liability offence, are cases in point. What people do, or what it can reasonably be expected they ought to do, is defined and determined in terms of a *de facto* good or right. Conformity to, or violation of, this standard is objectively determined and those who are convicted of violations are punished, regardless of their state of mind at the time.[11]

In subjective religion, people begin to rise to a sense of their freedom and of their independence from the world around them. They are freed from the dread of outward things and start to take a view of them as instruments of their lives. "The manifestation of the divine is no longer found in nature but in man; and even in man not as a natural existence, but only as a self-conscious, self-determined subject" (Caird, 1893b: 1.192). The divine is conceived as "...a spiritual will which stands apart from nature, and reveals itself to man mainly in the inner voice of conscience, the 'categorical imperative of duty'" (Caird, 1893b: 1.192). Objective religion evolves into subjective religion because the consciousness of the self and the divine "...disturb the order of the objective world into which they are intruded" (Caird, 1893b: 1.191). For example, when Antigone buries her brother, Polynices, she acts under the aegis of duty, despite the fact that her uncle Creon, king of Thebes, has forbidden that Polynices be buried. This disturbs the order of the objective world; the dry dust that Antigone sprinkles over her brother, in the words of the breathless sentry who witnessed the incident and reports it to Creon, was scattered "...in the manner of holy burial" (Sophocles: *l*. 271).

The kind of morality subjective religion implies identifies the good as something which is internal to consciousness and established by its own operations. The good has fled from the prison of nature and found more commodious accommodations in the human mind and heart. Goodness may be variously construed and defined thereby, but it is up to the human

---

10 Critics might respond that at least alienated labour under capitalism has the *choice* to sell its labour power to the capitalist, unlike human beings under the domination of Marduk and his consort. In response, I would say that Marx saw the condition of labour under capitalism as a life and death struggle. The worker has no choice but to go to work, for it is only by selling his labour power to the capitalist that he is able to survive (Marx, 1963: 120–34).

11 People are usually not happy about being punished for traffic violations, of course, but that is because their thinking represents another stage of moral consciousness. The type of consciousness which devises traffic laws and treats their violations as strict liability offences belongs to first-stage moral thinking. Having said this, moral or legal *theory* cannot be done at the level of first-stage moral thinking because it depends upon a view of the self which has been interiorized. A self which is simply an object out there in the world cannot frame moral or legal theories, no matter how "objective" they otherwise may be.

subject to make those determinations. Abandoned by the good, nature is not necessarily amoral for, through the categories of the human mind, it can be conceived from a moral point of view and treated accordingly. This marks a great advance on objective morality because the self has become a subject and sees the object in terms of a self-conscious relationship to it. Thus, "the mind is continually bringing that object more and more within the net of its categories, and changing its aspect" (Caird, 1883: 186–7). Caird identified this kind of morality primarily with Kant[12] though, in less systematic forms, it represents the whole of subjective moral theory from Hobbes to the present.

The last stage of religious consciousness is absolute or universal religion. Here at last, consciousness attains the concept of the religious idea, thereby uniting the inner and the outer and the subject and the object. The only concept which is able to do this is the idea of God. "[T]he idea of God is one with the unity which is at once the presupposition, the limit, and the goal of our divided consciousness of the world and of ourselves. ... To know God as God, is to know Him as the Being, who is at once the source, the sustaining power, and the end of our spiritual lives" (Caird, 1893b: 1.195). In objective religion, God is wholly other, an object out there in the world before whom we tremble with a sense of weakness. In subjective religion, God moves inside us and speaks through conscience, the inner voice of reason, or the categorical imperative. Neither type of consciousness is adequate to the idea of God, for God is the organic unity of the inner and the outer, the subject and the object, the knower and the known. This idea is gradually revealed in the evolution from objective to subjective to absolute religion. Absolute religion is the kind of religion experienced on the Day of Pentecost when Jesus, who was once objectively present but had died, takes up residence in the hearts of the disciples. Then a sound from heaven is heard as of a rushing mighty wind, filling the house where the disciples are seated. The sound in the room embodies the feeling in their hearts and they come to know God, in Paul's words, as the one in whom "we live, move, and have our being" (Acts 17:28).[13] "Thus, the perfect revelation of what the object is, is also the return of intelligence to itself, or rather the discovery that in all its travels, it has never really gone

---

12 For an example of Caird's treatment of Kant's moral philosophy, see Caird (1889: 2:143–405; 1893b: 1.330–347).

13 Paul's words were originally addressed to "certain philosophers of the Epicureans, and of the Stoics" (Acts 17:18). These philosophers represented the first stage of religious consciousness since, according to Luke, they thought the Godhead was "like unto gold, or silver, or stone, graven by art and man's device" (Acts 19:29). They were also on the threshold of subjective religion for they had raised an altar with the inscription, "TO THE UNKNOWN GOD" (Acts 19:23), something which would be impossible at the objective stage where the divine is always an identifiable object among other objects in the external world. This corresponds with Caird's (1893b: 1.260–85) view of Greek religion as mediating the transition from objective to subjective religion.

beyond itself. The highest fruit of knowledge is the deepening of self-consciousness" (Caird, 1883: 187).

To find the kind of morality absolute religion implies might seem like an exercise in futility. Morality always involves the quest for the good or the right, whereas here we seem to have achieved it. It was this sort of conundrum which prompted F.H. Bradley to observe:

> Reflection on morality leads us beyond it. It leads us, in short, to see the necessity of a religious point of view. It certainly does not tell us that morality comes first in the world and then religion: what it tells us is that morality is imperfect, and imperfect in such a way as to imply a higher, which is religion (Bradley, 1927: 314).

This reservation did not prevent Bradley from developing ideal morality, however, for the simple reason that there is no limit to the moral sphere. In ideal morality, "It is the moral duty to realize everywhere the best self" (Bradley, 1927: 219). The best self is the self which tries to realize a social and a non-social self, the first in its direct and immediate, and the second in its indirect and mediate, relations to others. As reflection on morality may lead us beyond religion, this is not a practical desideratum because there is no end to the process of self-realization. A more Cairdian interpretation would be to say the following: since the process of self-realization consists of uniting the inner and the outer and the subject and the object in fuller expressions of the self, and this process, in turn, is distinctive of religious consciousness, Bradley's ideal morality is, in fact, the morality of religious consciousness, even though he wants to distinguish between them. If it is objected that Bradley's ideal morality does not include the idea of God, the logical response would be that, while this is true superficially, the idea of God is nevertheless the source, the sustaining power, and the end of the process of self-realization since it is the only idea, the concept of which is adequate to explain such a process. Certainly the self which is developing, and can go on developing indefinitely, cannot function in that capacity, so there is good reason to believe that Bradley and Caird are closer on the religious nature of ideal morality than first meets the eye. If this is true, then Bradley's ideal morality is a good example of the kind of morality implied by religious consciousness.

Does Caird's social and moral philosophy have any contribution to make to contemporary social and moral theory? I think it does. The most important contribution of his social philosophy is the insight that social theory which strives to be empirically scientific, as Comte's did, must understand itself in terms of its own epistemological presuppositions. Too often, social theory wears the mantle of empirical science without realizing what this involves. Empirical science of any type makes certain presuppositions about the relationship between knowing and being that must be made explicit if it is not to go beyond its bounds. Empirical science is knowledge gained by observing subjects of objects under controlled conditions. As such, its theory cannot bridge the gulf between knowing and being because empirical science depends on the distinction—and difference—between the subject which knows and the object which is known. Empirical science can come to a knowledge of objects *qua* objects, but it needs to be limited, not to make room for faith, as Kant had said, but to make room for itself.[14]

To conclude, it is clear that Caird's moral philosophy has enormous importance for contemporary moral theory. In particular, it comes with the insight, as few moral theories do, that there are stages of moral development and one size does not fit all. Most Western ethical theory today is the progeny of Enlightenment theories dating back to Hobbes (contract theory), Hume (utilitarianism), and Kant (deontology) respectively. For all their insights and assets, none of these theories seems to recognise fully that moral development is a process and that different people (and societies!) are at different points along the way. This is not ethical relativism but an organic view of morality. Like Caird, Hegel did not write a book on ethics, but he articulated the organic theory of morality in its seminal form to the modern world.[15] Many of the thinkers he inspired have followed him in this regard so that their views of morality have to be inferred from other areas of their thought.[16] Furthermore, they developed the organic theory before—and often far better than!—later figures like Jean Piaget, Lawrence Kohlberg, Carol Gilligan, and others who have garnered so much attention. In Caird's case, his ethics can best be inferred from his views about the evolution of religion. This effort is well worthwhile for, among other things, we come to realize thereby that most of what goes by the name of ethical theory today is really second-stage moral thinking addressed to a second-stage moral audience. There is nothing wrong with this, provided everyone concerned is aware of what is going on, but, alas, that is rarely the case. Instead, from Hobbes onward, the thinkers concerned have understood themselves to be articulating a universal theory of morality, and their audiences have generally responded in kind. Needless to say, this has created a lot of misunderstanding on both sides and—though I cannot argue the point here—is one of the principal reasons why moral theory so often seems to be spinning its wheels in the sand. For those interested in ethical theory, Caird's insights into the developmental nature of moral consciousness are sufficient reason for making him a *cause*

---

14 For Caird's detailed discussion of the consciousness that informs empirical science (which, *qua* consciousness, is very similar to the consciousness of objective religion), see his account of the Hegelian logic (Caird, 1883: 151–85).

15 For one of the best introductions to Hegel's ethics, see Walsh (1969).

16 There are exceptions to this, the most notable being F.H. Bradley who not only wrote on ethics, but developed a detailed account of the stages of the moral life. See especially Bradley (1927), Chapters 5, 6, 7, and "Concluding Remarks". For an analysis of Bradley's ethics and the psychology which informs them, see MacNiven (1987).

célèbre and for promoting *The Evolution of Religion* to the level of required reading.

References

Bradley, F.H. (1927), *Ethical Studies, 1876*, 2nd edn. (Oxford: Clarendon Press).

Caird, E. (1883), *Hegel* (Edinburgh and London: William Blackwood and Sons).

Caird, E. (1889), *The Critical Philosophy of Immanuel Kant*, 2 vols. (Glasgow: James Maclehose and Sons).

Caird, E. (1893a), *The Social Philosophy and Religion of Comte*, 2nd edn. (Glasgow: James Maclehose and Sons).

Caird, E. (1893b), *The Evolution of Religion*, 2 vols. (Glasgow: James Maclehose and Sons).

Caird, E. (1898), "Biographical Introduction", in W. Wallace, *Lectures and Essays on Natural Theology and Ethics*, E. Caird (ed.) (Oxford: Clarendon Press), pp. vii–xl.

Caird, E. (1899), "Memoir", in John Caird, *The Fundamental Ideas of Christianity*, E. Caird (ed.) (Glasgow: James Maclehose), pp. ix–cxli.

Caird, E. (1903-04), "Idealism and the Theory of Knowledge", *Proceedings of the British Academy*, 2, pp. 95-108.

Caird, E. (1904), *The Evolution of Theology in the Greek Philosophers*, 2 vols. (Glasgow: James Maclehose and Sons).

Caird, E. (1907), *Lay Sermons and Addresses* (Glasgow: James Maclehose).

Comte, A. (1909), "The Religion of Humanity", in *A General View of Positivism*, trans. J. J. Bridges (London).

Comte, A. (1988), *Introduction to Positive Philosophy*, ed. Frederick Ferré (Indianapolis: Hackett).

Hegel, G.W.F. (1988), *Lectures on the Philosophy of Religion* (1827), ed. P.C. Hodgson (Berkeley: University of California Press).

Haac, O. (ed.) (1995), *The Correspondence of John Stuart Mill and Auguste Comte* (New Brunswick, NJ: Transaction Publishers).

MacNiven, Don (1987), *Bradley's Moral Psychology* (Lewiston: Edwin Mellen).

Marx, K. (1963), *Economic and Philosophical Manuscripts* (1844), in *Karl Marx: Early Writings*, ed. T.B. Bottomore (Toronto: McGraw-Hill), pp. 63–219.

Mill, J.S. (1969), "Auguste Comte and Positivism" (1865), in J.M. Robinson (ed.), *Essays on Ethics, Religion and Society, Collected Works of John Stuart Mill*, Vol. 10 (Toronto: University of Toronto Press).

Seth, A. (1890), Review of *The Critical Philosophy of Immanuel Kant*, *Mind*, os 15, pp. 266–79.

Sophocles, *Antigone*.

Walsh, W.H. (1969), *Hegelian Ethics* (London: Macmillan).

Darin R. Nesbitt

D.G. Ritchie's Ethics

Introduction

While D.G. Ritchie is perhaps best known for his revision of evolutionary theory, his application of the concept of social organicism, and his early efforts to reconcile Darwin and Hegel, in general his writings were concerned principally with ethics and politics (Simhony, 2001: 8; Ritchie, 1905: vi). Ritchie was part of the second generation of British Idealists—those influenced by T.H. Green and Edward Caird—who critically examined empiricism, scientific naturalism, and individualism in order to better direct social philosophy toward consideration of some of the most intractable social, economic, and political concerns of late Victorian society. As a social theorist, Ritchie tackled conceptual and philosophical issues raised by the advancement of scientific perspectives and concepts in social philosophy. Here one of his enduring contributions involved the grafting of idealist views on teleology, purposefulness, and the role of human consciousness onto scientific models of evolution. As a political theorist, Ritchie shared fears raised by academics, public officials, and social activists who watched with varying degrees of consternation and dismay the deterioration of community and social bonds in the face of emerging urbanisation and industrialisation. As a philosophical idealist, Ritchie shared the lexicon of the inseparability of society and the individual, the moral nature and purpose of the state, and notions of self-development and self-realisation.

Ritchie was a respected teacher and a devoted scholar, and his legacy has only recently been systematically explored after almost a century of comparative neglect.[1] Ritchie's published works reveal an active mind and provocative approaches to the study of ethics, and his writings exhibit a conceptual clarity and semantic precision that are not typically considered distinguishing characteristics of the British Idealists. His ethical theory contains elements that can be traced to a variety of influences. Darwin and

---

1   For an introductory survey of Ritchie's writings and life, see Nicholson (1998: pp. vii–xxviii). Recent efforts to resuscitate Ritchie and his legacy may be found in Neill (2003), Weinstein (2002), Boucher (2004), Sweet (2004), and den Otter (1996).

the classical British utilitarians were certainly important to the development of his system of ethics insofar as his notion of "evolutionary utilitarianism" was essentially a revision of naturalism and utilitarianism. From Green he inherited the belief that the concept of the self must be social in nature, from Plato and Aristotle that the idea of the good citizen is meaningless unless such a citizen resides in a good society, and from Kant and Hegel the doctrine of the unity of self-consciousness and the purposiveness of nature and human institutions respectively. Given such diverse influences, Ritchie sought to provide a more compelling account of the relationship between the individual and society, a reworking of citizenship based on a revised utilitarianism and idealist evolutionism.

Citizenship for Ritchie meant the idea of self-development and self-realisation, and free citizens were those who acted rationally by making choices in accordance with their better interests and common good. In the Victorian period, industrialisation, urbanisation, free trade, the expansion of voting rights, the increasing advances brought about by scientific and technological discoveries, and the improvement of information and communication forced a reconsideration of the requirement of citizenship and the role of government. Industrialism in particular became a target of criticism, and social legislation that aimed to improve working conditions essentially entailed an abandonment of individualism as an organising principle of social and economic policy. Most of the legislation dealing with social and working conditions was based on a notion of "collectivism" derived from Bentham's maxim of the "greatest happiness for the greatest number". In light of the absence of a more satisfactory collectivism within the British tradition, idealists sought to revise social and political theory concerning the purpose of the state, the nature of liberty or freedom, and the relationship between freedom and authority. Moreover, the existence of social and economic inequalities and human suffering meant that self-realisation remained an unrealised ideal and hence Ritchie argued that the state had a moral responsibility to create proper conditions for individual self-development.

The purpose of this chapter is to show that Ritchie's work on politics and ethics is important to examine and understand — even if, upon closer scrutiny, it is flawed in some ways. The intention here is to examine the effect of evolutionary theory and social organicism on Ritchie's ethical theory. Ritchie insists that the good of a community is the only criterion for judging what is right for individuals to do, and the good of the community is equivalent to the good of its citizens. He also consistently claims that citizens are the product of a society, and that their rights must be judged from the point of view of the society as a whole, and not the society from the point of view of the individual. Ritchie's "collectivism" was based on the centrality of social institutions to the progress of humankind. Yet his "metaphysics of ethics" implies an agency notion of equality, the recognition of others as moral beings capable of making choices and voluntarily undertaking obligations. This metaphysic is substantially more individualistic than Ritchie led his readers to believe, in spite of his efforts to use metaphysics to show the social nature of knowledge and individuality. Ritchie's metaphysics combined with his revision of evolutionary theory and utilitarianism leads to a form of *individualised ethical collectivism*. At a minimum, it remains an open question whether his metaphysics and his revised utilitarianism are ethically coherent and consistent.

Evolutionary Theory: From Natural to Social Evolution

Late Victorian quests for human understanding and social explanation were informed by the idea that evolution provided the key to revealing the secrets of nature and of human existence. Biological evolutionary theories in particular shaped notions of social and scientific development throughout the 1870s and 1880s. The doctrine of evolution influenced political, social, and cultural thought, principally through the works of Herbert Spencer, T.H. Huxley, and Benjamin Kidd. Just as mathematics influenced Plato and Aristotle and physics moved Locke and Kant, evolution was, Ritchie observed, "the great scientific revolution" of the 1800s (Ritchie, 1893: 41, 52). The British Idealists, though, did not have a uniform attitude about the proper influence of the sciences on philosophy. In his *Prolegomena to Ethics* Green lamented the tendency to subsume fields such as moral theory under the physical sciences. He remarked that "the theory of descent and evolution opens up a vista of possibilities beyond the facts, so far ascertained, of human history, and suggests an enquiry into the antecedents of the moralised man based on other data than the records which he has left himself…. Man will then have his ascertained place in nature, as perhaps the noblest of the animals but an animal still" (Green, 1883: §5). For Green, evolutionism and naturalism appeared to represent a danger to ethics by treating humans as if they were merely natural beings.

Ritchie adopted a critically supportive position towards evolutionary theory, insisting that the theory of natural selection should be used to understand and explain social conditions (Ritchie, 1889: 1–2). He directed his attention toward how normative or ethical judgments could be made to fit within an evolutionary framework and thus determine the extent to which evolution revealed ethical ends. Ritchie was appalled by the way in which natural selection was deployed in support of market fundamentalism and social inequalities, and his *bête noire* was the formidable Spencer. Darwin's *The Origin of Species* suggested that species evolved in competitive circumstances between individuals and between different animal species for sustenance and other necessities. Those individuals and animals best adapted to their environment tended to survive and increase at the expense of those less well adapted. Spencer's "New Radicalism" meant that ideal societies were those characterised by maximum competition, with the consequence that those individuals who could survive intense social competition were superior. Such competition was a form of progress that revealed increasing social complexity and integration and a decreasing role for the state, particularly in social policies designed to ameliorate poverty and labour exploitation. Spencer appealed to an evolutionary explanation of spontaneous social adjustments in which individual decisions and actions generate social changes and adaptations. Hence progress, Spencer averred, would be vitiated by a turn to collectivism and an active state.

Ritchie raised a number of objections—some profound and others pedantic—to Spencer's use of social organicism. The theory of evolution does not necessarily prove that the "fittest" creatures survive the evolutionary process. The only conclusion to draw is tautological: those creatures who do survive are most capable of surviving. Ritchie also objected to the notion that human beings can be grouped into natural species or varieties like animals and plants because they belong to different national, linguistic, cultural, religious, and occupational groups. At any rate, humans must be distinguished from other species on the basis of *sui generis* characteristics such as the ability to use, exploit, and change nature; the use of language, writing, and painting to communicate observations and reflections; a "free purposelessness" (Ritchie, 1895: 54) that allows for art, architecture, sculpture, and painting; and because they consciously organise relations or communities to become members of self-governing societies. In fact, closer scrutiny of the doctrine demonstrates that "rational selection" (Ritchie, 1895: 100) frequently counteracts natural selection. Social, as distinct from natural, evolution implies organisation and the ability—however limited—to change the direction of evolution. Indeed, Ritchie remarks that "[c]ustoms—and customs are laws in their primitive form—are habits regarded as right, because, having been adopted, they have proved conducive to the welfare and success of the tribe or nation; but customs tend to survive long after the circumstances which called them into being have changed" (Ritchie, 1889: 1–32). Natural selection, Ritchie insists, must be supplemented with a theory of "social inheritance" to explain the role of customs, habits, and traditions in the evolution of society. He rejected the idea that political and social institutions could "spontaneously" or "accidentally" emerge from the process of human evolution—human beings demonstrate an ability to imitate and also to reflect upon customs, traditions, and social institutions. For Ritchie, the very fact that customs and laws can persist in spite of their not infrequent deleterious effects on progress is proof that human intentionality and design can coexist within evolutionism.

If some of Ritchie's contemporaries were perhaps seduced by the metaphor of social organicism to describe societies, he himself frequently emphasised the need to apply it judiciously. There was certainly nothing novel about organicism as a conception in the history of political thought, one that could trace its origins to Plato (Ritchie, 1902a: 168).[2] The metaphor is typically used to support a notion of social growth that is purposive in nature and interdependent in the sense that individuals stand in relation to society as a parts-whole relationship in which the flourishing of one depends upon that of the other. Ritchie cautions that those who "apply the conceptions of organism and evolution to society as if they were adequate in politics as in biology, while they may give a correct account of the origins of society, leave us without a criterion by which to judge of the goodness or badness of any social condition. The only logically available criterion would be the ultimate success of any given society in the struggle for existence" (Ritchie, 1893: 28). He explains that "[f]rom the point of view of biology and of natural selection in its biological sense, the only matter of interest is the continuity and persistence of the race" (Ritchie, 1902b: 22). Moreover, evolutionary theorists had not adequately explained how humans, as part of nature, could theorise about nature and indeed change it (Ritchie, 1902b: 229). In short, Ritchie's principal concern was to warn social philosophers and ethicists against "crude applications of biological conceptions to social evolution" (Ritchie, 1902b: 164–5).

That said, given that organisms display purposiveness and consciousness, social organicism implied rational regulation that provided justification for state action. Ritchie believed that natural selection might help to explain the content of our ethical judgments, although he denies that natural selection by itself can explain the ultimate nature of right and wrong. If society is best imagined as an organism, then such a conception intimates organisation, purposiveness, and direction, and consequently citizens and public officials can shape and direct society. Ritchie identified a number of advantages of the metaphor. Social organicism corrected what he saw as a distressing tendency by some of his contemporaries to neglect the role that political and social institutions play in the development of individuals and society. It is the purpose of political and social institutions to encourage the process of differentiating the individual citizen from his or her social environment and to create conditions in which citizens can achieve self-realisation — a process Ritchie describes as "socialism." Social organicism also draws attention to what is socially useful, and "in appealing to social utility, we are appealing to something that can be tested, not merely by the intuitions of an individual mind, but by experience" (Ritchie, 1906: 103). Ritchie felt that a philosophy that incorporated evolu-

---

2 See also Freeden (1996: 197–204) and Morefield (2002) and (2004).

tionary themes would be a powerful ally in the fight to improve the social condition of society (Neill, 2003: 321).

Ritchie was able to adapt popular enthusiasm for evolution to idealist purposes by highlighting the developmental aspect of evolution and by arguing that evolutionary doctrine presupposed a spiritual unity. In short, evolutionary and biological science revealed for Ritchie the mutual interdependence that conditions the relations among individuals and between individuals and their society, and also the very real possibility that rational democratic control can be used to guide and direct individuals and societies. Ritchie appeared particularly interested in the idea that social cohesion and durability can be regarded as having some ethical value. Curiously, he did not attempt to directly address the conclusion that natural selection means that institutions and practices that cease to serve the purposes of social cohesion and durability will perish. In fact, he embraced the notion that natural selection entailed a notion of conflict, although he was quite clear that its proper manifestation was through the conflict over ideas.

Ritchie wished to articulate a theory of evolution that recognised human purpose and will without relying solely on a spiritual account of the development of human consciousness and purpose. He states that the social organism doctrine in fact points to a form of social organisation in which individuals recognise a "corporate consciousness" that implies a purposive and active state (Ritchie, 1891: 22). Ritchie attempted to restore a certain dignity to political and social institutions in light of evolutionary theory. He adapted evolutionary theory to show how morality and reason were reified in social institutions and consequently accessible through understanding certain recognised and established institutional and moral practices. He was convinced that such institutions supply visible examples of the volitional element of human societies. Drawing out the implications of critical perspectives towards social and political institutions is one of the primary objectives of speculative metaphysics.

Speculative Metaphysics and Ethics

According to Ritchie, a "complete account of the basis of ethics and politics" must demonstrate how every human being may potentially share in the recognition of the consciousness of universal reason (Ritchie, 1895: 96–7). Ritchie's optimism about evolutionary theory was based on his conviction that its supporters were in fact demonstrating an underlying unity of phenomena that lent support to philosophical idealism. Speculative metaphysics is, according to Ritchie, the philosophical approach to knowledge that acknowledges relations between man and nature. He states that "there is an eternal self-consciousness we are logically compelled to believe, and that it is in some way present in our individual selves; but in what way is a matter of speculation" (Ritchie, 1893: 15). In general, the British Idealists tried to demonstrate that there can be no absolute divisions between mind and nature or between the individual and the state. And Ritchie insisted that a proper ethical theory must originate with a conception of the self as rational and universal, albeit a self imperfectly realised in the universal reason manifested in social institutions. If Ritchie's approach to this stage has Hegelian and Platonic echoes, his speculative metaphysics reveals a certain Kantian influence that may have unintended consequences for his ethical theory. Ritchie reinterpreted the doctrine of the unity of self-consciousness and transformed it into one that revealed the social nature of knowledge and understanding.

The chief weakness of evolutionary ethics, Ritchie held, was its unsatisfactory account of the distinction between an *ought* and an *is*, between normative claims and statements of fact (Ritchie, 1905: 115–6). Ritchie was unimpressed by the explanation of self-consciousness advanced by proponents of evolutionary theory. All too frequently, evolutionism confused origins with development. After all, the origins of knowledge and its validity are, as Ritchie notes, quite different things. The issue is not that individuals struggle for existence but rather that they "*know* that they are so engaged, are capable of looking round on what they are doing, of reflecting, of comparing results and considering some good, some bad, some to be desired and others to be avoided" (Ritchie, 1889: 15).

According to Ritchie, "the presupposition of knowledge was found to be the presence of a Self which is eternal and which yet is never completely realised in any one of us, and which thus remains as an Ideal perpetually urging to its realisation" (Ritchie, 1893: 22–3; see Ritchie, 1902a: 80). Ritchie's idealism means that consciousness is not the product of material causes but rather that the self is an agent, a participant, in the rationally unfolding and unified universe. The presumption is that "some things must be absolutely certain, if anything whatever is to be even probable; that mere change and flux are inconceivable, unless there is something stable and permanent" (Ritchie, 1902a: 84). This principle of unity permeates Ritchie's thought and is presupposed in his analyses and solutions to epistemological, scientific, social, and ethical problems (Boucher and Vincent, 2000: 153).

It is necessary, Ritchie argues, to posit metaphysical propositions such as the claim that a knowing self implies unity and purpose in nature, in spite of the fact they cannot be verified in the way that scientific facts may be. The accumulation of empirical facts is only meaningful if such data are combined with other forms of knowledge. Perhaps the most important form of knowledge is that provided by inference. The particular facts and elements of experiential knowledge must be integrated into a more holistic framework in order to be called knowledge. The unifying force in Ritchie's epistemology was reason, the development of logical connections to explain causality. Reality was for Ritchie holistic, unified, and synthetic, and drawing logical or causal connections between events and objects could only be achieved if reality was presumed to represent a unified whole. Linked to the view of reality as a unified rational structure and process is the principle of coherence: the test for the truthfulness or falseness of claims. Ritchie used the principle of coherence elsewhere, for example, to show that the conception of society as organic logically leads to a greater rather than a reduced role for the state.

For Ritchie, science is systematised knowledge in which some degree of unification has been attained. Philosophy, too, is systematic, but the knowledge at which philosophy aims will not necessarily use the same methods as those which have proved successful in extending scientific knowledge (Ritchie, 1905: 266). In fact, ethics and politics are more difficult subject-matters than mathematics and physics because the facts the former deal with are so diverse and complicated (Ritchie, 1902b: 106). While Ritchie devoted considerable effort to showing how science and philosophy are distinct fields of knowledge—after all, he explains poignantly, "[p]hysics and chemistry will not explain the perception of a picture, nor the meaning the picture has to the spectator, who recognises what it is about and judges it beautiful" (Ritchie, 1905: 110)—he nonetheless believed that both science and philosophy share certain assumptions about the nature of reality and the universe. Science is not advanced merely by an increase in the number of facts and generalisations about them, but also on the basis of hypotheses and theories that try to explain the manifold of phenomena we experience. This, Ritchie insists, is what science and philosophy share: that the universe is a whole, is coherent, and is intelligible. However, philosophy deals with meanings, values, and ends that are not necessarily quantifiable.

Nonetheless both science and philosophy assume unity and intelligibility. Since science and philosophy share the assumption that knowledge is possible, Ritchie argues, "[k]nowledge is only possible on the assumption of the absolute validity of the principle of contradiction, or to put it more widely, of the principle of coherence in thinking: the incoherent cannot be true, the true must be coherent, though the seemingly coherent is not necessarily true unless we suppose all experience exhausted" (Ritchie, 1905: 198). He insists that the principle "in its most abstract form and in its more concrete applications is valid because without it experience and the sciences would be impossible" (Ritchie, 1905: 78). The principle of coherence will force observers to ask whether an experience "as interpreted by the individual (and it must be interpreted by concepts in order to be communicated to others) cohere with the rest of his experience (as interpreted) and with the experience of others (as interpreted and communicated by them)" (Ritchie, 1905: 87; 1895: 192). Thus for Ritchie, both scientific inquiry and philosophical analysis have a necessary social dimension where tests of truth and falsehood are established through observation, hypothesis, and interpretation. Philosophy ought to seek general laws as scientists seek to understand physical and causal laws. Ritchie, however, believed that philosophy involves an analysis of human motives and actions and thus must always be interpretive.

Ritchie's objective was not so much to reconcile philosophy and science but rather to show how both are intertwined and necessary for human advancement. He clearly sympathised with the general theoretical and practical aspirations of the sciences. The central question for Ritchie, therefore, is whether there can be a science of ethics, and his reply is that a historical science tracing ethical ideals and social ends is certainly possible, but it would have little if anything to say normatively. As Ritchie observed, "science may say such and such a nation is happier, more stable, more highly developed; it does not say which is *best*" (Ritchie, 1905: 254). Moreover, the necessary feature of general scientific laws had disturbing consequences for the nature and meaning of human conduct. Human freedom "consists not in a mysterious exemption from the law of cause and effect, but in [the] capacity for thinking and so rising above the mere blind processes of nature" (Ritchie, 1902b: 197). Ritchie was convinced human beings could select ideals best suited for human life and reject those found to hinder or undermine social good. To treat ethics scientifically means to accept Aristotle's dictum that systematic study requires comprehension of the method appropriate to the subject-matter. Ritchie rejected the implication that individuals and society were determined in some manner by universal or necessary laws such as those found in biology and physics.

Ritchie argued that social theorists and philosophers must "go behind" the phenomenal existence of institutions to examine their ethical importance. As an idealist and, therefore, influenced by the presumption that knowledge was both contextual and more importantly relational, it is unsurprising that, for Ritchie, institutions play a key role in the development of ideas. Yet speculative metaphysics involves the effort to assess critically the principles upon which social and political institutions are based, and a conception of a unity of self-consciousness. For humans to be *selves* properly conceived—to be moral agents—requires a conception of the unity of the self. Moreover, it was necessary to find manifestations and processes of reason not simply in the minds of individuals but also in social and political institutions. His metaphysics was meant to reinforce the social dimension of knowledge, and highlighted the need for each generation of citizens to (re)interpret its individual and collective experiences. He explains: "We come to know our own individuality by knowing that of others. Self and other selves mutually interpret each other" (Ritchie, 1905:

249). For Ritchie, society is a *community of self-interpretation*. Individuals interpret their experiences and communicate them to others in order to deepen their understanding of human existence and social life. Within this putatively social conception of knowledge, however, resides a self that must — to be a moral agent — distinguish itself from others — this is what Ritchie calls the recognition of an "antagonism" between self and others, individual and nature.[3] This "true self" must logically be separate from the very institutions and society it assesses and critiques — in short, a subjective epistemology and individualist ontology of the self that will impact his ethical theory.[4]

The Self, Individuality, and Community

Rather than interpreting natural and social evolution as justifying a competitive ethics, Ritchie saw a different form of ethics lying at its base, one that incorporated purposiveness, rationality, and cooperation. Evolution also implied a notion of human and social progress, and thus a conception of perfection that was partly inspired by Aristotelian and Kantian ethics and by Hegel's notion of the Idea realising itself in the world through human self-consciousness. For Ritchie, the chief ethical doctrine that received his most critical attention was intuitionism, an ethical approach that had hardened into an ideology that undermined social progress. The central political manifestation of intuitionism, Ritchie held, was the doctrine of natural rights found in Locke, Rousseau, and Spencer. The doctrine of natural rights once served a useful purpose of justifying challenges to the authority of tradition and appeals to private judgment, reason, and the conscience of the individual. Ritchie applauded the natural rights theorists who played a crucial historical role in supporting the rights of individuals against traditions and customs that had lost their usefulness. However, the excessive individualism of the doctrine, in Ritchie's mind, meant it needed to be reconsidered in light of social progress and evolution. His metaphysics ensured rejection of the doctrine of natural rights. An alternative account of the relationship between individuals, society, and the state became one of Ritchie's main tasks, a form of *socialised individuality* within the context of an historically expired individualism.

The gravamen of Ritchie's objections to natural right and social contract theories is their effort to defend individual rights on the basis of *a priori* principles and values. Ritchie condemns this approach as incoherent

---

[3] In his review of *Darwin and Hegel*, Wm. J. Eckoff writes: "For a generation to whom Darwinism is the dominant working hypothesis, Hegelianism is the fittest metaphysics. Mr. Ritchie has done well in recognizing the relation. He has done better in preserving a large core of Kantian Criticism in his Hegelianism" (Eckoff, 1894: 174).

[4] J.S. Mackenzie remarked that Ritchie's idealism was not "sufficiently grounded against Subjective Idealism. The statement that objectivity means 'validity and coherence for others selves as well as for self' can hardly be called clear" (Mackenzie, 1906: 105).

because (a) there are no rights prior to or independent of society, and (b) the theory provides no criterion for determining how to resolve disputes over those rights that may conflict with others. Ritchie embraces the doctrine of recognition, that "liberty in the sense of positive opportunity for self-development, is the creation of law, and not something that could exist apart from the action of the State" (Ritchie, 1895: 139–40). Rights to liberty, equality, and to property are claims that need social and political support. Ultimately society recognises rights on the basis of their indispensability to social life or as having a prudential, useful role to play in the regulation of social life. Ritchie insisted that reference to individual needs, wants, and interests without a corresponding conception of society or community is an "abstraction." As he insists, it is "obvious that there is no meaning in an individual's right unless there are corresponding duties imposed on other individuals" (Ritchie, 1891: 78). The only conclusion is that natural rights must be recognised from the point of view of society. From Ritchie's perspective, challenging natural rights doctrines clears the way for discussion of social, political, and economic issues and problems on their own merits.

Ritchie's critical assessment of intuitionism and natural rights doctrines required him to reconsider conceptions of the self, the individual and the community, and the role of the state. One of Ritchie's concerns was the persistent view that "[t]he individual is thought of, at least spoken of, as if he had a meaning and significance apart from his surroundings and apart from his relations to the community of which he is a member….You can say nothing about him, or rather it, except that it is not any other individual" (Ritchie, 1891: 11). To regard the individual and the state as if they were opposites not only, Ritchie argues, undermines any meaningful assessment of the proper role of government but also tells us nothing about whether in any particular case or instance government action is required. (Ritchie, 1891: 12, 98) Ritchie's critique of natural rights theories was a reaction to *a priori* assumptions about the nature of individual rights and those social theories that failed to recognise the essential role that society played in the development and formation of individuals. However, Ritchie did not reject the use of all *a priori* claims and principles. By its very nature, ethical theory will have to import some notion of duty or what ought to be done, but what duty a citizen has at this moment will depend on the current context and the stage of moral development of the society of which this citizen is a member. Ritchie is clear: "Duty is *a priori*; duties depend on experience" (Ritchie, 1905: 236).

Ritchie's metaphysics and ethics suggest two distinct but interrelated conceptions of the self: an eternal self and a communal self. The metaphysics posits that a self is implied in the simplest act of knowledge, and thus Ritchie insists that to explain how knowledge is possible requires that we recognise an "eternal Self" that provides an ideal by which we can judge our conduct and development. The correlate is the social or communal self, a member of a society whose central personality and legal characteristics are formed by living in a community. Thus a person is not a mere product of nature but rather is created by the social institutions that comprise a society, and the function of such institutions is to forge an individual's personality by developing the process of recognising other selves (Ritchie, 1893: 149). A "true self" or a "person" is found not in separation from others, but in a community with others; we cannot "separate our own interests in an abstract way from the interests of others, nor theirs from ours" (Ritchie, 1891: 97). For Ritchie, self-consciousness as an operative principle was expanded to include the consciousness of others. From this convergence emerged a notion of community and a reconciliation of the requirements of individual personality and sociality.

Each and every society, Ritchie argues, agrees to observe certain basic conditions of common life, which in a modern state means creating and sustaining rights and duties for its members. A society whose members are incapable of recognising a conception of the common good is no society at all. As he explains, the "personal satisfaction of the individual cannot exclude, but must include, the realization of social well-being" (Ritchie, 1902b: 181). The use of a theory of social organicism to undergird self-realisation and social well-being is a central feature of Ritchie's view, one which he finds in Plato's ideal polity (Ritchie, 1902a: 150–1, 164). It is, as Ritchie admiringly notes, a state wherein the welfare of the whole, and not this or that part or individual, becomes the guiding principle. He insists that a "society of one hundred individuals for the promotion of a particular end is something more than the aggregate of a hundred individuals working independently towards the same end" (Ritchie, 1891: 25). Organicism usually means that the parts of an organism – in the political or social sense, individuals – are mutually dependent on each other. Hence the value and worth of each part of the organism are derived from the whole and, by extension, the whole represents something different from the sum of its parts. Ritchie imbued the social organism with moral characteristics so that its constituent parts were in fact moral actors seeking self-realisation which could only occur within society.

Unquestionably the relationship between the individual and the social organism is one of the most controversial elements in Ritchie's theory.[5] The social organism analogy is a central *motif* throughout Ritchie's writings. The social organism has "a continuous life within which its individ-

---

5   See for example Freeden (1986: 94), Robbins (1982: 11), Vincent and Plant (1984: 91). One of Ritchie's contemporary reviewers, F.C. Montague, stated that "the doctrine of the social organism is much more likely to be used in the interests of tyranny than of forbearance. A man regards his limbs as mere means to his well-being, and to secure his well-being will cut off a leg as readily as a Jacobin would guillotine a class" (Montague, 1891: 580–1); see Sweet (2004: 17).

ual members arise and perish, a life which has to be cared for over and above the sum of individuals at any given time existing" (Ritchie, 1895: 98). For Ritchie, the "person" is not a mere natural agent but is shaped by the conscious work of laws, customs, and religions. It is the purpose of the modern state to continue the work done by families, clans, cities, churches, universities, corporations, and unions in the development of individuals. Thus Ritchie explains that the state has as its end "the realisation of the best life by the individual. This best life can only be realised in an organised society—i.e., in the State; so that the State is not a mere means to individual welfare as an end; in a way the State is an end to itself" (Ritchie, 1891: 102). Yet Ritchie does use the theory of social organicism to demonstrate some limitations on state and societal intervention. For example, he writes that the "main reason for desiring more State action is in order to give the individual a greater chance of developing all his activities in a healthy way" (Ritchie, 1891: 64). He also claims that all "salutary State action must be such as will give individuals so far as possible the opportunity of realizing their physical, intellectual, and moral capacities" (Ritchie, 1902b: 56–7). Even more interesting is his remark that the notion of social organicism is simply "a means towards the well-being of individuals" (Ritchie, 1895: 123). Moreover, Ritchie states that the "modern State in its idea (i.e., what modern constitutional States are tending to become) does not … differ absolutely in character from voluntary associations" (Ritchie, 1902b: 50). But if Ritchie qualified the social organism metaphor so extensively, what value does it have to his view as a whole?

The modest organicism Ritchie deployed can be explained on a variety of grounds, some consistent with his general philosophical orientation and others less so. He was fairly consistent with his reservations about the use of organicism to describe societies. Hence he remarks that the "conception of organic growth, if properly grasped, clears away mischievous abstractions in politics and in history; but politics and history are not thereby turned into branches of imaginative biology" (Ritchie, 1891: 100). Social organicism was also necessarily circumscribed by the incorporation of a "humanist ethic" whereby individuals need to consider in their conduct and actions "the well-being of humanity as a whole, or at least of human society in some fairly large sense" (Ritchie, 1902b: 178). Perhaps most importantly, the inherent logic of relational idealism functions to limit state action. Just as individuals must assess their actions by reference to social ends, it follows that political institutions must too—that is, that the state could not possess its own rationale for existence.

Less apparent throughout Ritchie's ethical theory is an underlying Kantian influence. Ritchie notes that a "great part—in some ways the more important part—of human life lies outside the region that the State can directly affect" and that conduct "is only morally right if it is done from right motives, and external compulsion can only affect the outward actions" of a citizen (Ritchie, 1902b: 75). Ritchie, though, does insist that a citizen who abstains from wrongdoing merely through fear of punishment is "very imperfectly moralized" (Ritchie, 1902b: 75). And while Ritchie was seeking to defend a more active form of citizenship where the good citizen would be something more than a law-abiding person, he admits that the state oversteps its authority if sanctions are applied to citizens who fail to recognise positive duties toward others. One may well ask whether these limitations on the theory of organicism are consistent (or inconsistent) with his overall efforts. It may be that such limitations are consistent with his metaphysic of ethics, and function to individualise his social ontology.

Ritchie followed other idealists by trying to break down the hard conceptual division between "society" and the "state" that had developed within liberalism. Viewing *society* as an organism meant for Ritchie that the state differed from other organisms or associations in that its objective was to pursue the common good, and that consequently the state was the only association in which all those in society were members. Viewing *the state* as an organism meant that, in addition to the state's representational function, decisions made and policies enacted by public officials could be tested and assessed on the basis that the well-being of all citizens must be taken into consideration. In short, Ritchie believed that democratic principles and values would be better supported and advanced by regarding society as an organism.

Ritchie's "System of Ethics"

Ritchie's system of ethics grounds moral purpose within the state—a state whose function is to help individuals to achieve self-realisation through participation in a community animated by and directed toward a common good. In the most general sense, ethics for Ritchie meant the study of human conduct and society. Ethics deals with what is good, whereas politics concerns itself with trying to forge good citizens. Ethics, he insisted, is the science of man as capable of realising an ideal in conduct, and any ethical theory that fails to acknowledge the presence of an ideal to all human efforts and institutions is fatally flawed (Ritchie, 1893: 26; 1905: 282-3). A "metaphysic of ethics" will inquire how humans come to have an ideal of conduct and how they are to realise this ideal in practice. The "art of ethics" will involve a practical consideration of obligations and duties, a task Ritchie assigns both to public leaders and citizens. The search for the good and the attempt to realise it in society creates an inseparable connection between ethics and politics. The practical realisation of sociability and the conditions under which such realisation is possible provide the subject-matter of ethics.

Ritchie's *evolutionary utilitarianism* is based on the notion that the criterion by which actions and decisions should be taken is that of social, not individual, utility. He was convinced that a reconsideration of the social and political implications of evolutionary theory would reveal important ethical principles such as social progress and the relational or organic features of social life. Ritchie also believed that utilitarianism can be refined so long as "utility" is understood as "social well-being" or "consideration as to what conduces most to general social well-being" (Ritchie, 1902b: 11, 37). He considered Bentham's "greatest happiness of the greatest number" maxim to be overly "arithmetical" or abstract, and hence believed it was better for utilitarianism to openly adopt the principle of the common good: "the highest development of individual capacities compatible with the coherence and continuance of the society as a whole" (Ritchie, 1902b: 62). Ritchie was also prepared to interpret utilitarianism to mean "expedience", which he regarded as any action or policy that would lead to the greater physical, intellectual, and moral well-being of mankind (Ritchie, 1891: 107). Ultimately, if there is an ethical criterion that takes priority over all other claims, it must be social well-being.

Ritchie's utilitarianism was inspired less by Bentham's hedonic calculus and J.S. Mill's qualitative utilitarianism, and more by Plato's explication of the concept of utility. According to Ritchie, Plato deployed a compelling notion of utility that avoided the fatal flaw of drawing ethical judgments on the basis of individual feelings. He applauds Plato for recognising that the ideal polity is one in which stability and harmony are organising principles. Perhaps more importantly, Plato appeals to individual reason and the lessons of human experience, to the need to educate citizens, and to the use of discipline and reason to counteract or at least moderate individual instincts and impulses. He also insisted that the Platonic emphasis on scientific achievement had the positive effect of bolstering the argument that it is the business of educated and disciplined citizens to direct their attention to the health of the state and to provide guidance (Ritchie, 1902a: 168). The associationist and individualist psychology undergirding Bentham's and J.S. Mill's utilitarianism meant that neither could adopt a coherent notion of common good in spite of the emphasis they placed on assessing actions, policies, and laws on society as a whole. For Ritchie, the effort to measure balances of pain and pleasure is a hopeless project, although he does agree that the existence of pain and unhappiness are powerful incentives to initiate practical reforms. Ritchie rejected egoistic utilitarianism but emphasised the importance of social organisation to individual well-being.

Classical utilitarianism understood the moral end of the happiness of mankind in two, not necessarily consistent, ways: (a) as attempting to quantify and aggregate individual preferences and (b) as providing a notion of social utility and thus in principle supplying a measure of progress. Like natural rights doctrines, utilitarianism, having served its reformative and felicitous historical purpose, must be modified by the theory of evolution, by replacing the hedonic calculus with a clear scientific basis for social organisation. Idealist evolutionism is an expansion of the principle of self-realisation, and self-realisation is a key element of Ritchie's thought. His contention is that ethics must deal with freedom because "morality implies freedom, and freedom implies the *conscious* direction of action towards an *end*"; consequently, "the conceptions that we have to examine to start with are *consciousness* and *end*" (Ritchie, 1905: 280). Ritchie, however, substantially revised ethical conceptions such as free will, freedom, and equality in light his idealist approach. He rejects the claim that individuals possess "free will", not because individuals are incapable of deliberation, choice, and action—these Ritchie was insistent upon—but rather because the "mischievous" effect of free will is to obscure the manner in which individual characters and personalities depend on their social environment and to neglect the ethical significance of political and social institutions. The ethical end for the individual must always be a social end or a common good.

For Ritchie, the main problem confronting modern states was whether "equality of social conditions" can be attained, without the loss of opportunities for human well-being that should be enjoyed by all rather than a select few. He regarded the belief that citizens are naturally equal as "dogma" , although he was adamant that differences in terms of wealth, position, or status were "due to the influence of social institutions, and not to any original, innate, or inherited characteristics" (Ritchie, 1893: 64). Nature demonstrates there are wide physical and intellectual differences between individuals, but the existence of such natural inequalities, Ritchie argues, is not sufficient to justify "artificial inequalities" among individuals such as social status and wealth. The main challenge is to distinguish between natural and artificial inequalities, and determine to what extent the latter are the proper result of the former. Consequently, equality "as a principle is ultimately dependant on utilitarian considerations" (Ritchie, 1902b: 34). Ritchie condemns social, economic, and political inequalities not because individuals are "born free and equal", but rather because such inequalities led to "constraint, suspicion, cringing deference, contemptuous indifference" (Ritchie, 1902b: 39). Elsewhere, Ritchie explained that the ideal of human equality "which alone is necessarily implied in an idealist system of ethics, would be more correctly expressed as their potential membership of a common society. It is only in so far as we can think of humanity as a possible society that we can regard human beings as equal moral units" (Ritchie, 1895: 253–4). Equality is based on the capacity for human society, but may vary in practice according to what kinds of social "compromises" can be made.

The ethical criterion—and test of individual actions and government policies and laws—"must consider every measure solely from the point of view of the probable effect of it on the welfare of the community as a whole, now and in the future" (Ritchie, 1902b: 65). This emphasis on what is "socially useful"—that decisions and actions benefit the existing community—essentially comprises the ethical end for Ritchie. Elsewhere, he explains that the ethical end is equivalent to the interests of human society (Ritchie, 1895: 111), and that a decision or action can be justified "only on the grounds of its success and on the better condition of some very considerable number of human beings which results from that success" (Ritchie, 1895: 233). The emphasis Ritchie places on what is verifiably useful certainly explains his reluctance to base individual rights on a conception of human agency—that human beings have inherent traits or characteristics from which eternal principles can be a guide. What he calls "legal rights"—those rights that are codified and hence formally recognised by the state—"may be explained by reference to the past, but can only be justified if it is shown that they subserve social well-being now and are likely to do so in the future" (Ritchie, 1893: 29).[6] Ritchie does note the existence of "moral rights", claims of individuals upon others not formally recognised in law, but such rights are based on an individual capacity "residing in one man of controlling the acts of another with the assent and assistance, or at least without the opposition of, public opinion" (Ritchie, 1895: 78–9).[7] Since Ritchie defined freedom or liberty as "opportunities of self-development" (Ritchie, 1895: 140), the extent to which individuals are free depends greatly upon the kinds of external and social constraints placed upon the ability to achieve goals and aspirations.[8]

Whether the topic is capital punishment, the distribution or redistribution of private property, the enforcement of contractual obligations, freedom of speech and association, and even the presuppositions of democratic governance and decision-making—all were to be assessed or tested by his conception of social utility. Thus Ritchie offers three questions that citizens and public officials must consider in appraising a given course of action: (1) does the end or objective proposed by some particular measure lead towards our ultimate end? (2) are the proposed means such

---

6   He also refers to legal rights as "practical rights" (Ritchie, 1895: 154).
7   The criterion specified for limiting conduct is whether it is possible and safe to do so (Ritchie, 1895: 161).
8   Ritchie explains further that liberty "in general is too ambiguous a term to permit us to decide how far the right to liberty is a right which ought to be recognised by a well-regulated society. The principle that the liberty of everyone should be limited only by the equal liberty of every one else has been shown to be incapable of any literal application as a fundamental principle of society; on the contrary, it is a principles which is either absurd or anarchical, or both" (Ritchie, 1895: 147).

that they will secure that end or objective? (3) will the advantages arising from the means outweigh the disadvantages by reference to the common good? (Ritchie, 1902b: 62–3)[9] We can call these the *coherence*, the *efficacy*, and the *common good* tests respectively. Ritchie applied these criteria to the issue of censorship, and replied that because of the fact of diversity of opinions regarding what counts as immoral, mischievous, and vile literature, the goal of a "common opinion" concerning literature is incoherent. In addition, given that government officials cannot possibly be competent and unbiased critics, censorship subsequently fails the efficacy test. Finally, because it is uncertain to what extent suppressing literature (and consequently freedom of the press) interferes with socially useful literature, censorship also fails to pass the common good test.

In general, Ritchie's criticisms — directed at the inadequate conceptions of social good by intuitionists and utilitarians — have merit. It is not evident, however, that he provided a compelling, or even well-considered, substitute. Certainly "social well-being" was meant to be such a substitute, but a less sympathetic critic of Ritchie might well respond that the positive tests and calculations of social utility could be used by perfectly sane, rational, and well-intentioned people to derive various, if not contrary, results. In spite of Ritchie's effort to demonstrate otherwise, his idealist evolutionism may offer no certain guidance in the event of conflicting judgments about what ought to be done. It is one thing for observers far removed from historical events to judge and assess the actions and decisions of others, and another to attempt to do so when directly immersed in contentious policy issues. It is also rather difficult to decipher a phrase such as "[o]nly in a society of equals who are, as it were, his 'other selves,' can an individual realise the best life possible for himself" (Ritchie, 1891: 172). Does it mean that individuals need to *consider* the interests of others in the course of their daily lives and conduct? (In this case, are individuals ethically bound to evaluate their plans and projects in light of others' plans and projects?) Or does it mean that individuals must have the *same* interests and objectives? It is difficult to understand what Ritchie meant by this, and one supposes it is another instance of what Henry Sidgwick called the "unsystematic character" of Ritchie's more constructive claims (Sidgwick, 1895: 385).

Ritchie's practical ethics reveals a complex ethical foundation influenced by a substantially revised utilitarianism that places self-realisation, the common good, and perfectionist considerations at its core.[10] Like Green, Ritchie condemned any society that limited the opportunities for its citizens to cultivate their faculties and talents. He believed that the evo-

---

9 See Bernard Bosanquet's similar views, in his 1899 *The Philosophical Theory of the State*, on criteria determining the place of compulsion (Bosanquet, 2001: 186–7); see Sweet (1997: 172).
10 See Weinstein (2001).

lution of social progress meant that there was an emerging consensus that it was both possible and desirable to alleviate human misery. Ritchie's preference for the well-being of society represents a shift from Green's strongly moralised and character-based ethic. Ritchie's intention, it would seem, was to provide a practical and efficiency-based claim that meeting human needs will benefit everyone. The good that individuals are to pursue must be in some manner or to some extent a "common good." The self to be realised must be a self in harmony with others. The expansion of social well-being to include all citizens represents social progress. Ritchie's efforts at articulating such an ethics is significant because it aims to have a strong practical dimension: its task is to reject (or caution against) abstractions and raise socially relevant issues and questions that respect context, circumstance, and place. His theory also informs its readers that a fully-developed individual life is best realised in the performance of social functions.

Conclusion

Ritchie sought to explicate the role and purpose of social and political institutions and human agency and volition within an evolutionary context. He proclaimed that idealist evolutionism was collective, cooperative, and progressive, and enabled individuals to grow and develop their potential fully. Even though by Ritchie's day *laissez-faire* individualism was largely a spent force—at least in Britain and in most other liberal-democratic states—his critique of liberalism through evolutionism required an even greater state intervention in the economy and society, in order to provide all individuals with a measure of security and wider opportunity to participate in society and to develop themselves more fully. Ritchie was also attempting to restore a certain dignity to politics, by ensuring that the language of evolution and organism were applied judiciously to social thought and explanation—in an way that revealed its usefulness but also its limitations. Ritchie's notion of usefulness presupposes experiment and discussion, a process—supplemented on the basis of education—that is essentially democratic and moderately collectivist, relying on people working together to find common solutions to collective problems.

Ritchie's ethical theory has, however, what some consider "antinomies."[11] On the one hand, Ritchie's Platonic-Hegelian influences led him to view society as an organism, whose social and political institutions represented an unfolding of universal reason and progress. On the other hand, Ritchie's Kantianism is founded on a notion of self-determination from which citizens' capacity for social life is based on rules and laws they have made themselves. To be free in this sense, meant not a rejection

---

11 See Gaus (2000: 181) and Morefield (2002: 150).

of the pursuit of self-interest but rather a recognition of the moral duty to pursue a common good in spite of one's self-interest. Ritchie insists that the ideal of equality must be pragmatically derived and based on practical considerations. Yet he also argues that the basis for equality is self-consciousness and the capacity for self-reflection.

Nevertheless, one may well question whether these two conceptions of equality can fit together into a coherent ethics. Admittedly, Ritchie located such ideals within social practices and institutions, but he is also wedded to the notion that ideals can be generated through critical self-reflection. He saw no inherent difficulty with this approach, because he stipulates that self-realisation entails both a notion of good for the individual and good for the community. In any event, Ritchie's account of self-realisation attempts to provide an answer to this concern, and to supply a link between ethics (what is good for individuals and society) and politics (how to forge and to provide appropriate institutional conditions for good citizens).

References

Bosanquet, B. (2001), *"The Philosophical Theory of the State" and Related Essays*, William Sweet and Gerald F. Gaus (eds.), (South Bend, IN: St Augustine's Press).

Boucher, D. (2004), *The Scottish Idealists: Selected Philosophical Writings* (Exeter: Imprint Academic).

Boucher, D. and Vincent, A. (2000), *British Idealism and Political Theory* (Edinburgh: Edinburgh University Press).

Den Otter, S. M. (1996), *British Idealism and Social Explanation: A Study in Late Victorian Thought* (Oxford: Clarendon Press).

Eckhoff, W. (1894), Review of *Darwin and Hegel*, *Political Science Quarterly*, 9/1 (March), p. 174.

Freeden, M. (1986), *The New Liberalism: An Ideology of Social Reform* (Oxford: Clarendon Press).

Freeden, M. (1996), *Ideologies and Political Theory: A Conceptual Approach* (Oxford: Clarendon Press).

Gaus, G. (2000), "Liberalism at the end of the century", *Journal of Political Ideologies*, 5/2, pp. 179-99.

Green, T.H. (1883), *Prolegomena to Ethics*, A. C. Bradley (ed.) (Oxford: Clarendon Press).

Mackenzie, J.S. (1906), Review of *Philosophical Studies*, *Mind*, 15/57.

Montague, F.C. (1891), Review of *The Principles of State Interference*, *The Economic Journal*, 1/3.

Morefield, J. (2002), "Hegelian Organicism, British New Liberalism and the Return of the Family State", *History of Political Thought*, 23/1, pp. 141-70.

Morefield, J. (2004), *Covenants without Swords: Idealist Liberalism and the Spirit of Empire* (Princeton: Princeton University Press).

Neill, E. (2003), "Evolutionary Theory and British Idealism: The Case of David George Ritchie", *History of European Ideas*, 29, pp. 313-38.

Nicholson, P.P. (ed.) (1998), *The Collected Works of D.G. Ritchie*, Vol. 1 (Bristol: Thoemmes Press).

Ritchie, D.G. (1889), *Darwinism and Politics* (London: Swan Sonnenschein & Co.).

Ritchie, D.G. (1891), *The Principles of State Interference* (London: Swan Sonnenschein & Co.).

Ritchie, D.G. (1893), *Darwin and Hegel: With Other Philosophical Studies* (London: Swan Sonnenschein & Co.).

Ritchie, D.G. (1895), *Natural Rights: A Criticism of Some Political and Ethical Conceptions* (London: Swan Sonnenschein & Co.).

Ritchie, D.G. (1902a), *Plato* (Edinburgh: T & T Clark).

Ritchie, D.G. (1902b) *Studies In Political and Social Ethics* (London: Swan Sonnenschein & Co.).

Ritchie, D.G. (1905), *Philosophical Studies* (London: Macmillan and Company).
Robbins, P. (1982), *The British Hegelians 1875–1925* (New York: Garland Publishing Inc).
Sidgwick, H. (1895), Review of *Natural Rights, Mind*, 4/15 (July), p. 385.
Simhony, A. and Weinstein, D. (eds.) (2001), *The New Liberalism: Reconciling Liberty and Community* (Cambridge: Cambridge University Press).
Sweet, William (1997), *Idealism and Rights* (Lanham, MD: University Press of America).
Sweet, William (2004), *Early Responses to British Idealism*, vol. 2: *Responses to D. G. Ritchie and Bernard Bosanquet* (Bristol, UK: Thoemmes-Continuum).
Vincent, A. and Plant, R. (1984), *Philosophy, Politics and Citizenship: The Life and Thought of the British Idealists* (Oxford: Basil Blackwell Limited).
Weinstein, D. (2001) "The new liberalism and the rejection of utilitarianism", in Avital Simhony and David Weinstein (eds.), *The New Liberalism: Reconciling Liberty and Community*, pp. 159–83.
Weinstein, David (2002), "Vindicating Utilitarianism", *Utilitas*, 14: 71–95.

Carol A. Keene

The Interplay of Bradley's Social and Moral Philosophy

The social and the moral philosophy of F.H. Bradley are closely intertwined in light of his theory of self-realization, for it is in the context of his seeking to answer the question, "What is the self to be realized?" that they take form. It is this question, with its formulation "borrowed" from T.H. Green, yet rooted in the Aristotelian ethics that dominated Oxford in Bradley's undergraduate days, that gives a thematic unity to *Ethical Studies* (1876), his initial "epoch-making" work.[1] It is this quest for a definition of "my true self" that provides a springboard for his wielding of the Hegelian ethic as well as an antidote both to the atomistic individualism of Mill and to the barren formalism of an admittedly exaggerated Kantianism. In using the Hegelian view as a corrective to these equally one-dimensional views of the self, Bradley puts forth the doctrine of "My Station and Its Duties", often taken as a statement of his moral philosophy, but mistakenly so.[2] Faulted for its own one-sidedness from a moral perspective, "My Station" ultimately fails as a response to the question of what is "my true

---

1   On Bradley having "borrowed" his "formula", though he cannot remember from whom, "perhaps Green", see Bradley (1999c; 255–6). He did attend four of Green's lecture series (G.S. Morris Papers, Bentley Historical Library, University of Michigan), and a few of his undergraduate essays bear Green's comments, as Peter Nicholson has recently confirmed in correspondence with me. For his undergraduate essays and "Notes on Green's Lectures on Moral and Political Philosophy", see Bradley (1999a: 1–136). His "Notes on Green's Lectures on Presokratic Philosophy" are included in the forthcoming expanded edition of the *Collected Works of FH Bradley*, vols. 1–5, titled *F.H. Bradley: Notebooks, Papers and Correspondence*, in InteLex's Past Masters series. For a petition to Green that he signed as a member of an essay society in June 1872, see Bradley (1999d: 1–2; 2004). On the Bradley/Green relationship, see Nicholson (1990).

    Bradley discussed the dominance of Aristotle's ethics at Oxford in the 1860s with G.S. Morris, as the Morris Papers reveal. Though one clearly finds elements of Aristotelian ethics in Bradley's ethical writings, his moral theory does not bear an Aristotelian label. On this relationship, see Crossley (1977), and Glover (1970: chapter 1).

    Regarding *Ethical Studies* being "epoch-making", see Bosanquet (1924: 57–8). See also Muirhead (1931: 228–238).

2   Ralph Ross (1951), in omitting Essays VI and VII (in which Bradley develops his own moral theory), contributed to this mistaken view, as did Sabine (1915), Krook (1959) and Wollheim (1969). See Nicholson's discussion (1990: 6–53) of this mistaken view and of labeling Bradley a political conservative. On the latter, see also Nicholson (1984) and Trott (1996).

self". The dialectic of *Ethical Studies* culminates with an ideal morality of self-realization, in which the ideal self is inclusive of the social self of "My Station" as well as an ideal social and an ideal non-social self — and it is a morality that issues, moreover, in religion. The purpose of this essay, then, is to sketch Bradley's moral theory and the manner in which his social philosophy is interwoven with it.

A Few Preliminary Remarks

There are, however, a few matters that require clarification from the outset. First, in the present ethical climate, with its enthusiasm for "applied ethics", it is well to point out that, for Bradley, moral philosophy is a speculative venture, not one ordained to practice. For him, it is not the function of the moral philosopher to devise ultimate principles by which determinations can be made as to what is right and wrong or to engage in casuistry.[3] Rather, the philosopher's function, whatever the branch of philosophy may be, is to understand *what is*. Secondly, in *Ethical Studies*, Bradley does not draw any sharp distinction between social and political philosophy, though notes to the second edition of this work, published posthumously (1927), suggest that he saw a need to clarify this matter.[4] Moreover, the direction of the Bradleian dialectic in *Ethical Studies* underscores that his social theory, embryonic as it is, is subordinated to a concern larger than that of determining the nature of the relation between the individual and society. Society for him is a moral organism, and hence his social thought cannot be dissociated from the moral impulse that prompts it. Thirdly, given that Bradley's discussions germane to the present essay appear mainly in *Ethical Studies*, the caution that he himself urged — namely, that this work rests upon metaphysical and psychological presuppositions — should be observed. Fourthly, in each of his major works, Bradley states that it is not his intent to devise a system, chiefly because he does not know where a given branch of philosophy begins or ends. Hence, in lieu of system-building, Bradley — whose forte is the essay — examines selected issues to which he seeks to give a thematic unity.

Because the initial essays in *Ethical Studies* provide a framework for Bradley's moral theory, a few words, however selective, must be said about them as well. The opening essay, "The Vulgar Notion of Responsibility in Connexion with the Theories of Free-Will and Necessity", sets

---

[3] Though Bradley does not object to casuistry for discovery of moral principles, he repudiates any attempt to draw up a code and determine the rightness or wrongness of a particular case by reference to it. See Bradley (1935b: 104–16). See also Bradley (1999c: 250–3, 395–6) and Vincent (1999).

[4] See Bradley (1927: 163n1, 173–4n2, 198n4). Bradley acknowledges that his usage of "social" shifts from referring to multiple spheres of family, profession, and state, to the state alone, without warning the reader.

forth certain criteria for an adequate theory of morality using, as a methodological springboard, the views of the "plain man", the typical individual of everyday life with his ordinary commonsensical notions, who holds that morality involves responsibility and accountability.[5] If an individual is to be held morally responsible and to have a given deed imputable to him, he "must act himself, be now the same man who acted, have been himself at the time of the act, have had sense enough to know what he was doing, and to know good from bad" (1927: 9). With these criteria, however, the theories of Free-Will and Necessity both fail. The Free-Will theory is inadequate because it necessarily entails a capricious will of the moment, thereby voiding the possibility of any principle of enduring sameness and hence of moral accountability. The doctrine of Necessity is untenable, too, because, in considering the self a mere collection of sensations held together by the laws of association, it rests upon a psychology that cannot ground personal identity. Though both theories can be faulted in other respects as well, their lack of a principle of self-sameness suffices to strike them out of play.

In Essay II, Bradley proposes self-realization as the unconditional end of morality. Setting about to determine what self is to be realized in morality, he suggests that if we look to the self of everyday life, we see that, living in multiple spheres, it wants a holistic world in which these spheres are harmonious, not fragmented or pitted against one another. Moreover, the everyday self has some ends subordinated to serve wider ends. Ultimately such broader or larger wholes are themselves included in one all-encompassing whole. Though some ends may not be so subordinated, still "if the life of the normal man be inspected, and the ends he has in view (as exhibited in his acts) be considered, they will roughly speaking be embraced in one main end or whole of ends", presenting itself as "an ideal of life" or "a notion of perfect happiness" (1927: 9). Thus, the self which we seek to realize is the "self as a whole", the self as a "consistent" and "harmonious" system (1927: 74n1). Marked by our finitude, by our relativity to others, our only avenue to such realization, however, is to be an active member of an infinite whole, one that is self-contained, self-related, and, in that sense, without limit or end. " 'Realize yourself as an infinite whole' means, 'Realize yourself as the self-conscious member of an infinite whole, by realizing that whole in yourself' " (1927: 78). But this, as Bradley admits, is only a formal response, one that is not advanced, moreover, by the one-sided

---

[5] Bradley's use of the "plain man" has received criticism because of its susceptibility to ambiguity and attendant difficulties of interpretation and translation into philosophical theory. See Sidgwick (1876), and Mackenzie (1928); reprinted, together with Edward Caird's 1876 *Academy* review, in Sweet and Keene (2004). For Bradley's reply to Sidgwick, see Bradley (1877, in Bradley, 1935: 677–81). On the relation between "vulgar" morality and Bradley's moral theory, see Kendal (1928, and Gardiner (1992). See also MacEwen (1996) who targets the ambiguity of such phrases as "the normal man" and "living people".

views of Hedonism (with its focus upon concrete particularity) and Kantianism (with its preoccupation with abstract universality) — positions that he explores, respectively, in Essays III and IV. Thus, the bedrock questions remain: What is the whole that I am to join in order to realize my true self? What is my true self?

The Social Self: My Station and Its Duties

At the heart of any social philosophy is ultimately the question of whether the self is solitary or solidary, and how such terms are to be defined. Though this question so posed falls prey in the final analysis to the fallacy of the false alternative for Bradley, it is nonetheless a useful point of departure from which to highlight his social theory.[6] Seeking to checkmate the tide of individualism long upheld in British socio-political thought, Bradley takes primary aim at the version of this tradition receiving attention in his day, namely, that emanating from Bentham, Mill, and the psychologist Alexander Bain — the trio which he called "the School of Experience". Opposing their view that society is no more than an artificial aggregate of bare particulars called "individuals", Bradley advances the theory that society "is an organism and a moral organism", apart from which the individual is a mere fiction (1927: 162).[7] Refraining from metaphysical argumentation on the grounds that the metaphysical position of this "School", being "mere dogmatism", warrants "no more than counter-assertion", and that he himself is not yet equipped with a metaphysics, he takes his stand on "the teaching of experience" (1927: 165–6). In refusing to plunge precipitously into a metaphysical discussion of the nature of the individual, Bradley proposes to stand by the facts in an effort to illustrate and vindicate his thesis that the individual — taken as real outside an organic community — is a vicious abstraction. His war against abstractionism, waged on the ground of his theory of feeling or immediate experience, is the Ariadne's thread that unifies his thought from his initial work — *The Presuppositions of Critical History* (1874) — to his final publication, the second edition of *The Principles of Logic* (1922).

In Essay V of *Ethical Studies*, he wages this war phenomenologically, proportioning his methodology to the self of everyday life. Considering a typical Englishman by way of example, he seeks to show that this Englishman is what he is because he was born and bred as a member of a social organism in a web of social relations that have penetrated his very being.

---

6   On the fallacy of false alternative, see Bradley (1922: 139n8, 166n17, 430n29; 1914: 238).

7   See also Wright (1984) for criticism of Bradley's organic view of society, and Banchetti (1922), both for similarities between Bradley's and Hegel's views in this, the most Hegelian of Bradley's essays in *Ethical Studies*, and for discussion of whether the social whole can meet the necessary conditions for being an organism. See also Milne (1962: 56–86, 165–83), and Stanley (1996).

Hence, even if he were to be the sole survivor of his nation, he still would not be the "mere individual" as understood by Mill.

Yet, some may argue that, at least at birth, this Englishman was a "mere individual", before custom and education could forge his sense of identity with others. For Bradley, however, "the teaching of modern physiology" trumps any view that sociality is merely acquired *à la* Mill. For physiology teaches that, from the first, a child has "an inner, a yet undeveloped nature, which must largely determine his future individuality", a nature, moreover, that is already inclusive of certain hereditary traits—a fact that precludes his being viewed as some bare particular even at birth (1927: 168).[8]

While denying that sociality is *solely* acquired, Bradley clearly grants that custom and education have roles in the process of socialization. Indeed, he maintains that the immediate tender care given to the child impresses habits upon him, forging his solidarity with other people before he knows himself as "this I" set over against others. In a classic passage anticipating his later, more fully developed, doctrine of feeling—of a primordial level of experience wherein awareness and being are one without as yet any formally drawn distinction between self and not-self—Bradley writes:

> His earliest notions come mixed to him of things and persons, not distinct from one another, nor divided from the feeling of his own existence. … the breast of his mother, and the soft warmth and touches and tones of his nurse, are made one with the feeling of his own pleasure and pain; … he does not even think of his separate self; he grows with his world … and when he can separate himself from that world, and know himself apart from it, then by that time his self, the object of his self-consciousness, is penetrated, infected, characterized by the existence of others. Its content implies in every fibre relations of community. He learns, or already perhaps has learnt, to speak, and here he appropriates … his country's language, and it carries into his mind the ideas and sentiments of the race. … He grows up in an atmosphere of example and general custom, his life widens out from one little world to other and higher worlds, and he apprehends through successive stations the whole in which he lives, and in which he has lived. (1927: 171–2)[9]

Born into, and enveloped in, a vibrant world of custom, the child, as he maturates, finds his life widen from the familial world to encompass his social position and profession as well as the state. "To be himself he must

---

8   In this second edition, Bradley questions whether "civilized tendencies" are hereditary and whether race can be an effective bond of unity; he also repudiates his interchanging "race" and "nationality" (1927: 180n1, 169n1). It is convenient to note here that, given Bradley's usage of "man" and masculine pronouns, I have retained such usage in this essay.

9   On the doctrine of feeling, see Bradley (1909: 40–64 [in Bradley (1914: 159–98)]). In his view, his account in *Appearance and Reality* lacked a "proper psychological treatment"; see Bradley (1999d: 65–6). See also Crossley (1989) and J. Bradley (1996).

go beyond himself, to live his life he must live a life which is not merely his own, but which ... is intensely and emphatically his own individuality" (1927: 163). No either/or here: true individuality weds the solidary and the solitary, with feeling or immediacy being the ground both of one's identity with others and one's own particularity.

With this social theory in hand, Bradley explores "My Station and Its Duties" specifically as a moral theory. "My Station" holds that we live in multiple spheres that prescribe our duties relative to our station in each, whether it be the family, our profession, or the state. By making my will one with the universal will of the social whole, with the duties prescribed and assigned to me in terms of my place and function in society, I realize the good will, that is, the moral will, and sustain the traditions of my society as well.[10] This dynamic interrelationship of "My Station", characteristic of social organicism, not only accords more with the teaching of experience than does the atomism of "the School of Experience", but it signals as well "My Station's" advance over the one-sidedness of Kantianism with its merely formal universal will.

Although Kant was correct in holding that, in order for the self to be realized, it must be equated with "the good will" in some sense, he had the sense wrong. If I am to realize the good will, it must be a concrete universal, a universal that has no real existence except in and through particular or private wills, a universal that entails the identity — to use Kantian principles — of homogeneity and specification.[11] Bradley's *provisional* thesis, then, is that "My Station", because it offers a concrete universal, has the wherewithal to overcome certain defects of a Kantian ethic. One advantage is its avoidance of capriciousness. Although "within limits I may choose my station according to my own liking, yet I and everyone else must have some station with duties pertaining to it, and those duties do not depend on our opinion or liking" (1927: 176). That my station is a matter of choice is important to underscore. For it shows that Bradley's own view yields neither to the status quo nor to gender determined stations. What I have to do and realize is a given in the various spheres of the organized community, not subject to my wish or whim. Moreover, the universal of "My Station" is truly objective as a "real identity of subject and object", unlike the purportedly objective Kantian universal, which, while claiming to be independent of this or that person, shows itself to be subjective (1927: 177). For, in bifurcating the moral whole, in separating the inner from the outer side of systems and institutions, the Kantian ethic fails to provide us with an objective moral content whereby we can secure our

---

10 For a defense of Bradley's case for holism, see Crossley (1977b), and Pettit (1985–6), though the latter adds "a consequentialist flourish" to social holism.

11 See Bradley (1927: 74). Throughout *Ethical Studies*, Bradley is unconcerned with clarifying his relation to Kant, though he took copious notes on Kant's works, far more than on the works of any other philosopher.

self-realization. "My Station", in contrast, as a theory of social holism repudiating such bifurcation, admits of an objective specification of my duties. By making my will one with the universal will already embodied in social institutions and traditions, I both perpetuate its outer existence and realize myself. The universal and the particular, hence, form an indivisible reality, whereby solidarity obtains between the self and its social system, and in this "My Station" surpasses the abstract universal of Kantianism. Finally, "My Station" claims to have overcome the fixed Kantian antithesis between the sensuous self and the non-sensuous moral ideal, between the "is" and the "ought". For, in maintaining that personal morality consists of oneness with the universal will—that is, the will of the actual moral world—it thereby denies identification with the "false self", the self opposed to the good will.[12]

Yet, for all of its advantages over a Kantian formalism, "My Station" is not without defects. However, before exposing them, Bradley examines popular conceptions that would be critical of this theory. One such conception is embodied in the thesis that, either there is some absolute rule of morality (constant throughout the ages for all peoples of all cultures), or else all morality is relative (subjective) and thus no morality at all. But this thesis, Bradley claims, offers only another false alternative. First, history shows that there is no fixed or absolute moral rule. A given society's customary morality changes across time, individuals considered good in one era may not be so considered in another, and what is considered right in one country may be considered wrong in another. In short, given our historicity, some kind of moral relativism is our only alternative. Moreover, the historical character of the development of "the true nature of man" precludes our having absolute moral notions falling from the heavens, because humanity's true nature, the perfect oneness of personal wills with the will of the whole, is still being worked out (1927: 189–90). But, secondly, though "My Station" upholds such an evolutionary view of human nature, it nonetheless maintains that at every stage in this process there is still the "solid fact of a world so far moralized. There is an objective morality in the accomplished will of the past and present, a higher self worked out by the infinite pain, the sweat and blood of generations, and now given to me by free grace and in love and faith as a sacred trust" (1927: 190). Hence "relativity", as used in "My Station", has a sense that is not reducible to mere "subjectivity", because it does not necessarily entail the eradication of an objective or "absolute" element. Nor does the relativism of "My Station" spell morality's demise by reducing it to capriciousness. For "My Station" safeguards against "relativism" in the latter sense by main-

---

12 See Bradley (1927: 181–2, 179n1), where Bradley acknowledges a failure to have warned the reader that his identification of personal morality with oneness with the will of the actual moral world was only provisional.

taining that what individuals must do depends upon their station in the social organism, not upon private wish or whim. A masterful technician of meaning-oriented analyses, Bradley uses this methodological tool to suggest that "relative" and "absolute" each have more than one meaning, with the consequence being that the aforementioned thesis fails because it fails to acknowledge the plural senses that such terms may have. He also cautions that "evolution", as used above, "gives us over neither to chance nor alien necessity, for it is that self-realization which is the progressive conquest of both" (1927: 190). Given the intellectual climate of his time, however, Bradley does consider whether "My Station" remains tenable on a Darwinian understanding of "evolution". He concludes that the Darwinian view mutilates "My Station", stripping it of its teleological orientation to the true nature of human reality and of its right "to speak of humanity realizing itself in history, and of myself finding in that movement the truth of myself worked out" (1927: 192).[13] Still, it leaves unscathed the right and duty to pursue self-realization through identification with the actual moral world, a world which, given its current social institutions and traditions, provides a content that is "absolute" in the sense of being "objective".

Another problem with "My Station" for some is that it offers no system of what is right and wrong in particular cases. But this view is rooted in an erroneous assumption about the nature of moral philosophy, which is simply "to understand morals which exist, not to make them or give directions for making them" or "to make the world moral" (1927: 193; see also Bradley, 1922: 270; and Bradley, 1930: 399). The view that holds moral philosophy responsible for supplying us with particular moral rules confuses two different kinds of judgment: reflective and intuitive; it is the latter that tells us what in particular cases is right and wrong, not the former. The world of categorical imperatives is not the world of everyday conduct. But neither is intuition a mode of apprehension that excludes understanding and its implicit judgments.

As to *how* I am to know what is right or wrong, the reply of "My Station" is: through custom and example. Moreover, if I embrace the spirit of my community, with its beliefs about right and wrong, then this whole, which through acculturation has become part of me, will provide a solid basis for my intuitive subsumptions (1927: 196) and thereby safeguard my judgments against being reduced to mere individual opinion. Thus, while "My Station" offers no codification of what is right and wrong in particular cases, still it clarifies the nature of that general foundation upon which our intuitive subsumptions depend. Hence it withstands the criticism of those

---

13 Bradley refuses to commit himself to whether evolution is teleological here, though later in *Ethical Studies* he suggests that such an orientation can be justified by faith.

who, in asking that it provide more, show their misunderstanding of philosophy's task.

Still another notion that is sharply rebuffed by "My Station", given its provision of an objective moral foundation, is that we should be better than our world. "If you could be as good as your world, you would be better than most likely you are, and … to wish to be better than the world is to be already on the threshold of immorality" (1927: 199). Although we may have a duty to try to make ourselves and our world better, this is to be done on the basis of the actual moral world and in harmony with its general spirit, not from the basis of private ideals that one sets against the moral world. But to move beyond the actual moral world even to social ideals, however much grounded in that world, is to move beyond "My Station".

Regarding the defects of this theory, Bradley first observes that it does not square with moral life as we know it, since it fails to account for the moral struggle that individuals experience between "the good self" and "the bad self". Secondly, it offers no guarantee that identifying one's self with duties prescribed by one's society secures one's realization, since one's society may well be in a "confused and rotten" condition (1927: 203). Thirdly, individuals may have to sacrifice themselves for the community, thereby being robbed of seeing their realization in fruition.[14] Fourthly, in holding that the self to be realized is the social self as defined by its station in the visible organism of the state and its sub-spheres, "My Station", in effect, nullifies the private selves of all. For it considers members of the social organism to be real only from the standpoint of their identification with the universal will of the community. By so reducing individuals to their social self, "My Station" at once renders them narrow and one-sided and reveals its own narrowness and one-sidedness, its spurious use of the phrase "personal morality", and its inadequacy to explain that whole in which we find our true self.

"My Station", moreover, is predicated on a moral world in a process of historical development, a world that therefore neither is nor can be consistent. Seeking to surmount such inconsistencies in the customary morality of its community, the everyday self may turn, in Bradley's view, to "cosmopolitan morality" (1927: 204).[15] By becoming aware of what other societies consider to be right and wrong and of what has been so thought in the past, the everyday self can develop a notion of goodness that is not restricted to some particular country and time. But if one's true self cannot be realized in one's society, then "My Station" fails as a moral theory, and the duality of the "is" and the "ought", which "My Station" had claimed to overcome, becomes all too real.

---

14   See Bradley (1894–5) wherein he argues that self-sacrifice is not unconditionally moral.
15   Bradley (1894–5) further entertains the possibility of an international community and morality.

Ideal Morality

In Essay VII, Bradley sets forth his own moral theory, seeking to justify pursuit of social reform as well as of interests not directly social. In so doing, he explores whether morality and self-realization are the same thing, thereby targeting the issue of how morality relates to other spheres of life. This issue is of import not only to his theory of morality, but to his later espousal of an all-pervasive relativism as well, for on that view, no aspect of our nature is unconditionally supreme, however much each within its own limits is admitted to have a relative supremacy.[16]

That morality and self-realization are in some sense different, is suggested by popular views. The everyday self, for example, does not consider artists or scientists to be moral simply because they are good artists or scientists. But neither does this self hold that morality can be closeted off from such aspects of life. As for Matthew Arnold's suggestion that morality covers only nine-tenths of our life, it falters because of its coarse fragmentation of life into parts.[17] Moreover, morality's dictate is "to be a good man in all things and everywhere, to try to do always the best, and to do one's best in it, whether in lonely work or in social realization to suppress the worse self and realize the good self" (1927: 215). This dictate suggests a qualified co-extensiveness of morality with self-realization. Stated otherwise, morality is coextensive with self-realization, but self-realization taken *only* in the sense of realization of the good self. However, as Bradley points out, two habits of thought may obscure this position: (1) the restriction of personal morality to social relations, and (2) the consideration of morality as necessarily entailing disagreeable duties. But, the former has already been faulted in criticism of "My Station", and the latter rebuffs the plain man's notion that individuals can be considered good even if goodness becomes natural and pleasant to them.

Some might nonetheless argue that, unless there is some region of indifference, the absurd consequence follows that we must be moral in every insignificant detail of our lives. Bradley faults this argument for failing to recognize that morality's distinguishing feature is its formal object, the realization of the good will, not the field from which it draws its material. Still it might be urged that, in principle, certain regions of life, such as fields of amusement, cannot be moralized, because actions therein are done naturally, without reflection and deliberate choice. This view, how-

---

16 See Bradley (1914: 470; 1930: 443, 449).

17 See Bradley (1927: 215) and Arnold (1873). For a comparison of the moral theories of Bradley and Arnold, see Krook (1959). For additional remarks on Arnold, see Bradley (1927: 315–9). In a letter of 1 February 1922 to his sister Emma Bradley Bull, who apparently had suggested that Bradley was too caustic in his remarks about Arnold, he wryly remarked: "You were quite right, for it's a mistake always to overdo that kind of thing. And really it was rather unjust—though he more than deserved it"; see Bradley (1999e: 257–9; see Bradley, 2004, vol. 5: L186).

ever, involves a twin error: "a mistake as to the limits, and a mistake as to the character of the moralized self" (1927: 217). In addressing this dual error, Bradley follows Aristotle, maintaining that whatever comes under the will's control is in the moral sphere. Forged by a series of will-acts, not inborn, our character thus becomes so interwoven with our being that it becomes our second nature, with good (or bad) behavior unreflectively issuing from it. Because formed by conscious volition, habits remain imputable and, thus, are not exempt from morality. Having trounced arguments favoring a region of indifference, Bradley contends once again that morality is coextensive with self-realization, but with "self-realization in the sense of the realization of the ideal self in and by us" (1927: 219). What, then, is the ideal self?

The ideal self, for Bradley, consists of: (1) the ideal as realized in society, namely, my station and its duties, (2) the ideal social self, inclusive of the social virtues of my station realized to perfection, such as the "perfect types of zeal and purity, honour and love", and (3) the ideal non-social self constituted of the ideals of truth and beauty (1927: 220). Put otherwise, the content of my ideal self has a threefold origin: (1) the objective or actual moral world of my station, which is its foundation and most important contributor, (2) the ideal of social perfection, and (3) the ideal of non-social perfection. The first we come to know through example and custom; the second, through an imaginative and abstractive extrapolation from witnessing the type of excellence in some individuals and projecting an ideal type, realized to perfection in none. As for the third, Bradley has very little to say other than that ideal morality is rooted in the ordinary morality of society, though he will nonetheless affirm that morality's *genesis* is not *solely* social.[18]

Cognizant of customary morality's resistance to any notion of a non-social perfection, he readily grants that non-social virtues may lead indirectly to the good of others. But he insists that the creative realization of one's intellectual or artistic nature is an end in itself, not subordinated to any form of social perfection or dictate. Yet he does not deny a social origin to either science or art, suggesting, again, that even non-social ideals develop within the context of a communal touchstone.

> To say, without society science and art could not have arisen, is true. To say, apart from society the life of an artist or man of science can not be carried on, is also true; but neither truth goes to show that society is the ultimate end. ... Man is not man at all unless social, but man is not much above the beasts unless more than social. (1927: 233)[19]

Bradley adds that there is nothing easier to suppose than that a life dedicated to art or inquiry would be considered a "sheer waste" by many,

---

18 On the ideal self, see Bradley (1927: 219–25).
19 See also Bradley (1930: 368, 381–2n1, 469n1).

given their predilection for identifying virtue with altruism (1927: 224). But was such a life immoral? "No", replies Bradley, "it was not *therefore* immoral, but may have been *therefore* moral beyond ordinary morality" (1927: 224). With this, he leaves the burden of proof to those who contend otherwise. But his claim that a life devoted to realization of non-social ideals may be "moral beyond ordinary morality" invites questions regarding how the three sources of content for the ideal self stand to one another.

May an individual "trample on ordinary morality" in order to become a good scientist or artist (1927: 225)? Or, from another side, may an individual take up a profession which society views as moral, but which, judged by his own ideal, is not moral? For Bradley, such questions require practical insight for their resolution, not abstract reasoning, since they involve the practical issue of colliding duties, where ordinary morality is being neglected or opposed in the name of some higher morality. Because they take root in complex, individual cases, efforts to define one class of duties as, in the abstract, higher than another class are, moreover, of no practical use. The everyday self, too, agrees that "the man who can give moral advice is the man of experience, who, from his own knowledge and by sympathy, can transport himself into another's case; … and the man of mere theory is in the practical sphere a useless and dangerous pedant" (1927: 226). Though "the man of experience" may well be a valuable guide to anyone involved in a head-on collision of duties, Bradley, unlike Mill, does not appeal to him to valuate or determine the hierarchical order of the diverse contents of "my ideal self". For judging the relative worth of the various aspects of our life is the task of the philosopher.

Regarding the relation of the ideal spheres (social and non-social) to the real sphere of my station, Bradley suggests that even "My Station" permits neglect of some duties, since—in a given case—an individual may have several duties and yet be able to perform only one. Then, too, society allows laws to be broken in the name of obedience to some higher law, as evidenced in its refusal to mete out strict justice to criminals, in its showing mercy through pardoning. Such examples suggest that in ideal morality, as in "my station", the question is simply what duty is to be done and what left undone in particular circumstances. "[I]f an artist or man of science considers himself called upon, by duty to art or science, to neglect, or to commit a breach of, ordinary morality, we must say that, in the abstract and by itself, that is not to be condemned" (1927: 226).[20]

Some might object, however, that no one has the right to set oneself above the morality of one's community. Yet even "My Station" admits

---

20 See also Bradley's posthumously published "On the Treatment of Sexual Detail in Literature" – in Bradley (1935)—written in 1912 at Elinor Glyn's request, her *Three Weeks* having been censored in Britain in 1907. He urged her to publish it under her name, but she declined; see Bradley (1999e: 172-3; 2004, vol. 5: L115).

such a right in excusing the soldier, for example, from society's general prohibition against killing. But, if "My Station" admits such exceptions, there is nothing in principle to prohibit an appeal to the ideal in order to justify overriding customary morality or breaking the law. Hence individuals have the right in principle, says Bradley, to disregard duties of ordinary morality in the service of a higher morality and to challenge moral institutions. But he cautions that exercising such a right must be seriously assessed, taking into consideration possible repercussions that might undermine the spirit and institutions of the social organism.[21]

Turning to the form of the ideal self, Bradley reconsiders the relation of morality to self-realization, observing that, while the everyday moral consciousness does not exclude morality from other dimensions of life, it does distinguish between moral excellences and such other excellences as health and luck, beauty and strength. But if there is more to goodness than the moral good or the good will, then morality is self-realization from only one point of view, "the sphere of the personal will" (1927: 229).[22] Still, all self-realization, because it involves will, can be considered from the moral point of view.

Bradley is quick to underscore that, while my will as realizing the ideal will is the good will, the good will is not merely mine. For it presents itself as a *universal* will, not in the sense that everyone does or should do what I do, but in the sense that, if they were I, they would either have to do what I must do or be immoral. The good will further presents itself as *one* will, in harmony with itself. Hence, my project to realize my ideal self by making my will one with the good will is a project to be "a harmony and system" (1927: 230), without internal discrepancies, without contradiction. But it is a project that is ultimately doomed to fail because, while I can become more and more good, one, and real, I can never *be* a perfect system since my bad self does not wholly cease to exist. Such is a mark of our finitude. Thus, while personal morality is positive as self-identification with the ideal self, it must also be negative in the sense of transforming the bad self — and the forever residual and unsystematized natural material of the

---

21   See Bradley (1927: 227). Though Bradley considers ideal morality in the abstract a "higher" morality than that of "My Station", he questions what sense "higher" and "lower" have when applied to morality. His tentative response anticipates his metaphysical notion of perfection: "The perfect is that in which we can rest without contradiction, … the lower is such because it contradicts itself, and so is forced to advance beyond itself to another stage, which is the solution of the contradiction that existed in the lower, and so a relative perfection. … On this view the higher is above the lower … because it is the harmony of those elements which in the lower were a standing contradiction" (1927: 249).

22   See also Bradley (1927: 237n1, 243–4n1). The Good, rather than simply moral good, becomes the focus in Bradley's later writings; see, e.g., Bradley (1914: 1–10). In Bradley (1930: 336), he defines Goodness as "the fulfillment of desire", but elsewhere (1914: 2n1), he claims that desire should be excluded from this definition, redefining the Good as consisting of "satisfaction", of "contentment and absence or suppression of unrest". He will also later exclude desire from his definition of volition in his *Mind* articles on the will in 1902–1904 (see Bradley, 1935: 476–594).

whole self—into the good self via the assertion of the good will. Morality, then, is intrinsically a process involving contradiction, requiring us to wholly realize that which we can never realize wholly, our ideal self. As Bradley states: "Where there is no imperfection there is no ought, where there is no ought there is no morality" (1927: 234). Morality thus must perpetuate that hiatus between the "ought" and the "is" which constitutes its lifeline and yet plunges it into self-contradiction, or else it must cease to be. It is this self-contradictory character of morality itself, this felt discrepancy in our moral life, that prods us, in good Hegelian fashion, to seek out a still wider sphere of life wherein such contradiction can be reconciled—the sphere of religion.

But, instead of turning next to religion, Bradley takes up the subject of selfishness and self-sacrifice in Essay VII, an essay in which the significance of psychology to his thought is writ large.[23] It is an essay, moreover, that serves not only to clarify his ideal morality but to further develop it by addressing some questions that might be raised against it. First, there is the question of why the good self, and not the bad self, realizes my ideal self. This entails setting forth a theory of what the good self and the bad self are. Secondly, given pleasure's role in Bradley's own theory, there is the issue of how his position differs from that of hedonism.[24] This is crucial because he holds that, whenever the self affirms itself in something, it receives pleasure from that thing, is satisfied, and comes to have a "heightened self-feeling", an intensified awareness of self as pleased (1927: 269n1). Thirdly, because of his claim that pleasure is the feeling of self-realizedness, of self-affirmation, there is the question of whether his moral theory can handle the phenomenon of self-sacrifice.[25]

Considering the good self and the bad self, Bradley explores the suggestion that they can be defined, respectively, as the unselfish self and the selfish self. One obvious objection to so distinguishing them is the thesis of universal selfishness—namely, that *all* human action is "selfish" since we do what we do for the sake of our own pleasure. But this thesis, Bradley argues, merely yields the tautological result that I do what I want to do, a result that the egoistic theory itself generates in claiming that the sole crite-

---

23 On the import of psychology for Bradley's moral theory, see Wollheim (1969 and 1975), MacNiven (1987), Crossley (1989), and my introductions to Bradley (1999b), and to Bradley (1999d, 2004, vol. 4). My dissertation (Keene, 1969) also examined the interrelationship of Bradley's social, moral, and religious philosophy as well as his metaphysics and psychology, relative to his theory of self.

24 See Bradley (1927: 269n1). For different senses of 'hedonism' used here, see MacEwen (1996) and Nicholson (1990: 18–9). On the Utilitarian version, see also MacNiven (1984) together with his book noted above (1987), and Crossley (2000). The sense of hedonism that Bradley will attack here is primarily that of egoistic hedonism, where one's own pleasure is the end, the moral good.

25 Bradley discusses this phenomenon elsewhere as well (1883a; 1930: 366–80; 1999a: 253–74). The last also considers moral and non-moral perfection, virtue and happiness, the good and the bad self, and the relation of *Moralität* to *Sittlichkeit*.

rion for determining what I want to do is that I do it. Moreover, attempts to obviate this result by changing the mode of expression to "I do what I want to do *because* I want to do it"' fail. For if the 'because' clause signals that it is want that moves me, then the statement again simply reduces to the tautological expression. But if this clause is interpreted so as to mean that I do everything as a means to the feeling of my private satisfaction, then it is false, for there are many actions that we do without a motive, for example, eating instinctively. From another angle, there are actions that we do reflectively, but without any ulterior motive, such as eating an apple rather than an orange. Finally, there are actions with a motive, where the act serves some objective, such as bringing happiness to another. Though some future feeling of my satisfaction may be my motive in such a case, and sometimes is, that it is only *sometimes* so, confutes the theory of *universal* egoism (1927: 257–62).

Bradley further argues that the hedonistic stance, resting on confusion of a pleasant thought and the thought of a pleasure, blurs the distinction between acting to realize a pleasant thought and acting for the sake of pleasure. Moreover, were pleasure to function as a motive, our action would be inexplicable, since a motive represents that which we desire and which so far we are without. Were my present pleasure, my felt pleasure, the motive of my action, then I would be acting to get what I have — a stance incompatible with the notion of motive. Though a pleasure we *think* of may well function as a motive or goal of our action in given circumstances, the pleasure we *feel*, the pleasure that accompanies an action of self-affirmation, Bradley contends, *never* does so.

Further, if we identify selfishness with pleasure-seeking, then, Bradley warns, we must curb our tendency to speak of pleasure as something apart from what is pleasant, because such a manner of speaking reflects the erroneous view that given experiences are bifurcated. Even when we distinguish pleasure and pain through our reflective acts, the distinction is relative only, since they remain intrinsically inseparable aspects of our feeling-whole. To consider pleasure, then, simply as belonging to the self as some self-thing, standing over against a not-self, is untenable.[26] Still another telling point against the hedonistic premise of *universal* selfishness is that we do not call *all* actions "selfish" nor *all* individuals "selfish".

Given that the identification of selfishness with pleasure-seeking fails, Bradley suggests that selfishness be redefined as "thinking only of yourself" (1927: 274). But if selfishness entails that we are self-conscious beings who consider all objects as mere means to our personal comfort, then selfishness must exclude action from passion, a non-deliberative action, and hence, once again, not all actions can be viewed as "selfish". Furthermore, all sorts of wrong-doing are not called "selfish"; for example, pride and

---

26 See Bradley's "The Individual for Psychology", written in 1904 (1999c: 191–204).

revenge are not so called. Thus, the bad self clearly encompasses more than selfishness and, consequently, the suggestion that it be identified as the selfish self, while the good self is the unselfish self, cannot stand.[27]

Exploring next the suggestion that the bad self and the good self can be viewed as two *hereditary* groups of habits, "egoistic" and "altruistic", Bradley offers a description of his experience of the two selves:

> I feel at times identified with the good, as though all my self were in it. .... And then again, there are certain bad habits and pursuits and companies with which perhaps I feel no less at home. ... I feel that, when I am good and when I am bad, I am not the same man but quite different. .... Nor is it only at different times that I feel so different, but also at one and the same time: I feel in myself impulses to good in collision with impulses to bad, and I feel myself in each of them. (1927: 276–7)

Bradley wields this description chiefly against Bain's psychology, seeking to show that the self-relatedness implied in self-conscious acts of a moral being challenges any view of the good and the bad self as being mere collections of desires and habits. That we can feel ourselves identified with our good self and our bad self, that we can be conscious of self in a determinate way as good against bad or bad against good, that the whole self can have an awareness of this duality falling within its own being — these facts not only reveal the inappropriateness of physical methodology and the language of mechanism in considering the self, but become mere fictions on the empiricist view. Broadening the base of his criticism, Bradley claims that hereditary qualities, however defined, cannot serve as the origin of the good and the bad self, since any inborn tendency can be moralized into good or turned into bad. In short, "a man's character is not the grouping of two descended heaps" (1927: 279n1).

Taking up another sense of "origin" of the good and the bad self, Bradley considers the moral development of children. Defining the good self as "the self whose end and pleasure is the realization of the ideal self", he looks to that in which the child takes a personal interest.[28] The first step in the child's development is feeling himself affirmed or negated in particular sensations, the ideas of which then become transferred to objects and form part of the content of his notions of them. Though the child comes to feel himself affirmed or pleased chiefly in relatively permanent objects, not transitory ones, his primary interest is with persons. For example, he

---

27 See Bradley (1927: 274-6). Bradley suggests (1927: 276 n1) that egoism may not always involve "mere pleasure or comfort", since it may be a selfish pursuit of an end, calling for sacrifice of one's own personal comfort.
 Bradley admits (1894) to errors in his criticism of Hedonism in Essay III, and acknowledges that in *Ethical Studies* he was warring more against individualism than hedonism. See also Bradley (1894–1895b: 383–4). In both he expresses a willingness to entertain a kind of hedonism that does not take pleasure as the sole good or ground itself in the psychology of Mill and Bain. See further Bradley (1924: 5n1).
28 See Bradley (1927: 279). On interest, see Bradley (1883b: 573-5 [in Bradley (1935: 138–41)]; Bradley (1886: 305-23 [in Bradley (1935: 181-202)]); and Bradley (1930: 75).

feels himself affirmed in the care of his mother satisfying his recurrent wants. Being always with her, he comes to feel her as part of himself, and when left alone, feels uneasy. He identifies her pleasure or discomfort with what is enjoyable or painful to himself. He discovers that she has a superior will that he cannot resist, a will that, moreover, can cause him painful consequences. He learns that in obeying her commands he feels himself affirmed and thereby pleased with himself (1927: 285–7).[29] Similarly, he learns that disobedience and his mother's displeasure are unpleasant and to be avoided. In short, the child discovers, in this initial unreflective stage of moral development, that good accords with himself and that bad does not. By emphasizing the unreflective character of this stage, Bradley seeks to disclaim the objection that his giving pleasure and pain such a central role in the child's moral education is geared to breeding calculating, young hedonists.

As for the bad self, "the self falls into bad habits in the same way in which it falls into good ones" (Bradley 1927: 295). Because the natural disposition of children at this pre-moral stage is a "chaos of appetites and propensities" that must be systematized "by repression here and encouragement there", and because the development of the good self as a process of habituation takes time, the emergence of bad satisfactions is inevitable (1927: 295). These, too, can be relatively permanent, since the immanence of the past in the present is a necessary condition of any habituation. Without some self-sameness, moreover, the facts of the moral world collapse, as the plain man has told us. But how is the transition effected from this unreflective stage of moral development to the stage of morality proper?

For the child to become a moral being, strictly speaking, three conditions must be met. There must be "knowledge of good, knowledge of evil, and self-conscious volition" (1927: 297). While feeling of evil is necessary for moral perception of it, it is insufficient here. Since morality implies the "ought" and hence imperfection, evil must be known as opposed to good or there is no morality proper. The self must knowingly will the good for its goodness, or knowingly will evil because it is evil.[30] That the whole self can psychically center its existence freely and self-consciously in that self in which it takes an interest, be it the good or the bad self, constitutes, moreover, the condition for imputation and responsibility. Bradley warns, however, that formal or absolute freedom of choice is a fiction. Since the self is concrete, filled with content, its freedom is always a conditioned

---

[29] Self-approbation is a key element of goodness for Bradley, signaling that morality's origin is not only social. See Bradley (1930: 381n1 and 346–63). Regarding the superior will, Bradley in the second edition qualifies his supposition that the superior will is moral, noting that "clearly it is not so wholly, and can be imitated when bad" (1927: 295n1*).

[30] See Bradley (1884: 286–290 [in Bradley (1935: 142–8)]). Regarding evil entailing knowledge of good, see Bradley (1883c: 415–8 [in Bradley (1935: 133–7)]).

freedom. Hence imputation and responsibility are always a matter of degree.[31]

The bad self and the good self, then, assume their specific character only at a self-conscious level. In the transformation from the unreflective to the self-conscious stage, the bad self gains a unity from its antagonism to the good that it previously lacked. The good self, by contrast, gains little, since it is already one with itself in light of its will being one with a superior will. Yet, in Bradley's view, it still acquires a new kind of unity—a self-conscious, and thereby a moral, unity.

As to why I find myself realized in the good self rather than the bad self, the answer lies in its responsiveness "to our real being", to our quest to be a harmonious system. The bad self, in contrast, is anarchical, "a heap of particulars", drawing a mere formal universality from self-consciousness (1927: 305). Though the everyday self can certainly will this or that evil because it is evil, it cannot always desire only evil, for it cannot rest in such felt self-alienation. Only the ideal self provides that teleological direction which the everyday self requires to realize the harmony that answers to its nature.

With Bradley's emphasis upon the self affirming itself in some relatively permanent object that pleases it and is responsive to its felt nature, the question arises as to whether his theory can explain self-sacrifice, a phenomenon usually opposed to self-assertion.[32] In considering this matter, Bradley suggests that self-assertion and self-sacrifice differ not in their contents, which in both may be drawn from multiple worlds, but in the uses to which these are put. Were I to use them to develop my individual perfection, then this would be self-assertion. Were I to use them to the loss of my private existence, in part or whole, in the interest of something higher, then this would constitute self-sacrifice. For example, I may devote myself intensely to some intellectual pursuit thereby jeopardizing my health, or I may give up my life for the welfare of others. In both situations, there is self-sacrifice but there is also self-realization. For, in both examples, I have identified myself with an ideal, with the good self, and hence, as a mode of self-realization, self-sacrifice "has a pleasure of its own" (1927: 310). Moreover, as a mode of self-realization, self-sacrifice involves

---

31 See Bradley (1927: 299, 302–3). In the second edition, Bradley remarks that "moral imputation in the end breaks down in principle (if you take it as ultimate and final)"; see Bradley (1927: 244–5n1). For further remarks on freedom, see Bradley (1927: 55–7; 1930: 385 n.1; 1935: 87–8; 1922: 79) See also Bradley (1902 [in Bradley (1935: 444–75)]).

32 See Bradley (1927: 309–12; 1930: 366–80). In *Appearance and Reality*, Bradley considers self-assertion and self-sacrifice as two methods of morality, arising from the divergence of harmony and comprehensiveness, the marks of perfection. Though his definitions of self-assertion and self-sacrifice in *Appearance and Reality* are basically the same as in *Ethical Studies*, in the former he emphasizes that self-assertion, while involving one's own good, must involve as well the transcendence of one's private being, since every self is a particularization of a common reality.

self-assertion, an assertion of its private will, but to its own negation. Hence what it realizes, it does not possess as a private good of its own; rather, its accomplishment goes beyond its individual existence.

To become a harmonious system is thus outside the reach even of the self-sacrificing, morally good individual. And, once again, we find that morality, in demanding of us a moral perfection that is not proportionate to our finite nature, reveals its own self-contradictory character. It enjoins us to overcome that hiatus between the "ought" and the "is" which is its lifeline. Jarred by morality's self-contradictory nature, we look elsewhere for the realization of "the true self" — the elsewhere, for Bradley, being religion. The completion of morality requires an invisible community with justification by faith, where one wills to believe that the ideal self of morality is real and realized in God, "the real ideal self", and that the union of the human and the divine is already worked out.[33] But to flesh out Bradley's view of the relationship of morality and religion is beyond the scope of this essay.

A Few Concluding Remarks

When *Ethical Studies* appeared in 1876, there was general agreement, regardless of philosophic persuasion, that here was a powerful, new voice in philosophy. Weaving different strands of thought — Hegelian, Aristotelian, Kantian, Platonic, and Hedonistic — into a theory that was distinctively his own, Bradley set forth an ideal morality rooted in the view of the social organism as a moral organism, a theory that eventually served as a touchstone for his fellow British idealists.[34] But as Bradley himself cautioned, the moral theory sketched in this early work had roots as well in metaphysical and psychological presuppositions. Clearly *Appearance and Reality* and its sequel, *Essays on Truth and Reality*, consider topics key to any metaphysical underpinning of Bradley's ideal morality. Both consider the nature and reality of the self, perfection and goodness, the matter of degrees of reality, goodness, and worth, and, of course, the Absolute. Both reexamine the relationship of morality to other aspects of life, including the special relationship between morality and religion and the issue of the nature of God. *Appearance*, moreover, highlights the essential role of self-approbation in the development of character, and addresses again the subject of evil as well as that of self-assertion and self-sacrifice. Further, *Appearance* and *Essays* both develop the theory of immediate experience — a doctrine pivotal to Bradley's thought as a whole and one much in

---

33 Although continuing to claim an intrinsic relationship between morality and religion, Bradley later distanced himself from a Christian view; see Bradley (1983) and Sprigge (1995). Other discussions of religion's role in Bradley's thought include Carr (1992), Frazier (1977) and Vincent (2000). See also Allen (1974), the thesis of which is that morality's contradiction is imposed by Bradley's metaphysics and unresolved by religion.

34 Regarding his relation to other British Idealists, see Nicholson (1990).

evidence in *Ethical Studies*. In recent years, Bradleian scholarship has yielded various fine discussions of the bearing of Bradley's work in metaphysics upon specific theories offered in *Ethical Studies*.[35] Similarly, the import of psychology for Bradley's moral theory is being addressed, spearheaded by the writings of David Crossley and Don MacNiven. This is a much welcomed trend, given Bradley's use of psychology as a norm of coherence for his philosophical work and his dedicating himself almost exclusively to psychology in the mid 1880s and in the decade from 1893–1902. His psychological articles — included in *Collected Essays*, save for "The Individual for Psychology" — consider sympathy and interest, pleasure and pain, desire and volition, and mental conflict and imputation, as well as feeling or immediacy, and clearly suggest further development of, and some substantive alterations to, the moral psychology offered in *Ethical Studies*.

That there are changes in Bradley's moral thought across the years is suggested, moreover, by Bradley's own ambivalence toward *Ethical Studies*, as I have discussed elsewhere.[36] In 1881, he described it as "d____d erbärmlich", requiring a new book.[37] Though in 1893 he wrote that it still represented his views "in the main", he also remarked that he would have rewritten it, had there not been "the decay of those superstitions against which it was largely directed" (1930: 356n1). In 1901 he asked, "Am I a dog to return to its vomit?"; and in 1906 he stated that the work included certain views no longer held by him (1999d: 196–7).[38] His subsequent expressions of an intent to reissue it, an intent initially expressed in 1914 in the Preface to *Essays*, stemmed from his growing recognition of the work's historical role. That he waited a decade, however, before initiating any systematic preparation of a second edition, suggests at best a lack of enthusiasm to do so. The notes to the second edition, written during the two weeks or so before his death in September 1924, are sparse. Nonetheless, they hint at changes regarding his views about hedonism, the homogeneity of the social organism or nation, the ideal self in religion, the restriction of union with the divine to the human and divine, and several psychological issues, to cite but a few examples.

Recently published materials from the Bradley Papers do show that from time to time in his last decade he made other notes about ethical topics, principally in the later entries of MS BK L, in MS BK W, and in his reading notes. These reveal his desire to reconsider the question of moral measurement, the matter of comparative judgments, and the issue of

---

35 In addition to previously cited discussions of this nature, see Armour (1996), Candlish (1978), MacNiven (1996), and Sweet (1996).
36 On Bradley's ambivalence, see my "Introduction" to Bradley (1999d).
37 See Bradley (1999d: 32–3, headnote).
38 See also Proverbs 26:11 and Bradley (1999e: 29–30).

degrees of moral desert. They signal, further, his willingness to explore conscientiousness as morality's highest end, to examine the development of morality into instinctive behavior, and to consider hedonism and "my station" as both justified if embedded in ideal morality. They also include further comments regarding punishment, casuistry, teleology and value, religion and morality, the Good and moral good, and self-realization and self-sacrifice. Then, too, there are remarks underscoring advantages of the formula of self-realization, together with an acknowledgment of the vagueness of this formula and its principally negative role in *Ethical Studies,* a role that revealed more what he denied than what he stood for. Though by no means exhaustive, this cursory survey should suffice to show the range of issues to which Bradley returned. Moreover, because these notes generally are more illuminating and more developed than those in the second edition, they should receive consideration in any effort to view Bradley's ethical writings as a whole.

Despite shortcomings in the eyes of critics and of Bradley himself, his theory of ideal morality, sketched in *Ethical Studies,* continues to show a certain resilience in its capacity to contribute to ethical thought in the 21st century. Grounded in a social holism, it has a kinship with contemporary communitarianism. Then, too, given the fiduciary relationship of professions to society, it offers as well a framework for branches of professional ethics, with its prescription of duties relative to station in society, its virtue emphasis, and its suggestiveness as to the manner in which a professional ethic may be informed by ideals social and non-social. It is open, moreover, to an ethics of caring, as shown in Bradley's now classic descriptions of the care given to the English child and in his rejection of rule-oriented moral theory. But this openness extends not only to the health care professions which have nurtured an ethics of caring, but to feminist ethics as well, especially when coupled with Bradley's version of moral relativism, a relativism that acknowledges both the evolution of functions within society and the individual choice of station in a gender-neutral fashion.[39] Further, his theories of self-realization and of the moral development of children have proved to offer instructive insights when considered relative to such theories as those of Piaget, Kohlberg, and Gilligan.[40] Lastly, several of his ethical discussions remain germane to such recurrent meta-ethical topics as the nature of criteria that any moral theory must meet in regard to the related issues of responsibility and accountability, why one should be moral, whether morality is autonomous, and what the relation is between morality and other spheres of life.

---

39 See Austen (1996).
40 See MacNiven (1987), Crossley (1989), and Austen (1996) regarding Bradley and these other theorists.

As J.S. Mackenzie remarked so perceptively of Bradley in reviewing the second edition of *Ethical Studies*: "The chief difficulty in reading his writings lies in their bright allusiveness and in the fact that his views on any subject are hardly ever to be found completely at any one place or in any one book" (1928: 238). To tie together the various threads within Bradley's writings, however, requires comprehensive or sustained studies. Such work might not only systematically identify the metaphysical and psychological presuppositions underlying his early ethical work, but explore as well whether these presuppositions are supported, developed, challenged, or ignored in his later thought. An interesting sidelight of such an approach might well be consideration of the extent to which, and manner in which, *Ethical Studies* informs Bradley's metaphysical writings. Another pathway to consideration of the development of positions taken in *Ethical Studies* would lie in the exploration of the relation between *Ethical Studies* and Bradley's other ethical writings. With few exceptions, this area has largely been ignored.[41] But if we are to have the full benefit of Bradley's thought in consideration of theoretical issues in ethics today, then we must continue to bear in mind that this philosopher, who was noted for his preoccupation with refinement and revision of his thinking, had almost a half century to reflect upon the issues addressed in, and generated by, *Ethical Studies*.[42]

References

Allen, R. (1974), "Self-realization, Religion and Contradiction in *Ethical Studies*", *Idealistic Studies*, 4, pp. 276–85.

Armour, L. (1996), "The Unity of Moral Principle and Bradley's Absolute", in P. MacEwen (ed.), *Metaphysics and Religion of F.H. Bradley* (Lewiston: Edwin Mellen), pp. 1–37.

Arnold, M. (1873), *Literature and Dogma* (London: Smith, Elder, 1873).

Austen, A. (1996), "A Feminist Reconstruction of Bradley's Ethical Idealism", *Idealistic Studies*, 26, pp. 17–28.

Banchetti, M. (1992), "My Station and its Duties", *Idealistic Studies*, 22, pp. 11–27.

Bosanquet, B. (1924), "Life and Philosophy", in J. H. Muirhead (ed.), *Contemporary British Philosophy* (London: Allen & Unwin).

Bradley, F.H. (1877), Reply to Sidgwick, *Mind*, o.s. 2, pp. 122–5; reprinted in Bradley (1935).

Bradley, F.H. (1883a), "Is Self-Sacrifice an Enigma?" *Mind*, o.s. 8, pp. 258–60; reprinted in Bradley (1935).

Bradley, F.H. (1883b), "Sympathy and Interest", *Mind*, o.s., 8, pp. 573–5; reprinted in Bradley (1935).

Bradley, F.H. (1883c), "Is There such a Thing as Pure Malevolence?" *Mind*, o.s. 8, pp. 415–8; reprinted in Bradley (1935).

Bradley, F.H. (1884), "Can a Man sin against Knowledge?" *Mind*, o.s. 9, pp. 286–90; reprinted in Bradley (1935).

Bradley, F.H. (1886), "Is there any special Activity of Attention", *Mind*, o.s. 11, pp. 305–23; reprinted in Bradley (1935).

---

41 Exceptions include Crossley (1976), Johnson (1984) and MacNiven (1996b), which offer differing perspectives on whether "Some Remarks on Punishment" launched an attack on the view of punishment in *Ethical Studies*. Though an aside here, see MacIntyre (1994) for a comparison of Edmund Pincoff's *Quandaries and Virtues* and Bradley's *Ethical Studies*.

42 This paper was submitted and accepted for publication in April 2005.

Bradley, F.H. (1894), "A Personal Explanation", *International Journal of Ethics*, 4, pp. 384–6.
Bradley, F.H. (1894–5), "The Limits of Individual and National Self-Sacrifice", [written c. 1878], *International Journal of Ethics*, 5, pp. 17–28, reprinted in Bradley (1935).
Bradley, F.H. (1894–1895b), "Rational Hedonism", *International Journal of Ethics*, 5, pp. 383–4.
Bradley, F.H. (1902), "On Mental Conflict and Imputation", *Mind*, n.s. 9, pp. 289–315; reprinted in Bradley (1914), pp. 444–75.
Bradley, F.H. (1909), "On our Knowledge of Immediate Experience", *Mind*, 18, pp. 40–64; reprinted in Bradley (1914), pp. 159–91.
Bradley, F.H. (1914), *Essays on Truth and Reality* (Oxford: Clarendon Press).
Bradley, F.H. (1922), *The Principles of Logic*, 2nd ed. (Oxford: Clarendon Press).
Bradley, F.H. (1927), *Ethical Studies*, 2nd ed. (Oxford: Clarendon Press).
Bradley, F.H. (1930), *Appearance and Reality*, 2nd ed. (Oxford: Clarendon Press).
Bradley, F.H. (1935), *Collected Essays*, 2 vols. (Oxford: Clarendon Press).
Bradley, F.H. (1935b), "Mr. Sidgwick's Hedonism" (1877), in *Collected Essays*, 2 vols. (Oxford: Clarendon Press), vol. 1, pp. 71–128.
Bradley, F.H. (1935c), "On the Treatment of Sexual Detail in Literature", in *Collected Essays*, 2 vols. (Oxford: Clarendon Press), vol. 2, pp. 618–27.
Bradley, F.H. (1983), "An Unpublished Note on Christian Morality", ed. by Gordon Kendal, *Religious Studies*, 19, pp. 175–183.
Bradley, F.H. (1999a), in C.A. Keene (ed.), *Collected Works: F. H. Bradley: A Pluralistic Approach to Philosophy, 1865–1882*, vol. 1 (Bristol: Thoemmes Press).
Bradley, F.H. (1999b), in C.A. Keene (ed.), *A Focus on Metaphysics and Psychology, 1883–1902*, vol. 2 (Bristol: Thoemmes Press).
Bradley, F.H. (1999c), in C.A. Keene (ed.), *Collected Works: F. H. Bradley: Refinement and Revision, 1903–1924*, vol. 3 (Bristle: Thoemmes Press).
Bradley, F.H. (1999d), in C.A. Keene (ed.), *Collected Works: F. H. Bradley: Selected Correspondence, 1872–1904*, vol. 4 (Bristol: Thoemmes Press).
Bradley, F.H. (1999e), in C.A. Keene (ed.), *Collected Works: F. H. Bradley: Selected Correspondence, 1905–1924*, vol. 5 (Bristol: Thoemmes Press).
Bradley, F.H. (2004), *Correspondence*, 2 vols. in *The Philosophers* (Charlottesville, VA: InteLex).
Bradley, F.H. (forthcoming), *F.H. Bradley: Notebooks, Papers and Correspondence* (Charlottesville, VA: InteLex).
Bradley, J. (1996), "Process and Historical Crisis in F.H. Bradley's Ethics of Feeling", in P. MacEwen (ed.), *Metaphysics and Religion of F.H. Bradley* (Lewiston: Edwin Mellen), pp. 53–90.
Candlish, S. (1978), "Bradley's My Station and its Duties", *Australasian Journal of Philosophy*, 56, pp. 155–70.
Candlish, Stewart (2006), *The Russell/Bradley Dispute and Its Significance for Twentieth Century Philosophy* (Basingstoke: Palgrave Macmillan).
Carr, S. (1992), "F.H. Bradley and Religious Faith", *Religious Studies*, 28, pp. 271–86.
Crossley, D. (1976), "Bradley's Utilitarian Theory of Punishment", *Ethics*, 86, pp. 200–13.
Crossley, D. (1977), "Self-Realization as Perfection in Bradley's *Ethical Studies*", *Idealistic Studies*, 7, pp. 199–220.
Crossley, D. (1977b), "Holism, Individuation, and Internal Relations", *Journal of the History of Philosophy*, 15, pp. 183–94.
Crossley, D. (1989), "Feeling in Bradley's *Ethical Studies*", *Idealistic Studies*, 19, pp. 43–61.
Crossley, D. (2000), "Early Criticisms of Mill's Qualitative Hedonism", *Bradley Studies*, 6, pp. 137–73.
Frazier, A.M. (1977), "F.H. Bradley's Analysis of Religious Consciousness", *Idealistic Studies*, 7, pp. 239–51.
Gardiner, P. (1992), "Bradley and Moral Philosophy", in J. Hopkins and A. Savile (eds.), *Psychoanalysis, Mind and Art* (Oxford: Blackwell), pp. 191–204.
Glover, J. (1970), *Responsibility* (London: Routledge and Kegan Paul).
Ilodigwe, Damian (2004), "Bradley, Ethical Studies, and Dialectic: Self-Realisation and its Equivocations", *Bradley Studies*, 10, pp. 65–87.

Keene, C.A. (1969), *F.H. Bradley's Theory of Self*, Ph.D. dissertation, Saint Louis University, 1969 (Ann Arbor, MI: University Microfilms, 1969).

Johnson, P. (1984), "Bradley and the Nature of Punishment", in A. Manser and G. Stock (eds.), *The Philosophy of F.H. Bradley* (Oxford: Clarendon Press), pp. 117–30.

Kendal, G. (1982), "Bradley and Moral Engagement", *Philosophy*, 57, pp. 373–9.

Krook (1959), *Three Traditions of Moral Thought* (Cambridge: Cambridge University Press).

MacIntyre, A. (1994), "My Station and its Virtues", *Journal of Philosophical Research*, 19, pp. 1–8.

Mackenzie, J.S. (1928), Review of the second edition of *Ethical Studies*, *Mind*, 37 n.s., pp. 233–8; reprinted in W. Sweet and C.A. Keene (eds.) (2004), *Early Responses to British Idealism: Responses to F.H. Bradley, A.S. Pringle-Pattison and J.M.E. McTaggart*, vol. 3 (Bristol: Thoemmes Continuum), pp. 29–35.

McEwan, P. (1996), "Bradley's Critique of Mill's Utilitarianism", in P. MacEwen (ed.), *Ethics, Metaphysics and Religion of F.H. Bradley* (Lewiston: Edwin Mellen), pp. 122–53.

MacNiven, D. (1984), "Bradley's Critiques of Utilitarian and Kantian Ethics", *Idealistic Studies*, 14, pp. 67–83.

MacNiven, D. (1987), *Bradley's Moral Psychology* (Lewiston: Edwin Mellen).

MacNiven, D. (1996), "Metaphysics and Ethics in Bradley's Idealism", in P. MacEwen (ed.) *Metaphysics and Religion of F. H. Bradley* (Lewiston: Edwin Mellen), pp. 91–110.

MacNiven (1996b), "Bradley and MacIntyre", in J. Bradley (ed.), *Philosophy after F.H. Bradley* (Bristol: Thoemmes Press), pp. 349–65.

Milne, A. (1962), *The Social Philosophy of English Idealism* (London: Allen & Unwin).

Morris, George S., "George S. Morris papers, 1852–1889 and 1910–1915" (Bentley Historical Library, University of Michigan).

Muirhead, J.H. (1931), *The Platonic Tradition in Anglo-Saxon Philosophy* (London: Allen & Unwin).

Nicholson, P.P. (1984), "Bradley as a Political Philosopher", in A. Manser and G. Stock (eds.), *The Philosophy of F.H. Bradley* (Oxford: Clarendon Press), pp. 116–30.

Nicholson, P.P. (1990), *The Political Philosophy of the British Idealists* (Cambridge: Cambridge University Press).

Pettit, P. (1985–6), "Social Holism and Moral Theory", *Proceedings of the Aristotelian Society*, 86, pp. 173–97.

Ross, R.G. (1951), *Ethical Studies: Selected Essays* (Indianapolis: Bobbs-Merrill).

Sabine, G. (1915), "The Social Origin of Absolute Idealism", *The Journal of Philosophy, Psychology and Scientific Methods*, 12, pp. 169–77.

Sidgwick, H. (1876), Review of *Ethical Studies*, *Mind*, o.s. 1, pp. 545–9.

Sprigge, Timothy (1995), "Bradley and Christianity", *Bradley Studies*, 1, pp. 69–85.

Stanley, M. (1996), "The Paradox of the Individual", *Bradley Studies*, 2, 51–62.

Sweet, W. (1996), "Bradley and Bosanquet", in J. Bradley (ed.), *Philosophy after F.H. Bradley* (Bristol: Thoemmes Press), pp. 31–56.

Sweet, W. and Keene, C.A. (eds.) (2004), *Early Responses to British Idealism: Responses to F.H. Bradley, A.S. Pringle-Pattison and J.M.E. McTaggart*, vol. 3 (Bristol: Thoemmes Continuum).

Trott, E. (1996), "The Self and the Social Order", in P. MacEwen (ed.), *Ethics, Metaphysics and Religion of F. H. Bradley* (Lewiston: Edwin Mellen), pp. 110–9.

Vincent, A. (1999), "Bradley and Sidgwick on Philosophical Ethics", *Collingwood Studies*, 6, pp. 110–26.

Vincent, A. (2000), "Mr. Bradley and God", *Bradley Studies*, 6, pp. 104–24.

Wright, C. (1984), "The Moral Organism", in A. Manser and G. Stock (eds.), *The Philosophy of F.H. Bradley* (Oxford: Clarendon Press), pp. 77–97.

Wollheim, R. (1969), *F. H. Bradley*, 2nd ed. (Harmondsworth: Penguin).

Wollheim, R. (1975), "The Good Self and the Bad Self: The Moral Psychology of British Idealism and the English School of Psychoanalysis Compared", *Proceedings of the British Academy*, 61, pp. 373–98.

Stamatoula Panagakou

The Religious Character of Bosanquet's Moral and Social Philosophy[1]

Introduction

Bernard Bosanquet (1848–1923) was not only one of the leading figures of the "second generation" of British Idealism, but perhaps the most prolific. As the author or editor of some 20 books, and of well over 200 articles and reviews, his writings range over logic, metaphysics, epistemology, aesthetics, religion, social policy, and political philosophy. Bosanquet is particularly well-known for his social and political philosophy—primarily, his *The Philosophical Theory of the State* (1899)—and essays and books on this topic appear from his earliest writings until just before his death.

Interestingly, however, Bosanquet wrote relatively little on ethics. He had a lifelong interest in social ethics and social policy, devoted much of his life to work with the Charity Organisation Society, and what he wrote in the area tended to focus on what we might today call applied ethics—such as *Some Suggestions in Ethics* (1918, 2nd edn. 1919) and *Social and International Ideals* (1917). And, while one finds discussions concerning value in his Gifford Lectures—*The Principle of Individuality and Value* (1912) and *The Value and Destiny of the Individual* (1913)—and a few essays, such as his 1903 inaugural address at St Andrew's "On the Practical Value of Moral Philosophy",[2] Bosanquet never wrote at length directly on ethical theory.[3]

---

1   This essay draws upon my "The Kingdom of God on Earth: Religion and Ethics in the Philosophy of Bernard Bosanquet", in a collection of essays on British Idealism entitled *Anglo-American Idealism: Thinkers and Ideas*, ed. James Connelly and Stamatoula Panagakou (Oxford: Peter Lang, 2009).
2   Bosanquet (1903a).
3   There has been some discussion of why this is so. Sweet (1999a) argues that Bosanquet held that Bradley had already provided a critique of existing moral theories, that he believed that moral theory could not provide any complete set of principles that would allow one to determine how to act morally, and that, in any event, any such principles would be insufficient for his primary concern of moral education and social reform.

It is plausible to claim that this is because Bosanquet's views on ethics are to be found within a larger context — namely, in his account of religion. Bosanquet developed his moral and social philosophy frequently in contexts that are focused on religion, and his ethical views are founded on his analysis of religion and presuppose the hermeneutic framework of his logic and metaphysics. An analysis of Bosanquet's views on moral and social philosophy, then, clearly involves his views on religion and religious consciousness,[4] and requires both a focus on the dynamic relation of faith and morality and an investigation of the logical connection between religious and ethical consciousness.

Consistent with the spirit of Bosanquet's analysis, then, I approach his account of moral and social philosophy by beginning with a discussion of his reflections on religion. To do this, I begin by clarifying what Bosanquet means by religion, and explore how his understanding of religious consciousness relates to his theorising of the finite-infinite self. More specifically, I look at how the individual's moral quest is articulated through the soul-transforming processes of self-transcendence and of the dialectic of the finite-infinite, and show that Bosanquet's views on religion are fundamental to his metaphysics of the self.[5] The attainment of the real, or true, self is based on the formative influence of the religious consciousness. Moreover, the realisation of the best life, which is the end of the state *qua* state, depends on a social ethics that represents the effort of individuals to affirm the good in all levels of social existence. Bosanquet articulates this

---

4   Bosanquet uses both terms indiscriminately; I follow his usage.
5   Self-transcendence and the dialectic of the finite-infinite sustain Bosanquet's metaphysics of the self expounded in the two volumes of his Gifford Lectures, *The Principle of Individuality and Value* (1912) and *The Value and Destiny of the Individual* (1913). Although Bosanquet refers to the "finite-infinite" or "self-transcendent" nature of the human individual as meaning one and the same thing (Bosanquet, 1913: 225), I would argue that "self-transcendence" and the "finite-infinite" character are, in fact, two distinct, yet logically, essentially, and fundamentally interrelated processes. Self-transcendence is made possible because of the finite-infinite nature of the human being and "leads to the affirmation of the spiritual world (the world of value and coherence) within the finite centre" (Panagakou, 2005: 45, 25n). The dialectic of the finite-infinite depicts the relation between the finite aspect and the infinite aspect of the self, and shows the character of the individual's development and realisation. The finite condition refers to the imperfect and incomplete nature of the human being; infinity refers to the inherent potential for completion, perfection, and coherence that drives the individual towards higher forms of self-realisation. See Panagakou (1999a, 2001). The meaning of the infinite is best understood in its contrast to the finite: "The finite is that which presents itself as incomplete; the infinite that which presents itself as complete, and which, therefore, does not force upon us the fact of its limitation. This character belongs in the highest degree of self-conscious mind, as realized in the world above sense; and in some degree to all elements of that world — for instance, to the State — in as far as they represent man's realized self-consciousness. It is the nature of self-consciousness to be infinite, because it is its nature to take into itself what was opposed to it, and thus to make itself into an organized sphere that has value and reality within, and not beyond itself. If false infinity was represented by an infinite straight line, true infinity may be compared to a circle or a sphere" (Bosanquet, 1905: xxvii). I have adopted Bosanquet's usage of the terms "infinity" and "infinite" — a usage that derives from his discussion of Hegel's philosophy. The "root-idea" of infinity, in the Hegelian sense, "is self-completeness or satisfaction" (Bosanquet, 1905: xxvi).

social ethics by elucidating the meaning of religion from a philosophical point of view. Religion offers the logical foundation that sustains the agonistic ethos expressed in morality. Indeed, for Bosanquet, the essence of religion is faith in the reality of the good as the only reality. In the sphere of morality, we acknowledge that the good should be real and, despite the obstacles of finiteness, we seek to realise it in practice. The claims of morality lead us to a higher level of spiritual awareness that is embodied in the idea of religion.[6] The dynamics of faith sustain the ceaseless movement of the self towards the attainment of the good. Ethical consciousness is essentially related to religious consciousness.

This essay is divided into three parts. In the first part, I discuss the immanentist perspective of Bosanquet's account of religion. Immanentism refers to the idea of finding and affirming the divine element in our lives in seeking to achieve perfection and self-realisation. In employing the immanentist perspective for theorising religion, Bosanquet shifts the focus from the transcendent and the supernatural to what he considered to be the true conception of the spiritual world and the ethical nature of social existence. This requires, however, a systemic analysis of Bosanquet's idea of religion, which has two constituent parts: what I call the structuration discourse and the substantiation discourse. The second part of the essay is devoted to an exposition and assessment of Bosanquet's philosophical understanding of the reality of the spiritual world as the world of truth, beauty, and goodness. I explore Bosanquet's philosophical hermeneutic of the spirit which draws upon his interpretation of Platonic, Christian, and Hegelian sources, and discuss the relation between the true conception of the spiritual world, religion, and self-realisation. Finally, I focus on the application of Bosanquet's theory of religion to the practical context of ethical life. According to Bosanquet, human beings are capable of building "the kingdom of God" in the present life through self-transcendence and by contributing to the common good. Thus, spiritual union—i.e., what Bosanquet refers to as the "body of Christ"—is the result of a firm belief in the reality of the good as the only reality that both sustains and guides the individual's endeavour to affirm the right will and the real self. Connected with this is Bosanquet's notion of one's "station and its duties"—a notion which plays a central role in Bosanquet's moral philosophy: it offers an effective medium for maintaining the aims and purposes of ethical life, sustains the ethical consciousness, and enables the moral development of the individual.

---

6   Bradley holds a similar view concerning the relation between religion and morality: "Reflection on morality leads us beyond it. It leads us, in short, to see the necessity of a religious point of view. It certainly does not tell us that morality comes first in the world and then religion: what it tells us is that morality is imperfect, and imperfect in such a way as implies a higher, which is religion" (Bradley, 1988: 314).

The Immanentist Perspective

Bosanquet's account of religion is based on what we may call the immanentist perspective.

Bosanquet's views on religion have been much contested.[7] This may not be surprising, as he was rather indifferent to the traditional beliefs of conventional Christianity. Instead of presenting God as an almighty power beyond this world who is master of the universe, Bosanquet defended a thoroughly humanistic conception of Christ that challenges central assumptions of traditional theology.[8] Bosanquet often criticised the authority of the clergy, and stressed the need for reading the New Testament independently of the guidelines of an "old-fashioned theology";[9] he regarded worship and religious observance as having only instrumental value in the understanding of the essence of religion;[10] and he had no belief in miracles and the supernatural.[11]

Despite his criticisms of institutionalised or dogmatic religion, Bosanquet took religion seriously.[12] He asserted that religion "is the only

---

7   For example, the Personal Idealists Andrew Seth Pringle-Pattison, Hastings Rashdall, and Clement C. J. Webb argued against Bosanquet's notion of an impersonal God (Tsanoff, 1920; Webb, 1922-3; Robbins, 1982; Patrick, 1985). Sell does not think that Bosanquet succeeded in bringing Idealism closer to Christian thought (Sell, 1988, 1995). Panagakou (1999b) and Sweet (2000) argue for the importance of Bosanquet's philosophical views on religion, and reflect on the connection between Bosanquet's theorising of religion and his ethics. See also Sprigge (2006, 2007).

8   Bosanquet writes: "Christ himself claims his divinity not apart from his humanity, but in it and because of it. The double nature is a figment of theologians; it is the Son of Man who as such is the Son of God. This, we are well told, has always been the voice of religious devotion, though not of doctrinal theology" (Bosanquet, 1894-5: 443).

9   In "The Kingdom of God on Earth", Bosanquet identifies some ideas and beliefs of the "old-fashioned theology" that can distract the human being from the true meaning of religion. Beliefs such as rewards and punishments in heaven, God as a master in heaven whose commands in the Bible we must obey, and the authority of the clergy to interpret the will of God, are all "fancies that men have had, just as though they were children, and being children, knew that they must be treated like children" (Bosanquet, 1899a: 114). To benefit from the teaching of the New Testament, we need to free our minds from the dictates and principles of the traditional theological discourse. See Bosanquet (1899b).

10 According to Bosanquet, the function of prayer, worship, and religious observance is to assist individuals in their daily endeavour to realise the good. What is religious in "systems of creed and ritual, or, more generally, of feeling and practice" is "all that which contributes to keep true religion alive in the heart. Praise and supplication, so far as they do not help in this, seem not to be religious *at all*" (Bosanquet, 1920a: 71).

11 For Bosanquet, spirituality properly understood is not superstition. Sprigge (1992), following W. James, describes this attitude as "refined supernaturalism" in contrast to "crass supernaturalism." The crass supernaturalist conceives of the supernatural as "a realm of concrete existence distinct from our ordinary natural world from which occasional influences emanate" (Sprigge, 1992: 105). For the refined supernaturalist, however, "special divine interventions, such as miracles, are mere superstition having nothing to do with real spirituality, except as symbols suitable for a more primitive stage of human culture than the present" (Sprigge, 1992: 105).

12 Sweet notes: "Though critical of religious dogma and doctrines, such as the personality of God and the existence of an afterlife, Bosanquet held that religious faith itself should be treated with respect" (Sweet, 2003: xxix).

thing that makes life worth living at all" (Bosanquet, 1920a: vii), and stressed the role of Christianity for the development of spirit and the advance of civilisation.[13] Bosanquet, like Caird, regarded Christianity as the "Absolute Religion" in terms of representing the most developed form of religious consciousness. Following Green (1888), he focused on the essence of Christian life and distinguished it from the theoretical edifice of dogmatic theology. His short treatise *What Religion Is* (1920a) contains his reflections on the real meaning of religion so that people may appreciate the essentials of their faith and avoid the distortions caused by superstition. Bosanquet's analysis of religion is, instead, structured around an immanentist approach, and vindicates the spiritual significance of the finite mind for the apprehension and realisation of the axiological cosmos. Bosanquet put religion at the heart of his philosophical system and made it the foundation of his moral philosophy. The attainment of the real self, the empowerment of the individual, the building of character, and the ideal of ethical citizenship constitute principal concerns in Bosanquet's discourse on ethics.

What is "religion"? In an encyclopedia entry on "Religion (philosophy of)", Bosanquet writes that religion is "that set of objects, habits, and convictions, whatever it might prove to be, which [one] would rather die for than abandon, or at least would feel himself excommunicated from humanity if he did abandon" (Bosanquet (1999a [1902]: 33). More broadly, we see religion "[w]herever a man is so carried beyond himself whether for any other being, or for a cause or for a nation, that his personal fate seems to him as nothing in comparison of the happiness or triumph of the other, there you have the universal basis and structure of religion" (Bosanquet, 1920a: 5).[14]

What is the immanentist perspective? I will use the term "immanentism" to refer to Bosanquet's idea of affirming the divine in our actual lives whilst endeavouring to achieve perfection and self-realisation. Rather than focus on a transcendent notion of God who stands outside human experience, an immanentist view holds that, because of our spiritual character, we all participate in the divine and we are able to realise it as goodness in our lives.

The realisation of the good is the ultimate "task" of the individual as a social being. The immanence of the divine is revealed whilst the moral self is actualised. God is identified with the idea of the good. This identifica-

---

13 "The spirit of Christendom, [...] and the modern spirit are on the whole convertible terms; and when we speak of culture, humanity, civilisation, as indicating moral aims and duties, we use these terms in the sense practically defined for us by the mind of Christendom" (Bosanquet, 1893a: 73).
14 Again, Bosanquet writes "Whenever, then, we find a devotion which makes the finite self seem as nothing, and some reality to which it attaches itself seem as all, we have the essentially religious attitude" (Bosanquet, 1913: 235). See the discussion by Sweet (2000).

tion is indeed present in traditional theology; Bosanquet, however, stresses the humanistic element and reshapes the perspective of conventional Christianity. He concentrates on the connection between the world of values and practical ethics, and shifts the focus from a notion of God as a Being dwelling in a transcendent realm to what occurs in this world. This world is the world that sustains the unceasing efforts of individuals to reach a higher ideal and contribute to the progress of civilisation. Religion (faith in the reality of the good as the only reality), then, is the foundation of morality. It supports the individual's spiritual need to overcome the limitations of finiteness and expand the frontiers of the self. In its effort to overcome finiteness, the human being follows morality (faith in the reality of the good) which is an area of self-realisation sustained by religion (faith in the reality of the good as the only reality).[15] The relation between religion and morality here is crucial. Religion and morality differ, of course, in their ways of conceptualising the good; but the difference is a matter of degree, not of substance. Nevertheless, religion is the force that motivates the spiritual restructuring of the self. Religious consciousness is the matrix that shapes ethical consciousness and maintains the activity of the moral self. Religion is the source of a higher spiritual awareness — not just a medium for intensifying the apprehension of a moral ideal. Thus, religion takes logical precedence over morality, because it makes possible the substantiation of ethical consciousness that underlies the formation of the moral self.

To appreciate the immanentist character here, it is important to look more closely at Bosanquet's idea of religion. Bosanquet employs two levels of analysis when he refers to religion. I call them "the structuration discourse" and "the substantiation discourse", respectively. In general, the structuration discourse conceptualises that particular type of disposition which expresses "the essentially religious attitude" (Bosanquet, 1913: 235); it focuses on the natural impulse that motivates the self to seek spiritual expansion and integration into a more inclusive reality. The substantiation discourse focuses on a specific form of consciousness which refers to the essence of religion as a case of self-transcendence: self-transcendence as one's unity with "perfection in the form of good" (Bosanquet, 1913: 226). These notions need some further explanation.

The structuration discourse refers to the constitutive elements of the religious attitude. The religious attitude is a mental predisposition — a sort

---

15 Bosanquet writes, "the good is indeed real, as morality claims that it should be; but there is something more; for in the end nothing else is real. And so you can be good, though you are not good, because as you are and as you stand, you yourself are not real" (Bosanquet, 1920a: 11). Bradley expresses a similar view: "The main difference [between religion and morality] is that what in morality only is to be, in religion somehow and somewhere really is, and what we are to do is done. [...] The importance for practice of this religious point of view is that what is to be done is approached, not with the knowledge of a doubtful success, but with the fore-felt certainty of already accomplished victory" (Bradley, 1988: 334).

of inherent motivating force that stimulates the self's spiritual movement beyond itself and thus prepares the ground for the individual's moral development. The religious attitude signifies, firstly, the sense of unity with a greater reality and, secondly, the human being's absorption into a world to which it is devoted and loyal. Devotion and loyalty to an object or an idea characterise "the essentially religious attitude", which has four main features. First, the absolute nature of the spiritual attachment: X would rather die than abandon his/her faith because X affirms his/her own humanity in being united with the reality expressed by the object or idea of the religious devotion (Bosanquet, 1999a [1902]: 33). Second, the ultimate moral function of the spiritual attachment: X experiences a strong and overwhelming feeling of unity with a reality beyond oneself — a reality that is inclusive and represents completion and coherence. This feeling of unity provides the human being with confidence and optimism; the resistance of the atomistic shell of the self is fading and X's potential of achieving a more substantial degree of self-realisation and fulfilment is vigorously activated. Third, the experience of transference to a higher ethical order: X has a sense of being absorbed in, and united with, a higher perfection that gives spiritual satisfaction and completion. And, finally, the absolute supremacy of a reality represented by the object or idea of religious devotion: X perceives his/her being as nothing in comparison to the reality to which one is attached (Bosanquet, 1913: 235–6).

This structuration discourse refers to the "mechanism" that sustains the articulation and function of "the essentially religious attitude." It illustrates the dynamic propelling of the self towards a new state of being in which the individual finds completion and fulfilment. The structuration discourse focuses on this natural impulse to unity — the force that motivates the self to seek spiritual expansion and integration into a more inclusive reality. The will of the human being to transcend the limitations of its finite condition and move towards coherence and completeness stems from the religious consciousness.

The substantiation discourse, on the other hand, concentrates on the nature and essence of religious consciousness. Religion presupposes self-transcendence — although this is not to say that "every sense of attainment or self-transcendence by the conquest of externality, is religious" (Bosanquet, 1913: 226). The type of self-transcendence which is characteristic of the religious consciousness is self-transcendence that involves "recognition of a higher perfection." The finite self seeks unity with this higher perfection and achieves a more complete state of being described as unity "with perfection in the form of good" (Bosanquet, 1913: 226). The quintessence of religious consciousness, or religion, is faith in the unity of the self with the reality of good that embodies the idea of a higher perfection. What we have in religion, Bosanquet explains, is the practical recognition of the absorption of the finite will in the will for perfection, that is, in the will for good, as the real and actual will dominant in the universe. [...] The finite mind so far as religious accepts as its true self an actual perfection, which alone is real, and in which evil is absorbed and annihilated. With this perfection it identifies itself by faith, that is to say, in the will to be, allied with the judgment of what is, disowning its finite imperfections and those of the world, and treating them as nothing—but, it must be added, not as non-existent (Bosanquet, 1913: 245–6).

Religious consciousness involves the recognition of the relation of finite will to the real will. *Ethical* consciousness depicts the individual's effort to attain the real self and affirm the real will; this is accomplished through faith—and faith is provided by religion. Both types of consciousness, religious and ethical, are manifestations of the spirituality of the human being—that is, the ability of mind to apprehend values and realise them in actual life despite the constraining conditions of temporality and finitude. Spirituality makes individuals capable of reaching a higher level of fulfilment in their engagement with the world. It enables human consciousness to perform the double task of reaching out and returning to itself in order to make the finite mind (one might say) a shrine of goodness and perfection and, thus, instantiate the immanence of the divine. The divine—the world of value and higher perfection—is "revealed" in the agonistic ethos of individuals who daily confront the challenges of finiteness and seek a greater degree of reality and completion in their lives. The empowerment of the self, which is attained through the spiritual force of transcendence, involves the opening up of new paths to self-understanding and personal enlightenment. Immanentism finds the essence of religion in the faith which sustains the impulse to unity with a reality greater than our immediate selves: "In a word, religion *is* just the weld of finite and infinite" (Bosanquet, 1920a: 62).

Bosanquet articulates the immanentist perspective through his analysis of the "absolute standpoint" as elaborated in two essays: "The Part Played by Æsthetic in the Development of Modern Philosophy" (1888–9), and "The Civilisation of Christendom" (1893a). The absolute standpoint relates to modernity. It establishes a new way of apprehending our being in the world, and provides an epistemological framework for the substantiation and expression of modern consciousness. The absolute, or modern, standpoint conveys "a sense of rational freedom" which is "the conviction that man can meet with nothing that is outside himself, in the sense of being necessarily and fundamentally superior to his rational nature and incapable of being faced or dealt with by it (Bosanquet, 1888–9: 85).

The absolute standpoint reflects the foundations of a humanistic hermeneutic of the spirit, which is the philosophical outlook that shapes the immanentist perspective. The absolute standpoint depicts the highest stage in the realisation of consciousness and provides a new way of understanding the relation between the world and the individual. It does so, by establishing a worldview that affirms the importance of the individual as a thinking agent, and by cultivating the idea of rational freedom. Reason is our weapon against the various impediments to the affirmation of values in our lives. Reason provides human beings with the necessary confidence, strength, determination, and knowledge to face serious difficulties and solve problems without having to resort to erroneous sources of explanation or adopt a fatalistic attitude towards the complexity of life. Let me explain.

According to Bosanquet, hardship, adversity and hazards are everywhere. Finitude generates obstacles which make the path to perfection difficult. At the level of practical ethics, the human condition is characterised by finiteness or, better, by the ceaseless conflict between the limitations of finitude and the reality of more complete and coherent states of being. It is the nature of the individual to be both finite and infinite; the constant effort to resolve, or overcome, this contradiction is depicted in the moral life. Externality might be hostile (physical disasters); belief systems might be flawed (superstition); and individuals might not always be capable of living up to the highest moral standard — but this is only a part of the story. The regressions and disruptions that might have a negative impact on the way to coherence and perfection are counteracted by the individual's urge to reach a higher state of unity and completion. This urge is inherent in the soul, and pushes towards a more substantial degree of self-realisation. The absolute (modern) standpoint signalled an era in which the will to self-determination becomes dominant. In dealing with the complexity of experience, the consequences of natural phenomena, and all sorts of impediments to the good life, humans use reason to think, analyse, and decide the right course of action. Having entered a concrete and robust phase of development, mind is conscious of its ability to triumph over those obstacles that beset its trajectory to freedom. The human spirit, confident of its power, confronts the enemies of its perfection. Rational freedom is gained and affirmed as individuals come to realise that they are masters of their own lives. The absolute standpoint celebrates the spiritual independence of the human being and signals the beginning of a new chapter in the evolution of human consciousness.

Bosanquet explores the link between the absolute standpoint and absolute religion, and assesses the contribution of Christianity to the crystallisation of a new spiritual outlook, in three seminal essays: "The Civilisation of Christendom", "The Part Played by Æsthetic in the Development of Modern Philosophy", and "The Evolution of Religion."[16]

In "The Civilisation of Christendom", Bosanquet discusses the role of Christianity in the emergence and articulation of the absolute standpoint.

---

16 Bosanquet notes that his article is inspired by Caird's *The Evolution of Religion* (1893).

He employs his dialectical understanding of the history of mind to chart the path to modern consciousness. The substantiation of the absolute standpoint follows the spirit's odyssey through time. Classical antiquity, Christianity, and the Enlightenment formulated conditions conducive to the genesis and consolidation of the absolute standpoint. Christianity, however, occupies a key position in the unfolding of developments leading to a new era of self-understanding. According to Bosanquet, Christianity affirmed the value of the individual—a principle that has Greek and Roman origins (Bosanquet, 1893a: 75-6). He then writes: "I connect it [the absolute standpoint] in particular with Christianity, from which religion it was in fact derived by the great men who first proclaimed it in the time of Goethe and of the French Revolution" (Bosanquet, 1893a: 80).

The long journey of the spirit reveals conceptual links, continuities, and constructive transformations that mark historical periods and show the dialectical synthesis of ideas reflected in the evolution of new worldviews. In "The Part Played by Æsthetic in the Development of Modern Philosophy", Bosanquet notes that the absolute standpoint expressed a conviction which was characteristic "of the progressive civilisation of Christendom", and claims that it was "this conviction which took philosophical form at the time of the French Revolution in the doctrine of the absolute or the objective idea" (Bosanquet, 1888-9: 86). Although the absolute standpoint attained its proper philosophical expression in the late eighteenth and the beginning of the nineteenth century, its fundamental characteristic—i.e., spirit that progressively reveals itself immanently—was already present in the religion of Jesus and of St. Paul. The absolute standpoint "excludes accident, caprice, and with these the vulgar idea of the supernatural" (Bosanquet, 1893a: 78). Furthermore, it sustains the idea of immanent divinity—an idea that Bosanquet attributes to the spiritual heritage of Christianity (Bosanquet, 1893a: 84).

Bosanquet's analysis in "The Evolution of Religion" plays a strategic role in the overall development of his views on philosophical psychology and ethics. Bosanquet notes that the most developed form of religion, or the third phase in the evolution of religious consciousness, is the "Absolute or Spiritual Religion"—which is also described as the "Religion of the Absolute, or of the recognized Unity between the Self and the World" (Bosanquet, 1894-5: 443-4). Like the absolute standpoint that signifies the highest stage in the unfolding of consciousness, the absolute religion refers to the highest phase in the realisation of religious consciousness. The idea of the absolute religion is adequately expressed in Christianity, provided that the latter is properly understood. The immanentist perspective, in adopting the principles of the absolute standpoint, suggests a new hermeneutic of the essence of religion, and inaugurates an exegetical path that is free from superstition and the supernatural.

The idea of religion as the consciousness of unity between the self and the world (Bosanquet, 1894–5: 435) also underpins Bosanquet's analysis of the metaphysics of the self. As we have seen, the attainment of the real self occurs within the social whole.[17] Bosanquet, like Plato and Aristotle, sees the social nature of the individual as indispensably related to a sound moral, social, and political philosophy.[18] This is because society is the structure that nurtures ethical life. Family, civil society, the state and the international community, offer channels of ethico-social co-operation that, logically, support the realisation of the real, or true, self, and fortify the real will. The notion of society as a common project is premised on the moral imperative of the idea of the good. The good is realised in everyday life—not in the unknown territory of an otherworldly realm. The ceaseless effort to realise the good signifies the moral development of the individual. The realisation of the good is a complex, continuous process that involves the often unacknowledged work of men and women who comprise an ethical fellowship of minds—a "unity of spirits" that transcends the limitations of finiteness (Bosanquet, 1919: 159).[19]

Religion, then, acknowledges the importance of the social nature of the individual for the articulation of religious sentiments. Social anthropology shows that, from primeval times, forming a group and the act of worship mark the beginning of social and ethical awareness (Bosanquet, 1999a [1902]: 36). Ethics presupposes self-transcendence and sociality; society offers the framework of self-realisation. There is an organic unity between the individual, society, and the world—a unity that sustains the journey of the self towards affirmation and completion (Bosanquet, 1999a [1902]: 34).

This process of self-realisation restructures and transforms the spiritual content of the individual. The real self represents the unity of the human being with a greater reality in the form of a higher perfection. The ethical

---

17 This is a belief widely shared among the British Idealists. Boucher writes of them: "The test of a morally worthwhile existence is the extent to which the individual attempts to do God's work in the world by achieving his or her own potential and contributing to the common good" (Boucher, 1997: x).

18 Plato and Aristotle "regarded the good for man as, in its nature, capable of realization only in a community of souls or selves, and did not think of separating the study of the good of the individual from the study of the good of the community" (Bosanquet, 1999b [1902]: 203).

19 This is a key issue, particularly in the debates between Bosanquet and the Personal Idealists. The realisation of the good is seen as a project of the human spirit in which all participate according to their own ability. Bosanquet notes that "My battle [for the good] is continuous with yours, but it is not quite yours; yours helps me in mine, but it is not quite the same. We are sent on diverse missions, and all of them are necessary to the good" (Bosanquet, 1920a: 42). Yet elsewhere he writes that "We may be contributors to a supreme good without having capacity for it in our immediate selves. All lives colour all" (Bosanquet, 1919: 160). A person can make an indirect contribution to a supreme good. Indeed, "Nearly all mankind rest in unvisited tombs, and leave behind them a common undistinguished work" (Bosanquet, 1919: 87). But although the anonymous effort might not receive explicit public recognition, it does represent a very important contribution to the world of value (Bosanquet, 1919: 76–7). I am grateful to Peter P. Nicholson for drawing my attention to this point.

consciousness maintains the individual's will to fight against imperfection, strive towards the attainment of the real self, and affirm the good. Ethical life is characterised by the ceaseless effort of human beings to overcome obstacles, contradictions and adversities, and achieve a greater part of the axiological cosmos both within and outside the self. Ethical life, however, is supported through and through by religion, whose essence is faith in the reality of the good as the only reality. This faith nourishes and strengthens the ethical consciousness, and sustains the spiritual path to inner awakening and salvation.

The Reality of the Spiritual World

Bosanquet's analysis of religion is premised on the reality of the spiritual world—by which he means the world of values that is characterised by completion, coherence and perfection. Bosanquet, like Bradley, affirms the humanism of Idealism, defending the doctrine that the values of truth, beauty and goodness are immanent in finite minds (Bosanquet, 1905; Bradley, 1999 [1904]). Bosanquet's essay "On the True Conception of Another World" (1886) offers a philosophical investigation into the nature of the spiritual world, the findings of which buttress the immanentist discourse on religion.[20] In this essay, Bosanquet clarifies how the "other" world should be understood, and where the distinction between "this" and the "other" world is to be found. He also explains the difference between the philosophical and the popular conception of the supra-sensuous world, distinguishes between a true and false form of spiritualization, and prepares the ground for ideas and arguments that appear later in essays that deal more explicitly with religious themes.[21]

The true conception of the spiritual world is indispensable for understanding the essence and meaning of religion. Bosanquet presents the spiritual world, first, as a world immanent in finite minds, and, second, as a whole that does not need any reference outside itself to be completed. In "Life and Philosophy", he reminds the reader that the reconciliation of "the other world" with "this world" started long ago with Plato who paved the way for immanentism.[22] Christianity and Hegel continued and

---

20 This essay was first published in 1886 as a prefatory essay to Bosanquet's translation of a fragment from Hegel's *Aesthetics*, entitled *The Introduction to Hegel's Philosophy of Fine Art*. Here, I use the 1905 second impression of this book.

21 For example, Bosanquet (1899a), (1899b), (1893a), (1893b), (1893c), (1893d), (1888–9), (1894–5), (1999a [1902]), (1913), and (1920a).

22 Bosanquet acknowledges that Idealism has progressed since Plato, yet he is adamant that all Idealist philosophers should unreservedly recognise Plato's contribution to a proper theorising of the idea of the spiritual world. In a review of books by Italian Idealists, he reproaches Croce and Gentile for not having paid enough attention to this fact: "We know that it is wrong to look to Plato for modern idealism; but that he laid the ghost of the two-world theory, and initiated the impulse which led in Christianity to the idea of human-divine unity, I

completed this project (Bosanquet, 1924: 55). In art, philosophy and religion, then, human beings experience "the great types of social excellence" which are "the achievements of beauty, knowledge, and goodness" (Bosanquet, 1919: 40). Ethical life provides the domain wherein the spiritual world (the world of values) is articulated through the experiences, institutions, and structures that shape the life of man as a member of the social whole. Through their interaction in the context of ethical life, individuals become aware of their inherent capability to expand and transform — in other words, to achieve a greater degree of self-realisation. Art, philosophy, religion, and the institutions of social organisation enable the self to transcend spiritually the apparent limitations of its specific spatiotemporal determinations, and "discover" its spiritual heritage that encapsulates the toil and achievement of minds throughout generations. In the social whole, the soul is moulded by its engagement in the processes and events of everyday life. As the self strives to attend to "the more real"[23] by removing the obstacles that stand between its momentary manifestation and its true being, it appropriates a more substantial part of the axiological cosmos and thus affirms a greater degree of reality.

The values of the spiritual world are the heartbeat of a meaningful and morally rewarding life. Socio-ethical self-realisation is related to spiritual self-realisation. The social whole provides the framework wherein spiritual imperatives influence the character of a social dialectic. In the ethical laboratory of society, the moral self asserts its spiritual constitution as the narrative of its social being unfolds. The understanding of the meaning of institutions, the appreciation and enjoyment of beauty, the use of reasoning and judgment, the effort to make a positive contribution to society — all these are experiences that reinforce paths of communication between the self and the world of values. During this process of transcendence and expansion, a greater degree of reality is attained by the finite-infinite self, and the significant role of the finite centre as the locus of the realisation of values is recognised. Transcendence strengthens the infinite aspect of the human being, and brings the self closer to perfection and self-realisation.[24] The supra-sensuous world presupposes the sensuous world, considering that it depends on the latter for its practical manifestation. The spiritual world is logically and essentially related to the world of the senses. The two worlds are inseparable: the sensuous world provides the necessary

---

should have said was certain. I do not think that these scholars [Croce and Gentile], learned as they are, have full and genuine sympathy with the Hellenic mind" (Bosanquet, 1920b: 368).

23 The phrase is borrowed from Bosanquet's "Plato's Conception of Death" (Bosanquet, 1903b: 109).

24 Gaus notes that the finite aspect of our nature imposes limits on our quest for perfection; this is why absolute perfection, "a coherent self encompassing all values", is impossible (Gaus, 1994: 419). However, although absolute perfection cannot be achieved, the self nevertheless strives for perfection through its endeavour to realise the good and assert the infinite dimension of its being.

framework for the development of spirit in consciousness. Belief in the supreme values of truth, beauty, and goodness underpins the common effort of individuals to raise the tone of society as a whole. The universe of values (the spiritual, or the "other", world) is affirmed in the processes and relations that substantiate the accomplishment of moral purposes.

Bosanquet's conception of the spiritual world has nothing to do with the popular conception of the "other" world. Bosanquet makes clear that his philosophical approach excludes superstition and the supernatural (Bosanquet, 1899b: 142; 1905: xxxii; 1920a: 28–33). Miracles; contemplation of a paradise existing in a future life; and belief in a remote world of disembodied spirits or ghosts: these are features of the popular conception of the "other" world—a conception that fails not only to grasp the true essence of the spiritual, but also, to explain the meaning and significance of the spiritualization of the natural body. Bosanquet, whilst discussing Hegel's idea of spiritual being, clarifies what the spiritualization of the natural body is:

> According to Hegel, it is only in the human form that intelligence can for us find its full expression. The notion of a spiritual body other than and incompatible with the natural body does not arise. Spirit exists in the medium of consciousness, not in a peculiar kind of matter. The spiritualization of the natural body is not to be looked for in an astral or angel body, but in the gait and gesture, the significance and dignity, that make the body of the civilized man the outward image of his soul, and distinguish him from the savage as from the animal. The human soul becomes actual itself, and visible to others, only by moulding the body into its symbol and instrument (Bosanquet, 1905: xxxiii–xxxiv).

The spiritualization of the natural body does not mean abolition of its material form. It is a characteristic of the human individual that signifies the ability of the self to realise values in the context of everyday life. To employ the terminology of the 19th century, spiritualization distinguishes the "civilized man" from the "savage" and from the animal. The crucial point here is the identification of what, in principle, constitutes the essence of individuality, and the establishment of a logical connection between perfection and the self. Spiritualization refers to the self's capacity for perfection, and describes the process of affirming infinity (the world of values) in one's life. It depicts the nature of the individual's moral odyssey: the continuous fight against the limitations of finiteness, and the striving towards the attainment of a more real self. Bosanquet uses Goethe's phrase "die to live" (or "dying to live") to illustrate this unique "soteriological" element of the metaphysics of the self.[25] Bosanquet's practical ethics is structured around this "die to live" metaphor. In order to assert our conti-

---

25 Bosanquet discusses "dying to live" in his "Plato's Conception of Death" (1903b), and in chapter VII of *Some Suggestions in Ethics* (1919). See also a brief mention of this term in relation to the principle of immanence (Bosanquet, 1999a [1902]: 35).

nuity with the world of values, we must overcome anything which holds us back and that lacks harmony and completion. The conquest of the sources of distraction, fragmentation, and contradiction means "death" to those aspects of experience that "tie" us to the less real. By overcoming these obstacles, the self comes closer to its truth, the will becomes more real, and the idea of the good obtains a deeper affirmation in life. A new beginning dawns, and brings "death unto sin" and salvation.[26]

The idea of spiritualization describes the individual's self-realisation in terms of value affirmation. False conceptions of the spiritual world cause harm to individuals and threaten social cohesion and the common good. Bosanquet regards the realisation of values in our lives as the revelation of divinity in human spirit in the present (one and only) world. "Divine revelation", in this context, represents the achievement of civilisation and the organisation of life according to reason so that individuals can achieve the best in them. This is a process which articulates the life of spirit over centuries and generations.[27] The world of values is substantiated in the sensuous world that contextualises the individual's self-realisation.

In *The Philosophical Theory of the State*,[28] Bosanquet discusses how individuals realise the spiritual world of values whilst living in the organised social whole — the "state". Bosanquet's use of the term "state" refers to that broader and inclusive whole that provides the possibility for ethical life. The role of the state, therefore, is not exhausted in the functions of government, bureaucracy, and administration.[29] The state represents the ultimate organisation of the political community in terms of sovereignty, territorial boundaries, and comprehensiveness of a moral purpose. It is the frame-

---

26 In discussing the redemptive character of the Crucifixion and Resurrection of Christ (as understood by St. Paul), T. H. Green lays the foundations for the philosophical perspective that is reconfirmed in Bosanquet's interpretation of the phrase "dying to live." Green writes: "The death and rising again of the Christ, as he [St. Paul] conceived them, were not separate and independent events. They were two sides of the same act — an act which, relatively to sin, to the flesh, to the old man, to all which separates from God, is death; but which, just for that reason, is the birth of a new life relatively to God" (Green, 1888: 232-3).

27 T.H. Green expressed a similar view: "God is for ever reason; and his communication, his revelation, is reason; not, however, abstract reason, but reason as taking a body from, and giving life to, the whole system of experience which makes the history of man. The revelation, therefore, is not made in a day, or a generation, or a century" (Green, 1888: 239-40).

28 *The Philosophical Theory of the State* went through four editions (1899, 1910, 1920, and 1923), and was reprinted several times. Gaus and Sweet (2001) produced the latest edition, annotated and with a lengthy scholarly Introduction. In the present essay, all references to *The Philosophical Theory of the State* are from a reprint (1925) of the 4th (1923) edition. For a reassessment of Bosanquet's philosophical theory of the state, see Panagakou (2001, 2005).

29 Bosanquet writes: "I use the term 'State' in the full sense of what it means as a living whole, not the mere legal and political fabric, but the complex of lives and activities, considered as the body of which that is the framework. 'Society' I take to mean the same body as the State, but *minus* the attribute of exercising what is in the last resort absolute physical compulsion" (Bosanquet, 1912: 311, 1n). Elsewhere, he notes that the state exists "to promote good life" (Bosanquet, 1925: 302). Bosanquet's analysis reflects the Greek conception of political life as a common moral enterprise of rational human beings: "For us, then, the ultimate end of Society and the State as of the individual is the realisation of the best life." (Bosanquet, 1925: 169).

work of the ethical life: an inclusive whole which sustains the institutions that shape the real will. Ethical life emancipates the self from its subjectivity by propelling it into the realm of social experience and the formative influence of institutions. Bosanquet refers to the institutions of family and property, district or neighbourhood, class,[30] and the state. He regards them as ethical ideas, that is, "constituent elements of the mind, which are also purposes" (Bosanquet, 1925: 276). Institutions express the spiritual evolution of humankind and fulfill a pedagogical function by providing channels through which the individual apprehends values and attains freedom.

As the individual strives to attain completion and perfection, a higher level of spiritual awareness is achieved. The self is restructured; the soul is recast: a more substantial degree of self-realisation is acquired through self-transcendence. Education offers an example that shows the moral significance of the soul-moulding process. Bosanquet invites his readers to reflect on the Resurrection and compare it to the development of a child :

> Does any man wish to see a far nobler miracle than the Resurrection, — not the recalling of a dead organism to life, but the elevation of an animal soul into membership of the supra-sensuous or spiritual world? *Then let him observe the education of his child*. The metaphors of old religion may now seem awkward and erroneous, but their language was not at all too strong for the facts which we *must* learn to see (Bosanquet, 1893b: 143).

This is a powerful statement that challenges established views and obliges us to expand our hermeneutic horizons. Bosanquet uses this example in order to stress the logical inseparability of the sensuous and supra-sensuous world, but also to provide an eloquent illustration of the principles elaborated in "On the True Conception of Another World." The education of a child demonstrates that the spiritual world is indeed "present, actual, and concrete" (Bosanquet, 1905: xvi). Bosanquet focuses on human experience and employs probably the most mystical and sacred moment of the life of Christ to describe an instance of self-realisation and social ethics that shows the immanence of the spiritual world and its affirmation in the present life.

The true conception of the spiritual world refers to "the world of beauty, and goodness, and truth" (Bosanquet, 1893b: 137).[31] It is in the values of

---

30 For Bosanquet, the term "class" does not denote an economic category or a political institution expressing privilege, hierarchy, and rigid social stratification. On the contrary, it "indicates the type of position and service involved in one's occupation […]. In principle, as an ethical idea, it takes the man or woman beyond the family and the neighbourhood; and for the same reason takes him deeper into himself" (Bosanquet, 1925: 291).

31 When Bosanquet answers, in the negative, the question "Are we Agnostics?" — in response to T.H. Huxley's essay "Agnosticism" (Huxley, 1889; reprinted in Huxley, 1892) — his claim is that, in their rejection of a spiritual world, agnostics miss the point. Bosanquet writes: "I am not objecting to a man being an Agnostic in opinion, but to his calling himself an Agnostic in the

truth, love, and beauty, that one's "unity with God and with the whole of being" is "solid and plain" (Bosanquet, 1920a: 28).[32] Bosanquet focuses on the immanent and ethical nature of the divine element. The spiritual world encompasses values whose apprehension enables the human being to reach a higher level of self-realisation. Recognition of the true nature of the spiritual world relates to the development of ethical consciousness, i.e., the type of consciousness which sustains the individual's membership of a social whole. The social whole, with its institutions understood as ethical ideas, offers the logical framework that "accommodates" the individual's quest for completion and perfection.

For Bosanquet, the teachings of Plato, Jesus, St. Paul, and Hegel constitute landmarks in the history of the mind to grasp the real meaning of the spiritual world. He regards Christianity as the religion that focused on the notion of immanent divinity — a conception that threw new light on the understanding of morality. Bosanquet's analysis of the Pauline doctrine of justification by faith shows the socio-ethical character of Christian faith:

> [Being one *in* and *with* Christ] are the two aspects of Paul's doctrine. Being one *with* the risen Christ, means that the particular believer has put away his bad will, is dead to sin, and has thoroughly submitted his heart and soul to the dominion of the good will, that is, the mind of Christ. Being one *in* the risen Christ means that the society of believers form what Paul calls the "body of Christ", that is, a spiritual unity which is Divine and yet human, and as wide as humanity. Faith means realizing this oneness in and with Christ (Bosanquet, 1899b: 151).

This passage deserves particular attention. Being one in and with the risen Christ means redemption and salvation, yet Bosanquet directs our attention to the ethical, not to the mystical aspect of this union. Divine oneness represents the ultimate stage in the moral development of the self: it signifies the transformation of the finite-infinite being in its striving for perfection. Being one in and with the risen Christ is self-realisation as completion and perfection. The "body of Christ" represents the spiritual unity of humans in the social whole — a unity affirmed in the moral will for the good. The kingdom of God is realised here on earth whilst individuals go about their daily activities guided by the moral imperative to do good.

---

sense that the name is to indicate his attitude with reference to the spiritual world" (Bosanquet, 1893b: 132). Bosanquet sees in agnosticism a regression in the development of religious consciousness — that the agnostic re-introduces erroneous beliefs which should have been abandoned after the new era of spiritual understanding brought about by the absolute standpoint.

32 In *What Religion Is*, Bosanquet uses two phrases to express the unity of the self with the supreme good: "unity of love and will" and "unity of will and belief" (Bosanquet, 1920a: 20, 30, 33). In addition, he slightly modifies his standard triptych of values: he refers to love, beauty, and truth (Bosanquet, 1920a: 28, 31), instead of goodness, beauty, and truth. Goodness seems to metamorphose into "the supreme good." It is possible that, by this shift, Bosanquet intended to show the substantive relation between the Christian concept of love and the Platonic idea of the good.

Religion, Ethics, and Self-Realisation

The preceding analysis of the immanentist perspective and of the true conception of the spiritual world has shown that, in Bosanquet's philosophy, religion is indispensable to morality, ethical consciousness, and the process of self-realisation. The understanding of religion as belief in the good as the only reality, sustains the real will, strengthens the individual's determination to fight against evil, and justifies the human being's endeavour to realise the true self in the present (and only) world.

Bosanquet's essay "The Kingdom of God on Earth" illustrates the practical aspect of his philosophical views on religion, and has a strategic position in his account of the essence of religion and faith. In this essay, Bosanquet uses the notion of our "station and its duties"[33] to show how the good is realised in this world—in the victory of the right will and the real self over the bad will and the bad self. But he also discusses religion and morality in terms of ethical citizenship and self-realisation in the community.[34] The kingdom of God is realised in society through individuals' effort to contribute to the common good and attain the best life. It is present in the ethical life of human beings who firmly believe in the good as the only reality and integrate this faith in the moral will—the will that sustains the process of self-realisation and nourishes the desire for perfection. The commitments, duties, rights, and responsibilities, which constitute the ethical fabric of social life shape the character of the individual and provide the context for the formation of the real self. The kingdom of God, far from being a transcendent realm, is immanent: it signifies a state of goodness and perfection that exists in man and society.

> All that we mean by the kingdom of God on earth is the society of human beings who have a common life and are working for a common social good. The kingdom of God has come on earth in every civilized society where men live and work together, doing their best for the whole society and for mankind. When two or three are gathered together, co-operating for a social good, there is the Divine Spirit in the midst of them (Bosanquet, 1899a: 121).

The Kingdom of God, therefore, is contained in one's consciousness of the good, in the spirit of human fellowship, in the development of civilisation. The kingdom of God on earth is instantiated through love and self-transcendence and permeates the whole of being. It is anticipated in the individual's conquest over the bad self and the bad will, and is "pres-

---

33 This idea is likely taken from F.H. Bradley's *Ethical Studies* (1876; 2nd ed., 1927). Bosanquet was impressed by Bradley's analysis. Indeed, according to Helen Bosanquet, Bernard "seems to have contemplated writing a book on Ethics, which was forestalled by Bradley's *Ethical Studies*" (H. Bosanquet, 1924: 34).

34 According to William Sweet, Bosanquet "presents an analysis of the nature of the human individual and the community that was taken up later in his political philosophy" (Sweet, 1999b: xviii).

ent" in the moral law that keeps society together. The divine aspect of the human being is affirmed in the individual's capability to pass from the narrow self of daily atomistic wants and claims to a self that wholeheartedly seeks union with greater realities. This spiritual hunger of the individual for states of being which bring the self closer to its real nature constitutes the driving force of self-transcendence and thus self-realisation.

The idea of the immanence of the kingdom of God is best represented in the moral (right, or real) will: we find God's will in our own right will. The crystallisation of the right will and the formation of the real self are essentially related to one's station and its duties. One's station and its duties depicts one's position in society — not in terms of social class, but in terms of the roles, commitments, functions, rights and responsibilities that characterise human life. From their station in society, individuals engage the world around them. But one's station and its duties are also the vehicle of ethical consciousness: "it is the very heart and spirit of our little individual life" and "gives the reason for doing what we ought to do" (Bosanquet, 1899a: 117).

One's station involves a variety of functions and relations that generate responsibilities and obligations, feelings, affections, and loyalties. Take, for instance, the case of a woman—Helen. She is a mother, a daughter, a lawyer, an executive member of her professional association, a member of a human rights NGO, a volunteer in an organisation for the protection of women against violence, an amateur photographer, and a talented violin player. All these roles, which constitute various aspects of Helen's station in society, refer to capacities and powers that enable her to maintain herself in the world, lead a meaningful and morally rewarding life, exercise her real will, and achieve self-realisation. From her station and through her various duties, she fights against the obstacles to the good life and contributes to the common good. In order to sustain her right will and fulfil her roles, she has to rise above her momentary desires and overcome the limitations of a narrowly conceived self-interest. For instance, in her role as a daughter, she might decide to postpone a trip to the countryside (which would allow her to relax , and provide material for her photography), in order to keep her elderly mother company. In doing her duty, Helen manages to transcend the obstacles posed by the wants of the finite self (e.g., the desire to go on an excursion), and assert her real will. We have here an act of self-transcendence that strengthens the ethical consciousness, and enables the individual to adopt a greater vision of life—a vision that prioritises moral duty, commitment, and love over the demands of atomistic individualism. Helen's decision to choose the right course of action and put her mother's well-being above her own immediate satisfaction shows her emotional and spiritual maturity. She challenges the insularity of the "narrow" self, and follows her real will—that is, the will which would enable her to reach fulfilment, salvation, and freedom.

For Bosanquet, salvation depicts the individual's spiritual battle against the restrictions of finiteness and the absorption of the self into the world of values. As the self opens up to goodness, beauty, and truth, it becomes a communicator of values and a shrine of the axiological cosmos. The path to salvation leads to gradual emancipation from the "tyranny" of the various limitations stemming from finite being. The human being is divine in the sense that the potential for a union with the reality of the good is inherent in the soul—God's will is the will to do good. The human being asserts itself in the effort to "go out of itself" and expand the frontiers of the self in the vast, rough sea of ethical experience. This is a pilgrimage that brings about "death", "redemption", and "rebirth." The enemies of perfection are defeated every time that the individual, guided by the real will, asserts a completer state of self-realisation. The self is redeemed: it becomes stronger, more real, more divine and thus, more human. But this process of "reaching out" which results in one's spiritual unity with the supreme good is neither an easy nor a "painless" affair. "Salvation", Bosanquet writes, "is the entrance to the strait gate and the thorny path" (Bosanquet, 1920a: 4). Religious faith may bring salvation that can be seen as an "idyllic" situation of fulfilment and peace (Bosanquet, 1920a: 5), yet it "does not seem to promise exemption from suffering" (Bosanquet, 1920a: 53). As Bosanquet explains:

> It is crude and pagan, perhaps, to say that all good comes by suffering, and I do not say it. But religious faith seems to mean a going out of oneself, which may be exultant, but can hardly fail at times to put the finite being on the rack (Bosanquet, 1920a: 61–2).

Bosanquet devotes the sixth chapter of *What Religion Is* to the topic of suffering. How does Bosanquet understand the function of suffering in relation to religion, and how does he integrate it into the logic of his discourse on self-transcendence, salvation, and self-realisation? For Bosanquet, suffering is a fact—a universal and inescapable fact deriving from the nature of the finite world. Suffering "belongs on the one hand to the religious spirit, and on the other to the finite world" (Bosanquet, 1920a: 59–60). It is embedded in the conflict that characterises the ontological constitution of the self in its double nature as finite-infinite.

Bosanquet contextualises his reflections on suffering in the broader framework of his discourse on the metaphysics of the self. His analysis of suffering relates to the familiar theme of the hazards and hardships of finite selfhood (Bosanquet, 1912, 1913). Suffering and salvation are premised on the double nature of the individual. The finite element drags the self back to patterns of behaviour and ways of being that impede the individual's potential for perfection. But, simultaneously, the impulse to transcend the limitations of finitude and unite with the world of values propels the self towards a dimension of being that is more substantial spiritually and more coherent logically:

> What I am urging is rather that our true personality lies in our concrete best, and that in desiring its development and satisfaction we are desiring an increase of our real individuality, though a diminution of our formal exclusiveness (Bosanquet, 1913: 284).

The finite-infinite self, because of its transcending dynamic, is equipped with the ability to make the most of its inherent potential for self-realisation. The human condition is the source of suffering — yet it is the conflict of opposing forces within the psyche that produces salvation and rebirth. The conflict brings both suffering and victory.[35]

In this spiritual conflict that takes place in the domain of consciousness, salvation means to achieve the real self. As the real self emerges triumphant, the actual self — the self of the momentary desires and satisfactions — suffers defeat. The attainment of the real self becomes a reality because the individual believes firmly in it, remains confident of his/her ability to acquire it, and has unshakable faith in the reality of the good as the only reality. The entire process of self-realisation presupposes religious faith (Bosanquet, 1920a: 53–4).

Salvation means the victory of the self against insularity and isolation. It depicts the emergence of the real self which is a state of being that the actual self appears to contradict. In instantiating the logical link between subjectivity and the sphere of social realisation, one's station and its duties can be regarded as the vehicle that brings the individual to the gates of salvation, self-realisation, and freedom. The various roles and responsibilities associated with our position in the social whole reflect a system of values which encapsulate the essence of ethical life, that is, a harmonious relation between the well-being of the individual and the common good. Human beings have the capacity for achieving the good life whilst realising the ideal of ethical citizenship. Bosanquet explains:

> There are the simple duties of honesty and thoroughness in all work; there is education; there is wise and painstaking help of our neighbours; there is wise management of societies or clubs which we have to do with; there is forming an enlightened judgment on trade questions and on questions that concern us as citizens; and there is the attempt to make the tone of our society a little higher, more full of real interests, more free from vice and vulgarity. Every man is responsible for the

---

35 Bosanquet writes: "A word like 'victory', or 'in the end', becomes deceptive if we press it as meaning an event, an occurrence. What it means to say is, I take it, that though all appearances good is supreme. And, saying so, it does not leave us with empty words or empty hands. It gives as much of good as our spirits can contain. [...] It only requires us to rise above the appearance, and keep our unhesitating grasp on the reality which is wholly good" (Bosanquet, 1920a: 41–2).

tone of the society in which he moves, and for the influence which he spreads round him, hour by hour (Bosanquet, 1899a: 119).

Life in the organised social whole offers the environment wherein individuals fulfil their obligations and co-operate for the accomplishment of shared social ends. Social fellowship is by nature ethical. In carrying out their duties, humans make their own unique contribution to the well-being of the social organism, and strengthen the ethical consciousness — the source of the right will and the real self. However, the bad will and the bad self have not been entirely abolished in the sphere of ethical life. Although the individual seeks perfection and is absorbed in the moral quest for the good, the process of completion and self-realisation might, at any time, regress because of the finite aspect of the human being. The ethical life cannot abolish finiteness; but it can successfully minimise its negative impact on the individual's endeavour to affirm a greater part of reality. The bad self and the bad will might exist, yet they are not real — that is, they do not embody the world of values. The individual strives for wholeness and perfection; there is an impulse within the self that drives it towards more complete and fulfilling states of being. How is this *nisus* to the whole sustained? Where does the foundation of self-realisation lie? What is the source of ethical consciousness? At this point, the link between religion and ethics in Bosanquet's philosophy becomes more than evident. In order to win the battle against the bad will and the bad self, we must will the good and have faith in the reality of the good as the only reality. We need religion.

Conclusion

In this essay, I have focused on Bosanquet's views concerning the relation between religion and ethics. Bosanquet's writings on religion are deeply concerned with ethics; their purpose is to help to describe and articulate how to revitalise morality and how to promote the self-realisation of human beings. These works present, within a broadly metaphysical context, a way of understanding the nature of morality as it is — or should be — engaged in within a social setting.

Bosanquet places religion at the heart of his moral and social philosophy, emphasises the importance of Christianity for both the development of Western civilisation and the spiritual progress of humankind, and provides a unique account of the connection between religious and ethical consciousness. His analysis of religion reassesses traditional theological discourse in the light of a humanistic hermeneutic. Bosanquet's account of the attainment of the real self and the crystallisation of the right, or real, will shows the importance of religion to his moral philosophy. For Bosanquet, religion means faith in the reality of the good as the only reality, and refers to one's unity — in love and will — with the supreme good.

These principles guide the moral will, fortify the ethical consciousness, and sustain the dynamics of self-realisation.

The preceding analysis of the relation between religion and ethics in Bosanquet's philosophy focused on three main topics: the immanentist perspective; the true conception of the spiritual world; and ethics, self-realisation, and the social nature of "the kingdom of God." We have seen the links between the absolute standpoint, the immanence of the world of values, and the metaphysics of the self, and also seen how Bosanquet's account of religion is indispensable to his ethics. For Bosanquet, religion underpins moral thinking and strengthens the individual's quest for perfection and completion. Religious consciousness is the spiritual source of ethical consciousness.

The immanentist conception of religion is structured around the connection between the world of values and the moral realm of action and self-realisation. Immanentism stresses the idea of the divinity of the human being—i.e., the self's capacity for perfection and for accomplishing the ends of ethical citizenship. In this context, individuals affirm "God's" will in their own right will. Bosanquet articulates the immanentist perspective through his discussion of the absolute standpoint—the hermeneutic framework of modern consciousness. The absolute standpoint refers to a distinctive outlook which affirms the value of human agency and the empowering character of rational freedom. Mind is thus revitalised and a new worldview emerges that heralds a revaluation of the individual.

Bosanquet's views on religion draw upon his theory of the nature of the spiritual world. For Bosanquet, the spiritual world is immanent and contains the values of truth, beauty, and goodness—values that the individual seeks to attain during the process of self-realisation in the context of ethical life. Membership in a social whole means ethical fellowship and thus spiritual unity. Human beings are able to achieve a more complete state of selfhood in co-operating for the realisation of the common good. The link between the essence of religion and the moral character of one's station and its duties demonstrates that "the kingdom of God" is found on earth—in the endeavour of individuals to realise the right will, fight against the limitations of finitude, and contribute to the well-being of the community. Self-realisation represents the individual's salvation from the bad will that hinders one's unity with the reality of the good.[36]

---

36 I am grateful to Professor William Sweet for his comments and suggestions on an earlier version of this paper.

References

Bosanquet, B. (1888-9) "The Part Played by Æsthetic in the Development of Modern Philosophy", *Proceedings of the Aristotelian Society*, 1/2, pp. 77-97.

Bosanquet, B. (1893a) "The Civilisation of Christendom", in B. Bosanquet, *The Civilization of Christendom and Other Studies* (London: Swan Sonnenschein; New York: Macmillan), pp. 63-99.

Bosanquet, B. (1893b) "Are We Agnostics?", in B. Bosanquet, *The Civilization of Christendom and Other Studies* (London: Swan Sonnenschein; New York: Macmillan), pp. 127-59.

Bosanquet, B. (1893c) "Old Problems Under New Names", in B. Bosanquet, *The Civilization of Christendom and Other Studies* (London: Swan Sonnenschein; New York: Macmillan), pp. 100-26.

Bosanquet, B. (1893d) "The Future of Religious Observance", in B. Bosanquet, *The Civilization of Christendom and Other Studies* (London: Swan Sonnenschein; New York: Macmillan), pp. 1-26.

Bosanquet, B. (1894-5) "The Evolution of Religion", *International Journal of Ethics*, 5, pp. 432-44.

Bosanquet, B. (1899a) "The Kingdom of God on Earth", in B. Bosanquet, *Essays and Addresses*, 3rd edn (London: Sonnenschein), pp. 108-30.

Bosanquet, B. (1899b) "How to Read the New Testament", in B. Bosanquet, *Essays and Addresses*, 3rd edn (London: Swan Sonnenschein), pp. 131-61.

Bosanquet, B. (1903a) "On the Practical Value of Moral Philosophy. Inaugural Address Delivered October 21, 1903" [at the University of St Andrews] (Edinburgh and London: Blackwood).

Bosanquet, B. (1903b) "Plato's Conception of Death", *The Hibbert Journal*, 2/1, pp. 98-109.

Bosanquet, B. (1905) "On the True Conception of Another World", in B. Bosanquet, *The Introduction to Hegel's Philosophy of Fine Art* (London: Kegan Paul, Trench, and Trübner), pp. xv-xxxv.

Bosanquet, B. (1912) *The Principle of Individuality and Value: The Gifford Lectures for 1911 delivered in Edinburgh University* (London: Macmillan).

Bosanquet, B. (1913) *The Value and Destiny of the Individual: The Gifford Lectures for 1912 delivered in Edinburgh University* (London: Macmillan).

Bosanquet, B. (1917) *Social and International Ideals: Being Studies in Patriotism* (London: Macmillan).

Bosanquet, B. (1919) *Some Suggestions in Ethics* 2nd edn (London: Macmillan).

Bosanquet, B. (1920a) *What Religion Is* (London: Macmillan).

Bosanquet, B. (1920b) Review of G. Gentile, *Sommario di Pedagogia come Scienza Filosofica*; G. Gentile, *La Riforma della Dialettica Hegeliana*; L. Vivante, *Principii di Etica*; A. Shannon, *Morning Knowledge: The Story of the New Inquisition*; J.A. Smith, *The Philosophy of Giovanni Gentile*. Mind, n.s. 29, pp. 367-70.

Bosanquet, B. (1924) "Life and Philosophy", in J.H. Muirhead (ed.), *Contemporary British Philosophy. Personal Statements. First Series* (London: George Allen & Unwin), pp. 51-74.

Bosanquet, B. (1925) *The Philosophical Theory of the State* (London: Macmillan).

Bosanquet, B. (1999a [1902]) "Religion (philosophy of)", in W. Sweet (ed.), *The Collected Works of Bernard Bosanquet, Vol. 1: Selected Essays* (Bristol: Thoemmes Press), pp. 29-39.

Bosanquet, B. (1999b [1902]) "State (philosophy of)", in W. Sweet (ed.), *The Collected Works of Bernard Bosanquet, Vol. 1: Selected Essays* (Bristol: Thoemmes Press), pp. 203-15.

Bosanquet, H. (1924) *Bernard Bosanquet: A Short Account of His Life* (London: Macmillan).

Boucher, D. (1997) "Introduction", in D. Boucher (ed.), *The British Idealists* (Cambridge: Cambridge University Press), pp. viii-xxxiii.

Bradley, F.H. (1988) *Ethical Studies*, 2nd ed. rev. / with additional notes by the author; with an introduction by R. Wollheim (Oxford: Clarendon Press).

Bradley, F.H. (1999 [1904]) "On Prof. James's 'Humanism and Truth'", in C.A. Keene (ed.), *Collected Works of F.H. Bradley, Vol. 3: Refinement and Revision, 1903-1924* (Bristol: Thoemmes Press), pp. 205-18.

Caird, E. (1893) *The Evolution of Religion*, 2 Vols (Glasgow: James Maclehose; New York: Macmillan).

Gaus, G.F. (1994) "Green, Bosanquet and the Philosophy of Coherence", in C.L. Ten (ed.), *Routledge History of Philosophy, Vol. VII: The Nineteenth Century* (London and New York: Routledge), pp. 408–36.

Gaus, G. F. and Sweet, W. (2001) (eds.), *The Philosophical Theory of the State and Related Essays by Bernard Bosanquet* (South Bend, IN: St. Augustine's Press).

Green, T.H. (1888) "The Witness of God", in T.H. Green, *Works of Thomas Hill Green*, ed. R.L. Nettleship (London: Longmans), Vol. III, pp. 230–52.

Huxley, T.H. (1889) "Agnosticism", *The Nineteenth Century*, Vol. 25, No. 144, pp. 169–94.

Huxley, T.H. (1892) "Agnosticism", in T.H. Huxley, *Essays upon Some Controverted Questions* (London and New York: Macmillan), pp. 329–77.

Panagakou, S. (1999a) "The Concept of Self-Transcendence in the Philosophy of Bernard Bosanquet", *Collingwood Studies*, 6, pp. 147-64.

Panagakou, S. (1999b) "Religious Consciousness and the Realisation of the True Self: Bernard Bosanquet's Views on Religion in *What Religion Is*", *Bradley Studies*, 5/2, pp. 139–61.

Panagakou, S. (2001) *Self-Transcendence and the Dialectic of the Finite-Infinite in the Philosophy of Bernard Bosanquet: Metaphysics, Religion and Political Philosophy* (University of York, D.Phil. thesis, unpublished).

Panagakou, S. (2005) "Defending Bosanquet's Philosophical Theory of the State: A Reassessment of the 'Bosanquet-Hobhouse Controversy'", *The British Journal of Politics & International Relations*, Vol. 7, No. 1, pp. 29–47.

Patrick, J. (1985) *The Magdalen Metaphysicals: Idealism and Orthodoxy at Oxford* (Macon: Mercer University Press).

Robbins, P. (1982) *The British Hegelians, 1875–1925* (New York and London: Garland Publishing).

Sell, A.P.F. (1988) *The Philosophy of Religion, 1875–1980* (London and New York: Croom Helm).

Sell, A.P.F. (1995) *Philosophical Idealism and Christian Belief* (Cardiff: University of Wales Press).

Sprigge, T.L.S. (1992) "Refined and Crass Supernaturalism", in M. McGhee (ed.), *Philosophy, Religion and the Spiritual Life* (Cambridge: Cambridge University Press), pp. 105–25.

Sprigge, T.L.S. (2006) *The God of Metaphysics* (Oxford: Clarendon Press).

Sprigge, T.L.S. (2007) "Bosanquet and Religion", in W. Sweet (ed.), *Bernard Bosanquet and the Legacy of British Idealism* (Toronto: University of Toronto Press), pp. 178–205.

Sweet, W. (1999a), "Social Policy and Bosanquet's Moral Philosophy", *Collingwood and British Idealism Studies*, 6, pp. 127–46.

Sweet, W. (1999b) "Introduction", in W. Sweet (ed.), *The Collected Works of Bernard Bosanquet, Vol. 1: Selected Essays* (Bristol: Thoemmes Press), pp. xi–xxxvii.

Sweet, W. (2000) "Bernard Bosanquet and the Nature of Religious Belief", in W.J. Mander (ed.), *Anglo-American Idealism, 1865-1927* (Westport, CT: Greenwood Press), pp. 123–39.

Sweet, W. (2003) "Introduction", in B. Bosanquet, *Essays in Philosophy and Social Policy, 1883–1922, Vol. 1: Essays in Aesthetics, Ethics, Religion and Metaphysics*, ed. W. Sweet (Bristol: Thoemmes Press), pp. xi–xxxvii.

Tsanoff, R.A. (1920) "The Destiny of the Self in Professor Bosanquet's Theory", *Philosophical Review*, 29, pp. 59–79.

Webb, C.C.J. (1922-3) "Mr. Bosanquet on Contemporary Philosophy", *Church Quarterly Review*, 95, pp. 160–5.

David Boucher

Henry Jones: Idealism as a Practical Creed

Introduction

Of the British Idealists, Henry Jones was the only Welshman. He was born at Llangernyw in Denbighshire, 30 November 1852, and died after a long and painful battle against mouth cancer, 4 February 1922. In this chapter, I want to outline Jones's philosophical universe in order to discern the moral and social as well as metaphysical principles in terms of which he approached theoretical and practical problems. I will then take an example, that of heredity, to demonstrate how these principles inform his mode and method of argument, and contribute to the conclusions relating to moral character, social issues and practical policies.

Jones within the Idealist Traditions

In 1920–1, Jones delivered the Gifford Lectures that were to be his philosophical testament, and testimony to his powerful optimistic religious personality in the face of adversity, not only in illness but in having lost three of his six children, and seeing a fourth taken prisoner during the First World War in Turkey (Jones, 1922). His adopted home was Scotland, where he was an undergraduate and assistant under Edward Caird, and whose chair of moral philosophy he inherited in 1894, against strong competition from John Watson and David George Ritchie.

Jones was one of the most faithful of the Idealists to Hegelianism. Hegel has been vilified for the practical outcomes of his philosophy. In his defence, however, he believed philosophy impotent in matters of practical instruction because "it always comes on the scene too late to give it" (Hegel, 1952: 7).[1] Jones departed significantly from Hegel in maintaining a very strong connection between theory and practice. No one, not even T.H. Green or Caird, propagated Idealism "with a more daring abandon-

---

[1] This, of course, is what Hegel is trying to impress upon his readers when he compares philosophy to the owl of Minerva.

ment and passion and a more genuine enthusiasm than Jones' (Metz, 1938: 302).

Jones had an unflinching conception of the public role of the academic as a reformer and opinion leader. All social injustice was an affront to the dignity of the person and an impediment to moral progress. Education was the key to emancipation, and it was to permeate every aspect of society, not only in the elementary and secondary schools he championed in Wales and Scotland, but also in the broadening of participation in university education to women and the working classes. Idealism, for him, was a religiously driven crusading philosophy, as the titles of some of his most famous books bear witness: *Social Responsibilities: Lectures to Businessmen*, *Idealism as a Practical Creed*, and *The Working Faith of a Social Reformer*.[2] Jones was the only one among the British Idealists knighted for his services to his country. Whereas much of his writing is directed at a broader audience and intended to have practical effect, he was nevertheless capable of serious and sustained philosophical argument and criticism, in which he expounded and defended the philosophy of Idealism, not so much against its predecessors (although like his fellow Idealists he could not ignore the immense popular appeal and practical effect of the theories of Herbert Spencer)[3] as against the variations of Personal Idealism, and neo-idealism critical of the Absolute Idealism he espoused.[4]

Jones was an ardent Absolute Idealist, confident that materialism and subjectivism, the dominant philosophies for much of the nineteenth century in Britain, were noticeably diminished in their appeal. The Benthamite utilitarians had passed their mantle on to the hands of the Idealists (Jones, 1910: 77, 197). Hegelianism was, for Jones, the philosophy most closely attuned to modern life, and whose principles saturated the theoretical and practical life of the times. He took modern philosophy to be the type of enquiry derived from Hegel and associated with the greatest modern minds (Jones, 1909a: 12). Hegel's achievement was to refuse to acknowledge the dualism between knowledge and reality, whereas previous philosophers, even Kant, had attempted their reconciliation. Kant had made the advance of making reality conform to thought, and hence rejected the Cartesian starting point of making thought conform to reality. Kant nevertheless always started with the dualism of knowledge and reality, making the latter, as things in themselves, beyond the grasp of the former. He nevertheless saw the essential relation between thought and

---

2   See also Jones (1905b, 1909, 1910).
3   See, for example, Jones (1883; repr. 1997). Jones could refer to him as "the philosopher who more than any other represented the stupidity of the English people" (Jones, 1908a). Also see Jones (1910: 43).
4   See, for example, Jones (1891, 1893, 1895a, 2004).

reality, but it never became so essential to him to as to be *constitutive* of both terms. In discovering over and over again that each term only had meaning in relation to its opposite, Kant's philosophy implied what was to become explicit in Hegel, namely, the subordination of terms to their unity and regarding them as elements in the unity: "Kant's task to the end was that of reconciling differences, that of Hegel was to differentiate a unity" (Jones, 2004: 121).

Jones's self-confidence, commanding presence and resolution of will, while positive in helping him overcome the disadvantages of his background and stand against the narrowness of religious dogma, nevertheless made him less sympathetic to tendencies of thought that turned away from Hegelianism. He was aware of this failing and much regretted it (Jones, 1921a).[5] Jones was dismissive of the opponents of Idealism who he believed were wholly preoccupied with criticism, and contributed nothing to the development of philosophical enquiry (Jones, 1909a: 12–13). The tendency was, he believed, towards dividing philosophy into special departments, exercising the duty to criticise, but not having the right. What he meant was that valid criticism must derive from "some consecutive and ultimately constructive theory of existence" (2004: 106–7). Critics knew that mind and its objects have to be reconciled, but they do nothing to bring about the reconciliation, and instead criticise Idealism from dualistic points of view (2004: 109). Jones addressed himself to critics close to home, those who were Idealists opposed to monism, such as Rudolf Lotze and Andrew Seth Pringle-Pattison, or critics like James Martineau and L.T. Hobhouse, who, although not overt Idealists, had sympathy with certain of its doctrines. The principal exception he made was a sustained attack on Herbert Spencer (1883), whose inimical and pervasive influence he deplored, and, more than any other thinker, represented "the stupidity of the English people" (1908a: 8).

Jones was a social liberal and, were it not for the class analysis and class conflict preached by socialism, he could easily have found a home in the Labour Party. Political activism was a hallmark of all but a few British Idealists, but there were none more socially committed, more patriotic, and more idealistic in the political sense than Jones. He was small of stature, but had huge presence and personality which inspired audiences wherever he spoke, and inspired his students to devote themselves to "good works" and public service—among them Thomas Jones, who influenced government thinking on social policy for more than four decades. Because Henry Jones preached idealism with the fervour and conviction of a

---

5   In a similar vein, Jones wrote to his son, H.H. Jones, "I have far too little respect for the ordinary run of professional philosophers, nor have I taken enough trouble to follow what younger men have had to say. I don't want any philosophy or poetry except the very best and I want it stored for a while like port wine" (Jones, 1921b).

prophet, he could also just as easily turn people against him. He supported the British cause in the First World War, and lost one of his own sons in the carnage, as did Seth Pringle-Pattison, and he could barely tolerate those young men who did not volunteer to do their duty. Among them was John Anderson whom Jones scorned for not wearing a uniform to one of his classes. Anderson never forgave him, and in Sydney, where he was a leading Marxist and the founder of the school of Australian Realism, the enemy was always idealism in its various guises, whether it was those who represented it in Adelaide and Melbourne, such as William Mitchell or W.G. Boyce Gibson, or those, such as Green who encapsulated its spirit. Anderson lectured on Green well into the 1940s.

Like Caird, Jones littered his philosophical writings and speeches with religious and poetic references, refusing to acknowledge artificial divisions in the unity of experience as a whole. Poetry could in its imagery lead us to the same truths as philosophy, but without the endless argumentation. This was possible because, in his view, all modes of thought were converging upon a common form of explanation, that of evolution. It was to be found in the sciences, particularly biology, in poetry, politics, religion and philosophy, and when understood correctly, it amounted to nothing more than the Hegelian principle of emanation. Evolution was a powerful colligating hypothesis in terms of which to understand the universe, and instead of explaining the later stages of the process in terms of the earlier, the earlier was conceived as having the latter nascent in it. The higher explains the lower, and not the lower the higher, as Darwin and Spencer maintained.[6] Although in one sense it could be said that all the disciplines were converging on the "Truth", in so far as a coherent and unified understanding was emerging, Jones nevertheless believed that our understanding and investigation of the universe rests on postulates, colligating hypotheses, or unquestioned assumptions, such as the unity of experience, and the immanence of God expressing himself in us and through us. Truth is never a destination, we are always on the way to achieving it, and philosophy is never a finished system with ultimate validity, and those who think it is have misunderstood the nature of metaphysical enquiry (Jones, 1893: 161).

---

6   For a fuller discussion of the issues, see Boucher (1992, 1997).

The Nature of Philosophy and the Unity of Experience

Consistent with the character of Idealism, Jones contends that philosophy is a process—not a fixed system—that takes as its task reflection upon experience. Philosophy lifts the given in experience to consciousness and reflection, and does not rely upon anything outside of experience upon which to base its conclusions (Jones, 1893: 162).[7]

The hypothesis of unity is, for Jones, the prerequisite of all Idealist philosophy.[8] Unity, or the idea of "a One in the Many" (Jones, 1910: 205), is not opposed to difference, but is not content with abstract dualisms, such as those between the mind and its objects, the subjective and objective, or appearance and reality (Jones, 2004: 292). When faced with a dualism, the unity that transcends it does not obliterate the opposites. It is one of the opposites itself, which includes, or presupposes, its correlative opposite. The fact that opposites mutually implicate each other and are correlative does not mean that they are co-ordinate. Furthermore, from acknowledging the existence of differences, or opposites, it cannot be assumed that knowledge entails unifying differences, nor does it entail colligating discrete entities into coherent systems. If we acknowledge that opposites are correlative and mere abstractions if taken in themselves, then the question of "bringing them together cannot arise" (Jones, 1909a: 266). In fact, the relation between the self and not-self, for example, needs to be interpreted differently. The not-self only finds meaning in the self, and it is the self which unites and identifies the not-self with itself. On the principle of identity in difference, or unity in diversity, Jones argued that: "*Spirit comprises its differences without annulling them*: it possesses them and yet distinguishes them from itself" (Jones, 1905a: 33).

Because the universe is a unity, there is no absolute distinction between the modes of thought by which we comprehend it. Science, poetry, religion and philosophy, all sovereign in their own right, are not autonomous alternative conditions of life, but instead differing and mutually inclusive aspects that complement, rather than rival, each other (Jones 1896: 4). Art, morality and philosophy, for example, do not have separate objects. Each is not restricted to the separate spheres of beauty, the good, and knowledge, respectively. They are pervasive throughout the whole of reality. For Jones, there is an "ultimate affinity" between all forms of experience. Their insights are reasoned expressions of the intelligibility of the universe (Jones, 1905c: 6). In other words, they may reach the same conclusions as philosophers, having travelled to them by different routes. Poetry, for example, "reaches the results of philosophy by short cuts, and without the

---

7   This section draws upon some of the material used in Boucher (1990) and Boucher and Vincent (1993: chapter 2).
8   See Jones (1904–5: 452; 1906–7: 761).

endless linkage of argumentation" (Jones, 1902: vii).[9] Poets are the first to apprehend the greatest philosophical ideas (Jones, 1896: 31). In Britain, the poets Browning, Wordsworth and Tennyson, and its literary heroes Carlyle and Coleridge, have comprehended far greater truths than the unadventurous British philosophers, stultified by caution (Jones 1902: vii–viii), and incapable of reaching such truths. The time, Jones believed, was propitious to restore to humanity "the consciousness of the unity of the world..." (Jones, 1893: 170).

Poetry and philosophy are not distinct modes of thought and in the great philosophers they are almost indistinguishable (Jones, 1909a: 10, 153–60). The unity of poetry and philosophy, and their intimate affinities with the other forms of experience, were daily being vindicated, in that they were all converging upon, and working through, the same hypotheses. The concurrence of conclusions in science, religion, art and philosophy was testimony for Jones that they were coming closer to the very heart of reality itself. Their purpose, he maintained, was "to reveal unity in difference, whether that unity be a law of thought, or a principle of life" (Jones, 1909a: 208).

In Jones's view, if reality was to be intelligible, modern philosophy had to assume that it is a rational system whose organizing principle reveals itself in every part.[10] The universe is a rational or spiritual unity. The hypothesis that art, morality, philosophy and religion all hold is "that this world of ours and the soul of man are saturated with spiritual significance" (Jones, 1909a: 145). The rational interpretation of this spiritual unity must assume that its subject-matter is itself rational. The occasion for knowledge is destroyed if the rationality of the universe is denied (Jones, 1909a: 271). This, of course, is the Hegelian principle that the Real is the Rational, and it is subject to the same qualification. Jones's philosophy of history postulates the idea that Freedom is gradually revealing itself in the world. Under oriental despotism no one was free, in the Greco-Roman world some were free, namely citizens, and in the modern world all are free. That which contributes to the gradual revelation of freedom is real, and therefore rational. Slavery in the ancient world was real because it saved thousands of prisoners from being slaughtered, and hence contributed to the march of freedom on earth. Slavery in the modern world is an affront to the freedom achieved and is not therefore rational. That which fails to contribute to the revelations of freedom merely exists, and cannot claim rationality. In other words, not everything that exists is rational, only the real is rational. For Jones, the hypothesis of the existence of God and of the spiritual unity of the universe is a condition of all rational experience, and is thus not just an hypothesis, but "an absolute postulate"

9   Cf. Jones (1924: 58, 205, 225).
10 See Jones (1895a: 372–5; 1902–3; 1910).

(1909a: 296), whose loss would constitute the loss of the significance of life (1909a: 198).

Idealism is a profoundly religious philosophy in the hands of Jones and the principle of the unity and spiritual purpose of the universe is exactly that "hypothesis of the Nazarene teacher as to the nature of God" (Jones 1909a: 296). You could not be on firmer philosophical ground than that occupied by Jesus, "the ancient idealist" and forerunner of Hegel's teachings. Jesus himself subscribed to the principle of "the real is the rational" when, in far more eloquent language, he contended that "The earth is the Lord's, and the fullness thereof" (Jones, 1895b: 10). Jones, who rejected Divine Transcendence, argued that Jesus was not set apart, nor differentiated, from humanity by his divinity and unity with God. Jesus revealed to us the divine character of our own natures. There is something of the Divine in all of us. Divine and human nature are unified in the love that God had for Jesus, and that both have for humanity (Jones, 1909b: 106). In the Absolute, humanity is emotionally and intellectually united. The love and truth of men and women are no different in character from God's, with the exception that God is the ideal manifest in His children. Human beings, on the other hand, are always in the process, or "on the way", to realizing this manifestation (Jones, 1896: 329). The process, although divine, is also human activity in that it is the free expression of spirit. The individual, in expressing the will of God, pursues his, or her, own highest will and, in conforming to the law which is his, or her, fundamental nature, obedience is offered to God. Drawing upon his familiar idealist doctrine of unity in diversity, Jones argues that: "The unity of divine and human within the spiritual life of man is a real unity, just because man is free; the identity manifests itself through the difference, and the difference is possible through the unity" (Jones, 1896: 341).

The Unity of experience in which spirit reveals itself in, and knows itself through, the expressions of individuals entails a further hypothesis upon which modern thought has converged, and in terms of which all experience is understood. In Jones's view, it was no coincidence that the idea of evolution should have become the dominant conception of the day (Jones, 1909a: 23), because it implies that very identity in difference that the spiritual unity of experience demands if it is to be conceived as a process being realised in the development of freedom and reason in the human character.[11]

Jones was at the forefront of applying philosophical principles to social and educational reform. He published four articles in the *Hibbert Journal* on "The Working Faith of the Social Reformer",[12] in which he argued for the relevance of philosophy in dispelling the confusions of metaphoric

---

11 See, for example, Jones (1896: 69, 195, 198,199, 1893. 164, and 1910. 100, 206, 220, 231, 255).
12 See Jones (1905–6: 42–62, 294–313, 550–69, 761–81). These articles are reprinted in Jones (1910).

language in the social sciences; discovering and articulating the ideals by which the social worker is motivated; and, explaining and justifying the extension of state action in prosecuting those ideals. The ideals, because they are social, are always moral, and any social enterprise promoted by the state is not to be welcomed or condemned as a matter of course but, instead, assessed in terms of its contribution to "moralising our social relations as they stand" (Jones, 1910: 114).

I now want to show how Jones applied his principles to a specific problem that was both theoretical and practical, and which had policy implications. The principle of the unity of experience predisposes Jones to employ a formalized method of analysis. He characteristically portrays each problem in terms of a dualism, for example, those between Nature and Spirit, subjective and objective, genetic and cultural and determinism, the cosmic and ethical processes, and Individualism versus Socialism. He then demonstrates how each side of the dualism is ill-conceived and misunderstood, and proceeds to arrive at a unity which demonstrates that both sides of the purported opposition are in fact one, and that neither is independent of, nor possible, without the other.

Heredity — Character and Environment

The questions posed by the debate over heredity were of crucial importance for social policy. The different answers had different implications for our conception of what a rational and responsible person is, and for his or her relation to society.

Jones, as a critic of naturalistic evolution and a proponent of "spiritual" evolution, used Hegelian principles in order to undermine Herbert Spencer's conception of a social organism. Social cohesiveness is an internal relation and not something imposed from outside. It is not accidental or fortuitous in that, should it be broken, the parts of the social organism are reduced to abstractions devoid of meaning (Jones, 1883: 193). If the whole and its parts — society and the individuals who comprise it — are severed from each other, they have no existence: "They exist in and through each other, and are constituted by their relation" (Jones, 1883: 208-9). In an allusion to the criticism by Personal Idealists that the Absolute Idealists diminish and destroy personality, Jones adds that this is not a denial of the individuality of the parts of the social organism. On the contrary, it is an affirmation of their mutual implication and acknowledgement that the welfare of each and the welfare of the whole are integrally connected. Such a view of society, of course, has implications for how one understands heredity. The issues revolve around both biological and social heredity, and this raises questions about biological and environmental determinism. One of the principal areas of debate concerned the issue of inherited character as a mechanism of social evolution.

Herbert Spencer gave emphasis to the survival of the fittest and natural selection as important evolutionary mechanisms, but they were not the whole story in the explanation of the process. Despite considerable evidence to the contrary and the importance of the theory of inheritance developed by the post-Darwinian August Weismann, Spencer clung tenaciously to the Lamarckian idea of inherited or acquired character.[13] An acquired character is a modification brought about by influences outside of an organism and believed to be transmittable to offspring. Devoted neo-Lamarckians, including Spencer, attributed mature moral sentiments and a strong sense of duty to the transmission of inherited characters. While Darwin never explicitly rejected it, the idea of inherited characters became less significant for him, whereas for Spencer it was at the basis of his whole system.[14]

Darwin's theory of inheritance relied upon the idea of pangenesis, which postulated that all cells throughout the body gave off gemmules that circulated and eventually came to rest in the germ-cells and were transmitted to offspring. Gemmules were purportedly given-off by all tissues at every stage of their development, and therefore every unit of the organism would be represented in the germ-cells at every stage of their development, capable of reproducing themselves, and enabling the characters of one generation to be perpetuated into the next (Doncaster, 1921: 140). Herbert Spencer, for example, used the case of a white woman married to a white man in the United States who reportedly gave birth to a black child some years after having sexual intercourse with a black man, as evidence of the existence and efficacy of pangenesis. The important point for Spencer was this: organs or parts of the body modified by use, disuse, healthy living or other external factors continuously give-off gemmules and thus are capable of being inherited.

For Spencer, the idea of inherited characters became the single most important issue in evolution. The answer to whether character could be inherited had important implications for how education, ethics, sociology and politics were to be conceived (Spencer, 1893a: 456). The implication was that the condition of those degenerate and poor, having inherited certain characters (including moral character), should not be alleviated for fear of perpetuating undesirable traits.[15]

Discoveries of the common properties of cells in cytology, systematized in the work of Weismann, undermined the scientific basis of the theory of inherited characters. He was an admirer of Darwin, but rejected his theory

---

13   For an excellent account of the Spencer/Weismann debate see Freeman (1974).
14   Spencer (1887: iv) makes this quite clear.
15   The opposite, of course, could also be contended. Jensen (under the pseudonym of H. Ingerman) believed that the modification of the environment by socialism would introduce for the common good admirable, worthy habits and high ideals with the propensity to become inherited by the human race. See Jensen (1909: 20).

of gemmules as "wholly imaginary" (Weismann, 2003: xiii). Weismann was a proponent of the self-sufficiency of natural selection as the only mechanism of evolution, and thus a critic both of Darwin and Spencer. Darwin had thought that Spencer's "physiological units" were very like his gemmules. They are similar in that they assume small units multiplying by fusion, but are nevertheless quite different. As Weismann puts it: "Spencer's units are the elements which exclusively compose the living body; while Darwin's gemmules only give rise to cells, i.e., they are elements which are present for the special purpose of bringing about heredity, without anything being specified as to their share in the composition of the living body" (Weismann, 2003: 6).

Put simply, Weismann maintained that that part of "germ-cells" collectively responsible for heredity is "germ-plasm" or "soma", while the remainder of the body comprises "body-plasm". Germ-plasms — or, as he came to call them, "ancestral germ plasms" or "*ids*" (Weismann 2003: 12) — are contained in the chromosomes in the nucleus of the cell. Weismann contended that germ-plasm is distinct from the body-plasm, and therefore acquired modifications to the body cannot be transmitted because the reproductive germ-cells are unaffected. Germ-plasm gives rise to body-plasm, but not *vice versa*. Reproductive germ cells contain within themselves that which is to be transmitted and are unaffected by the environment. The child is like the parent because of germinal continuity, i.e., not because the body produces its own germ-plasm, but because parents and children are produced from the same pool of germ-plasm. Weismann's hypothesis to account for variation is that, since each individual contains different combinations of ancestral germ-plasm, there will be variations in the development of their bodies.

Weismann encountered a good deal of opposition. Romanes defended the idea of inherited character in the name of Darwin, and Haeckel took Darwin's conclusions to new and misleading extremes (Di Gregorio, 1894: 134). Spencer was foolish enough to attack Weismann's theory, and in the exchange which ensued further discredited the validity of his own scientific hypotheses.[16]

In sum, the conclusions drawn were that the environment had no appreciable effect upon the child, who is almost wholly the product of the potential encoded in the genetic make-up of his or her forebears. The environment provided the opportunity for the flourishing of inherent traits, but could not initiate anything new, nor stimulate development beyond an inherited capacity. A capacity may, over successive genera-

---

16 See Spencer (1893b),Weismann (1893), Spencer (1894), Weismann (1895), and Spencer (1895). In coming to understand the terms of reference of the controversies surrounding the evolution debate in the nineteenth century, I have benefitted enormously from reading Freeman (1974) and Richards (1987).

tions, become accentuated by means of natural selection, bringing about internal genetic modifications, ostensibly unaffected by external environmental factors.

Jones's approach to the problem was to set out the dualism between, on the one hand, a character that is genetically fixed, and, on the other hand, one that is moulded by environmental factors—that is, the dualism between Nature and Nurture. Both views undermine our conception of the person as a free and rational moral agent. Both views deny the possibility of a moral character capable of self-improvement. The significance of this, of course, casts doubt on the Victorian reverence for character which implied the suppression of animal instincts, and the promotion of self-improvement, individual self-consciousness, manifesting itself in individual responsible behaviour (Collini, 1980: 217). Individuality simply meant self-realisation in the context of social relations.[17]

How, then, could the opposition between character and environment be transcended, and at the same time preserve the idea of free moral agency? Character and environment, he argued, constitute a unity whose relation is not one of mutual exclusion, but instead one of mutual inclusion (Jones, 1910: 52). For Jones, the denial of the inheritance of acquired characters in itself was an important conclusion because, far from diminishing the importance of heredity, it gave emphasis to all those aspects of character that were biologically inherited. Jones was typical of idealists in subscribing to the idea of the socially constituted self. Apart from our social relations, human beings are nothing. Our minds and bodies owe everything to the sustenance of the social environment. Jones contended: "Organised society is the means of all our knowing and the impelling power of all our doing"; "[W]e literally owe our soul to our environment" (Jones, 1913: 27 and 32).[18] When we are born, we begin as moral entities, but not as mere receptacles into which to pour the social inheritance. Moral theory must reconcile individualism with the social elements of our character. The individual and society, or character and environment, are not opposed. Darwinian evolution, in giving emphasis to the adaptation of character to environment, has minimised the extent to which *we* adapt the environment to our characters. Character and environment are related, not by mutual exclusion, but by mutual inclusion. The power and meaning of both lies in their relation. The social environment is not a causal factor in the development of character, but a condition which facilitates and circumscribes the sorts of development that can take place (Jones, 1889: 5). We do not inherit tendencies, but potential faculties. We may vary in the capacities we inherit, but it is only by means of interaction with the environment that we can achieve self-realization. The larger the inherited

---

17 See Vincent and Plant (1984: 101–12) and Freeden (1978: 170–7).
18 See Jones (1919a: 178) and Jones (1919b: 94).

powers and capacities, the greater is the opportunity that any given environment brings. The more meagre the inherited endowment, the less the environment can do to develop or repress it. Jones argues:

> And relative to his animal progenitors, it is because the hereditary powers of the child are so great that the nature of his environment is so important. You can swing a canary's cage in the most immoral surroundings without detriment to the bird; but to place the child there is to come near to making a calamitous result inevitable. (Jones, 1910: 170)

The human spirit mediates the environment in being conscious of it, and the social world is constituted anew as it is mediated in every individual's mind and will. In internalizing the world we infuse it with spiritual significance, elevating it to a higher plane and realising our own selves in the process.[19] The moral attributes constitutive of character are not inheritable. Good and evil are values that structure peoples' lives, and have no existence apart from those who will them; they presuppose rational will. We inherit capacities, or powers — a constitution — that flourishes when in contact with the social and physical environment. What the individual inherits, in addition, is not a moral character or the vices of the parents, but a social legacy of language, culture, morality and political traditions which provide the conditions of personal spiritual growth. The inherited social tradition is recreated in each act of appropriation, and constitutes a partnership between the generations. Society is a moral partnership, and each person constituted of and by it, is his or her own society individuated. Rational self-consciousness is the organic relation that makes moral life possible in the social whole. Social relations are not a qualification of, nor addenda to, individual human personality; they are "the inmost content and reality of it" (Jones, 1910: 233). The social organism is neither biological nor mechanical. It is a self-conscious unity of free individuals upon which morality is conditional, and from which duties and obligations follow and form the very cohesiveness of society. Individual and social welfare, individual aims and purposes, are inseparable from the welfare and aims of the whole (Jones, 1883: 200, 207, 209). Free will, upon which society and the individual are premised, is negated if it is allowed that antecedent inherited character or external environment determines the will. Consciousness mediates, converting the antecedent and external into the self, making all action self-determined (Jones, 1888: 320–6). Freedom itself is not an adverbial addition to our character, but an achievement which is always in the process of making. It is a power or capacity that uses the environment in the unending process of realising itself through reason.

The significance of the new findings about the genetic material coded into the germ-plasm, and thus the strength of Weismann, was that, in the

---

19 See Jones (1913: 31–2) and Jones (1910: 48, 52, 56, 169; Jones, 1883: 197–9; Jones, 1912: 33).

political sphere, one could argue that the moral characteristics of the parents are not inherited by the child, but acquired as a result of the environment interacting with and producing character; if one brought up the offspring of criminal and degenerate parents in a different environment, its character would not be tainted by those of its parents. We cannot assume, Jones contended, that evil dispositions are inherited and will surface in the child irrespective of the environment. It is such an assumption that has deterred the better-off classes in society from adopting the offspring of the poor, for fear that their characters may manifest the "tendencies which destroyed their parents" (Jones, 1910: 160). Jones contends that: "each child is a new beginning; and the way to virtue, so far as internal conditions are concerned, is as open to the child of the wicked as it is to the child of the virtuous" (Jones, 1910: 176).

Spencer's harsh social theories concerning the improvement of the moral fibre of the human stock of society by means of the principle of the survival of the fittest could, therefore, be dismissed with reference to the new biological evidence. Jones took every opportunity to emphasise that people were aware that, through social legislation, the human will could make a difference to the condition and moral character of the poor. For example, during his lecture tour of Australia, he spoke in Sydney on the relation between the child and heredity. He argued that legislation cannot directly improve character, but it could improve the environment upon which character depends for its development. The child is shaped by the environment that retards or promotes the realization of potential. Heredity, Jones argues, has little to do with what a child is. The child's character is the result of the interdependence between child and environment, first around the hearth of the fire, and then within the society as a whole. Wise legislation should be used to improve homes and the general conditions under which people live. Such legislation was imperative because, once a character had been formed, there was little that anyone could do to change it. In Adelaide, Jones contended that the bad will has an alchemic effect upon the opportunities afforded it and transforms them into its own baseness. The social conditions for improvement must be laid in youth, and examples set which the child can strive to emulate. This was the view he had expressed at the annual conference of the Charity Organization and Relief Societies eleven years earlier, when he declared his lack of faith in charity that was not informed by an understanding of social principles. Charity which did not discriminate between those whom it was helping encouraged pauperism and increased poverty, thus injuring both the recipient and the community. The most important aim of the statesman and the social reformer, Jones believed, was to reform character.[20]

---

20 See Jones (1908b, 1908c, 1897: 33, 39–40).

References

Boucher, D. (1990), "Practical Hegelianism: Henry Jones's lecture tour of Australia", *Journal of the History of Ideas*, 51, pp. 423-52.

Boucher, D. (1992), "Evolution and Politics: The Naturalistic, Ethical and Spiritual Bases of Evolutionary Arguments", *The Australasian Journal of Political Science*, 27, pp. 87-103.

Boucher, D. (1997), "Introduction", in D. Boucher (ed.), *The British Idealists* (Cambridge: Cambridge University Press, 1997), pp. xiv—xx.

Boucher, D. and Vincent, A. (1993), *A Radical Hegelian: The Political and Social Philosophy of Henry Jones* (Cardiff: University of Wales Press).

Collini, S. (1980), "Political Theory and the 'Science of Society' in Victorian Britain", *The Historical Journal*, 23, pp. 203-31.

Di Gregorio, M. (1984), *T. H. Huxley's Place in Natural Science* (New Haven: Yale University Press).

Doncaster, L. (1921), *Heredity in the Light of Recent Research* (Cambridge: Cambridge University Press).

Freedon, M. (1978), *The New Liberalism* (Oxford: Oxford University Press).

Freeman, D. (1974), "The Evolutionary Theories of Charles Darwin and Herbert Spencer", *Current Anthropology*, 15, pp. 211-34.

Hegel, G.W.F. (1952), *The Philosophy of Right*, tr. by T.M. Knox (Oxford: Clarendon Press).

Jensen, H. (1909), *The Rising Tide* (Sydney: Workers Trust).

Jones, H. (1883), "The Social Organism", in A. Seth and R.B. Haldane (eds.), *Essays in Philosophical Criticism* (London: Longmans), pp. 187-213; reprinted in D. Boucher (ed.), *The British Idealists* (Cambridge: Cambridge University Press, 1997).

Jones, H. (1888), "Morality as Freedom", *Time* (London).

Jones, H. (1889), *Wales and Its Prospects* (Wrexham: no date; preface dated 1889).

Jones, H. (1891), *Browning as a Philosophical and Religious Teacher* (Glasgow: Maclehose).

Jones, H. (1893), "The Nature and Aims of Philosophy", *Mind*, n.s. 2.

Jones, H. (1895a), *A Critical Account of the Philosophy of Lotze: The Doctrine of Thought* (Glasgow: Maclehose).

Jones, H. (1895b), "The Higher Learning in its bearing upon National Life in Wales, an address delivered June 28, 1895" (Bangor: University College of North Wales).

Jones, H. (1896), *Browning as a Philosophical and Religious Teacher* 3rd ed. (Glasgow: Maclehose).

Jones, H. (1897), "Corporate and Individual Charity", Sixth Annual Conference of the Charity Organization and Relief Societies of the U.K. (Glasgow).

Jones, H. (1902), "Introduction", in P. Janet and G. Séailles, *A History of the Problems of Philosophy* (London: Macmillan).

Jones, H. (1902-3), "The Present Attitude of Reflective Thought Towards Religion", *Hibbert Journal*, 1, pp. 228-52.

Jones, H. (1904-5), "Mr. Balfour as Sophist", *Hibbert Journal*, 3.

Jones, H. (1905a) *The Philosophy of Martineau* (London, Macmillan, 1905).

Jones, H. (1905b), *Social Responsibilities: Lectures to Businessmen* (Glasgow: Maclehose).

Jones, H. (1905c), *The Immortality of the Soul in the Poems of Tennyson and Browning* (London: Philip Green).

Jones, H. (1905-6), "The Working Faith of the Social Reformer", in four parts, *Hibbert Journal*, 4, pp. 452-77.

Jones, H. (1906-7), "Divine Immanence", *Hibbert Journal*, 5.

Jones, H. (1908a), "The Growth of Freedom", *Sydney Morning Herald*, 15 July.

Jones, H. (1908b) "Evolution of Man", *Brisbane Courier*, 1 August.

Jones, H. (1908c), "Child and Home", *Sydney Morning Herald*, 9 July.

Jones, H. (1909a), *Idealism as a Practical Creed* (Glasgow: Maclehose).

Jones, H. (1909b), "The Idealism of Jesus", *Hibbert Journal*, supplement for 1909, 81-106.

Jones, H. (1910), *The Working Faith of the Social Reformer* (London: Macmillan).

Jones, H. (1912), "The Immanence of God and the Individuality of Man", Provincial Assembly Lecture, Manchester (Manchester: Rawson).

Jones, H. (1913), *Social Powers; three popular lectures on the environment, the press and the pulpit* (Glasgow: Maclehose).

Jones, H. (1919a), *The Obligations and Privileges of Citizenship – a plea for the study of social science: Three lectures inaugurating the Sharp Lectureship in Civics and Philanthropy, Rice Institute Studies*, VI.

Jones, H. (1919b), *Principles of Citizenship* (London: Macmillan, 1919).

Jones, H. (1921a), Letter from Henry Jones to Lord Haldane, 2 June 1921. NLS, Ms 5915, fols. 35 and 36.

Jones, H. (1921b), Letter from Henry Jones to H.H. Jones, 25 July 1921, Thomas Jones Collection, Class U, vol iii, fol. 228/2. National Library of Wales.

Jones, H. (1922), *A Faith That Enquires: The Gifford Lectures delivered in the University of Glasgow in the Years 1920 and 1921* (London: Macmillan).

Jones, H. (1924), *Essays on Literature and Education* (London: Hodder and Stoughton).

Jones, H. (2004), "Idealism and Epistemology", in D. Boucher (ed.), *The Scottish Idealists* (Exeter: Imprint Academic); originally published in *Mind* n.s. 2 (1893).

Metz, R. (1938), *A Hundred Years of Philosophy* (London: Allen and Unwin).

Richards, R. (1987), *Darwin and the Emergence of Evolutionary Theories of Mind and Behaviour* (Chicago: University of Chicago Press).

Spencer, H. (1887), *The Factors of Organic Evolution* (London, Williams and Norgate).

Spencer, H. (1893a), "The Inadequacy of 'Natural Selection', II", *Contemporary Review*, 63.

Spencer, H. (1893b), "Professor Weismann's Theories", *Contemporary Review*, 64.

Spencer, H. (1894), "Weismann Once More", *Contemporary Review*, 66.

Spencer, H. (1895), "Heredity Once More", *Contemporary Review*, 68.

Vincent, A. and Plant, R. (1984), *Philosophy, Politics and Citizenship* (Oxford: Blackwell).

Weismann, A. (2003), *The Germ-Plasm: A Theory of Heredity* (Bristol: Thoemmes Press); originally published (London: Walter Scott, 1893).

Weismann, A. (1893), "The All-sufficiency of Natural selection: A reply to Herbert Spencer", *Contemporary Review*, in two parts, 64.

Weismann, A. (1895), "Heredity Once More", *Contemporary Review*, 68.

Leslie Armour

Metaphysics, Morals, and Politics
McTaggart's Theory of the Good and the Good Life

Introduction

J.M.E. McTaggart's moral and political views have occasioned surprise and even consternation. People are used to fitting political views into a few common clusters and McTaggart's do not fit in any. Moral theories based on metaphysics are no longer common, and McTaggart's is unashamedly and unabashedly metaphysical. Finally, many of McTaggart's beliefs seem paradoxical.

Like most radical conservatives, he believed that all values in the end attach to individuals; the only values are the states of mind of sentient creatures.[1] But like most communitarians, he believed that human beings — indeed all sentient creatures — are tied together by unbreakable bonds and that these communities are what make their lives worth while.[2]

He was a traditionalist who revelled in the ceremonies and small politenesses of the Cambridge society within which he lived most of his life and believed that much of what was good in it was founded on tradition. Yet he battled for the admission of women and for women's rights generally and almost always for the rights of underdog.

He was a rationalist who had mystical experiences and who believed that the most important thing in the world was the emotion of love, and his marriage to Elizabeth "Daisy" Bird, a New Zealand woman with whom he shared all that he did, was said to be idyllic. But though they lived a very

---

1 See McTaggart (1934a).
2 This view is rooted in McTaggart (1918: 151–96), but its metaphysics is developed in *The Nature of Existence*, Vol. 2, Ch LXIV, in which McTaggart tries to show that "the value of a whole is not in any or all of its parts" (1927: §788). His argument in essence is that the highest order values are those of love. All the love is "in" the individuals and yet the total value depends on their relations even though the *totality as such* has no value. But one must be careful. Though in (1918: 189) McTaggart insists that the ultimate end of political life is an organic society and also that the only way to it is through our present society, he denies that it is right to make our *present* society an end. In the First World War, patriotism may have dimmed his vision, but I think he would always have maintained this view.

quiet and private life, this did not blind him to the concerns of others, and, at a time when it was very unpopular to do so, he defended the rights of homosexuals.

His own thinking was rooted in the work of Hegel,[3] but his long critique of Hegel led him to revise much that that philosopher said and to abandon the rest, including the theory of the Absolute. His own metaphysical idealism was unyielding and yet he incorporated ideas from his "realist" Cambridge colleagues, especially Bertrand Russell (who had been his pupil) and G. E. Moore.[4]

Finally, he believed in moral responsibility and opposed "fatalism". Nevertheless he insisted that he was a kind of determinist himself, and he believed in the importance of the future — although his most celebrated argument was intended to prove that time is unreal.[5]

His writings were deeply metaphysical, and yet his interest was practical. For he was concerned with the idea of the good life and the means by which we might live it. I shall argue that this was not a man fraught with tensions and forced by them into contradictions, though it requires careful thought to see how the bits might be put together.

McTaggart's theory of the good life is metaphysical. He thinks, that is, that if you understand the ultimate nature of reality, you will understand how to conduct your own affairs and how to participate in the life of your community.

The truth about the universe is that it consists of timeless loving spirits; the truth about us is that we are caught in an illusion of time and separation. The good life consists of seeing through the illusion as best we can.

McTaggart's argument is that anyone who understands his metaphysics will see at once the general outlines of the good life, though he would have been the first to deny that morality can be reduced to a set of simple rules.

---

3   The way that he develops his own moral views in relation to Hegel can be seen best in McTaggart (1918), especially in Chapter IV.

4   Peter Geach (1979: 174-5) has suggested that McTaggart was unduly influenced by Moore's ethics. Moreover, McTaggart's famous argument about the unreality of time owes much to Russell's account of definition, and McTaggart's account of the irreducibility of first person statements derives from Russell's accounts of egocentric particulars.

5   "Fatalism", e.g., the doctrine that it was always necessary that Napoleon should die on a certain day — an "event fixed independently of all other events" — is explicitly attacked in McTaggart (1906: §139, p. 170). The Napoleon example appears in a footnote. Yet McTaggart insists there and in (1921; 1927), that determinism is true in the sense that all events have causes. I shall argue that the resolution of this seeming contradiction lies in the fact that McTaggart, in a grand Cambridge tradition that goes back to Ralph Cudworth in the seventeenth century, was an *organic determinist,* i.e., he believed that individual organisms are determined by their own natures. Squaring these elements of a more common *systematic determinism* which applies to the whole of reality will require some attention. The final version of the argument about time occupies Chapters XXXIII and LI in Vol. II of *The Nature of Existence,* but "the futurity of the whole" is the subject matter of Chapter LXI. Geach (1979: 170) quotes McTaggart as saying "Heaven is as future as tomorrow's breakfast." McTaggart (1934b) insists that there is a causal relation between eternity and what appears in time, and that the future is the most important direction.

Very much of the discussion which follows must be addressed to the relevant questions of metaphysics and its bearing on ethics and politics. I shall almost always simply describe what McTaggart says and does, but on two occasions — in the account of "determining correspondence" and in the account of "time" — I shall suggest a way of rescuing vital steps in his argument without which his system would, I think, collapse.

The heart of the matter for McTaggart is that all the value of the world is in the conscious states of sentient beings and that the most valuable of such states is love. Love is a relation of perfect sharing, such that each participant enjoys the experience of the other and neither seeks any advantage beyond this sharing (1921–7: §460–70). He says "love is a liking which is felt for persons, and which is intense and passionate" (1921–7: §460). He goes on to say that it is neither benevolence nor sympathy. Benevolence he thinks of as a desire to do good to others, while love is an emotion. We may desire to do good for those we do not love and, though sympathy is an emotion which goes with love, we may also have sympathy for those we do not love. Finally, love is not necessarily associated with pleasure. It is precisely the feeling of sharing in extreme intimacy, of being so conjoined that the other person is almost (but not quite) a part of ourselves (1921–7: §469). In the end, "no condition [is] necessary for love except that the lover should be conscious of his unity with the beloved" (1921–7: §470). Notice that it is the *sharing* and not some perceived quality that McTaggart thinks makes for love. It would be bad taste to say, "I only love her because she has such good legs" and strange to say "I only love her because she can resolve quadratic equations and understands quantum physics." And love, if it is genuine, is not wiped away by grey hair and wrinkles. But one must be wary. McTaggart wants lovers to keep their independence though they share their experiences. People have sometimes imagined being wholly absorbed into another being, especially God, but McTaggart believed that each centre of experience is timeless and is not only indestructible but has always existed, i.e. has existed at each moment of apparent time.

If we could grasp reality we would find, according to McTaggart, that we love many people intensely. We actually are closely related to one another in this way within apparently large defining groups of perceivers, and related only slightly less closely to all other perceivers. For McTaggart thinks that our love is most intense only for others whom we directly perceive (1921–7: §473). But he thinks that only illusion keeps us apart from those we directly perceive and, importantly, from those we shall eventually indirectly perceive and will love only somewhat less intensively.

Were we to experience reality we would neither have nor be able to conceive any desire for any other state except the one of intense love in which we found ourselves, and, therefore, it would be absurd to consider alternatives. The illusion is so great that we must struggle to imagine it.

Practically, both our own moral lives and our political existences reflect our illusions. Even in this illusory state, however, we can choose political relationships and systems which reflect both the fact that only individuals are loci and sources of value and the fact that the values we are most attached to are those that demand a community.

Our task, here, then is to look first at how McTaggart comes to this momentous — and surely, to a mind filled with up-to-date ideas, surprising — conclusion, and then to explore the way in which he believes that it enables him to construct a moral and political philosophy. Finally, I will try to dissolve the apparent paradoxes.

McTaggart's Metaphysics of Love

McTaggart believed that, at bottom, the timeless loving spirits that comprise the real are joined together in natural communities. How can he know that this is so? Apart from the fact that we do have some experience and know for this reason that something exists and that it has some degree of complexity, what we have to go on, in McTaggart's view, when we come to formulate descriptions of reality, are truths of a quasi-logical kind. When we formulate our moral and social concerns we do know, certainly, that we experience love and that we value it more highly than other experiences, but we do not know from experience that love is associated with the core of reality. Logically, we might always be deceived. It is what we can infer from a small number of basic principles to which we have logical commitments that should persuade us of the nature of reality.

In fact, McTaggart's metaphysics is based on a very small number of basic and seemingly innocent principles. It has been suggested by Peter Geach that there are only three.[6] More likely there are at least four and one other principle (which one might call a metaphysical principle of morals) which are necessary to make his ethics and his political philosophy work. But none of the principles is as simple as it looks.

The first principle, the principle of sufficient description, asserts simply that anything that is real must have what McTaggart called a description sufficient to distinguish it from everything else. The second is that reality consists of substances — the principle, as I shall call it, of substantial predication. The third is the principle of infinite divisibility. A fourth is the principle of determinacy. I will discuss these first, and leave the central value

---

6 Peter Geach says there are ultimately three principles: The principle of sufficient description, the principle that every substance has parts, and thus parts within parts *ad infinitum,* and the principle of ontological determinacy (see Geach [1979: 124]). I will argue there is also what I will call the principle of substantial predication, and that to make McTaggart's ethics work there has to be a principle of the value of consciousness.

principle, the metaphysical principle of morals — that consciousness is valuable and that its value is associated with love — for separate discussion.

The reasons that McTaggart gives for each principle are quasi-logical. He suggests — though he does not spell out his method — that in each case our discourse would become unintelligible without the principle in question. I call this "quasi-logical" because McTaggart most often does not try to prove that the denial of the principle would amount to a contradiction, though in some arguments, e.g. about time, he does draw on the claim that a contradiction would result from the denial.

The Principles of Sufficient and Exclusive Description and of Substantial Predication

The principle of sufficient description — which McTaggart calls the principle of "the dissimilarity of the diverse" (McTaggart, 1921: §99) — holds that if something exists it must be distinct. Now it is easy to find descriptions which *locate* things. Such accounts Bertrand Russell called *definite* descriptions. One and only one thing is "the oldest star in the galaxy", unless two or more are of the same age. Similarly, "fattest man in this room" will probably be good enough. If two men are equal in weight, we can add "the one with the Harvard Ph.D." and such until we get down to one. Some philosophers have thought that "definite descriptions" like this are enough, but McTaggart noted that while these are "exclusive descriptions", they are not "sufficient". They involve chains of descriptions. Other "substances" are involved — not just the oldest star, but the galaxy; not just the fattest man, but the room, and so on. Such chains must end somewhere, and anything that really exists as a distinct thing then must be a terminus of some such chain. What we need are descriptions that involve at least one characteristic which belongs to the particular substance and to no other. For unless something has some characteristic of its own, there must be a sense in which it does not really exist as a distinct entity. The characteristic cannot be just whatever is designated by a proper name — if there is any such characteristic[7] — for then it is in some sense empty. This is simple enough. As Peter Geach suggests, we could start with Adam and Eve and identify people by their place in that order. But this would not work if there were an infinite number of people.

McTaggart's beliefs about distinctness and identity stem from his views about what it is to exist, but they are also related to his moral and political

---

[7] If one says that one sees a red patch, "red patch" might just be a proper name like "Fido", or "red" might designate a place in the standard spectrum. In the "proper name" case, it represents one's decision. Your dog is named Fido if that is what you name it, just as the Queen Mary II has the name its owners and the Queen gave it. But there is not a characteristic "Fidoness" and the ship acquires no new character, except the character of having a name, when someone names it.

views, for they provide a world in which moral responsibility is possible. People exist as distinct agents, and their actions have precise outcomes.

We will see that his view about substances bears on his idea of love, and that the notion that people are not mere aggregates of characteristics is very important to him. Of course, on the face of it, most substances are not people, though McTaggart contends that the others are illusions. Nonetheless, it is his contention that there *are* an infinite number of substances. For he believes that a substance is anything that has qualities and relations but is not itself a quality or a relation and is also not a fact.[8]

Substantial Predication

We now need to explore the sorts of things that can have the necessary descriptions and be substances. One might think that there are only qualities in the world or qualities and relations. That is, if we start to describe the elephant in the zoo we may list his characteristics — greyness, four-leggedness, bad-temperedess, intelligence, and so on. And we may think that when we get them all listed there will be nothing left. Together, they *are the elephant*. But McTaggart says on the contrary, that, by and large, characteristics of the elephant cannot be predicated of one another. It is not the greyness that is four legged nor its intelligence that is bad-tempered. It is the elephant that has these things.

There is at least a very large class of things such that its members are particular occasions of or manifestations of various properties. Indeed the properties themselves only really exist as and when they are expressed, or at least as potentialities for expression. Such potentialities must themselves be particular features of reality, so McTaggart denied that there could be real "possibilities" if by that one means purely abstract entities not embedded in any reality. There may be exceptions in one sense. The property of abstractness must be in some sense real, but it applies to abstractions — to abstract things, if you like — and the notion of an abstract thing is one that many people, among them McTaggart, want to analyse away.

If it is true that one must have both characteristics — qualities and relations — and something in which they are instantiated in order to have anything in the world, then to get a description of anything, one must describe a complex relation or set of relations between a set of properties and an occasion when a thing occurs. Characteristics which are not attached to specific occurrences of things — redness, for instance — are open and vague. There is red hair and there are red balls, but nothing is "just red". There has to be some quantity of redness at a point in some system. (It is

---

8   This last qualification — not being a fact — was apparently added to *The Nature of Existence*, §67 by McTaggart himself. See Geach (1979: 43).

important to McTaggart that this need not be a spatio-temporal system.) Such points are particulars; McTaggart called them "substances".

The Principle of Divisibility

All such substances, in McTaggart's system, are "infinitely divisible" in some dimension.[9] This turns out to be very important. For it plays a crucial role, however surprising that may seem, in McTaggart's "timeless loving spirits" thesis.

Every substance will have at least one characteristic and, in McTaggart's view, it will have very many because it will have every characteristic, either positively or negatively. McTaggart insists that if Smith is not an elephant, then he has the characteristic of being a not-elephant. Furthermore, relations will exist between each and every quality and between every characteristic and the substance concerned. (Characteristics include relations and qualities—so there will be relations between relations as well as between one quality and another.)

For each relation, according to McTaggart, there is a relational property. If you are my brother, we share the relational property of brotherhood. Various forms of what McTaggart calls derivative and repeating characteristics are thus generated (1921: §85–92).

In the end, he thinks that if we make clear that a simple substance would be a substance with no content, and therefore not a substance at all, we can take this proposition as self evident (1921: §167). Some substances are differentiated from themselves in respect of their content. That is to say that there is a property of *being* substance x, and it is not a property or relation *of* that substance (i.e., a property or relation which *characterises* that substance), but it is rather the property of *being* that substance.

This seems clear enough for some substances. For instance, if Abelard loves Héloïse it is not some of her properties (or all of them together) that he loves, for then he would equally love someone else if they had the same properties, or might cease to love Héloïse if some of her properties changed.[10]

Are *all* substances so differentiated? Let us suppose that one is not. Now if anything changes in that universe, or if anything is different in any sense in that universe, our hypothetical substance would cease to be. For any change would bring about a change in its relational properties—and then, on this hypothesis, it would be a *different* substance. But that would mean that it was not a substance within the meaning of the earlier argument

---

9   The idea of a "dimension" is essentially the idea of a property that varies in quantity or intensity and can be measured independently of all other properties. See McTaggart (1921: §162).
10 This is the view of people like McTaggart who think "till death do us part" is a sound doctrine. It is challenged by people who think that changes in characteristics justify divorce. But such people generally do not hold that they are married to everyone who might turn out to have a certain set of characteristics.

because it would exist only because its characteristics exist. This would make the existence of characteristics preeminent, that is, there would be no real substances, and we have seen that there must be.

Once we grant this, all that we need to get infinite divisibility is to show that each instantiated characteristic of a substance must itself *be* a substance with further division. Any instantiated characteristic is something that will have qualities and relations and an exclusive description. So the process is naturally repeating.

The Principle of Determinacy

Thus we have the principle of infinite divisibility, and this gives us three of the four principles. The fourth principle, the principle of determinacy, Geach urges, is necessary for McTaggart but not mentioned by him and, according to Geach, not finally justifiable. But he may be wrong about the last claim at least (Geach, 1979: Ch. 4).

McTaggart's theses so far entail that every property of every entity should be precisely describable. For this to be true, all such properties have to be determinate. There is a strong form and a weak form of this principle.

The strong form holds that predicates must not include logical alternands. That is, the characteristics of things are unitary, and things either have them or not. The weaker form admits that there are complex predicates and that things are not just A or B but may be A-or-B — that is, that they have options built into them. Those that are A-or-B can be either, independently of the causes that specify their existence conditions. Such properties seem to be required for quantum theory, for human freedom in the ordinary sense, and for the kinds of organic determinism that McTaggart subscribes to and that does not entail fatalism. McTaggart does not discuss the issue, but he is not committed to the strong form. The strong form would invalidate important elements in his philosophy.

What McTaggart opposed was the notion that whole universes or some things in them might be vague. It is true, of course, that when you look at a blue sky in which a white cloud is tinged with orange from the setting sun, it may be impossible to say exactly where the white ends and the orange begins. Painters struggle to convey this truth. But the blue patch and the orange patch are not, ultimately, *entities*. They are the visual effects of photons and water drops that are precisely determinate. In fact, properties become determinate because of certain relations to other properties. Redness does not exist vaguely in the universe but in precise patches with determinate limits which are determined by the other properties of red things.

A vital question is, evidently, just how does one property "determine" another. McTaggart seems to shed little light on this, but it would seem evident that the determination must, in his system, be quasi-logical. Sections 207 to 212 of *The Nature of Existence* deal with causality. Their upshot is that causality is really a relation of "intrinsic determination" between characteristics, i.e. qualities and relations. In McTaggart's view, every characteristic is what it is by virtue of its relation to all characteristics, but it is specifically the case that characteristics are linked by necessities that follow from the intrinsic nature of each of them, for his universe does not and cannot consist of chains of the push-pull "causation" that are traditionally called "efficient causation". His universe is not in time and does not have sequences of this sort. It is often thought that this would commit him to the fatalism he rejects, but it turns out that this is not so, for, though he does not say so, it turns out that what may be intrinsically determined are complex properties including alternands.

It is, in any case, McTaggart's view that it is a logical property of "existence" that the term applies only to entities which are not vague. For if vague things existed they would lack precise existence conditions and statements about them could not be said to be either true or false. McTaggart's certainty about this seems to have arrived simultaneously with his abandonment of the Hegelian dialectic.

Systems like Hegel's involve a dialectic in which there is a tension — for instance, between "being" and "nothing" — in which entities have a wavering existence. But philosophers sometimes fail to distinguish between vagueness and the possession of complex properties whose structure is expressible in the form of alternands — a-or-b or c-or-d-or-e, for instance. It was Hegel's contention that the dialectical tensions applied only to quasi-real entities short of the Absolute, and F.H. Bradley believed that the truly real was beyond the defects of vagueness. Both substituted the notion of "degrees of reality". So vague things just fall short of reality in the full sense. McTaggart denies the possibility of such degrees because he thinks that, in some root sense of "exists", everything intelligible must exist. Even illusions are what they are and have their own modicum of "existence", though only as misperceptions.

Properties become determinate by entering into relations with other properties. Redness and space-occupancy go together to make a red patch. We would have to ask if anything is ever finally determinate in this sense. In so far as entities are in time, they may not be fully or finally determinate because they seem to be in transition. If we follow a member of the class lepidoptera from egg to caterpillar to chrysalis to moth, we create the appearance of precise determinateness by freezing its development at crucial stages, but the underlying biological processes may prove more resistant, as Henri Bergson thought, to freezing like frames in a movie film. But McTaggart believed that time was unreal so this was not a problem for him.

If one puts all these conditions together what one gets is the requirement that a universe which contains an infinity of substances must have a sufficient description for each of its parts. But it would seem that an infinity of substances cannot be determined in this sense, for no list of determining conditions would be sufficient. There would always be some undetermined properties. In McTaggart's view, at any rate, the sufficient description would be infinitely long in a sense which made it vacuous: It would have no ending.

Determining Correspondence

This is what leads McTaggart to the celebrated doctrine of determining correspondence. He believed, that is, that this seeming impossibility had to be broken.

He believed that he could think of one and only one universe which would meet this condition. He offers both a technical description of the state of affairs and an example (1921: §195–206, 236). The technical description is quite simple. Suppose we have a whole with a set of parts, A, B, and C. (In fact, the number of parts can be infinite, McTaggart says.) Suppose, too, that A has a set of parts, and that B and C have sets of parts which exactly correspond to A's parts. Then suppose the correspondence between the two to be such that the nature of the parts of the parts is always determined by the original parts. This system can be extended to infinity, he says, in such a way that descriptions of one set of parts will determine descriptions of all the others.

This sounds puzzling, but the example McTaggart gives is not especially puzzling. The example represents the following situation: Imagine that there are in the universe three observers, A, B, and C. A perceives A's perceptions *and* B's perceptions. B perceives B's perceptions *and* A's perceptions. A perceives B's perceptions of A's perceptions. B perceives A's perceptions of B's perceptions. Equally, A and B perceive C's perceptions, C perceives his or her own perceptions *and* A's perceptions *and* B's perceptions — and so on for any combination of perceivers. This relation is continued to infinity (1921: §236).

It so happens that this example meets important conditions. We need to see just why, and what one ought to make of the fact. A perception is unique. You and I cannot have the same perceptions,[11] even if we have perceptions which have the same contents, for a perception is a content from a point of view. A perception of a perception, if such a thing exists, then, will

---

11   McTaggart does not, I think, address the problem of shared subjectivity. Many philosophers have held views that imply that God shares in each of our experiences. McTaggart's notion is that in reality we perceive one another's perceptions. This would fall short of a fully-shared subjectivity. Evidently McTaggart did not think this possible, though the matter deserves more exploration.

be just like the original perception except that it will have a different place in a certain order. It will therefore turn out that a description of the original perception together with a rule for generating the order of the perceptions of perceptions will, in fact, succeed in generating a description of the whole of the infinite series postulated. Thus we have a substance infinitely divisible in at least one dimension which nevertheless has a sufficient description. Or so one might think.

The difficulty with the example is this: It involves a series which is, indeed, infinite but whose members differ from one another by reason of their place in the series and in no other way. Here we have a case in which, apparently, context makes no difference. But, if that is so, then the principle of the dissimilarity of the diverse—the notion that if A and B are genuinely two things then they must be different in some respect—is false. And McTaggart was firmly committed to this principle.

In fact, alas, McTaggart would appear to have succeeded not in dissolving the contradiction but in denying one horn of the dilemma. What he is saying is that one perception is so like another that a perception of a perception is identical with the original perception. Thus we can understand how there can be an infinite series with a sufficient description. Such a description is necessarily finite, for otherwise it itself would go on to infinity without achieving the necessary determinateness.

This way out is too easy, for the argument was that reality *does* consist of an infinity of distinct things. To deny their distinctness is not an answer. Furthermore, the characteristics must be linked, as we saw, by some kind of logical necessity.

Now we do know something about how characteristics are linked. Basically they are linked in determinate-determinable hierarchies. That is, nothing is red unless it occupies a spatial surface. Nothing occupies a spatial surface unless it is part of a space-defining object. And so on until one reaches the "highest order determinable", the thing of which everything else is a determinate form.

What is needed for McTaggart's purpose is a series through which we may proceed by orderly and finite transformation rules from an original description to any member of an infinite series. Furthermore, this descent through a series must produce a series which meets the meaning conditions of a determinate/determinable hierarchy, for this is what is at issue: Reality does consist of determinate forms of determinable properties, and the properties must be linked in a logical order.

What might such a series be like? The uniqueness required to generate an infinity of descriptions must stem from something which by its nature must be unique. McTaggart was surely right to focus on perceptions. The problem is that perception is not enough.

The perceptions must have other characteristics as well. Perceptions, in so far as they are intentional activities of unique perceivers meet this requirement in a way which nothing else could. Each perception requires an "egocentric particular" to identify it. The claim that one must use an expression which stands for an egocentric particular to identify perceptions is related to but not identical with the claim that such expressions stand for some special entity. The particulars may be just original perceptions so far as the argument *here* goes, though the stronger doctrine — the doctrine that there must *be* an *ontological* self — can be defended. At any rate, of all the things which there are or might be in the universe, only perceptions are by their nature unique. Anything else can have more than one instance. Hydrogen atoms must be much like each other, geometrical shapes are universals, and so on. Actions are unique also in the sense that an act which is Smith's cannot also be Jones' act unless they are the joint authors. But actions are not objects. Nevertheless, McTaggart's notion of perception together with the notion of repeated quality will give us the clues which we need to find the solution.

If we conceive of the relevant series as consisting of experiences which are items of knowledge, and not *simply* systems of perception, we will get a series which may well have the required properties. Each experience is different from the one next to it because it represents a potential context which has become actualised by a specific content. In your life history, the potential for experiences which you started out with became actualised by the events which formed its content. Each experience was what it was and different from any other by reason of being your experience, being where it was in the sequence and so on.

Suppose we conceive of a universe whose primary parts consist of what we might call experience paths — each is a series of experiences or potential experiences which does or could compose the life and affairs of an individual. Now there is one perspective from which the universe consists of a set of events each of which is an experience. There is another from which, in this example, it consists of the lives and affairs of a set of persons. There is still another in which this set of persons, in turn, may be said to work out the destiny of civilisation, another from which they may be said to work out the destiny of human beings and so on. Each of these consists of a set of determinates of the next highest determinable. From any level, there could well be a set of finite rules determining two different things: (1) the way in which a given set of events determines the life of an individual, in which the lives of individuals determine the nature of a civilisation and so on, and (2) the ways in which one level generates the next. If this is true, then there would be a hierarchy which would meet McTaggart's conditions.

Thus it is possible that there is a world which meets McTaggart's conditions and does reconcile the alleged contradictions. It is somewhat more complicated than McTaggart supposed because it includes not only experiences (McTaggart's "perceptions" or whatever their real counterpart might be) but also knowledge. For one has knowledge when one understands how events go to form a human life of a certain sort, how lives of a certain sort go to make up civilisations and so on. (Notice: "go to make" does not imply a one-way relation. It may be that civilisations determine lives as much as lives determine civilisations, and that events shape our lives though our lives shape events. The relations, here, are more likely to be dialectical than anything else.) Knowledge does not consist in a mere accumulation of experience nor, one must surmise, in the mere delineation of rational principle.

There is, then, a universe which might meet the demands of the system so far developed, and a way of reading McTaggart which might sustain his position. The reader will already, I think, have concluded that many questions could still be raised about each of the basic principles and about their applications. *If* the argument stands, and *if* there is *only* one possible universe that meets the conditions, then, surely, as McTaggart thought, that is the universe that exists.

But most readers will hope that there is more to say. And there is. In fact, McTaggart was surely persuaded in part by his own mystical experiences — in the long Cambridge tradition of rational mysticism that goes back to Henry More — and by the fact that the most plausible theological tradition for understanding those experiences is that which holds, as Ralph Cudworth suggested, God is love.[12] McTaggart did not think there was a God, at least in the sense that there is a Master of the Universe. Though *Some Dogmas of Religion* assails traditional theism mercilessly on all possible grounds,[13] there is no doubt that McTaggart's main concern is that the reality of love is incompatible, as Cudworth thought, with the kind of Calvinist God who orders people about and determines everything. The love that we know in the world as individuals is the reality that there is. And ultimately all the individuals are equal. None is better or more real than any others. For each is capable of an infinity of richness. This is the ultimate basis of McTaggart's moral and political theory.

Without telling us — and without, I think, usually being aware of it himself — McTaggart is constantly calling on major strands of the tradition of western philosophy. Unfortunately, though he lectured often on the his-

---

12 Cudworth says that God is love "if by it be meant, eternal, self-originated, intellectual Love, or essential and substantial goodness, that having an infinite, overflowing fulness and fecundity dispenses itself uninvidiously, according to the best wisdom, sweetly governs all, without any force or violence… and reconciles the whole world into harmony." His final judgement is that "love in some rightly qualified sense, is God" (Cudworth 1678: 123; note that the page number is misprinted 117 in the three British Library copies. See also Cudworth 1845: 179). The Royston edition remains definitive, but the Harrison-Tegg edition has a rich index and also J.L. von Mosheim's still-valuable notes.

13 See (McTaggart, 1906: Chapters VI–VIII).

tory of philosophy he did not write such a history and, so far as I can find out, we do not have his lecture notes. But his community of timeless loving spirits is, after all, just the Christian Trinity (especially as expounded by Cudworth, and Locke thought Cudworth was the best expounder of its history) expanded to include us all.

The Principle of Value: Love, Goodness, and Sentient Beings

For our present purposes, McTaggart's philosophy can be seen as exemplifying the scholastic tradition of the convertibility of goodness and being. Love, in McTaggart's view, is the highest order value. And what is nearest the good is the most real. What it is not to be real is to lack something, to be imperfect. The timeless loving spirits grasped in their whole perfection lack nothing.

Like G.E. Moore, McTaggart denied that one can *define* goodness, but he insisted that one can identify it (1927: §787). This brings us to McTaggart's final principle.

McTaggart believed that consciousness is valuable and that its value is associated with love. He insisted first of all that there can be no good or valuable states except the states of conscious beings. It is true that we think that some paintings, some works of music, some examples of scenery and so on, are good. But it would be very odd to say that to protect the Mona Lisa we should lock it in a vault and allow no one to see it. Even a good photograph is not a substitute, and even if it were it might provoke the response that photography can damage the original.[14]

Ethics appears to be a practical study, however. Its purpose is to organise one's life. McTaggart asks what it is that one might achieve that no one would want to change. Love is the obvious answer, and if it is reciprocal it becomes even more obvious. If it happened to be true that genuine love never harmed anyone — and I think McTaggart believed this, though it takes some believing — then it would be truly obvious. Particular kinds of pleasure — often offered as an alternative — are evidently transitory in any case and, what is more, pleasure except in love can be an evil thing. McTaggart allows that pleasure always has a place, but its place is in the reality of love.

Aristotle recommended contemplation and Hegel liked to talk of "pure thought thinking about pure thought" as the work of the Absolute. We might think of this as perfection, but McTaggart finds it again empty without love. Does one pursue knowledge for the sake of having knowledge? Many people have thought so — perhaps Aristotle, St. Thomas, Spinoza

---

14 Lately the Bibliothèque Nationale in Paris has adopted the habit of not letting readers see the originals if micro-film or microfiche copies are available. But this apparently stems from their view that the only value of a book is in the understanding of the words. The new habit is disastrous because not all features of the original appear in the copy.

and Hegel are among them—but McTaggart thought not. (Think of someone who knew all the prime numbers between one and a trillion but nothing else.) Its place again is in the perfection of love which involved intimate knowledge of another human person.

One must be careful, however. This account of McTaggart may make it sound as if he is talking about the pleasant but perhaps vapid and vacuous relationship which one finds among the young as they sit and gaze into one another's eyes. But McTaggart means, of course, the interlocking of whole minds, and he means it in a way that preserves and protects the individuality of each. McTaggart's love would evaporate if one person simply dominated another and if the other was simply a reflection of his or her own mind. He intends a sharing of all the richness of which two—and more—developed human beings are capable.

The love that he writes about is, of course, the love of timeless loving spirits and it involves everyone in the universe, though we love some people even in eternity more intensely than others. His thesis is that we directly perceive the perceptions of some of the participants and only indirectly perceive those of others, for we begin with a finite set of original perceptions and there is an infinity of percipient beings. Whatever sadness we might find at not being members of some groups of such spirits will be made up, he thinks, by the delight that we will find in others.

The Principles and Problems of Timelessness

McTaggart insists that in some profound sense—though not, I shall argue, in quite the obvious sense—the loving spirits who make up reality are timeless.

There is a direct argument for this which derives simply from his metaphysical theory of the good and of values in general, and it is this rather than his technical argument that I think was always in the back of his mind. If the good and existence coincide, then, if love is the highest order value, existence is composed of loving states. But McTaggart argues that in such states there is no reason for anything to change.

His technical argument has occupied—and continues to occupy—many pages in books and learned journals, and it continues to have supporters, including Hugh Mellor and Gerald Rochelle. Those who have been puzzled deeply include C.D. Broad, A.C. Ewing, G.J. Whitrow, R.M. Gale, and J.R. Lucas—but also Rochelle and Mellor.[15] But I think, once again, that the argument hides more than it explicates about McTaggart's central concern.

I will explain the argument briefly and then say why I think this.

---

15 See Broad (1933–8: vol. II), Ewing (1951), Whitrow (1961), Gale (1968), Lucas (1973), Mellor (1991), the twelve essays in L. Nathan Oaklander and Quentin Smith (1994), and, most recently, Rochelle (1998a).

McTaggart begins his discussion of time by noticing that we require two temporal series in order to render intelligible our common notions of time.[16] One of these is the series which we designate by the words past, present, and future. The other is the series which we designate by the words earlier and later. McTaggart calls these series, respectively, the A and B series, and it will be convenient to adopt this lettering. The B series is the one which we usually think of as composing history: In it, everything has one and only one fixed place. Julius Caesar crossed the Rubicon earlier than the time at which the Roman Republic became the Roman Empire, but later than the time at which Cicero was born. All of these events were earlier than the birth of Christ but later than the death of Plato.

These positions never change. If event x was ever earlier than y, x is always earlier than y. This series is not, in itself, temporal for, in it, nothing changes. It is simply a serial order within which everything has a fixed place. The A series is the series which seems to contain change: For the events now past were present, and when they were present, they had been future. Every event is, at some time, past, present, and future. Without both series there is no time for, if we have only the B series, nothing happens, and, if we have only the A series, there is no reference point against which we may cope with the changing temporal predicates. (Whenever anything changes, it must change in relation to something which, for that purpose, must be regarded as unchanging through the relation. Thus if I know that time passes, I must be one person who lives—unchanged, in respect of being an observer—through the change. Otherwise, no one notices the change. If steel shrinks when it gets cold, it must do so in relation to some foot-rule which remains constant. Imagine that everything in the world shrank by a factor of one-half and that everything changed uniformly. How could anyone notice? Would that count as change?)

McTaggart says, however, that though both time series are necessary, the A series has a description which inevitably contains a contradiction: For it is both true of every event that it must have all three A-series predicates (pastness, presentness, and futurity) and true of every event that no event may have more than one. For what it means to be a present event is to be an event in time which is neither past nor future. One must suppose, of course, that one can overcome this difficulty readily enough: Events which are present, were future, and will be past. But now, rather than past, present and future, we have another series: was, is, and will be. The same objection will accrue to that. And so on. McTaggart urges that such an infinite series is vicious: For it re-locates the problem each time in the new series without change.

Two things seem clear to me: One is that McTaggart must be concerned about how we *talk* about time, for he writes both about our ordinary con

---

16 The discussion of time occupies McTaggart (1927: §§303–404 and §§710–85).

cept of time and also about our inability to express it without contradiction. He means to save much of what we think of when we think about time, for the concept of the future is important to him and a long chapter of *The Nature of Existence* is devoted to "the futurity of the whole".[17] And in fact he believes that there is a real series, the C series, that contains the non-illusory relations that remain when we have cleared away the debris from our merely apparent world.

McTaggart does not make himself fully clear about the matter. Robert Leet Patterson (1959) gives up on an attempt to explicate the C series doctrine with anything like completeness, and most authors ignore the matter. Gerald Rochelle (1998b) is the principal exception. Rochelle carefully delineates the notion of an a-temporal series which has the necessary properties. But I shall argue later that McTaggart needs a special kind of "temporal residue". If I am right, Rochelle does not solve *all* of McTaggart's problems.

I intend, in the circumstances, to adopt the following procedure: I shall first indicate an argument which has a structure like McTaggart's but goes more directly to the heart of the matter. I shall then ask what conditions the C series must meet and attempt to construct it so as to meet those conditions and also to meet the clearest of McTaggart's stated requirements for it.

It seems to me that we may get to the heart of the matter at once if we approach it as the problem of defining temporal expressions. It will turn out that this question, ultimately, is relevant in any case to the issue of the nature of time. McTaggart, like Russell, tended to think that meanings were carried by words and that words could be defined either by the use of other words or by pointing at their designata. Words like past, present, and future are peculiar in this way. If they are defined in terms of other words, a vicious infinite regress of words ensues: The past is what was future and then present. The present is what was future and will be past. The future is what will be present and then past. But "was", "is", and "will be" are expressions which pose the same problems. The reason for this is as follows: They function, in fact, to order events serially, and only other notions of serial order will suffice in their definition. Even then, the serial order must be of the same sort. Is it, then, an experience which gives meaning to our temporal life by way of reference in these cases? Not exactly: For we cannot point at the future and the past. The present is what we can point to, as I suggested in *The Rational and the Real* (1961: 59–61). We could then say that the future is what is possible but cannot be pointed at, while the past is what is now impossible, and the present is what can be pointed at. (In this way, we would assimilate some temporal notions of possibility and impossibility.)

---

17 See (McTaggart, 1927: Chapter LXI, §§727–39).

McTaggart wanted to limit the notion of real possibility to the notion that some characteristics imply others (1921: §35), but he did not explore this thesis at length. Thus, in effect, in his discussion of the C series, he proposes that the distinction between the past and future on the one hand and present on the other is factual — that is, that the distinction is between what is in my experience to be pointed at, and what *is* but is not in that experience. This leads to difficulties, as we shall see.

The account I gave in *The Rational and the Real,* though plausible, is not the best account for the explication of McTaggart's own system. For it makes of the present something radically different from the past and from the future.

But the notion of meaning and the reality of ontological status of meanings are crucial. We find the past and future not in experiences but in meanings. When we look at a printed page, we usually think that the black marks on the paper are more real than the meanings of the words they bear. What McTaggart must hold is that the meanings are more real than the black marks on the paper. The meanings we are sure of. That the marks are on paper is an educated guess which an expert might confute. (Perhaps the stuff is really thin metal or plastic.)

Pastness is not to be found in an experience, but in a meaning. When we say we remember something, we may be referring to something present — a memory image — though we may not. But even when we are speaking of a memory image, we call it a memory because it means or intends something past. Similarly, to speak of the past is to use language so as to give it a certain function. All the historical evidence, be it books or mounds, art works or shards, is in the present. Its *meaning* is in the past.

The difficulty is that present carriers must bear those meanings, and that is why, in part at least, the problems that McTaggart raises arise. For there are two senses of being in the past.

In one sense, to be in the past is to have a meaning which belongs to the set of meanings which comprise the past. On the other, to be in the past is to be an event which is not present.

This last notion is, in fact, contradictory: Nothing can be an event and not be an event now for, on that supposition, it *is* not an event; it *was* an event. It is this contradiction which McTaggart exploits, though he does not see the significance of it.

He *does* however grasp the solution to the problem. On the face of it, any ordinary temporal series is an exclusionary series. It is the case, that is, that to be an event at one moment of time excludes the possibility of being an event at another moment of time. What *is* at one moment is at *that* moment and not at any other moment.

To say this is merely to describe the condition of the bearers of the meanings and not that of the meanings themselves. They do not have the same relation to time. Indeed, they accumulate and may be said to *be* at *all* moments. In an inclusion series, what *is* at any earlier moment will *be* at *any* later moment as well.

Julius Caesar is not now crossing the Rubicon. But the meaning of that sentence which describes his crossing *is* with us now, and it is part of the set of meanings which comprise the past. Those meanings accumulate. Furthermore, they have a real order of their own which is the order of meanings. It is only in meaning that there is a past and a future. All else is in the present, and we can define expressions like "past" and "future" in just that way: the past is the set of meanings which are established but do not comprise the present. The future is the set of meanings which are not established but are open.

We shall certainly have to ask just what such a view means to and for us. Briefly, all the data which we receive and are aware of comprise the immediate present. But we do not live in the immediate present. If we did, we could not understand sentences, follow music, or perform intentional actions. We transcend the present in meaning. The meanings involved are, of course, the meanings of sentences like "Caesar crossed the Rubicon", "Jefferson studied agriculture", "Mark Antony liked girls" and so forth.

The situation, then, is that we are timeless beings struggling in a world of illusion. The meanings of many events in our lives lie in the past or in the future. The "meaning of life", in the sense of the purpose and the goal of any individual human life, indeed lies in the future. But it is the meaning of what we say and do now that lies in the future not, on McTaggart's apparent view, the events themselves.

McTaggart never seems to explain this situation, but an explanation is possible given what he does say. The truth about it is that we are timeless loving beings, but this is not how we experience ourselves. This timeless state is not now a feature of our consciousness.

What could be lacking in our present states that brings this about?

McTaggart's account of love demands intentional activity: "Love is a liking which is felt by persons, and which is intense and passionate" (1927: §460). It must be developed in a series of conscious acts. It cannot come to consciousness in any other way, and it seems likely that, even if McTaggart is right, we are currently a long way from the termination of this series. Like other specimens of the present, these acts may well have their existence in an eternal present whose successive relations are simply given by their relation to and distance from the final goal and so they may be elements in the real C series. There will, of course, be another series which is the order of errors in our current perceptions, and McTaggart called this the D series. But the future and the past are composed of the meanings attached to the sentences expressing these acts.

This explains how we can be a-temporal creatures living in what appears to be a temporal illusion, and so, if it is correct, this dispels one of the apparent contradictions in McTaggart's system.

Freedom and Determinism

It raises obvious problems, though, about freedom and determinism. The reality is that the timeless states of which we are now conscious are determined, but the world in which our intentional acts take place is not determined in the same way. Our personal lives are certainly not without determination. McTaggart says such a view would make morality impossible, for nothing would be predictable.

Our actions though are chiefly determined by our characters. This is a kind of organic determinism. We are determined by our own characters, not by something extrinsic to them. Characters determine action, but characters need not be determined in the same way. McTaggart, though he eschews fatalism explicitly as we saw, is unclear about this and once again he seems to need a notion of complex alternands as properties or predicates. Our characters tend to determine that if something happens, one of a determinate set of alternatives will follow. McTaggart did allow a distinction between intrinsic determination and extrinsic determination which could provide the seeds for this.

He believed that, in the end, we would reach the state of bliss which he thought to be reality. His certainty has to do with his views about the ways in which finite sets of original characteristics can determine infinite chains of characteristics, and this theory is too full of complexities for us to be certain that he is right. Once again, however, the simple consideration that everything permitted by a determinate system happens if one goes on long enough[18] might suffice.

Seeking Glimpses of Reality

What should we do in the meantime? Obviously we should look for the moments of love which appear in our lives. Obviously, too, we should work together to try to realise our inter-relations. Social responsibility and concern for others follow from this.

The demand for equality of opportunity and treatment follows from the fact that we all share the same ultimate reality and that we are equal in value.

McTaggart placed great value on community, and so he was a staunch defender of the Cambridge in which he taught and of the England in which he lived. But his own character in the end may have saved him from

---

18 What it is for something to be possible is for it to occur at least once in an infinite series of chances.

the bigotry of patriots. After the First World War there was an effort to recruit him in the battles against Bolshevism. He said he had exhausted what little capacity he had for hatred in hating Germans and could undertake no more.

The New Testament has it that the Kingdom of God is with us now. McTaggart has it that the reality of the timeless loving spirits is with us now. Both suggest that we live in a world in which the truth is obscured and we must try to see through it. McTaggart thinks that we will see through it but that we will be well advised to seek the signs of the real that peek through the illusion.

If we make a few changes in the arguments it is just possible that McTaggart is right. The needed changes are often in places where, as Peter Geach noticed, McTaggart adopted doctrines from Russell and Moore — Russell's theory of definitions and Moore's account of "defining" the good.

Conclusion

If McTaggart were right would it matter?

I think it would, for the only really good argument for equality — equality of all human beings, of men and women, of the apparently clever and others, of the immediately lovable and those who cache their virtues — is that everyone ultimately *is* equal. If people are not equal, it will not work to pretend that they are. The consequences are profound. They amount to accepting Pascal's adage that we should treat everyone as if they were saved, as if they were finally good and are destined for the best world there is. Pascal's argument did not cut as well as he hoped, for he did not really think everyone would go to heaven. McTaggart thought they were already there.

References

Armour, L. (1961), *The Rational and the Real* (The Hague: Martinus Nijhoff).
Broad, C.D. (1933-8), *Examination of McTaggart's Philosophy*, 2 vols. (Cambridge: The University Press).
Cudworth, R. (1678), *True Intellectual System of the Universe* (London: Royston).
Cudworth, R. (1845), *True Intellectual System of the Universe*, ed. J. Harrison (London: Thomas Tegg).
Ewing, A. (1951), *The Fundamental Problems of Philosophy* (London: Routledge and Kegan Paul).
Gale, R. (1968), *A Treatise on Space and Time* (New York: The Humanities Press).
Geach, P. (1979), *Truth, Love and Immortality* (London: Hutchinson).
Lucas, J.R. (1973), *Time* (London: Methuen).
McTaggart, J.M.E. (1906), *Some Dogmas of Religion* (London: Edward Arnold).
McTaggart, J.M.E. (1918), "Society as an Organism", in *Studies in Hegelian Cosmology* (Cambridge: The University Press), pp. 151-96.
McTaggart, J.M.E. (1921-7), *The Nature of Existence*, 2 vols., ed. C. D. Broad (Cambridge: The University Press).

McTaggart, J.M.E. (1934a), "The Individualism of Value", in S. Keeling (ed.), *Philosophical Studies* (London: Edward Arnold), pp. 97–110.

McTaggart, J.M.E. (1934b), "The Relation of Time and Eternity", in S. Keeling (ed.), *Philosophical Studies* (London: Edward Arnold), pp. 132–55.

Mellor, D. H. (1991), *Matters of Metaphysics* (Cambridge: the University Press).

Oaklander, L. and Smith, Q. (eds.) (1994), *The New Theory of Time* (New Haven, CT: Yale University Press).

Patterson, R. (1959), "A Critical Account of Broad's Estimate of McTaggart", in P. Schilpp (ed.), *The Philosophy of C. D. Broad* (New York: Tudor Publishing), pp. 115–70.

Rochelle, G. (1998a), *Behind Time* (Aldershot: Ashgate).

Rochelle, G. (1998b), *The End of Time* (London: Ashgate).

Whitrow, G. (1961), *The Natural Philosophy of Time* (London: Thomas Nelson).

Jan Olof Bengtsson

The Moral, Social, and Political Philosophy of British Personal Idealism

Introduction

The current view of personal idealism is that it represents a reaction within British and American idealism against the playing down of the importance and value of the individual person and the weakening of his metaphysical status in the systems of absolute idealism. Against this tendency, philosophers like Andrew Seth Pringle-Pattison in Britain and Borden Parker Bowne in the United States, in simultaneous *rapprochement* to Christian theism and renewed attention to concrete living experience as a whole, are perceived to have sought to create a theoretical space for the understanding of the meaning of personality while remaining largely within the shared idealistic outlook. The debate was an in-house affair, which concerned mere details or marginal differences of emphasis.

While it is true that in important respects the personal idealists remained idealists and that in this sense this was an in-house debate, it can be argued that this standard account of the relation between personal and absolute idealism, although it is largely true as far as it goes, tends to miss much of the nature and the importance of the dispute as well as of its historical origins. One of the reasons why the full significance of the debate has often been overlooked or poorly understood by historians of philosophy is indeed precisely its in-house aspect—the fact that, in important respects, the personalists did not break with idealism. Many twentieth-century philosophers simply dismissed personal idealism along with absolute idealism in a sweeping rejection of all idealism. But a closer look at the relation between the different forms of idealism reveals heretofore hidden perspectives and meanings highly pertinent to philosophical questions that are still very much with us.

Although the personal idealists joined the absolute idealists in their opposition to empiricism, utilitarianism, and "atomistic" liberalism, their epistemological, metaphysical, ethical and axiological focus on personality, human and divine, made for a very different form of idealism. It can be argued that the personal idealist criticism of the insufficient alternative to the jointly rejected positions set forth by the absolute idealists cannot be regarded as a mere esoteric quibble within the ranks of idealism. It is possible, I believe, to show that, in a broader historical perspective, the disagreement must be seen to have a deeper cultural, moral, and political significance in the intellectual history of western modernity.

While pointing briefly to the historical perspective in which this deeper meaning is revealed, my more limited purpose here is to present the distinctive positions in ethics and social and political philosophy of personal idealism, and more specifically of the work of three representative British personal idealists, Andrew Seth Pringle-Pattison (1856–1931), his brother James Seth (1860–1924), and Clement C. J. Webb (1865–1954) — who can, in my view, be regarded as typical representatives of personal idealism.[1] Although a broader historical context makes evident new dimensions of the significance and the historical lineage of their work (which in some respects were not fully perceived even by these figures themselves), a more narrow-focused discussion will introduce and familiarize us with their historical self-understanding in a way that should swiftly dispel doubts about the nature and the importance of the issues involved in this drawn-out intra-idealistic debate in the last decades of the nineteenth-century and the first decades of the twentieth.

The Parts and the Whole in the Philosophy of Personal Idealism

Distinguishing the moral, social and political philosophy of personal idealism from its epistemology and metaphysics, and concentrating on the former, raises the issue of the relation between these fields within a philosophy the systematic nature of which is, as in all idealism, fundamental. Here the positions differ somewhat among the personal idealists themselves; but perhaps these differences, and even those between the personal and the absolute idealists in these respects, should not be exaggerated. The

---

[1] Andrew Seth Pringle-Pattison was professor of logic and metaphysics at Edinburgh; James Seth was professor of moral philosophy at Edinburgh, after holding professorships in the United States, including one at Cornell University; Webb was Fellow of Magdalen College, Oxford, and the first holder of the Oriel (subsequently Nolloth) chair of the Philosophy of the Christian Religion. Other important British personal idealists are William Ritchie Sorley, J.R. Illingworth, Hastings Rashdall, and the later A.E. Taylor. In classifying them all as personal idealists, I follow the practice of historians such as Metz, Passmore, Copleston, Reardon, Sell, James, Boucher and Vincent. The term personal idealisim was first used by the American George Holmes Howison in the title of his main work, *The Limits of Evolution and Other Essays Illustrating the Metaphysical Theory of Personal Idealism* (1901). As William Sweet has shown, Howison objected strongly when the term was taken up by the British philosopher Henry Sturt, who diverged strongly from his own position in the direction of pragmatism. It is clear that Sturt's version is less representative and that Howison was right to protest. Likewise, J.M.E. McTaggart's version of personal idealism is highly idiosyncratic and falls outside the main current here outlined, most conspicuously, but not exclusively, because of his atheism.

definition and separation of the various sub-disciplines of philosophy are of course not merely part of a parallel, institutional history which to some extent shapes philosophy through an extrinsic logic of its own, and thus contingently. The relation is quite as much the reverse, as thought itself determines the configuration and relations of the various fields that together constitute philosophy. Yet sometimes the focus on these differences, even when they point to the variety of positions in substantial issues, can overshadow more important meanings of the latter that cut across the formal divisions among disciplines.

James Seth distinguishes ethics as a "science" from metaphysics, and proceeds, in his main work, *A Study of Ethical Principles* (1894; 17th edn, 1926),[2] to deal with it as such, in contradistinction to T.H. Green's metaphysical ethics. But in the second half of this book, he also sets out a metaphysic of morals, covering, like Kant but with different answers, the questions of the soul, God, and immortality. Seth explains at length the necessity of thus travelling "beyond the scientific explanation to one that is deeper and ultimate" (Seth, 1926: 361). He provides in his works a kind of ethical corollary to the work of his brother, Andrew Seth Pringle-Pattison (hereinafter: Pringle-Pattison), who was mainly a critical metaphysician and for the most part not directly concerned with ethics as such. Seth's metaphysic of morals is, however, similar to his brother's metaphysics. The importance of the difference between scientific ethics in a radical empiricist sense and metaphysical ethics in a pre-Kantian sense is plain enough, and the difference between a Kantian and a Hegelian position in this regard is considerable too. Yet Seth's distinction between a "scientific" and a "metaphysical" approach seems somewhat less significant with regard both to the development and the nature of the distinct positions that are characteristic of the school of personal idealism. The inspiration of British idealism in general was preponderantly ethical. This holds *a fortiori* for personal idealism, since its objections to absolute idealism were not least ethical in nature. But at the same time it is obvious that in each major personal idealist thinker, the inspiration and motivation are to some considerable extent metaphysical too.

Consequently, in line with the thinking of the personal idealists themselves, I will deal here not only with ethics as, in the case of Seth, conceived partly in separation from metaphysics, but with ethically relevant aspects of their metaphysics as well. It should be kept in mind however that the way in which they conceived of metaphysics, and the metaphysic of morals, was different from the Greenian and absolutist one. Needless to say,

---

[2] I use a late edition (the seventeenth, in fact; the work was successful, and must have been much used as a textbook), since Seth continuously made changes and amendments. Other relevant works of Seth are *Freedom as Ethical Postulate* (1891) and *Essays on Ethics and Religion* (1926).

the systematic integration of ethics and social and political philosophy in the personal idealists is quite as close as that of ethics and metaphysics.

The Continental European Background

For all its distinctively original and specifically British features, it is obvious that British absolute idealism must be understood, culturally and historically, in connection with the earlier German idealism that in so many important respects is its source and background. Less known is the extent to which British personal idealism too should be understood in connection with a continental European tradition, a tradition of more or less personalistic thought going all the way back to Friedrich Heinrich Jacobi's criticism of pantheism in the 1780's and the later F.W.J. Schelling's rejection of his own early absolute idealism in favour of a new kind of theistic personalism. Most of the central arguments against what can perhaps be termed the "impersonalism" of absolute idealism set forth by Pringle-Pattison in *Hegelianism and Personality* (1887; 2nd edn., 1893) had already been developed by these thinkers, by their successors among the so-called "speculative theists", and by R.H. Lotze, with whom Pringle-Pattison, like Bowne, studied in Germany (Bengtsson, 2006).

Although it is unclear to what extent the British and American personal idealists were aware of this earlier, continental tradition before Lotze, there can, I submit, be no doubt that in substance, their thinking is part of a broader current of personalistic idealism that runs through the whole of the nineteenth century. It was present in Britain to some extent even in the work of the later Coleridge, as well as in that of James Martineau. In Germany, personalistic idealism developed as a counter-current to the main line of idealism from Kant via Fichte and the early Schelling to Hegel. Its motives and inspiration seem to a considerable extent to have been the same as those at work in the British personal idealists' criticism of the absolute idealists many decades later, and in very different historical and cultural circumstances.

It should be added that not least with regard to its moral and political philosophy, personal idealism must also be understood as part of a general assertion of the value of personality in the nineteenth century. Even its insistence on the personality of God must be seen to some extent as a consequence of a new humanistic stress on the personality of man: it is no mere return to or reassertion of the orthodox Christian position.

Individual and Society: The Unresolved Modern Dialectic

My main argument will be that personal idealism contributed uniquely to the philosophical solution of a problem which, due to questionable assumptions of western modernity, has haunted it from the outset and still seems as pressing as ever: the relation between the individual and the social whole.

Enlightenment political philosophy focused on the individual, his rights, and his contractual relations to other individuals, but in these social respects, all individuals were alike: individuality did not imply unicity or singularity, or at least individuality in this sense was not important. Moreover, at least on the European continent, such Enlightenment theory was worked out within the social structure of the *ancien régime*, which retained in practice much traditional outer, social determination of human identity, although the slow shift to individualism had begun already during the Renaissance. With the French revolution and its European reverberations through the nineteenth century, this social order crumbled. But the consequences with regard to individuality were anything but unambiguous. The French revolution itself, alongside its liberation of the individual, and inspired not least by Rousseau, launched new social wholes, the People, the General Will, *la république*, the Nation, and foreshadowed in Babeuf's abortive efforts the later claims on behalf of the Proletariat. At the same time, and mainly in Germany, the Enlightenment—including the "atomistic" individualism of classical liberalism, political economy, and utilitarianism—was challenged by the new organicism and the new metaphysical wholes of romanticism, idealism, and historicism. While the revolution and its theorization in the early forms of German idealism further emancipated the individual from traditional social determination, romanticism stressed, often in *outré* ways, individuality as singularity, not least in the form of the "original genius", against the rigid, conventionalist pseudo-classicism of the eighteenth century—this latter was perfectly consistent with the uniform individuality of Enlightenment political thought. The idealization of the individual, in the more or less moral forms of the original genius, the hero, the "great man", was to shape western culture until the onset of the high modernist and postmodernist disintegration and negation of individual subjectivity that was to become a decisive feature of the intellectual climate of the twentieth century. Carlyle's and Emerson's paradigmatic expressions of this ideal remained influential throughout the nineteenth century.

The idealists and the romantics perceived clearly the problems of individualism in its Enlightenment form, as well as of its status in the post-revolutionary world. But in the light of two hundred years' subsequent historical experience, it is possible to see equally clearly the problems in their response to the new political and cultural situation. These have to do, on the one hand, with the nature of the romantic assertion of individuality and, on the other, with the nature of the new wholes that were at the same time, often seemingly paradoxically, introduced and defended.

It is hardly an exaggeration to say that, since this time, western society has been shaped by an unresolved dialectic of individualism — both of the Enlightenment and the romantic variety and in various combinations of the two — and collectivism, or a dominance of one or more of the various new larger wholes. Often the swing between them has been one between extremes, and as worked out on the scene of history, the dialectic and its consequences have not seldom been disastrous. At work in individual thinkers, its inexorable logic has also yielded strange theoretical results. From the beginning, romantic individualism had a nihilistic strain. The narcissistic self-assertion of the romantic poet soon ended in a will to self-extinction in the abyss of nature or some metaphysical whole or void.[3] This strain was reinforced and became dominant with the gradual dissolution of the subject, with Nietzsche and postmodernism broadly conceived. Sartre, the radical existential individualist, significantly threw himself into the arms of communism.

At the same time, classical liberals, unperturbed by any theoretical or political obstacles or criticisms, have insisted to this day on the sufficiency of eighteenth-century theory, sometimes without the slightest modifications. While some parts of the world have been ravaged by unprecedented collectivist totalitarian reactions in the name of the new romantic wholes, such liberals have periodically shaped the destiny of other, major parts. Although in some forms romanticism, and to some extent even Hegelian idealism, could momentarily serve restorative and conservative purposes in seeking to reinforce or recreate traditional social determination in the post-revolutionary chaos, the deeper momentum and cultural dynamic of romanticism, and not least of Hegel, was unambiguously part of the larger dynamic of modernity. Both in its new individualism and its new collectivism, romanticism was no less antitraditional than Enlightenment rationalism, and in the course of the nineteenth and twentieth centuries, for all of their surface clashes, these two wings of modernity showed themselves to be thoroughly interdependent and mutually supportive. Firmly wedded, they gave birth to the political ideologies of modernity.

The grandest of the syntheses of these opposites is undoubtedly that of Hegel.[4] In its distinct combination of rationalistic and romantic elements, it made the most ambitious claim to support at the same time as the new societal and metaphysical wholes and the rights of individuality. British absolute idealism, represented by thinkers like Green and Bosanquet, with its "new liberalism", is clearly among the most important attempts at synthetic thinking in the Hegelian line with regard to the modern problematic of individualism and wholes, despite its considerable departure from Hegel in other respects.

---

3   For a study of this romantic individualism, see Izenberg (1992).
4   In his own way, the later Sartre tried too, it should be admitted.

Personal Idealism and Liberalism

While sharing the absolute idealists' criticism of atomistic individualism, as well as their insistence on the importance of the state, it is the characteristic position of personal idealism to reject some of the their key philosophical assumptions. The reasons for their finding fault with the absolute idealist version of the synthesis are not just ethical or political, but also metaphysical, in accordance with what I have already said about the interlocking cohesiveness of the idealist systematicity. The difference between the personalists and the absolutists is not this systematicity itself, but the way in which the personalists focus on the category of the person. All of the various divisions between the two schools of idealism – concerning the issues of freedom, the meaning of self-actualization, the understanding of the common good, the value and destiny of the individual, the nature of God and of immortality – are, if not fully reducible to this understanding of personality, at least closely and systematically related to it.

It is the centrality of this category that defined the whole of the counter-current in continental European philosophy which constitutes the background of the later flourishing of personal idealism in Britain and America. Clearly, in the intellectual climate outlined above, there were distinct risks involved in ascribing to the category of the person such a decisive philosophical significance. Perhaps unavoidably, problematic forms of personalistic idealism soon emerged. If they did not fall prey to romantic pseudo-individualism and its dialectical opposite of self-annihilation, or to the cult of the daemonic super-personality beyond good and evil, they often used too loosely the category of the person, as a facile solution to complex philosophical problems.[5] The remarkable feature of idealistic personalism at its best, however, is that it managed to steer clear of most of the pitfalls of the intellectual landscape of the nineteenth century produced by the developments pointed to above. This is not least the case with the leading British personal idealists.

Pringle-Pattison was strongly influenced by the Scottish tradition of common sense and moral sense philosophy, particularly through his teacher, A.C. Fraser. Interestingly, the counter-current in German philosophy, at its very inception, was also shaped in important respects by this Scottish tradition, as F.H. Jacobi early on received decisive impulses from it. This influence is traceable not only in the elements of experiential epistemology, "realism", and the understanding of "faith" in Jacobi's work, but in his liberalism as well: there is a distinct flavour of the alternative, Anglo-Scottish Enlightenment especially in his doubts about the French revolution.[6]

---

5   At a late stage, Max Weber complained about this phenomenon in Germany.
6   See George diGiovanni (1994: 4-7, 18-21, 25-6, 35-6).

Many of the synthesizing idealists in the Hegelian — or Young or Left Hegelian — line claimed to have developed or to represent a view of the person and of society that avoided individualism, on the one hand, and a collectivism repressive of personality, on the other. Yet from the perspective of personal idealists like Pringle-Pattison, Seth, and Webb, their metaphysics and their metaphysical ethics were of a kind that must necessarily lead to failure. Towards the end of his important criticism of most of the main forms of contemporary liberalism, *Beyond Liberalism*, R.T. Allen concludes — against most dominant intellectual currents today — that

> What liberty and liberalism... need is a conception of the individual as a substance and a value in his own right, and therefore a unique, irreplaceable, and unrepeatable individuality, what Scheler called a 'value-essence'. European civilisation, and with it European law and liberty, is based on that idea, although its explicit philosophy has rarely recognised it and, increasingly in the modern world, has too often explicitly denied it. (1998: 235)

Like the personal idealists, Allen finds the absolute idealist position insufficient in this regard. But some of the problems with the absolute idealist view can be found already in Kant. Does not Kant's categorical imperative require us to respect humanity in all and to regard all men as ends and not merely as means? Kant forbids that we should

> not use each other just as means to *our own* ends. There is nothing at all about us not being essentially means for the realisation of something else. On the contrary, each of us has no value in and as himself. What has value... is rational humanity. We are only temporary embodiments of it, and, in Kant's philosophy as in the empiricism and rationalism which it tries to combine, the individual is such only by the accidents of his bodily location in space and time... There is no "autonomy of the person", only the "autonomy of reason" (Allen 1998: 234).[7]

In reality, then, "Kant's general philosophy offers uncertain support for human liberty" (Allen 1998: 234).

I suggest that some important elements of the kind of liberal philosophy that Allen calls for are in fact already available in the school of personal idealism. With its deepened understanding of personality and individuality, and without relinquishing universality, in this regard personal idealism improves not only on absolute idealism, but also on Kant's philosophy.

---

[7] Allen here uses a different concept of personality than Kant's, but his criticism in the last sentence can easily be reformulated as a criticism of the insufficiency of Kant's concept. Allen may, however, go too far when he writes that for Kant "Ideally and really, there is but one rational process of thought, and thus one substantive mind, from which we are separated by the nonrational and morally irrelevant effects of our bodies which cause us to have different experiences" (1998: 234). This is a controversial issue. Pringle-Pattison, in *Hegelianism and Personality* (1887; 2nd edn., 1893), took the position that this was not Kant's meaning, but a distinctive development, and distortion, at the hands of his successors, the absolute idealists.

Pringle-Pattison's Criticism of Absolute Idealism

Pringle-Pattison argued at length against the metaphysical reasons for, and problems with, the absolute idealist position regarding the nature and the status of individual personality, and also pointed to its ethical and axiological implications. In *Hegelianism and Personality* and *The Idea of God in the Light of Recent Philosophy*,[8] Pringle-Pattison seeks, at great length, to show how the main line of modern idealism fails to explain and rightly understand the manifold characteristics of finite beings. He accepts what is in fact the later Schelling's view that "the 'otherness' of the finite is not a logical transparency, but brings with it a real difference and important consequences" (1920: 415).[9] Hegel treats "notions as the ultimately real, and things or real beings as their exemplifications"; the "process of existence" is the evolution and realization of the notion of self-consciousness, of subject or spirit. But "if we start thus with an abstract conception, our results will remain abstract throughout"; "where or in whom the realisation takes place, of this nothing is said, or can be said, along these lines". Never really discussing human or divine self-consciousness or spirit but merely self-consciousness or spirit in general, Hegel fails to see that this is an abstraction, that "only *spirits* or *intelligences* are real"; "Absolute spirit is said to be realised in art, in religion, in philosophy; but of the real Spirit or spirits in whom and for whom the realisation takes place we are not told" (1893: 159–61).

Hegel intended by his notion of spirit or the concrete idea to do justice to the unity of as well as the distinction between God and man, rejecting Spinozistic identity of substance, without the one being reduced to the other. It was also intended to overcome the opposites of individualism and universalism. But the solution fails in Pringle-Pattison's view since spirit is not concrete "in the sense of designating an actual existence; it is concrete only with reference to the 'logical Idea' which preceded it". It remains the mere "notion of knowledge hypostatised", and as thus abstract, it

> unites God and man only by eviscerating the real content of both. Both disappear or are sublimated into it, but simply because it represents what is common to both, the notion of intelligence as such. They disappear, not indeed in a pantheistic substance, but in a logical concept. If we scrutinise the system narrowly, we find Spirit or the Absolute doing duty at one time for God, and at another time for man; but when we have hold of the divine end we have lost our grasp of the human end, and *vice versa*. We never have the two together... (1893: 163–4).

---

[8] His argument against Bosanquet in the famous debate at the Aristotelian Society (1920), which I will use here, repeats, *mutatis mutandis*, the arguments against Hegel and Green in *Hegelianism and Personality*.

[9] An introduction to the later Schelling's paradigmatic criticism of Hegel can be found in Andrew Bowie (1993); for an extensive treatment, see Manfred Frank (1975).

On Bosanquet's monistic view, Pringle-Pattison wrote, " 'the formal distinctness' of finite selves is an appearance due to 'impotence' and incidental to their finitude". It follows that merging of distinct selves in the absolute experience is either the result of their temporal striving or the eternal truth which the appearance of such striving somehow expresses. Pringle-Pattison insists against these positions that formal distinctness is "part of the fundamental structure of the universe" and is the "fundamental method of creation". Finite centres may overlap in content, but "they cannot overlap at all in existence; their very *raison d'être* is to be distinct and, in that sense, separate and exclusive, focalizations of a common universe" (1920: 258, 261, 264). The differentiation in space and time "may be regarded ultimately as only a mode of expressing the general fact of individuation—the fact that there are finite centres at all". The "perennial duel between individualistic and organic theories of society or between nominalism and realism, pluralism and monism" in philosophy can be overcome only by an Aristotelian emendation of the understanding of the concrete universal, which establishes the equivalent balance between the universal and the individual as interdependent and realizing themselves only in each other (1920: 265–7).

In line not only with Lotze but with a whole continental personalist tradition insisting on the givenness of reality in experience, Pringle-Pattison rejects the monists' attempts to explain away the characteristic features of the fact of the "relative independence and separateness" of created souls (1920: 285). Creation is a "creation of creators" (1920: 288),[10] of the otherness of selves with independent status and wills of their own. "[T]he character, the spiritual will, is the concrete personality. It is as such a will that man is independent. To be a self is to be a formed will, originating its own actions and accepting ultimate responsibility for them" (1920: 292). These selves are "real centres of existence and not points of intersection or radiating centres of a single force":

> if the individuals are simply pipes through which the Absolute pours itself, jets, as it were, of one fountain, there is no creation, no real differentiation, and, therefore, in a sense, no mystery. A self which is merely the channel or mouthpiece of another self is not a self. It is of the very nature of a self that it thinks and acts and views the world *from its own centre*. No supposed result of speculative theory can override a certainty based on direct experience…We are not simply an ideal (i. e. an imaginary) point through which the forces or ideas of the universe cross and pass. (1920: 288)

Pringle-Pattison compares the individual selves of a monism which treats them "as merely the channels through which a single universal consciousness thinks and acts" to "masks… of the one actor who takes all the parts in the cosmic drama" (1920: 433). For Pringle-Pattison, as for

---

10 The expression is Bosanquet's although he rejects the idea.

Schelling, reality is clearly a drama, but for them there are many actors. However, the "real otherness" of finite selves does not imply the opposite Spinozistic or Hegelian view, according to which there is no "divine self-consciousness except that which is realised in the finite individuals" and where the finite selves are alone real, "reducing God to the status of an abstract universal". The "comprehensive divine experience" is "other than, and infinitely more than, that of any finite self or of all finite selves collectively, if their several contributions could be somehow pieced together" (1920: 433–4).

Bosanquet, despite his acceptance both of the latter position and of Keats's "vale of soul-making", cannot admit that the end of the absolute is to "give rise to beings such as I experience myself to be" (Bosanquet, 1918: 88). Considering the desire for immortality as "the perpetuation and stereotyping of my present self in all its poverty and meanness" to be unworthy and irreligious, Bosanquet sees (according to Pringle-Pattison) the only alternative in "a desire to be fashioned more and more in the likeness of a perfect humanity" (Pringle-Pattison, 1920: 429). This is "not a desire for personal continuance at all" but an "identification with perfection… in the sense of merging our own personality altogether in that of the Perfect Being" (1920: 429). Against this Pringle-Pattison argues that

> Because I desire to be made more and more in the likeness of God, I do not therefore desire to *be* God. The development of a personality in knowledge and goodness does not take place through confluence with other personalities, nor is its goal and consummation to yield up its proper being and be 'blended with innumerable other selves' in the Absolute (1920: 428–9).

Against both Bosanquet and the mystics, Pringle-Pattison holds that this idea of blending "depends entirely on material analogies which can have no application in the case of selves", such as the one of the drop of water that rejoins the ocean. For the French Pietist Labadie, this was how God engulfed the soul "in the divine abyss of His Being". But, Pringle-Pattison objects, "in the case of a spiritual being" such engulfment means nothing but loss, "the extinction of one centre of intelligence and love, without any conceivable gain to other intelligences or to the content of the universe as a whole". A union of "knowledge and love and conscious service is… closer and more intimate by far than any which can be represented by the fusion of material things". It is in the "personality of the worshipper" that his value to God lies (1920: 429–30).

Only false mysticism implies what in Bradley's philosophy is described as the dissipation and vanishing of the personality in the absolute, or any disappearance of the distinction between the subject and object, as in *advaita vedanta*'s idea of non-differentiation from oneness with *brahman*.[11] The individual finite being is not "fused or commingled", is not "merged in the divine essence", not annihilated and "absorbed into the substance of that which it contemplates". Absorption cannot mean "being sucked under, as it were, and physically incorporated in the being of the object". Such talk is "completely illusory". Schleiermacher's attempt to "comfort the mourning widow by telling her that 'melting away into the great All' should be thought of as 'a merging not into death but into life, and that the highest life' has no meaning unless the living self survives to realize the fruition of the union". Schleiermacher is guilty of the "confusion between the conscious identification of our private will with the divine will and the cessation of the individual consciousness altogether" (1922: 116, 130, 163–5).[12] In strikingly strong terms, Pringle-Pattison dismisses what has often been considered the apogee not only of spiritual experience but of speculative sophistication. Hinting, like Jacobi, at the inner connection between radical monism and pantheistic speculative systems on the one hand and materialism on the other, he writes, for instance, that "with the less speculative and less truly religious minds the material metaphor becomes more and more dominant. We never know how deep our materialism goes." In what he calls "the higher mysticism", however, the finite being is absorbed only in the sense of being concentrated on the vision of God. The "joys of heaven for the genuinely religious man" are "a continuation and intensification of the communion he has already enjoyed" (1922: 160, 162).

The soul-making of the finite being must have the same value for the absolute as for the finite soul itself, and "[u]nless the souls are conserved as souls, it is hardly intelligible to speak of their moulding as in any sense the end or meaning of the world-process". For Bosanquet, " 'values' survive in the Absolute, but not persons". Pringle-Pattison notes Bosanquet's comment that "What has value is the contribution which the particular centre — a representative of certain elements in the whole — brings to the whole in which it is a member" (Pringle-Pattison, 1920: 278; see Bosanquet, 1912: 26). But again, for Pringle-Pattison, our contribution lies precisely "in being ourself, our particular, imperfect, but developing, self, the unique individual whom it has taken such pains to fashion"; its "contribution cannot lie in any of the qualities of the individual taken separately, for these are all universals, and as such must be already fully represented in the perfect experience of the Absolute" (Pringle-Pattison, 1920: 278–9). "Uniqueness belongs to the very notion of a self or consciousness"; none of

---

11 Pringle-Pattison does have a counterpart in *vedanta* however, in the *vishishtadvaita* school and its criticism against *advaita*.
12 This is a second series of Gifford lectures. The story of Schleiermacher and the widow is cited from Martineau.

my experiences, "in the sense in which it is my experience", can be that of another. Pringle-Pattison agrees with another British personal idealist, Hastings Rashdall, that it is meaningless to speak of "one consciousness as 'included in another'", or " 'a Mind which includes all minds'", and "of man as, in that sense, 'a part of God'" (1920: 433–4).

Seth's Ethical Unification of Individuality and Personality

With regard to the origin and status of individual persons, Pringle-Pattison turns against, on the one hand, pantheistic emanation or evolution or blind development and, on the other, arbitrary fiat or efficient causation as the mechanical manufacture of a separate article. Finite beings enjoy a kind of freedom that is wholly compatible with law and system, and which as such rules out both fatalistic determinism and pure contingency. This freedom, and the view of the finite individual from which it is inseparable, are of course central to ethics. But in this field, it was Pringle-Pattison's brother, James Seth, who best formulated the characteristic position of personal idealism.

Pringle-Pattison provided a deep metaphysical perspective on the characteristic nineteenth-century problematic of individual personality and wholes. Seth sets out his ethics by means of "scientific" investigation of ethics *per se*, a demonstration of the failure of hedonism (Epicureanism, utilitarianism) and rationalism (Stoicism, intuitionism, Kantianism) respectively, and of the necessity of a third position which does justice to the partial truths of both, the partial truths of feeling and reason respectively, by means of "their reduction… to the unity of a common life governed by a single central principle" (Seth, 1926: 186). Only after this does he consider freedom, and the related metaphysical questions of the soul and God, in his critical metaphysic of morals.

If the principle of hedonism is self-gratification, and that of rationalism self-sacrifice, Seth's unifying principle is self-realization, and the ethical position based on it—which he develops partly by drawing on the legacy of Plato, Aristotle, Christianity, and Butler—he calls "Eudaimonism, Or the Ethics of Personality".[13] But Seth is aware of the vagueness and the broad applicability of these terms, and thus of the need for a more specific definition of the self that is to be realized. The ethical problem turns out to be the definition and understanding of personality, and it is here that the distinctive position of personal idealism begins to emerge.

Seth's use of the term personality, and the way in which he distinguishes between personality and individuality, is more Kantian that that of other personal idealists. Clement C.J. Webb, devoting much space to purely historical investigations of the shifting meanings and usage of the

---

[13] This is the title of the third chapter of Part I of *A Study of Ethical Principles* (1926). In his use of the term eudaimonism, Seth was not alone among European personalistic idealists.

term person, defended a concept which more directly included individuality. Yet the importance of individuality is accepted by Seth too, even as part of personality in the full sense. It is for Seth the task of personality, the rational self, to discipline the individual, sentient self, to prune it of its egoistic, separative impulses, and shape it into rational moral character. To the self's theoretical organization of the data of sensation into rational synthesis or system by means of the transcendental apperception, corresponds its practical, moral organization, through the exercise of will, of the data of sensibility into a supreme moral end, purpose, or ideal. But at the same time, the person always includes this sensible individuality: "the person is always an individual; his personality acts upon, and constitutes itself out of, his individuality" (1926: 198; 257). "The true career for a man is that which will most fully realise his individuality" (1926: 257). Man's true self is also his total self; its rational, emotional, and active or volitional elements are to be symmetrically developed, "each in its perfection", "all in the harmony of a complete and single life" (1926: 254-5). The moral imperative is: "*Be a person*; constitute, out of your natural individuality, your true, ideal, or personal self"(1926: 199). This is the unifying, synthesizing principle. Through harmonization and subordination, this sensible individuality becomes "an element in the life of personality" (1926: 201).

Seth's description of the spontaneity, freedom and naturalness — "like that of the life of original impulse" (which characterizes the successful achievement of moral character and differs sharply from the "continual repression" of "the mere rigorist or negatively good man" [1926: 202-3]) — is strongly reminiscent of the position of Friedrich von Schiller. In line with Schiller's criticism of Kant, sensible individuality has a positive as well as a negative significance (1926: 253). Ultimately, sensibility can be subjugated only "with its transmutation into the enthusiasm of some great end", when it has become "organic to reason", "the dynamic of the rational life" (1926: 252). Personal idealism clearly preserves other and perhaps more of the distinctive themes of German neohumanism and *Bildung* than absolute idealism, in that such positively individualist elements (stressed also, e. g., by von Humboldt) are more easily reconcilable with it.

It is for this Schillerian ideal state that Seth uses the term self-realization, or "happiness", in the Aristotelian sense but with distinctly modern personalist additions: "The life of man's total selfhood is its own end, — a doing which is the expression of being, and the medium of higher and fuller being, of a deeper and richer unity of thought and sensibility" (1926: 204; 258-9). However, since the Good is not the actual, but the ideal which partially manifests its infinity in our conscience, their absolute coincidence is never fully or definitively attainable by the finite being (1926: 208, 210-1).

Through the combination in personhood of rational personality and individual content, rationalist formalism on the one hand and hedonist subjectivism and particularism on the other are superseded:

> The interpretation of personality as including individuality provides for the form of reason a content of sensibility, and thus secures a concrete view of the moral life: it discovers the universal in the particular. I am different from you, for we are both individuals; and since our individuality must colour our respective ideals of life, these ideals are, so far, different. But while it is the individual self that has to be realised, it is the complete self or personality of the individual, in whose common life the individuality of each must be taken up and interpreted as an element; and this secures a common ideal for all. (1926: 207)

Although Seth follows other post-Kantians in this concrete-substantial ethical supplementation of Kant, accepting Hegel's and Green's familiar criticisms of the abstract and formal nature of Kant's ethics, he also develops it further in the characteristic personalist direction, beyond the position of the absolutists. This can be seen in his stronger insistence on the ontological primacy of individuality in his formulations on concrete universality.

> The doctrine of the abstract universal, of pure rational selfhood, of form without content, is not less inadequate than the doctrine of the abstract particular, of mere individual sensibility, of content without form. In the moral, as well as in the intellectual sphere, the real is concrete, — the universal *in* the particular, such a unity of both as means the absolute sacrifice of neither. Such a moral realism at once recognises the truth of idealism, Platonic or Kantian, and supplements it by a more adequate interpretation of ethical fact. For, morally as intellectually, 'the individual alone is the real'. (1926: 198–9)

Significantly, before reaching his metaphysic of morals, Seth combines this view of ideal, universal personality and real, sensual individuality with a defence of a substantial, spiritual individuality. Strictly, the senses and the body are merely the "organ of a life that is, in its essence, spiritual", and the true self is "the soul or the spiritual self" (1926: 255); "in every man there is a soul, a self, unique and interesting, waiting for its development" (1926: 258). Thus beyond the self of mere transcendental apperception and practical reason, what was for Kant the individual, noumenal soul, somehow seems suddenly to enter personal idealism in a very different role than in Kant's philosophy. This represents another departure from the version of concrete-substantial ethics set forth by absolute idealism. Individuality is not *merely* the sensitive material out of which moral character is formed, and personality no longer *merely* the unity of such formed individuality and rational universality.

A similar position is hinted at by Pringle-Pattison. In his work there is, in fact, a tension between the Keatsian soulmaking by means of the shared content of the universe as immanent manifestation, on the one hand, and a more Platonic, spiritual, "daimonic" individualism of the kind of which Schelling and other early personalists developed different versions, and where an intelligible character was already either given in the mind of God or somehow chosen outside of time. Accepting the characteristic personalist emphasis on "the history of a life", Pringle-Pattison writes that "to take it as 'pure history' is to rob it of all significance", that "[w]e involuntarily regard it as the unfolding of a specific nature, the moulding of a mind and character in the play of circumstance or the stress of passion." Strangely, no attention is given here to the considerable difference between "unfolding" and "moulding". The important thing about this formulation, however, is that it shows how Pringle-Pattison too was prepared to accept that the soulmaking was not merely an existentialist self-creation, but an essentialist manifestation taking place through the life-history of the finite person. For all his adoption of immanentist positions from Hegel and modern biology, the rich complexity of Pringle-Pattison's philosophy is evidenced not least when it becomes clear that it still ties in with the sublime yet romanticized Platonism of Schelling's idea of the intelligible character, as when he speaks about the destiny of a self-conscious spirit as committed to itself and depending on a personal choice. He almost approaches a personalistic form of anamnetic reappropriation when he speaks of "the informing spirit of a beloved life — its 'idea', as Shakespeare calls it — lighting up the significance of individual acts or sayings, half-forgotten, as glimpses of a single soul", and of "a human mind and life to be realized as a divine idea or an individual purpose in the Absolute" (1920: 362–3).

Somehow, the spiritual individuality mentioned by Seth must be part of the picture when, immediately after mentioning it, he returns to the subject of "true doing" that springs from being, and expands on it by saying that "such doing is as unique as such being; the measure of it is found in the individuality of the worker. Each man, like each planet, has his appointed course, appointed to him by his nature" (Seth, 1926: 258–9). Yet because of the nature of personality, universality is still retained:

> The best ambition a man could cherish, both for himself and for his fellows, is that he and they alike may, each in himself, and each in his own way, so reflect the moral universe that none may have cause to travel beyond himself to find the fellowship of a common life and a common Good (1926: 259–60).

Although Seth expressed his position partly in Kantian and modern idealist terms, the notion of the person as containing in itself both universality and individuality was part of a long-standing tradition of western thought about the meaning of personality. In Seth and other personal idealists, this tradition was creatively renewed.

The Political Implications of Absolute Idealist Metaphysics

The problem with the ethical and axiological implications of the absolute idealist position with regard to individual personality, and especially with the social and political implications, is succinctly stated by R.T. Allen.[14] Allen accepts Bosanquet's view of positive freedom, his understanding of "how the individual does not stand over and against other individuals, institutions, society, and the state, but is essentially implicated in them, and that they can and do represent a better and higher level of himself below which he falls from time to time" (Allen, 1998: 232). At the same time he acknowledges that Bosanquet, despite being one of the leaders of the "new liberalism" with its sanction of the state's "active pursuit of specific goals", "by his doctrine of the limits of State action, reared a largely liberal politics upon Hegelian foundations", and even that he "went in his recommendations for policy no further than Hayek" (1998: 22). But he also clearly perceives what is nevertheless the ultimately precarious status of the individual in Bosanquet's political philosophy. For although merely hinted at in *The Philosophical Theory of the State*, the metaphysical and ethical positions set out in *The Principle of Individuality and Value* and *The Value and Destiny of the Individual* provide the background and foundation of the former work.

According to Allen, Bosanquet's "view of the relation of one person to another and to society is essentially a metaphysical one of their substantial identity" (1998: 232). For this reason, Bosanquet's criticism of "the supposed self-existent isolatable [sic] being", "the particular human being in his repellent isolation" (and so on), and his formulation that "The whole notion of man as one among others tends to break down; and we begin to see something in the one which actually identifies him with the others, and at the same time tends to make him what he admits he ought to be" (1998: 232),[15] have a very different meaning from the similar criticism of atomistic individualism in the personal idealists and from their development of the Kantian notion of rational personality.[16] Assuming with empiricism and analytical philosophy that "mind *is* its contents", and differing from them in drawing the correct inference from that assumption, namely "that minds with the same contents are, or are parts or functions of, one and the same mind", Bosanquet holds that there is "ultimately only *one* individual, namely, the Whole, the Absolute". The finite individual, being "distinct from the whole only by the accidents of bodily location,

---

14 This is not the place to comment upon the recent attempts to defend or resuscitate absolute idealism and not least the political philosophy of the absolute idealists. Its recent defence by a number of philosophers and historians is much needed after a century of simplifications and distortions.
15 Quoting Bosanquet (1923: xxxiii–xxxiv, 95), see Bosanquet (2001. 22–3, 120).
16 I add this observation to Allen's argument.

without which finite minds could actually merge and unite into higher unities", is in himself, Allen concludes, "nothing and has no value". His only value is "his contribution to the Whole, his performance as a cosmic functionary" (1998: 232).

As we have seen, these were the positions which Pringle-Pattison sought to refute philosophically in *The Idea of God*; earlier, in *Hegelianism and Personality*, he had historically explained the development of the idea of the single, identical transcendental self, hypostasized as the absolute, in German and Greenian absolute idealism. These were also the positions which Webb challenged in his Gifford lectures, *God and Personality* (1918) and *Divine Personality and Human Life* (1920). But their practical implications seem to become most clearly manifest in political philosophy. Because of its metaphysical and ethical background, there is an insidious ambiguity about Bosanquet's liberalism. "For, if in the end", Allen continues, "the individual person is nothing substantial in himself but only an adventitious collection of experiences, just why should he be treated with respect and allowed liberty of action?" If, as for Bosanquet, the answer can only be a utilitarian one, there can be no objection to overriding the individual person's liberty and dignity if by so doing more good can be achieved. Allen finds

> no explicit or implicit repudiation in Bosanquet's writings of Hegel's frank admission of the dispensability of the finite individual when the Whole, the World Spirit, has no more use for him. For all Hegel's incorporation of a level of individual rights and liberty within his rational state which will finally embody the Idea in an objective form, just as his own philosophy embodies it in a subjective form, in the end each person is but a disposable vehicle for the self-realisation of the *Weltgeist*, and intermediate levels of spirits of the time or nation can use any individual embodied spirit in whatever way best furthers the cosmic goal of the self-realisation of the Idea (1998: 232–3).

Although Bosanquet's Absolute is "a static one above time, though including time within itself, and not one coming into being in time and world-history", it "includes the same principle of the metaphysical and thence moral subordination of the alleged individual to higher unities and finally to the one Whole" (1998: 233).[17]

Individuality and Universality in Society

Perceiving clearly the potential dangers of this kind of position, before its more or less direct consequences could be studied in the totalitarian systems of the twentieth century, the personal idealists worked out an alternative which, while preserving some of the important truths of idealism, supplemented the view of the individual person that Allen calls for.

---

17 For a discussion of the Absolute as "static", see Tyler (2006: 157ff). For a more sympathetic reading of Bosanquet on the issue of the value of the individual, see Sweet (1996).

From Seth's view of the relation of individuality and personality, it follows that the moral life is always both individual and personal; the self is "enlarged and enriched", not sacrificed, by unselfishness, and individuality is preserved in the larger social good (Seth, 1926: 271). But since rational, autonomous personality is universal, its law makes possible society, the kingdom of ends, and constitutes in itself the common good (1926: 205). The moral imperative—forming sensible individuality into moral character—is both individual and social, it is the same for individual and social life. In the case of moral character and true self-realization, there is no conflict between egoism and altruism: "the most effective method of doing good is to be good… the truest care for others is to keep carefully the vineyard of our own nature" (1926: 287). Using his distinct concept of personality which includes but also transcends that of Kant, Seth writes that "The individual and the social are in reality… two aspects of the one undivided life of virtue, and their unity is discovered with their reduction to the common principle of personality", and continues: "The social life is, equally with the individual life, personal; and the personal life is necessarily at once individual and social" (1926: 276).

Personal idealism characteristically rejected hypostasized abstractions, the new appearance of a one-sided "Scholastic Realism, or substantiation of the universal" (1926: 277). Society has no "life of its own apart from its individual members; society is the organisation of individuals, and it is they who live, not it". Nor is society the organism of the romantics, but "the ethical organisation of individuals. Obviously, we must not isolate the organisation or the relation from the beings organised or related". Combining the Kantian and the individualized notions of personality, and preserving the truths of idealism's "new liberalism" in a deeper defence of individuality, Seth writes:

> A common personality is to be realised in each, and in infinite ways the life of each is bound up with that of all. Only, the individual must never lose himself in the life of others. As a person, he is an end in himself, and has an infinite worth. He has a destiny, to be wrought out for himself; the destiny of society is the destiny of its individual members… The ethical end is personal, first and last. As the individual apart from society is an unreal abstraction, so is society apart from the individual. The ethical unit is the person. (1926: 277)

Thus, when Seth calls this "true socialism", it is clear that it is something quite apart from the historical line that connects Hegelianism with Marxism, so-called real socialism, and national socialism, of the twentieth century.[18] And this despite the fact that Seth, in his chapter on "The Social Life", uses an inclusive definition of the state, presents a defence of state interventionism—which, in its general formulations, sometimes seems to

---

18 Elsewhere (Seth, 1926: 331), socialism, presumably in his view "false socialism", represents for Seth the "abstract extreme", opposite to "abstract… individualism".

go further than Bosanquet's—emphasizes the positive and not merely negative functions of the state, and holds an ambiguous view of the general will as the moral basis of legitimate state power; all these are positions that he shared with the absolutists. For Marx, it will be recalled, the human essence is man's true collectivity. For Seth, "Society exists for the individual"; and

> the individualism of the person is, in idea at least, synonymous with the true socialism, and the true democracy with the true aristocracy. For social progress does not mean so much the massing of individuals as the individualisation of the social mass; the discovery, in the 'masses', of that same humanity, individual and personal, which had formerly been discerned only in the 'classes'. The truly social ideal is to make possible for the many—nay, for all, or better for each—that full and total life of personality which, to so large an extent, is even still the exclusive possession of the few. Social organisation is never an end in itself, it is always a means to the attainment of individual perfection. (1926: 277–8)

We have already seen how Seth's application of the central idea of the concrete universal is significantly different from that of Hegelianism, which, with its generalist, impersonalist metaphysics in which the status of individuality and concreteness ultimately remained precarious, could hardly systematically integrate it. Seth's political no less than his ethical application of the concept exhibits his view of the ontological status of the individual. We can see his different stress on individuality in both his political and his ethical use of the idea, for instance in the following passage on cosmopolitanism and patriotism:

> The concentration of patriotism is not necessarily identical with narrowness and limitation… cosmopolitanism has proved a failure when subjected to the test of history… it resulted in individualism and social disintegration. We best serve humanity when we serve our country best, as our best service to our country is our service to our immediate community, and our best service to our community is the service of our family, and friends, and neighbours. For here, once more, we must be on our guard against the fallacy of the abstract universal. Humanity is only a vague abstraction until we particularise it in the nation, as the latter itself also is until we still further particularise and individualise it. The true universal is the concrete universal, or the universal in the particular; and we can well believe that in the life of domestic piety, of true neighbourliness, and of good citizenship, our best duty to humanity itself is abundantly fulfilled. (1926: 319)

The primacy of individuality in relation to social wholes is also stated clearly by C.C.J. Webb, against the background of his epistemological and metaphysical discussions of the relation of individual personality to impersonal orders of any kind. Reconnecting the partial truths of modern idealism to the tradition of classical natural theology, Webb analysed the classical option of elevating an impersonal rational order above the personal God. Swinging between the voluntarism of Ockham and the rationalism of Leibniz, philosophy had departed from the balanced, orthodox solutions of Augustine and Aquinas. Webb and other personal idealists return to the orthodox position, but with a new and specifically modern emphasis on the concept of personality and with new, modern meanings added to it.

For Webb, ultimate reality cannot be impersonal reason — but this implies no conflict between personality and reason. Pringle-Pattison innovatively develops the idea of creation to explain his view of reality as a dynamic unity in diversity. Webb uses a similar conception, explained by means of typical analogies, in order to harmonize reason and personality: "In the creative activity of the artist", Webb writes, "we seem to see Personality and Reason no longer contrasted but reconciled and at one" (Webb, 1918: 268); "the Intelligence which is manifested in the world-process must be thought of rather after the analogy of the dramatist than after that of the geometer" (1918: 270). Both Pringle-Pattison and Webb devote much space to the unavoidable questions involved in the co-thinking of personality and the Whole: whether the Whole and the absolute can at all be thought in personal terms, whether the concept of personality does not necessarily imply limits as well as mutual relations. This problematic was never quite so pressing for orthodox Christianity, since it conceived of three persons within one divine nature, and God was therefore not *a* person. Personal idealism, whether unitarian or trinitarian, insisted that the whole and the absolute could indeed be personal and be involved in personal relations. Created finite beings are not wholly independent, nor do they exist outside or alongside their creator, the personal absolute.

One consequence of this thoroughgoing personalism was that neither on the level of the absolute nor on that of the finite being could values be conceived as impersonal or as transcendent in relation to personality. Truth being seen as a value in this tradition, and values being realized only in persons, eternal truths can only be personal truths, not in the sense of relative, subjective truths, but in the sense of truths manifested by persons. Of course, finite beings manifest them only fragmentarily and relatively. Their ultimate ground is the absolute person, but precisely because this person is absolute, universality is not thereby lost. It is just that there can be no universality beyond that manifested in and by the absolute as personal. Persons and the society of persons are for Webb primary, not only in relation to rational truths and values, but to other impersonal entities, "principles, causes, or communities for which persons sacrifice themselves" (Webb, 1920: 243). The latter cannot be conceived "as actually existing otherwise than as they are embodied in persons, are carried out by persons, or consist of persons": "we shall hardly fail to find ourselves profoundly dissatisfied if we are convinced that the object to which persons have sacrificed themselves is never and nowhere realized except as an aim unfulfilled in any personal life as real as that which has been surrendered in its service" (1920: 243).

With an elevated poetic style, Pringle-Pattison appeals to the same "great experiences in life" which Bosanquet had invoked in support of impersonal transcendence — but in order to prove the opposite, "the absolute necessity of what I… call 'otherness'": "It takes two not only to make a bargain", but

> it takes two to love and to be loved, two to worship and to be worshipped, and many combined in a common purpose to form a society or a people. Surely, as the poet says, sweet love were slain, could difference be abolished; the most self-effacing love but ministers to the intensity of a double fruition… Selfhood is not selfishness — Surely the better the society… the more pervasive the spirit of membership — the more fully does each member realize and enjoy his own individuality. It is in individual foci that the common life burns: it is reflected to us from the countenances of our fellows. (Pringle-Pattison, 1920: 289–90)[19]

For Webb, not even the preference for an impersonal system of law over personal caprice implies "an ultimate preference for the impersonal over the personal, which we must needs carry over even into our notion of divine justice". For "there are persons to whose discretion one would commit oneself with far more confidence than to the generalities of a legal rule" (Webb, 1918: 257). "The truest Justice" includes Mercy, and "Mercy in the highest sense" vindicates for itself "the name of Justice". But this union can best be represented "as realized in a personality than after any other fashion" (1918: 257-8). Ideals can "survive or live at all" only "as included in a personal experience" (Webb, 1920: 246).

This characteristic personal idealist emphasis on individuality which never relinquishes objectivity and universality, is consistently maintained as Seth, too, works out in detail the social and political implications of his ethics. Social virtue is divided by Seth into two parts: justice (i.e., the negative maintenance of the sphere of individual liberty) and benevolence (i.e., the positive removing of obstacles and the creation of favourable conditions for self-actualization). While both may be political, justice is related to the community and has the state as its sphere, while benevolence is related to the individual and is exercised primarily in the private sphere of the family and of non-political associations.[20] But benevolence is "more just than justice, because it is enlightened by the insight into that 'inequality' and uniqueness of individuals which is no less real than the 'equality' of persons" (Seth, 1926: 282).

---

19 Only the first half of the line "sweet love were slain, could difference be abolished" is a literal quote from Tennyson's *The Princess*; the reference in the poem is the difference between man and woman.
20 Seth rejects as artificial the limitation of state action to justice.

The legitimate interventions of the state are for Seth mainly the ones that are necessary to prevent the chaos and injustice of unbridled individualism, and to secure the space, the opportunity, and the conditions for the individual to live the moral life — to develop his individuality to personal moral character. The state, like society, is not an end in itself, it exists for the sake of the individual person; it is, like society, the medium of his moral life (1926: 293). The moral life can never be forced by the state: "Not even God can *make* a man good", Seth writes in true Kantian spirit; "Goodness, by its very nature, must be the achievement of the individual" (1926: 278). The state as an ethical institution, furthermore, "cannot, without contradicting its own nature, contradict the moral nature of the individual" (1926: 287). The "ultimate sanction and measure of political obedience" is found in "the ethical value of the State as the vehicle of the personal life of its citizens". Its interference can therefore be "only with the individual" in the sense of the immoral, anti-social nature of sensible individuality, "not with the person". Moreover, the purpose of such interference "is always to save the person from the interference of other individuals" (1926: 295). Seth notes:

> The State restrains the expression of the individuality, that it may vindicate the sacred rights of personality in each individual. Its order is an improvement upon the order of nature; it is more discriminating, more just, more encouraging to virtue, more discouraging to vice. The political order foreshadows the moral order itself… (1926: 299)

But, interestingly, he adds that "The subject who remains loyal to this ideal has a right to rebellion if the state contradicts it" (1926: 300).

Personal Freedom

One of the most fundamental and significant differences between personal and absolute idealism is exhibited when Seth's view of the relation between the individual person, and society and the state; this receives a deeper metaphysical elucidation and explanation in his teaching on freedom in his metaphysic of morals. Pringle-Pattison's metaphysical discussion of this issue is related to his treatment of will. For Pringle-Pattison, as for many earlier, continental European personalists, will is related to intelligence in a "larger, directer form" (Pringle-Pattison, 1920: 339). As thus related, it is not "a meaningless freedom of choice" nor a "groundless act", not bare, abstract, "contentless will". It is a continuous "affirming and possessing one's experience, which is the characteristic, or at least the ideal, of the self-conscious individual" — a conception which he also applies to God (1920: 339–40). The external, impersonal forces of the universe, although acting on the individual person, do not determine his moral action, since he always makes his response and is thus transformed only according to "his deliberate choice" (1920: 292). Seth, however, discussed freedom at greater length. The question of the soul (or, as Seth frames it, of "the interpretation of man's essential being" [Seth, 1926: 366]) includes, as in Kant, the two inseparable questions of whether this being is reducible to nature or shares in a super-natural life, and of freedom. If man is reducible to nature, he is unfree, if sharing in a supernatural life, he is free; "the moral problem of freedom is... the problem of personality itself" (1926: 372).

With Kant, Seth concludes that freedom, or at least the idea of freedom, is the postulate of morality,[21] and that it is confirmed by the demands of the moral consciousness. Its acceptance may, Seth frankly states, necessitate a "surrender of metaphysical completeness in our scheme of the universe": materialistic as well as idealistic monism must be relinquished with the recognition of the experiential factuality of "free personality" and "a plurality of spiritual agents". Moreover, the same admission implies "the recognition of evil, real and positive, alongside of good, in the universe" (1926: 372). This understanding of the philosophical ramifications of the acceptance of freedom was characteristic of the whole of the "countercurrent" of personalism throughout the nineteenth century, ever since Jacobi's criticism of Spinozism in the 1780s. It was Schelling's new insights precisely regarding freedom and the real choice between good and evil that was the source of his break with his own earlier absolute idealism and of his criticism of Hegel in *Über das Wesen der menschlichen Freiheit* (1809), the work which, according to Heidegger, "shatters Hegel's *Logic* before it was even published" (quoted in Snow, 1996: 149).

With reference to the claims of evolutionary science, Seth questions the relevance of the philosophical attempts to interpret freedom in a way that would render it compatible with the outer necessity of nature—attempts of the kind that are today called "liberty of spontaneity" and "soft determinism":

> In our day... it is no longer scientific to recognise such a break as Mill... insisted upon, between outward constraint and inward determination. All the interests of the scientific ambition are bound up with the denial of freedom in any and every sense of the word; its admission means embarrassment to the scientific consciousness, and the surrender of the claim of science to finality in its view of human life. (Seth, 1926: 370)

With Kant, however, Seth insists that these interests must simply be supplemented by philosophy. But not any philosophy will do. For naturalism's alleged opposite, absolute idealism, being equally impersonalistic, was also equally deterministic. Liberty of spontaneity or soft determinism, a moral and political freedom of a kind allegedly compatible with meta-

---

21 Seth first set out this Kantian view (as already characteristically modified and enhanced by his personalism) in *Freedom as Ethical Postulate* (1891).

physical necessity, was the position of the absolute idealists too.[22] In contradistinction to both, personal idealism's defence of a deeper personal identity includes the dimension of moral freedom that it holds to be inseparable from such identity.

But if, as we saw above, each man, like each planet, has his own course, appointed to him by his unique, individual nature — if, according to personal idealism, his deepest identity is somehow already given and merely unfolded in the course of his life-history — then at least liberty of spontaneity, the freedom of "inward determination", would seem to be a natural, concomitant position. For personal idealists, there is indeed both inward and outward determination. They rule out pure liberty of indifference and the illusion of absolute subjectivist or existentialist freedom which Jacobi had already perceived to be quite as nihilistic as any pantheist or monist determinism. The personal idealists saw through and rejected this aspect of the typical modern dialectic. The determinations, Seth and others argue, are merely partial. Inner nature and outward circumstances provide a given, limited, determined moral sphere for the individual, but within this sphere, each is irreducibly free to choose between good and evil (Seth 1926: 397). And this choice is the moral imperative as understood by personal idealism — an imperative of which such freedom is of course the precondition: "Inner nature and outward circumstances are, as it were, the raw material out of which he has to create a character — a plastic material which, like the sculptor, he has to subdue to his own formative idea" (Seth, 1926: 379). Again, because of the individually determined confines, "the moral ideal takes a different complexion for each of us, and… no man's moral task is exactly like his brother's", yet "though it must be realised in a variety of concrete particulars, it may be realised in any particulars, without losing its universal significance" (1926: 379). Moral success or failure "is determined ultimately not by the material, but by the free play of the energy of the self" (1926: 380). And this requires that there is an active, synthetic, transcendental self which is separate from the material and from its successive experiences, a self which is not "resolvable into its phenomenal states" as in empiricism, psychology, and certain forms of absolute idealism (1926: 383).

Seth presses ahead, like Kant, with the question of the reconcilability of theoretical and practical reason — the question of the theoretical implications of the testimony of moral consciousness. He accepts, with Lotze, that freedom properly understood postulates uniformity of the law of causation as widely extended but not exclusive, as "instrumental, an organic instrument in the life of the self". But, he continues, "the supreme category of that life is freedom". For freedom means self-determination, not indetermination; "it presupposes, rather than negates, uniformity" (1926:

---

22   For the case against compatibilism, see Bernard Gendron (1976).

378). With the whole of the nineteenth-century personalist current, Seth's defence of moral freedom against materialist as well as absolute idealist "monism" goes considerably beyond Kant's position. Personal idealism finds Kant's view of freedom deficient in that it confines freedom to a noumenality that is so sharply distinguished from phenomenality as to render it empty and unreal. Even as a moral ideal it is onesided, the freedom only of the rational self apart from the necessity of sensible individuality. For Kant, "Good alone is the product of freedom, evil is the product of necessity" (1926: 397). The distinct personalist view of freedom, in contrast, is "freedom in choosing the evil equally with the good; only such a double freedom can be regarded as the basis of responsibility or obligation". Freedom is even "that which makes evil evil, and… that which makes good good" (1926: 397). Freedom can only have real moral significance if it is

> realised in the concrete life of motivated activity, in the apparent necessity of nature, which is thereby converted into the mechanism of freedom; not apart from this actual life of man, in the life of sheer passionless reason, which is not human life as we know it. By… constituting for it a purely rational sphere of its own, Kant has reduced freedom to a mere abstraction. What is left is the mere form of the moral life without its content. The content of human freedom can only be that life of nature and mechanism, of feeling and impulse, which Kant excludes as irrational. (1926: 397)

Hegel, again, sought to overcome this Kantian dualism, but only through the impersonalism of the closed—if dialectical—immanentism which sacrificed the reality of man's moral life with his freedom. In Hegel, both the finite self and its freedom are resolved into God or the Absolute and its higher necessity, while apparent evil is resolved into real good, or, "rather, both good and evil are resolved into a *tertium quid*"; they are both mere *entia imaginationis*, in Spinoza's term (1926: 400). With the whole early personalist tradition, Seth dismisses this as "too rapid an explanation"; negating instead of explaining the experiential facts, its unification cannot be the true one:

> Such an unethical unification might conceivably be a sufficient interpretation of nature, and of man in so far as he is a natural being, and even in so far as he is an intellectual being; it is not a sufficient interpretation of man as man, or in his moral being. The reality of the moral life is bound up with the reality of human freedom, and the reality of freedom with the integrity of the moral personality. If I am a person… I am free; if I am not… a person… I am not free. (1926: 401)

Webb on Autonomy and Authority

Only if I am a person, only if I have a full experience of the moral life and freedom, can I reach not only the highest conception of union and communion with God, a union "not only of thought with Thought, but of will with

Will" (Seth, 1926: 402), but the highest conception of God himself—which turns out to be crucial to ethics. This is a central tenet of personal idealism, harking back, as so many others, to the first half of the nineteenth-century. What we really do as self-legislative, Seth writes, is "re-enact the law already enacted by God; we recognise, rather than constitute, the law of our own being. The moral law is the echo within our souls of the voice of the Eternal, whose offspring we are" (1926: 434). For the moral ideal is no mere ideal, fiction, or human creation. It must also be real; the supreme reality must be the realization of the ideal.

Here the personal idealists agree with the British absolute idealists that the absolute is not realizing itself in time, history, and the consciousness of man. In the whole that is a plurality in unity of personal selves, neither God nor the universe is evolving or growing: against William James, but also against Schelling (who, as later German and other European personalists had already perceived, was in this respect even in his later thought still caught in the older German romantic pantheism), Pringle-Pattison holds that only finite beings undergo development (Pringle-Pattison, 1920: 373–4). Our awareness of the ideal attests its reality and actuality in original transcendent completeness, "the very note of moral and religious experience" (1920: 382–3). But since, in Seth's words,

> the moral ideal is an ideal of personality, must not the moral reality, the reality of which that ideal is the after-reflection as well as the prophetic hint, be the perfection of personality, the supreme Person whose image we, as persons, bear and are slowly and with effort inscribing on our natural individuality? (Seth 1926: 434)[23]

The rest of Seth's argument for the ethical necessity of the personality of God (in relation to finite persons), and for immortality (the last question or aspect of the metaphysic of morals), builds on arguments identical with those of his brother, Pringle-Pattison, and the whole of the earlier personalist tradition.

From this personal view of the absolute—a conclusion of both metaphysics and ethics—follows the deep ethical divergence between personal idealism, not only from Hegel, but from Kant. The personal idealists cannot accept human rational autonomy alone as the final word of ethics. This aspect of personal idealism was perhaps best formulated by Webb. Against Kant's application of his distinction between noumenal and phenomenal man as an explanation of the paradoxical appearance in his moral philosophy of "the judge on the bench" being identical with "the prisoner at the bar" (Webb, 1920: 122), Webb holds with Martineau (in his *A Study of Religion*) that "in the act of Conscience we are immediately introduced to a *Higher than ourselves that gives us what we feel*", and (as he writes in his *Types of Ethical Theory*) that "It takes two… to establish an obligation… The per-

---

23 Here, clearly, spiritual individuality is again suggested.

son that *bears* the obligation cannot also be the person whose presence *imposes* it... Personality is unitary and in occupying one side of a given relation is unable to be also on the other." The recognition of "another than I... another greater and higher and of deeper insight", who is indeed supreme over us — a personal God, immanent as well as transcendent, and with whom is possible the relation which Kant's epistemology cannot admit and which is "only to be described as personal intercourse" — is implied in our experience of the authority of the moral law, or of the moral law as the object of our veneration (1920: 123-4, 126, 132).[24]

This does not mean for Webb that the moral law does not have its own "intrinsic authority" (Webb, 1920: 129). We may even speak of it as self-imposed, in the sense that our reason unconditionally accepts its obligation. The disinterested recognition is indeed precisely how I know a command to be God's (1920: 132, 137). Kant's fear of religious fanaticism based on pious fancy was in itself commendable in Webb's view. But there was also, in Kant, "a defective sense for the specifically religious factor in human life" which led him to his conclusions in this regard, conclusions which Webb also finds philosophically untenable (1920: 129):

> We must acknowledge in obligation... an aspect of *autonomy*, but also of a *heteronomy*, which turns out on inspection to be really a *theonomy*. Such a heteronomy, however, is not a heteronomy in Kant's sense; for... it is involved in our notion of God that he is immanent in our reason and will, which notwithstanding he transcends. (1920: 132).[25]

Our recognition of the obligation is at the same time a recognition of its source "as the supreme and absolute Lawgiver over all rational beings". This "in no way impairs my freedom, since it is only through my free choice of the right that I am conscious of his demands upon me" (1920: 137-8). The development of historical criticism and the comparative study of religions in the nineteenth century had, in Webb's view, averted the risks of fundamentalist literalism that such a position would in Kant's days have increased (1920: 132).

With this development of Kant's ethics, Webb thus still insists on the value of Kant's recognition of authority, "the correlative of the notion of Obligation" (Webb, 1920: 131). Importantly, he sets this against the weakening of that recognition in Green's demotion of obligation and the consciousness of duty to a position secondary to that of the common good, and his linking of autonomy to Rousseauan democracy. By this move, the Kantian idea of the disinterested nature of obedience to the moral law was abandoned (1920: 131). Yet, at the same time, Kant's own considerations which made it impossible for him to admit the kind of heteronomy

---

24 See also Martineau (1888: ii: 27) and (1901: ii: 107ff).
25 These positions had been set forth long before by idealistic personalists in other countries (Webb himself here refers to a German, Julius Müller).

defended by the personal idealists precluded the only way to forestall a Rousseauistic use of autonomy. Since democracy and political self-determination tend to become principles corresponding to the insufficient pure autonomy of Kant's ethics, a supplementation of Kantianism is needed in politics as well. In this sphere, Webb holds, the risk is even greater of a disregard of Kant's distinction between noumenal and phenomenal man, of "the pursuit of the general happiness" being

> so plausibly represented as the whole content of public duty, the sole end of public action, that it is especially easy here first to think of a 'common good' rather than of a 'common obligation', and then to interpret this 'common good' in terms which really in the end are terms of individual happiness and pleasure. (1920: 135–6)

Webb not only dismisses utilitarianism, perceiving how absolute idealism in its politics could move into its vicinity. He also discerns the specifically modern, Rousseauist element in the "new liberals" — how theirs was no longer the old aristocratic, classical concept of the common good, traditionally taught at Oxford, but a subtly, or sometimes not so subtly, reinterpreted one. Webb's observations in this regard are considerably sharper than Seth's.

Yet for all their errors and onesidedness, the doctrines of social contract and the rights of man, Webb held, contained the truth that there is no legitimate authority without consent. But this truth needed to be supplemented by the partial truth of the doctrine of the divine right of kings, namely that authority and obligation cannot be deduced from consent. They derive "from an ultimate experience of the human spirit incapable of explanation in terms of anything other than itself" (1920: 137). The two truths correspond to autonomy and heteronomy/theonomy respectively, which are thus found also in social life (1920: 136–7). Webb agrees with Plato that society is the individual soul writ large (1920: 138). The authority of heteronomy is needed in social no less than in individual life. Without reverence for the law, obedience to it and to those who administer and execute it cannot be justified on any other ground than self-interest. And, Webb asks, how can there be reverence for a law whose authority is derived merely from consent (1920: 141)?

As we have seen, for Webb, not even the preference for an impersonal system of law implies an ultimate preference for the impersonal over the personal. The concept of an impersonal law — i.e., natural, moral law — was dominant in antiquity and the Middle Ages, Webb points out, and he thinks that it was only with the growth of a stronger sense of personality that its attribution to an author became more natural, i.e., the elevation of personality above the impersonal order. At the same time, however, historical knowledge and theological thought combined to make "the direct attribution to divine personality of the whole law obeyed by a political community" implausible. Thus modern society was left with the human imponent, and, more precisely, the human imponent as a collective, the principle of autonomy and consent (1920: 139–41). As this principle alone is neither true to moral experience nor politically viable, Webb insists on the necessity of a social counterpart to the personalistically reinforced authority of individual conscience, in the form of the personal lawgiver:

> the true ground of preference of free and popular institutions over despotic law lies not in this: that no one is really under *obligation* to obey any authority but one which is ultimately *his own*; but in this: that only where he has himself a say in appointing or accepting the vehicles of that authority can he be counted upon to acquiesce in their authority as — not his own — but the best representative he can find of God's. (1920: 142).[26]

On these grounds, Webb defends monarchic government, which:

> may rest as well as any other on the consent which is necessary to give to the community... the character of freedom or self-determination corresponding to the autonomy of the individual moral choice; while it is perhaps especially well qualified to bring before the imagination that other character of authority, in which it is representative of God. (1920: 143)

In their explanations of the concept of personality as implying a distinct relationship both with other human persons in society and with transcendence (and more specifically, the transcendent, divine person), the personal idealists creatively elaborated, in a new historical and intellectual setting, a characteristic theme of western thought on personhood — just as they had done in their ideas of the unity of individuality and universality.

Conclusion

The British personal idealists, as part of a deep and broad personalistic current in modern thought, presented a distinct, coherent worldview and a powerful alternative to the various philosophies they criticized. This is not least true of their moral, social, and political philosophy. The absolute idealists' new liberalism held out the hope of a philosophy equal to the new social reality and the problems of modern industrial capitalism. But, as I have argued, both the classical liberals and the idealist new liberals are caught in a characteristic modern dynamic which lacks the intellectual and moral resources to overcome the fatal dialectic of the extremes of individualism and collectivism. The absolute idealists certainly *claimed* to be able to do precisely this. There can be no doubt that they were aware of the reality of this problematic and endeavoured to present a solution. The questions with which they dealt were real indeed, and their perspective on them remains of considerable interest. Significantly, some conservative thinkers are prepared to admit the partial truths in the absolute idealists' view of

---

26 Webb here cites his own collection of addresses, *In Time of War* (1918), 51.

the state and society, despite their scepticism with regard to their specific idealist derivation.[27] But Hegelian conservatism, like romantic conservatism, is if not a wholly adventitious phenomenon, at least one which disregards the deeper cultural dynamic of modernity, and is likely to be carried away on its waves unless it is anchored in other and more properly congenial traditions. As Peter Nicholson has shown, not even Bradley can properly be regarded as a conservative thinker. But whether interpreted in a radical or conservative direction, the dynamic of which absolute idealism was a part made it impossible for the new liberalism satisfactorily to reconcile individuality, the larger social wholes, and the moral order.

It is not that the personal idealists were themselves wholly untouched by the modern dynamic of rationalism and romanticism that was intrinsically and necessarily linked to the fatal dialectic of individualism and collectivism. As I have pointed out, the nineteenth century elevation of personality itself was often fatally caught in spurious intellectual tendencies of the age. But the personal idealists' claim to our attention today is not least that they were able — and to a much greater extent than their contemporaries — to perceive important aspects and implications of this dynamic, as well as many of its historical sources and stages of development. All in all, personal idealism at its best, represented in Britain by Pringle-Pattison, Seth, Webb, and others, must be said to be part of what could perhaps be termed an "alternative modernity". For it managed, on the one hand, to appropriate the partial truths of modern idealism and liberalism and address the specific problems of modern thought and society, while, on the other hand, to retain a sufficient grasp on and continuity with the insights of the Christian and to some extent classical tradition, to be able to see through some of the problematic tendencies of modernity.

The key to this clearsightedness was the personal idealists' understanding the meaning and the implications of that complex and often elusive yet centrally important and unique concept: the concept of the person.

Setting against the "atomism" of the classical liberals an insistence on the social and metaphysical wholes, the absolute idealists failed to explain and assimilate the truths of the deeper or higher individuality of personality. Accepting the absolutists' criticism of classical liberalism and its underlying empiricism, as well as many of the general idealist positions with which they sought to replace it, the personal idealists perceived this weakness, and presented a clear analysis of its real nature.

While sharing with idealism and liberal theology a tendency towards a moralization of faith, their understanding of the concept of the person allowed the personal idealists to retain and even reinforce classical theism

---

27 Thus Roger Scruton adheres to the view of Hegel as a conservative thinker, at least in some important respects; R.T. Allen's endorsement of important elements in Bosanquet cited above is a conservative one.

against the drift of the age towards deism, pantheism, and ultimately atheism. Perhaps the reason why personal idealism has as yet received comparatively little attention in the renaissance of idealism studies is that most modern intellectuals are still caught in the constitutive dynamic of modernity, the main thrust of which is precisely the rejection of the theism, partial transcendence, freedom, and moral objectivism that personal idealism sought to defend in contemporary terms — what may perhaps be called the "pantheistic revolution" of modernity (and indeed of postmodernity). There is, thus, a broad range of cultural, psychological, and other factors at work, a whole orientation of the modern sensibility and not a purely philosophical consideration, which makes the personal idealist position seem implausible.[28] Drawing attention to the personal idealist alternative, let alone arguing for its merits, requires addressing this whole sensibility.

The attempt is worthwhile. For the characteristic achievement of the personal idealists was that they retrieved within the modern project itself, broadly conceived, the traditional western positions from which alone the fatal flaws and inner logic of the pantheistic revolution, the consequences of which we have had ample historical opportunity to study, could be laid bare. While not wholly escaping its influence, they pointed clearly in the direction in which the valid elements of Kantianism, idealism, and liberalism could be extricated from the rational-romantic dynamic of modernity. Ever since Hobbes, modernity had been unable to reconcile credibly, either in theory or practice, secular, appetitive individuality and the social and political whole. No version of individualism has been able to save either real individuality or the true universality that is one of the preconditions of its defence. Meaningful difference, and thus sweet love — and, less poetically, the value and dignity of the individual person — remained threatened. They still remain so in the postmodern world of a shallow, relativistic individualism without selves. Their defence still requires the elaboration of the notion of the concrete universal in combination with a more traditional, moral and spiritual conception of individual personality. The personal idealists suggested, in outline, how a viable moral, political, and social alternative could be conceived *within modernity itself*.

I have suggested that personal idealism supplies a needed deepening of liberalism, and in particular of idealism's "new liberalism". But in truth, the independent, integral, and philosophical character of this alternative becomes evident not least if we consider the extent to which it defies classification in terms of any standard ideological definitions, whether of liberalism, socialism, or conservatism. It is hardly correct to describe the early phase of what I regard as the unitary personalist current in the nineteenth century as a purely conservative reaction in Germany against radicalism and Young Hegelianism, as does Warren Breckman in his *Marx, the Young*

---

28 For the philosophical case, see e. g. Kohák (2002).

Hegelians, and the Origins of Radical Social Theory (1999).[29] As he is himself aware, Jacobi was clearly a kind of liberal, and, as I have pointed out, rather in the Anglo-Scottish tradition. This aspect of early personalism becomes even more evident when we turn to other European countries. At the same time that theistic and idealistic personalism became a support of conservatism in Germany, and the original radical impulse of idealistic pantheism was again released under the pressure of the political reaction which sought to extinguish its "dragon seed", the leading Swedish personal idealist, Erik Gustaf Geijer (1783–1847) drew distinctly liberal conclusions from the very same personalism. American personal idealism, while restating many of the older arguments, is most definitely part of modern liberalism in a broader, including a moral and theological, sense.

Webb's defence of authority and monarchy is reminiscent of the early German arguments that Breckman analyses. As such, it is proof of the continuity between early nineteenth-century personal idealism and the later British one. J.R. Illingworth, alluding to the divide in the Hegelian school in Germany, upon joining them called the members of this British school the "Greenites of the Right", and pointed to Pringle-Pattison as their leader; presumably Bradley and Bosanquet were in Illingworth's view the "Greenites of the Left" (Illingworth, 1917: 90).

But in Britain, we have seen how Seth defended a "true socialism" and was often very much in line with the "new liberalism". It is clear that the social and political aspects of British personal idealism cannot simply be classified as conservative. But it is true to say that almost all personal idealists preserved in their own way some of the essential insights of conservatism. Not only was for this reason their "socialism" something very different from what has passed under that name in the twentieth century, but their liberalism too was distinct from all other versions of liberalism. It could be said that, to the extent that there are recognizable similarities, the liberal, socialist, and conservative elements were modified, adjusted, and bent into conformity with the insights that were the distinctive property of personal idealism itself. And this holds also for the elements shared with absolute idealism and Kantianism. But perhaps this description does not do full justice to the contribution of the personal idealists. It might rather be the case that, from the core of these specific insights, there followed positions which, although sometimes similar to those of other thinkers and currents, are those of personal idealism alone.

---

29 See my (2000). The book under review has considerable merits in other respects.

References

Allen, R. (1998), *Beyond Liberalism: The Political Thought of F.A. Hayek and Michael Polanyi* (New Brunswick, NJ: Transaction Publishers).
Auxier, Randall E. (ed) (2008), *Focus on Jan Olof Bengtsson, The Wordlview of Personalism, The Pluralist*, 3/2.
Bengtsson, J.O. (2000), Review of *Marx, the Young Hegelians, and the Origins of Radical Social Theory*, *History of European Ideas*, 26/2.
Bengtsson, J.O. (2006), *The Wordlview of Personalism: Origins and Early Development* (Oxford: Oxford University Press).
Bosanquet, B. (1912), *The Principle of Individuality and Value: The Gifford Lectures for 1911* (London: Macmillan).
Bosanquet, B. (1918), "Life and Finite Individuality" (Aristotelian Society Supplementary Volume) (London, Williams and Norgate).
Bosanquet, B. (2001), *The Philosophical Theory of the State* (4th edn., 1923); new edn. with Introduction, notes, and related essays, ed. William Sweet and Gerald F. Gaus (South Bend, IN: St Augustine's Press).
Bowie, A. (1993), *Schelling and Modern European Philosophy* (London and New York: Routledge).
diGiovanni, G. (1994), "Introduction: The Unfinished Philosophy of Friedrich Heinrich Jacobi", in F. Jacobi, trans. G. diGiovanni, *The Main Philosophical Writings and the Novel Allwill* (Montreal and Kingston: McGill-Queen's University Press).
Frank, M. (1975), *Der unendliche Mangel an Sein* (Frankfurt am Main: Suhrkamp).
Gendron, B. (1976), "Is Political Freedom Compatible with Determinism?" *The Personalist*, 52/4, pp. 356–63.
Heidegger, M. (1971), *Abhandlung über das Wesen der menschlichen Freiheit*, ed. Hildegard Fieck (Tübingen: M. Niemeyer).
Illingworth, J. (1917), Letter to Wilfrid Richmond, 14 December, 1888, in Agnes L. Illingworth, *The Life and Work of John Richardson Illingworth* (London: John Murray).
Izenberg, G. (1992), *Impossible Individuality: Romanticism, Revolution, and the Origin of Modern Selfhood, 1787–1802* (Princeton, NJ: Princeton University Press).
Kohák, E. (2002), "The Person in a Personal World: An Inquiry into the Metaphysical Significance of the Tragic Sense of Life", in T. Buford and H. Oliver (eds.), *Personalism Revisited: Its Proponents and Critics* (Amsterdam and New York: Rodopi).
Martineau, J. (1888), *A Study of Religion: its sources and contents* (Oxford: Clarendon Press).
Martineau, J. (1901), *Types of Ethical Theory* (1885). 2 vols., 3rd edn., revised (Oxford: Clarendon Press).
Pringle-Pattison, A.S. (1893), *Hegelianism and Personality*, 2nd edn. (Edinburgh and London: Blackwood).
Pringle-Pattison, A.S. (1920), *The Idea of God in Light of Recent Philosophy*, 2nd edn. (New York: Oxford University Press).
Pringle-Pattison, A.S. (1922), *The Idea of Immortality* (Oxford: Clarendon).
Seth, J. (1926), *A Study of Ethical Principles*, 17th edn. (New York: Charles Scribner's Sons).
Snow, D. (1996), *Schelling and the End of Idealism* (New York: State University of New York Press).
Sweet, W. (1996), "F.H. Bradley and Bernard Bosanquet", in James Bradley, (ed.), *Philosophy after F.H. Bradley* (Bristol, UK: Thoemmes Press, 1996).
Tyler, C. (2006), *Idealist Political Philosophy: pluralism and conflict in the absolute idealist tradition* (London: Continuum).
Webb, C. (1918), *God and Personality* (London: Allen & Unwin).
Webb, C. (1920), *Divine Personality and Human Life* (London: Allen & Unwin).

Thom Brooks

Muirhead, Hetherington, and Mackenzie

To think is to take great risks[1]

Introduction

John Henry Muirhead (1855–1940), Sir Hector James Wright Hetherington (1888–1965), and John Stuart Mackenzie (1860–1935) are today not among the better known of the British Idealists. Indeed, there has not been any major work focussing on their distinctive philosophical contributions.[2]

Perhaps one reason why they are generally regarded as minor figures in British Idealism is because "they were nothing but 'Green parrots'" (Nicholson 1990: 1). It is true that all three were influenced strongly by the writings of T.H. Green, as well as Edward Caird, Sir Henry Jones and many others. Yet, it is equally true that Muirhead, Hetherington, and Mackenzie did far more than simply recycle what they had learned from Green. Indeed, all three were students at the University of Glasgow, and each were important figures in their own right — Muirhead and Mackenzie published an impressive amount of work by any standard, and Hetherington was knighted for his efforts in revitalising the universities in Exeter, Glasgow, and Liverpool.

In this chapter, my focus will be to present major themes and important contributions made by Muirhead, Hetherington, and Mackenzie. As so little is known about them — and so much more about more well-known figures in British Idealism — I will not explore the various connections between these three and their teachers, nor with Kant and Hegel. Nevertheless, there is much we have to learn from them.

John Henry Muirhead (1855–1940)

J.H. Muirhead was two years old and the third of four sons when his father, a lawyer by profession, passed away. Later, his mother moved her

---

1   Muirhead (1918a: 33).
2   Perhaps the only exception is Henderson (1989).

children to Glasgow. Muirhead first attended the Glasgow Academy and then, at the age of fifteen, entered the University of Glasgow where he studied for six years, befriending Henry Jones and J.S. Mackenzie. Here, he came under the influence of Glasgow's Chair in Moral Philosophy, Edward Caird, whom some have said was "probably the most lasting influence upon [Muirhead's] own thinking" (Harvey 1941: 88). It was at Caird's house that Muirhead met T.H. Green in 1874. Muirhead left Glasgow after winning a Snell Exhibition in philosophy, bringing him to Balliol College, Oxford to work under Green and R.L. Nettleship. In 1897, Muirhead joined what is now the University of Birmingham as Chair of Philosophy and Public Economy. After his retirement two decades later, he worked at both Edinburgh and Berkeley.[3]

During his lifetime, Muirhead published extensively, including over twenty books and more than seventy articles in the major journals of his day. Several of his books were co-edited with important figures such as H.J.W. Hetherington,[4] Henry Jones,[5] and Sarvepalli Radhakrishnan.[6] His reputation as a world class editor led to his becoming editor of the "Library of Philosophy" from 1888 until his death in 1941. Here, his duties were not simply to commission new work, but included providing written comments to authors as they prepared their manuscripts for publication.[7] Thus, Muirhead was able to leave his mark on much of the exciting new work of the period. Indeed, his Library published a number of important volumes, which included not only the first translations of Henri Bergson's work and Hegel's *Phenomenology of Mind*, but also F.H. Bradley's *Appearance and Reality*, D.G. Ritchie's *Natural Rights*, J.S. Mackenzie's *Elements of Constructive Philosophy*, and Bertrand Russell's *Introduction to Mathematical Philosophy*. Muirhead also edited the collection *Nine Famous Birmingham Men*, writing an entry on John Henry Newman.[8]

As an editor, therefore, Muirhead was not only perhaps one of the most influential philosophers in Britain at the time, but one of the best connected philosophers as well. He was even dubbed "one of the Elder Statesmen of the kingdom of philosophy" (Field 1933: 229). His connections with

---

[3] Those readers who wish to learn more about Muirhead's life should consult Sweet (2010), Boucher (1997: xl-xli), Harvey (1941: 88-91), and, especially, Muirhead (1942a). A short extract from this book can be found in Muirhead (1942b).
[4] See Hetherington and Muirhead (1918). I discuss this book in the section on Hetherington.
[5] See Muirhead and Jones (1921).
[6] See Muirhead and Radhakrishnan (1936).
[7] For example, see Mackenzie (1917: 3): 'My deepest thanks, however, are due to the Editor of the Library of Philosophy, Professor J.H. Muirhead, of Birmingham, for his most valuable encouragement and help, both while the work has been passing through the press and previously. He undertook the laborious task of reading it both before and after it appeared in proof, and his suggestions and criticisms have been of the greatest assistance'.
[8] See Muirhead (1909). His entry 'Cardinal Newman' appears on pages 183-224. This collection begins with an entry on Joseph Priestly by Sir Oliver Lodge.

so many important figures in Britain led him to edit a two volume *Contemporary British Philosophy*.[9] Here Muirhead assembled statements from leading philosophers in Britain on their own philosophies. The result is a set of fascinating self-portraits of philosophers, such as J.B. Baillie, Bernard Bosanquet, J.S. Haldane, L.T. Hobhouse, J.M.E. McTaggart, Russell, and F.C.S. Schiller, in addition to both Mackenzie and Muirhead. Muirhead's influence and the universal respect of him from the most important philosophers in Britain made such an achievement possible, a task that the others might not have been able to perform. What comes across in Muirhead's self-portrait is anything but an arrogant and snobbish figure. Instead, he is remarkably charitable and modest.[10] Nor did he let his high standing go to his head, as he was always quick to say that the best philosopher in Britain, if not the world, was Bradley, rather than himself.[11]

While he achieved much deserved recognition for his abilities as an editor, Muirhead's contributions to philosophy were greater than this. As noted above, he was a prolific writer in the leading journals of the day. Much of his work centred on defending an ethics grounded in the British Idealist tradition of Green, Caird, and Jones—one able to counter the growing criticisms of a later time. One example of his work in this area is his *Rule and End in Morals*, published in 1932.[12] It is essentially a detailed commentary, looking at ten important works that were circulating Oxford at the time, such as G.E. Moore's *Principia Ethica*, Pritchard's *Duty and Interest*, E.F. Carritt's *The Theory of Morals*, and H.W.B. Joseph's *Some Problems in Ethics*. In *Rule and End in Morals*, Muirhead engages each thinker, first presenting a charitable reading of his critic's view (indeed, his insistence on charity—rather than the desire to be harsh and overly critical—often frustrated his sympathisers), followed by thoughtful and often compelling critiques.

Yet, Muirhead made his name well before the publication of *Rule and End in Morals*. His first—and best—book was *The Elements of Ethics*, first appearing in 1892; it was also his most popular work.[13] It was instantly recognised as one of the most important contributions to ethics and, in the words of Henry Jones, was regarded as "the first attempt made in this country to state in a popular way the main ethical doctrines of the English

---

9   See Muirhead (1924 and 1925).
10 This is not to suggest that he did not have his moments, such as his review in the *International Journal of Ethics* of Schäffle's *The Impossibility of Social Democracy*, where Muirhead says: 'The book reads fairly well in its English dress, though the details of its toilet bear manifest signs of haste, and leave much to be desired' (Muirhead, 1892: 128).
11 See Muirhead (1924: 9): 'Mr. F.H. Bradley has been by general acknowledgement the foremost figure in British philosophy (perhaps in the philosophy of our time in any country) for the last generation'. See also Muirhead (1924: 316-17).
12 See Muirhead (1932).
13 See Muirhead (1910: 19-20).

Idealists" (Jones 1892: 113).[14] Upon the publication of a later edition in 1932, J.S. Mackenzie stated:

> The appearance of a new edition of Muirhead's *Elements* is a great event in philosophical literature ... It is certainly astonishing how fully, within a short compass, every problem of any importance that has been brought forward has been noted and discussed, usually in a way that may almost be taken as final ... Altogether, it can hardly be denied that it is incomparably the best general introduction to Ethics that we have. (1933b)

Not only do we find a number of developments in Idealist moral and social thought, but it is a book whose themes Muirhead would turn to again throughout his career. Thus, *The Elements of Ethics* is important not only as a significant development in British social thought, but it was also the cornerstone of Muirhead's thinking which helped make him a significant figure in his own right.

In *The Elements of Ethics*, Muirhead argues against the view that ethics is concerned with determining what is, in some substantive sense, "true". That is, he opposed a conception of truth in ethics that was fixed and eternal. Instead, he claims that ethics is concerned only with standards of right and wrong, not with right and wrong in itself, as it were. We determine these ethical standards in light of how each standard relates systematically to others. He says:

> I claim then for ethics that it is a science in as full a sense as any one of the physical or material sciences. It aims at *explaining* moral judgments, as astronomy aims at explaining the motion of planets, or geometry the properties of figures, by showing their place in a system which cannot exist as a consistent whole (or, in other words, cannot be recognised by reason as existing at all) without them. (1910: 27)

For example, following one of his own illustrations, we do not come to explain why theft is wrong by reference to any "moral sense" or a divination of God's will. Instead, it is best explained with reference to its inconsistency "with that system of mutual relations which we call social life" (1910: 27). That is, as theft is inconsistent with the respect for property rights and the proper exchange of property through contract, then it is wrong insofar as such property rights (including the use of contract) best enable the flourishing of mutual relations in other areas. Thus, no standard, judgement or act can be understood fully isolated from the entirety of its social context. No doubt such an enterprise is extremely com-

---

14 J.S. Mackenzie (1933a: 533) writes: "Muirhead's *Elements of Ethics* is so well known to readers of *Mind* that any general appraisement of it here would be out of place. It must suffice to say that I believe it to be quite the best general introduction to the study of the subject that we have in English; and that its successive editions supply an admirable index to the advance of ethical thought in this country." Mackenzie's review is all the more remarkable due to the fact that he, too, wrote an important work in ethics — which I discuss below — *A Manual of Ethics*, which was reviewed by Muirhead in *Mind* in 1893.

plex—an issue of which Muirhead was only too keenly aware. Nevertheless, much of his work aimed at demonstrating "the working of the idea of an inclusive order or world of experience in the life of the individual and of society as the principle of constructive ethics and politics" in this manner (1924: 324). This is a project that engaged Hetherington and Mackenzie as well, as we shall see below.

As with British Idealists before him, Muirhead was sensitive to the issue of how an idealist-inspired ethics can overcome the worry that it is a kind of pie in the sky form of rumination so complex it takes a life on of its own, rather than a crucial insight into ethics and social thought. For instance, he notes: "Philosophy at all times, like science, has had its roots in man's practical needs. To try to sever it from these is to cut it off from the springs of its life" (1924: 312). Perhaps Muirhead's drive to show how ethics is connected with everyday life was, in part, to overcome what he saw as unfair criticisms levelled at Green, who some saw as "a metaphysical Frankenstein".[15] (Muirhead's own views of Green's philosophy are best found in his lectures on Green, published in 1908 as *The Service of the State*.)

While it is well known that Green's philosophical ideas had a great impact on Muirhead, there is later a significant shift away from Green's emphasis on the importance of logic and metaphysics.[16] For Muirhead, Green's "exposition of the theory of right" was the most convincing part of his philosophy (1908: 60). Indeed, as stated in the subtitle of *The Service of the State*, Muirhead's lectures focus on "the political teaching of T.H. Green", rather than on any metaphysical underpinnings. Surprisingly, elsewhere he says of Green's *Prolegomena to Ethics*:

> To the present writer much, both of the metaphysics and the psychology of that great work, seems to possess little more than an historical interest, but the Lectures on the Principles of Political Obligation are as fresh and vital to-day as when they were delivered in 1879. (1896: 390)

Now, I would not want to suggest that Muirhead was *anti*metaphysics. In fact, he credits Scotland's "tradition of comparative detachment from theological dogma and *a metaphysical genius*" as its main virtues in resisting "the compromise of Positivism" (1927: 427).[17] Metaphysics was not a bad word or faulty science as such, in his eyes, and useful in a number of ways. However, ethics is distinct from metaphysics—a view that, as we will see below, J.S. Mackenzie challenges—and has only in common with

---

15   See Muirhead (1908: 8): "He [i.e., Green] has been attacked by humanistic writers as the prince of intellectualists, a metaphysical Frankenstein who spent himself in setting up as the ultimate truth of things a logical monster unrelated to human purposes."

16   We will see below how Mackenzie tries to revitalise the importance of metaphysics in light of Muirhead's contributions to moral and social theory.

17   Emphasis added. However, it is worth noting that we can find comments unsympathetic to metaphysics in his writings. For example, he says in his *Chapters from Aristotle's Ethics* (Muirhead, 1900: 155): "Philosophy is concerned with the reality that underlies the world about us, not with any metaphysical realities beyond it."

metaphysics the general position that "the value of our ideals [is located] in relation to experience as a whole" — a view in keeping with the systematicity of social organic relations Muirhead found central to the proper study of ethics.[18] Thus, his point is not that we should avoid the study of metaphysics — such a study might be useful in coming to understand the nature of relations of parts and wholes, which can aid us in ethical theorizing — but that metaphysics ought not to play as large a role in ethical thought that it did with other Idealists.

Returning to his divergence with Green's position, Muirhead had a particular desire to make moral philosophy speak more to concrete practices — in effect, to show the possibility of an Idealist brand of applied moral philosophy.[19] He says:

> Moral philosophy is sometimes thought of as an abstract study which treats of human life out of relation to definite circumstances of time or place. This is to ignore the fact that philosophy, like science, art, and religion, stands in organic relation to the age and nation whose philosophy it is. (1900: 1)[20]

How Muirhead attempts to do this is by arguing that all forms of human conduct are wilful choices directed towards some end or purpose. Our task is then to explain what rights we have, if any, in virtue of their relations to others and their enabling the pursuit of a common good. Here he says: "Right is thus at every point relative to society. In origin, contents, and in the condition of its maintenance, it depends upon society" (1908: 71). One result of this view is that different societies will possess different conceptions of rights (and, correspondingly, of what is wrong). This is not to say that all such conceptions are equally valid. Rather, Muirhead believes that some societies better conceive the relationships between the individual, the state, and the pursuit of a common social purpose than others. Further, we can see how one improves upon others, when we recognise how some might fail to grasp that the pursuit of one policy over another might lead to disunity rather than bringing individuals into greater organic relation.

Another of Muirhead's insights here concerns the nature of moral values. In his view, we can conceive of "right" and "good" as "objectively real". However, their reality was not a fixed and eternal fact. Anticipating Ronald Dworkin,[21] he says: "they are something there waiting to be revealed rather than creations of our own. But it is through and in us that they are revealed, for we also are their offspring" (1932: 86n1). He adds:

---

18 See Muirhead (1903: 366).
19 I do not wish to suggest that such a characterisation of Green is entirely fair. For example, see Brooks (2003).
20 See also Muirhead (1900: 21): 'The function of theory is not to carry us away into a region of abstraction and comparative unreality, but to put us into closer touch with fact'.
21 See Brooks (2007).

"Moral philosophy can only make explicit the principle which unconsciously controls his actions. It cannot give principle to them" (1900: 20). Thus, the task of moral philosophy is to *recover*, not *discover*, the purposes driving our actions. For Muirhead, whatever guiding principles we find help us better understand the value of any goodness in our actions. However, these principles are thought to be responsive to changing circumstances over time, and ought never to be applied as some timeless, fixed manner of social regulation.[22]

Muirhead's views of organic relations extended to his conception of the individual. The individual is a fiction if considered atomistically; it is only a fact when seen in his relatedness to others in society. He says:

> We never know man but as a member of some kind of society. He not only exists in a society, but is what he is in virtue of his relation to it ... The education which he receives is only possible by means of such social institutions as language, the family, the school, the workshop. The prizes he wins in battle, the property he acquires in trade, can only be secured to him in virtue of some form of social law and social justice, however rudimentary. In a word, his life takes its form at every point from the relation in which he stands to his social environment. (1910: 146).[23]

For Muirhead, the individual as such is not the proper subject of ethical study. Rather, it is "the good of man *as a citizen*, or *member of a community*"; "[t]he good of the individual ought never to be separated from the good of the whole of which he is a part" (1900: 23 [emphasis mine]). The good of the individual is, therefore, "the common good" that individuals in community share equally. This common good expresses itself as a "social purpose", that is, the pursuit of a particular end or good.[24] To illustrate, Muirhead says:

> It [i.e., human activity] has reference at every point to the larger whole in which the true life of the individual man is to be sought. Every act, therefore, however narrow its apparent scope, really points beyond its immediate object to the wider life as to the context which gives it meaning. (1900: 206)

How it is that we can demonstrate the way our actions and judgements systematically relate to an end or good is the task ahead of us,[25] and this view strongly indicates the strong influence of Green.

Likewise, in a clear rejection of utilitarianism, Muirhead emphasises that considerations of pleasure should not enter our calculus:

---

22 See Muirhead (1900: 20-1).
23 See also Muirhead (1918b: 103): "[I]ndividuality is something that is achieved in various degrees and possesses various values, not according to the degree of a thing's dissimilarity from other thing so its independence of them, but according to the range of its power to focalize and assimilate."
24 See Muirhead, "Introductory", in Hetherington and Muirhead (1918: 20).
25 See Muirhead (1910: 86).

> Pleasure, so far from being the end, is for the most part its enemy. It may be that there are pleasures which are good, or at least harmless, but no action which has pleasure for a motive can be truly human or good. In order to be good, an act must be done out of reverence for the reason which enjoins it, and without regard to the consequences to the sentient self, whether one's own or another's. As opposed to the theory that the end is pleasure for pleasure's sake, this theory has aptly been called the theory of duty for duty's sake. (1910: 126)

This rejection of pleasure as a guiding principle is found throughout the work of Muirhead, as well as Mackenzie and other idealists. What makes an action good is not merely that it seeks (even though it does not completely attain) an end that is good. Instead, an action is good in itself if the ideal it seeks is good, whether or not this end is satisfied. As Muirhead says, "the end or ideal in morals is not to be conceived of as 'some far-off divine event' which is some day to come to pass. It is daily and hourly realised in the good act itself" (1910: 202). If we take seriously the way in which our particular actions relate to the actions of others, then it becomes clear that certain kinds of actions cannot be performed by everyone at the same time. These non-universal actions, then, are not thought to relate to "the whole" (i.e., the actions of others in society). In fact, such actions help prevent the possibility of everyone acting in tandem and, thus, adding to societal discord.

For example, if someone were to commit theft or a murder, this action would be unethical because of how it relates to the actions of others. A thief steals from someone in order to possess the property of another, but the thief would not want her belongings taken from her by another thief. Likewise, murder is wrong because there would be no society if everyone murdered one another; the possibility of individuals working together towards a social purpose would be inconceivable. These actions are unethical not merely on the grounds that they cannot be universalised and performed by all in tandem (in a Kantian fashion), but *also* because they lead to the degeneration of society — they threaten the lives and well-being of the citizenry.

Finally, Muirhead adds, interestingly, that "In seeking wealth, power, position, the criminal seeks an object which has value only because of the recognition of the society of which the very existence is endangered by the crime" — this further illustrates that crimes are wrong because they are actions that cannot be universalised and which erode social bonds (1918c: 89). When we *do* perform acts that can be universalised, the opposite happens: society is rejuvenated, the well being of all is developed, and citizens act virtuously. Indeed, for Muirhead, virtue is acting in a way that ideally relates such a "part" (i.e., the particular action) to the "whole" (i.e., the actions of others).²⁶ As a result, he says: "the essence of all virtue is the control of action by the idea of the whole" (1910: 217).

The influence of Muirhead's views on the generation of philosophers coming of age in those years was, no doubt, inhibited by the sentiments aroused by the First World War—in particular, Germany becoming an enemy of Britain.²⁷ One can easily imagine the discomfort felt in the universities for those who thought that British philosophers should continue to be keen to develop the German Idealist tradition as it was received through Green and others before him. Muirhead published an essay in the Oxford Pamphlet series of 1914-5, entitled *German Philosophy and the War*.²⁸ This series seemed to be aimed at promoting greater interest in German intellectual movements, while remaining loyal to the British cause. We thus find other essays by Arnold on "British and German Steel Metallurgy" and Sonnenschein's "Through German Eyes".

In his essay, Muirhead presents just such a line, claiming that current developments in Germany represent "a violent break with the ideas for which Kant and the whole early idealist movement stood. It is a story of a great rebellion, I believe on the whole a great apostasy" (1915: 3). Part of the reason for this break, he says elsewhere, was that Germans "lost touch with common sense and missed the plain way of civilization in the mazes of abstract theory" (1918d: 22). The essay makes a case for why it is that the grand German philosophical tradition that includes Kant, Fichte, Hegel, and, later, Nietzsche had been so recently abandoned in Germany, noting that, for these thinkers, "[w]ar is not the continuation but the failure of politics" (1915: 12). Thus, Muirhead tried to separate militarism and war from the German Idealist tradition he cherished.

Was Muirhead ultimately successful here? Unfortunately, he was not. In an obituary in *Mind*, John W. Harvey (1941: 88) wrote:

> With the death of John Henry Muirhead at the end of last May there passed away the last representative philosopher who had drawn inspiration as pupil from the fathers of late nineteenth-century Idealism in Scotland and England, from Edward Caird and T.H. Green.

With Muirhead's passing, the Idealism that marked British thought lost one of its great proponents. But it was certainly not the case that Idealism died with Muirhead; others of his generation remained, and still others—R.G. Collingwood (1889-1943), C.E.M. Joad (1891-1953), A.C. Ewing (1899-1973), G.R.E. Mure (1893-1979), Errol E. Harris (1908-), Nicholas

---

26 Muirhead further distinguishes between different 'cardinal virtues', such as courage, justice, self-restraint, temperance, and wisdom. See Bk. 4, ch. 4, in Muirhead (1910).
27 It is well known that British Idealism "was decidedly on the retreat" by the end of the First World War (Boucher, 1997: viii). My suspicion is that part of the reason for this decline was not entirely due to other schools of thought 'disproving' Idealist insights, but major political events instead.
28 See also Watson (1916).

Rescher (1928–), Leslie Armour (1931–), Timothy Sprigge (1932–2007), and their students—would follow.

This leads us, then, to consider the life and works of two of Muirhead's close friends and colleagues, Sir Hector Hetherington and J.S. Mackenzie. Each draws inspiration from Muirhead's work and develops the ideas outlined above in new directions.

Sir Hector James Wright Hetherington (1888–1965)

Sir H.J.W. Hetherington was born in Cowdenbeath, Scotland and educated at the Dollar Academy, later entering the University of Glasgow in 1905 in order to study classics, economics, and philosophy. At university, like Muirhead before him, he came under the influence of Sir Henry Jones and was his assistant for a short period.

Shortly thereafter, Hetherington moved across the country, taking up prestigious positions and changing the face of higher education in Britain. In 1914, he became a lecturer in philosophy at the University of Sheffield[29] and, in the following year, was given a chair in philosophy at Cardiff. He was appointed the Principal of the Royal Albert Memorial College, Exeter in 1920. Hetherington quickly began paving the way for that college to be granted university status: today it is the University of Exeter. In 1924, Hetherington became Professor of Moral Philosophy at his alma mater, the University of Glasgow. But three years later he moved again, to the University of Liverpool, where, as its Vice Chancellor, he made a number of important economic and strategic improvements. Hetherington made his final move in 1936 back to the University of Glasgow, this time as its Principal. He was knighted in that same year.[30]

Hetherington's greatest legacy lies in his work restructuring and expanding the universities of Exeter, Glasgow, and Liverpool. The effort he expended in university administration prevented him from producing the huge corpus of works that we find with Muirhead and Mackenzie, but Hetherington was nevertheless a philosopher of high standing in his own right.

While the youngest of the three figures discussed in this chapter, it is natural to turn to Hetherington after Muirhead and before Mackenzie for several reasons. First, like Muirhead, Hetherington was an editor of note; Mackenzie did not edit volumes or journals. Hetherington's most important work was perhaps his well known collection *The Life and Letters of Sir Henry Jones*, in honour of his former mentor in Glasgow.[31] Second, unlike Mackenzie, Hetherington is not concerned with reformulating Muirhead's

---

29 Interestingly, T.H. Green was instrumental to the establishment of Sheffield College.
30 For more biographical information, see Hutcheson (1965).
31 See Hetherington (1922 and 1924). For an excellent look at the work of Henry Jones, see David Boucher's chapter in the present volume, as well as Boucher and Vincent (1993).

insights in ethics. Instead, his philosophical contributions arise from applying these insights more fully than Muirhead did, in areas such as education and the role of social institutions. These contributions are clearest in an essay "The Conception of a Unitary Social Order" (published in the years 1917–8) and in his *Social Purpose: A Contribution to a Philosophy of Civic Society* (1918) — a work dedicated to Jones, Mackenzie, and John MacCunn, and which he co-authored with Muirhead.[32] In this section, I focus on the general themes of Hetherington's work.

Hetherington shares with Muirhead the desire to make philosophy speak to everyday life, to address the real world, as it were, rather than let it exist as some form of idle speculation. Hetherington writes:

> We progress, therefore, not, as philosophers have supposed, by letting reason carry on its world of synthesis, of shaping the elements of our life into a growing form of unity, but by holding it to its subordinate function, and by releasing the infra-rational forms of life from its domination. In them lie the spring of progress, and the true unity of the self. (1917–8: 292)

Any progress in social and moral thought must take account of life as it is lived.

One new area that Hetherington takes account of is how distinct social institutions contribute to the pursuit of our social purpose, or common good. For him, social institutions are far more than a complex series of various social bodies, but rather a system where "a real identity of principle throughout" is manifest (1917–8: 301). The view of Idealist philosophers previously, he says:

> has been that what makes society possible at all is the presence in each individual will of an idea, which is also an ideal, of what life in society is. That idea requires the whole social world to express it; and it requires that world *as a whole* … That is to say, it regards society not merely as the result of the fact that man happens to need others to help him to attain his ends, but as a condition of there being any ends at all. (1917–8: 303–4)

Rather than focussing on how individuals relate to the state as such, Hetherington notes that individuals do not contribute to this whole merely as discrete individuals, but, again in keeping with Muirhead's views on the nature of the human being, a member of various social associations.

In particular, Hetherington discusses "institutions". Institutions are created from the individual's participation in social life, each embodying different conditions which permit the flourishing of a community's social purpose, or common good (1918a: 121). Furthermore, institutions are also self-educative. That is, they allow individuals to develop in greater

---

32 See Hetherington (1917-8) and Hetherington and Muirhead (1918), especially chs. 6 and 8-12.

detail—and in a more concrete fashion—the conditions permitting the community's social purpose to grow. (1918a: 122).

For example, Hetherington views industry as more than a means of making a material livelihood, but one of many important institutions that make up our social world (1918b: 178). As such, all institutions, not least industry, he says, "become constituents of the good life, and therein instruments of freedom and human value" (1918b: 179). Of course, one criticism we could raise is that, as it is practiced, institutions (such as industry) might not actually bring freedom to all members of society, as not everyone might find employment.[33] Hetherington's answer to this charge is instructive. He argues that society's refusal, say, for more generous welfare programmes, is the result of a reluctance "to revise the conception of the place of these things in human life"—such as a potential "lowering of our standards of comfort and a sacrifice of the leisure we enjoy" (1918b: 181). This reluctance prevents us from providing such welfare programmes—something we could do if we were willing to enjoy a lower standard of material living—and leads us to accept an industrial system that is less ethically satisfactory than it could be otherwise.

As a result, he says: "It is, therefore, not unfair to argue that the present industrial order maintains itself because we will that it should" (1918b: 181). Industry remains an institution that contributes to the flourishing of freedom for all. The fact that not all might benefit fully is not because of some defect in industry as such, but rather how we as a society elect to administer industry.[34] Indeed, Hetherington is not pleased with this state of affairs, in large part because it may lead to the stifling of the intellectual and creative abilities of citizens, especially those who perform physical labour.[35] Thus, he says: "Living his life among machinery, man finds himself reduced almost to the level of the tools with which he works" (1918b: 185).

Industry was not the only social institution that interested Hetherington; he was also concerned with education and the state (as well as the international relations of states to each other). His work on education is, in part, a restatement of common themes we find in earlier British Idealists.

---

33 Of course, how it is that we can reconcile the existence of poverty with the view that all citizens are entitled to social freedom is a charge that has also been levelled at Hegel.

34 He also claims that there is no reason to think why we could not exert greater democratic control over the large industrial organisations. The fact that we do not is indicative of our reluctance, not to control the influence of industry, but to suffer from any drop in anticipated material comforts as a result of greater regulation and restrictions. See Hetherington (1918b: 188).

35 See Hetherington (1918b: 185): "The real tragedy is that men and women have to spend day after day in such simple routine uninspiring tasks that not merely is bodily strength exploited but intellectual and moral alertness and sensibility are dulled and even extinguished. There is nothing in the whole course of many an industrial life to call forth the creative energies of man, nothing to develop mind and will in the higher sense."

For example, Hetherington held that the education of children should be about more than training them to become "useful" members of the workforce, although it is important that education does this.[36] Education should also endeavour to exercise and harness the intellectual and creative powers of students, allowing each student to be "at home in the worlds of Nature and of man, to train his will and feeling as well as his intelligence, to give him some appreciation of the values of life, and to train him in the endurance that is necessary for their pursuit" (1918c: 212). Ideally, education should be a free service provided by the state.

Hetherington's views on the state, however, are more distinctive. He writes:

> [The state] can never claim that the individual owes his final loyalty to it; or that in its service he should be prepared to sacrifice without question the duties that he owes to other institutions. When a conflict arises between the claims of the State and those of other associations, the State may not assume, as a matter of right, its own priority. Its claims must be tested by the same criterion as that which is applied to every other institution — the depth and seriousness of the purpose for which it exists, and its relevance to the progress of that whole Society which expresses all the ends and ideals of human life, and to which alone, therefore, the individual owes his highest obligation. (1918d: 228)

Unlike Hegel, for whom the state is composed of the totality of all social institutions in a particular order, Hetherington here seems to treat the state as one amongst several institutions. The totality, for him, is not the state, but rather the "whole Society". As institutions have legitimacy only insofar as they help us develop our "social purpose" or common good, institutions (such as the state) might lose their legitimacy when they become obstacles to the realisation of this purpose or good.

Note that Hetherington *seems* to treat the state as an institution, which looks clear enough in the stated passage. Yet he appears to contradict this remark shortly thereafter. Hetherington writes:

> It [the state] exists simply as a condition for the better life of other, genuine institutions. It is not itself an institution. It is, at most, an important piece of mechanism, for the upkeep of which we should be prepared to pay. But it plays no constitutive part in the individual life; and therefore never requires any moral devotion or service. (1918d: 250)

Here Hetherington seems to imply that not all institutions have an equal status. This is unproblematic; if institutions are legitimate only insofar as they enable us to realise our social purpose, then it would seem that we can have legitimate institutions where all are necessary but some play greater individual roles than others. The problem is that the state, here, is not an

---

36 See Hetherington (1918c: 211). It is also important for citizens to make intelligent decisions about which vocation is best for them to pursue in the workforce.

institution – which seems to contradict what we saw earlier: civil disobedience is justified insofar as the state loses its institutional legitimacy – and the view it "plays no constitutive part in the individual life" nor "requires any moral devotion or service".[37] The latter is a problem because it would seem that the state does play such a part for members in the civil service (and perhaps government officials as well) who provide their particular services to the state as a means of making a livelihood.

In addition, Hetherington acknowledges patriotism as "of the finest sort, which brings mind, feeling, and will to the service of country and nation" (1918e: 266). While not an "uncritical adherence to all that the State does", he adds: "Rightly enough, we value the man who believes in his country and who will stand by anything it does. He is a better man than one who thinks first of human duty, and serves his country according to the light he discovers there"; and one should think of the state as a mechanism for the fulfilment of common social purpose, rather than a means for pursuing one's private self-interest (1918e: 266). Thus, the state ideally should receive moral devotion, namely, in the form of patriotic allegiance.

In short, while there is much that is suggestive in Hetherington's account of the state, in parts, it appears to be inconsistent.[38]

Equally suggestive, but perhaps less problematic, are Hetherington's views on law. He argues that "a law plays the same part within an institution as the institution plays in the general system of social life. The institution makes and secures a level of social attainment; within the institution, the law does the same" (1918a: 129). As a result, Hetherington is led further in uncovering the myriad of ways in which individuals relate to one another in society, in a complex web of social institutions and laws. Furthermore – and not unlike Ronald Dworkin – Hetherington views law as an "articulation of certain moral principles … it expresses the values which the moral opinion of the community attaches to the different institutions within it" (1918e: 251). But these remarks are only suggestive insofar as is far from clear *precisely* how a law, say, requiring persons to wear seatbelts, has the various interconnections and implications Hetherington claims. Perhaps the closest we get to an argument for this claim is found in a discussion on the substance of legal rights. Here Hetherington writes:

---

37 Later Hetherington (1918d: 256) refers to the state as "an institution on which depends much of the progress of mankind".

38 I will only cite one such suggestive passage on international relations that I hope will elicit further interest and research in Hetherington's philosophical contributions: "International justice, like justice between individuals, requires, not so much that wars should cease, as that physical force should not be a consideration in determining the solution of questions to which such force is irrelevant. Wars would cease, then, as a matter of fact, because they would be perfectly meaningless. And the object of satisfactory international agreements is not primarily to secure peace, but to secure right, and thereby to make war impossible by making it as impotent to settle an international issue as the size of a man's muscles to settle a civil action" (1918e: 286).

> It [i.e., rights] rests, not on force, but on a view of the nature and ends of a given Society. Plainly, therefore, not every right, recognized or claimed, involves a corresponding duty; not merely in the sense that if I enjoy or desire a certain right, it is my duty to respect a similar corresponding claim on your part, but in the sense that in enjoying or in claiming my right, I rely upon a definite social construction, and therefore I must admit as binding upon myself the obligations which attach to my place in that construction. Every new privilege that an institution confers on its members is a more precise articulation of the order embodied in that institution, and involves a more precise obligation. (1918a: 130)

As before, our social institutions come together in one organic whole as "society", not as the state. What is interesting is the insight that rights and duties correspond to one another, not merely because I choose to claim, or enjoy, a given right; but, instead, because, in claiming a right, I rely on a particular picture of my place within the entirety of my society's social purpose (and rights are only legitimate insofar as they further this purpose). The rights we claim are embedded in our institutions and laws, as in Muirhead's view—and, again, foreshadowing Dworkin's later views on legal development. Thus, the process of understanding which rights, if any, we are entitled to is a process of recovery, not discovery, in an immanent development of law.

To conclude, perhaps the best statement of Hetherington's philosophical position is found in *Social Purpose*. He writes:

> We are bound to accept the test imposed upon us—Kant's maxim—that we should regard humanity always as an end, never merely as a means. But if it is true—as it has been the whole thesis of this book to prove—that humanity is a social creation, and that the individual comes to himself in association with institutions which are instruments of the enlargement of his mind and will, then it is not incompatible with this principle that he may find his best life in the service of purposes which are more fully or more consciously embodied in institutions or in persons other than himself. (1918b: 205)

Hetherington was not simply echoing Muirhead's position, but neither was his moral and social thought contrary to it. Hetherington's philosophical contribution lies in his efforts to spell out how Muirhead's many insights lend themselves to a new way of thinking about the relationship between the individual and society through a variety of social institutions. It is a great pity that, because of the time he invested in improvements and expansions at a number of important universities, Hetherington wrote comparatively little to improve and expand upon his highly suggestive remarks. Thus, we are unable to articulate as comprehensive an account of his moral and social theory as we can with either Muirhead or Mackenzie—to whom we now turn.

John Stuart Mackenzie (1860-1935)

J.S. Mackenzie was born near Glasgow.[39] He was orphaned in Buenos Aires as a boy and travelled back to Scotland, later attending Glasgow High School. In 1877, he entered the University of Glasgow where he was taught by Caird and Jones.[40] He took over as Caird's assistant, replacing Jones, after finishing his degree and obtaining a Clarke Fellowship. Soon after he won a Shaw Fellowship which took him to Edinburgh—where he succeeded W. R. Sorley in the fellowship. On Sorley's advice, in 1886 he went to Trinity College, Cambridge. There he befriended J.M.E. McTaggart, to "whom he converted from his early enthusiasm for Spencer to an admiration for Hegel" (Boucher: 1997: xxxix). Shortly after being elected a Fellow of Trinity, Mackenzie went to Manchester and, in 1895, accepted a Professorship of Philosophy at the University College, Cardiff, where he remained until 1915. He was also named a Fellow of the British Academy.[41]

Like Muirhead, Mackenzie was a prolific author, writing nine books and more than sixty articles in top academic philosophy journals. Indeed, his work appears in virtually every issue of the *International Journal of Ethics* for its first twelve volumes, sometimes contributing half a dozen book reviews in addition to articles. One major difference from both Muirhead and Hetherington is that Mackenzie believed that, to understand ethics properly, one had to be immersed in metaphysics—an area he became increasingly interested in later in his career.[42] Indeed, he thought his most significant contribution to philosophy was his major work in metaphysics, *Elements of Constructive Philosophy*. Here, I focus on Mackenzie's writings in moral and social philosophy.

Mackenzie's first work in this area was his first publication, *An Introduction to Social Philosophy*.[43] It was composed of his lectures delivered at the University of Edinburgh as part of his Shaw Fellowship. We can discern immediately certain themes that would develop much further later in his more notable works. Firstly, he argued that "[p]hilosophy is nothing if not systematic" (1890: 3). As we saw above with Muirhead and Hetherington,

---

39 A brief note on the spelling of his name. Conventionally, we might expect to spell his name, as some contemporary commentators do, as 'MacKenzie'. However, nowhere does he or others (such as Muirhead) ever spell his name any way other than 'Mackenzie'.

40 Of Caird and Jones, Mackenzie (1924: 233) said: "My philosophy, such as it is, owes most, I believe, to the teaching of Edward Caird. But I was always a somewhat recalcitrant pupil, in constant rebellion against what seemed to me his over-confident optimism. His disciple and successor, Sir Henry Jones, to whom also I owed a great deal, was even more remarkable than his master for the fervour of his convictions."

41 For further biographical information, see Boucher (1997: xxxix-xl), M. Mackenzie (1936) and Muirhead (1926: 277-8), and Sweet (2010).

42 See also Mackenzie (1914 and 1931).

43 Mackenzie (1890).

Mackenzie argues that philosophy's goal is to make explicit the proper relations of various ends, goals, rights, and so on, to each other. He adds:

> It teaches us to regard the pursuit of wealth, the pursuit of virtue, the pursuit of knowledge and wisdom, the pursuit of culture, the pursuit of political organisation, the pursuit of aesthetic satisfaction, the pursuit of religious truth, not as a number of separate ambitions which one man may choose and another may neglect, but as all essentially parts of a single aim which no one can renounce without in some degree ceasing to be human. (1890: 375)

Thus, particular actions—most especially ones we value, such as the pursuit and attainment of ends or rights—are best grasped in relation to other pursuits of ends or rights within a single system.

We also find Mackenzie beginning to explore what we might call, in contrast to Muirhead, a *re*introduction of metaphysics as a topic of great concern for ethicists. In the preface to the third edition of his *A Manual of Ethics*, Mackenzie says:

> The theory of Ethics must, I believe, in the end rest on Metaphysics; and what it is possible to do without Metaphysics can be little more than a clearing of the ground, and leading up to the metaphysical principles that are involved in the subject. The system of metaphysical truth, however, is like a city with many gates; and perhaps the student may enter it by the ethical gate as profitably as by any other. (1915: vii)

For him, not only was ethics an organic system composed of various parts, but ethics itself was part of something larger than itself, including both art and religion. How this "cosmos" of "universes" fits together is grounded in a rich metaphysical backdrop.

His *A Manual of Ethics*, mentioned above, was perhaps his most important contribution to moral and social thought, reprinted in six different editions between 1893 and 1929. It was instantly recognised as a great success;[44] Muirhead wrote that the book was "an earnest and striking contribution to the ethical literature of the time" (1893: 395).

There are several similarities between *A Manual of Ethics* and Muirhead's *The Elements of Ethics*. First, each was a textbook on ethics, written for the use of undergraduate students, that sought not only to present important positions in the field, but offer a novel position that was important in its own right. Second, both reflected the view that individuals are inherently social, Mackenzie saying: "Human beings do not drop out of the clouds", but become what they are through their social relations (1915: 372). Third, Mackenzie also felt a need to make philosophy speak to practices, that it must have "a most intimate bearing on practical life"

---

44 The editions of *A Manual of Ethics* are as follows: 1st ed. (1893), 2nd ed. (1894), 3rd. ed. (1897), 4th ed. (1900), 5th ed. (1915), and 6th ed. (1929).

(1894a: 161).[45] Fourth, Mackenzie likewise took the task of ethics to be to discern the rightness or wrongness of human conduct with reference to how these acts contribute to the common good (1915: 1). This led him to also adopt a view of society as an organic society, not dissimilar to Muirhead or Hetherington.[46]

However, there are a number of differences between the two works. Unlike Muirhead, Mackenzie thought ethics was a science rather unlike physical science: "A science, it is said, teaches us *to know*, and an art *to do*; but a practical science teaches us *to know how to do*" (1915: 11; emphasis given). A second difference between them was the special importance Mackenzie places on metaphysics as a way of understanding how the rightness or wrongness of our conduct relates to the pursuit of some common end. Interestingly, he says that his *A Manual of Ethics* was written "as closely as possible" to Green's treatment of ethics in *Prolegomena to Ethics*, a work we saw Muirhead had claimed was of no more than historical interest (Mackenzie, 1924: 242).[47] Mackenzie, however, is ultimately critical of Green's use of metaphysics, not because it is too strong, but because it is "too largely dominated ... by the doctrines of Kant" for his tastes (Mackenzie, 1924: 242).

What Mackenzie took to be a metaphysical approach did not, in many ways, employ language that was all that different from Muirhead's. For example, Mackenzie believed the social purpose, or common good, ought not to be understood as a process of self-realization, but, rather, "as the realization of a rational universe" (1896: 428n). He says:

> In other words, what is maintained is that the Universe is a Cosmos, a system of orders; and that, in finding any particular truths, we are discovering their place within that coherent whole. It is regarded as a comprehensive truth within which all other truths have a place. (1928: 30)

This view, for Mackenzie, entails a duty for all to enable the development of humanity. He says:

> Our rights and our duties are, as it were, two aspects of our powers, of our concrete personal development. To realize a complete humanity, so far as that is at any moment possible, is our only ultimate right and

---

45 See p. 171: "When I say that Ethics is practical, I mean merely that it unfolds and analyzes for us the ideal principle of life—an ideal which is indeed forever real, both in the sense that it is the deepest actuality in the nature of man and that it is continually realizing itself in the institutions and habits of social life; but which, though thus forever real, is also forever ideal." See also Mackenzie (1897: 358-9).

46 See Mackenzie (1918: 59), where he calls society "an organism of organisms', where 'each of these minor organisms is also an organism containing others within it' all within one 'spiritual whole".

47 See also Mackenzie (1915: 254): "[Green's *Prolegomena to Ethics* is] probably the most considerable contribution to ethical science that has been made in England during the present century." Elsewhere (1890: 47n2), he says that "the best examples of treatises on Ethics" are 'Kant's *Critique of Practical Reason* and Green's *Prolegomena*'.

> duty. The means to this realization, so far as these are at any time accessible, are what we claim; and our obligation is to use the means in the most effective way. (1896: 431)

This talk of "efficiency" appears often in his writings, and it may make us think of a kind of economic efficiency. This is not what he has in mind. Instead, he uses efficiency in that sense whereby a society can be said to be more efficient when it allows all persons to receive an education which will help the state to adopt intelligent policies over time—and help each person to develop his or her mental and spiritual life (1915: 336). A state that uses slavery or hereditary government officials is, in his view, weak and inefficient insofar as those with greater talent and abilities are prevented from taking their proper place. The state can thus be said to fail to realise its potential. The degree to which states fail to do just this is, correspondingly, their degree of inefficiency.

Mackenzie also focusses on how we are to understand "goodness", as in "the goodness of an act". For instance, he says:

> A good painter is one who *can* paint beautifully: a good man is not one who *can*, but one who *does*, act rightly. The good painter is good when he is asleep or on a journey, or when, for any other reason, he is not employed in his art. The good man is not good when asleep or on a journey, unless when it is good to sleep or to go on a journey. Goodness is not a capacity or potentiality, but an activity. (1915: 14)

Thus, ethics can only judge standards of goodness or wrongness of actions (1915: 28). This does not mean whether we have done good is determined by the "success" of our action. We need not produce a good result; all we need have is a good intention to perform a good act (1915: 132). This might seem like a contradiction. After all, if ethics judges actions and we perform, say, unsuccessful acts with a bad outcome (although performed with the best of intentions), why is our action not judged "bad"? Mackenzie's answer is simple: "A result is generally a resultant of several causes, of which the will of any particular agent is only one" (1915: 132). Here he tries to distinguish sharply between what we may call "the result" from "the action", and the view that actions should be our primary focus.[48]

In addition, Mackenzie defends a view of law as part of an organic society. He writes:

> This is the superficial aspect of legal and political rights; but if we accepted it as the final view, it would be just as superficial as the idea that words are made by the lexicographer and have no relation to the characters of those who use them. Laws and political institutions, like words, are a growth out of the general consciousness of a people. (1896: 434)

---

48 See Mackenzie (1915: 137).

Legislators might appear to be the creators of law, but they do no more than give external expression to a moral standard in community.[49] Which political and legal rights a community enjoys are reflective of what Mackenzie calls "the average standard of morality in a people" (1896: 436). This is not to say that the laws, as a community's moral standards, are right or correct in any objective sense. Indeed, he argues laws only have legitimacy insofar as they enable the flourishing of all in society (1896: 438). That is, we must ask ourselves in each case how each particular right makes "a rich and perfect life more possible than it would be without them" (1896: 439).[50] Not all laws in all communities are ultimately just, and many might need alteration, replacement or be removed from the legal code, although such laws are always reflective of the values of those governed by them.

Mackenzie also offers important insights into our understanding of justice in punishment, and he professes to have been inspired here by Hegel's account.[51] To begin with, Mackenzie recognises that, whatever the relationship between morality and positive law, the two will never be completely commensurate, insofar as crime is a more narrow category of wrongdoing than sin.[52] Punishment acts as "a vindication of the law" (1915: 432). Mackenzie writes that punishment is "a revelation of the fact that the law holds good although it has been broken" (1915: 432). Indeed, he believes that "[a] law that is not carried into effect is no law at all" (1928: 283). His views on punishment are primarily retributivist, and he argues that "[i]t is only when an offender sees the punishment of his crime to be the natural or logical outcome of his act that he is likely to be led to any real repentance" (1915: 432). In more Hegelian language, he adds:

> The place of punishment has been indicated as the recoil of guilt upon the offender, thereby asserting the majesty of law, and leading on, through this, to repentance and reformation. In this way 'the wheel comes full circle': the crime is wiped out—i.e. its essential nullity is exhibited—within the universe occupied by the criminal. (1915: 436)

Yet, one does find a certain tension in Mackenzie's writings, where he suggests that perhaps all that is necessary for criminal wrongdoers is that they be subjected to a kind of *treatment*, but not necessarily *punishment* as such. He follows the above quote with the remark that:

---

49 See Mackenzie (1896: 439): "Legal rights are like the dikes in Holland. They mark our triumphs over the waves of human selfishness and passion."

50 Also see at p. 441: "In the end we cannot accept anything as a right or as a duty, however venerable may appear to be its authority, however august its sanction, if it cannot somehow be made clear to us that it is an essential element or a necessary stage in the development of a full and perfect humanity." There is also the question of whether or not certain rights are best pursued without a system of penal sanctions. See Mackenzie (1896: 440).

51 See Mackenzie (1915: 432n2). On Hegel's theory of punishment, see Brooks (2004).

52 See Mackenzie (1915: 427).

> It is possible, however, that this revolution may be effected without the intervention of punishment. The guilt may be brought home to the mind, not by the working of it out within the universe in which it has arisen, but by rising to a higher universe. Education, for instance, may bring about this result. Modern humanitarian sentiment leads us, as far as possible, to seek to deal with criminals — especially young criminals — in this way, rather than by way of punishment. Where this is possible, the offence can be forgiven, because it no longer exists at the higher point of view. It must be remembered, however, that to say this is not to deny the validity of the preceding account of punishment. (1915: 436–7)

(It is worth noting that there were several debates on Mackenzie's discussion of punishment in *International Journal of Ethics*, although none of them pick up the line followed here.[53]) Elsewhere, in a reply to G.F. Stout's review of *A Manual of Ethics*, Mackenzie appears to adopt this second approach to punishing, as he tries to explain why his views on punishment are not a mere endorsement of simply adding "pain to evil" (1894b: 381).[54] Mackenzie says:

> Of course it should be remembered that this is merely a *Theory of Punishment*, — i.e., a justification of the practice of inflicting pain upon a wrong-doer. It is not at all incompatible with the view that it would be better to reform than to punish — i.e., that it would be better to raise a man into a higher world instead of merely completing the circle within his present world. (1894b: 382; emphasis given)

Unfortunately, Mackenzie thought the further exploration of such questions beyond social philosophy's remit and best handled by philosophers of law. In some debates on punishment today, theorists express ever greater concerns over the justification of hard treatment and its "success". What is interesting and suggestive about Mackenzie's view may be its attempt to endorse a variety of retributivism that allows a way out of hard treatment, without "doing nothing", as it were. Certainly, this is a view in greater need of study.

In short, Mackenzie's provocative writings were as prolific as Muirhead's, and he remains one of the most important early figures in social philosophy, considered by some at the time to be a pioneer in a new and emerging area of study. Here I have tried to demonstrate the ways in which his thought borrows from Muirhead and Hetherington, while acknowledging the greater sympathy Mackenzie gave to metaphysics and the distinctly different conceptions of society as an organism of organisms (on a cosmic scale) and of punishment.

---

53 For example, Mackenzie (1894b) and Mukerji (1914).
54 See also Mackenzie (1918: 160) — in the last discussion of punishment I have been able to find in his writings — where he says that "two wrongs do not make a right".

Conclusion

As noted at the beginning of this chapter, there has been no examination in detail of the thought of J.H. Muirhead, Sir H.J.W. Hetherington, and J.S. Mackenzie for nearly half a century: My aim has been to provide an introduction to their moral and social philosophies through an account of each's life and his main philosophical work. Given the importance of their contributions to idealist ethics and beyond, there is clearly need for greater attention and study of these three figures. May the work of Idealism's nearly forgotten sons again be recognised!

References

Boucher, D. (ed.) (1997), *The British Idealists* (Cambridge: Cambridge University Press).

Boucher, D. and Vincent, A. (eds.) (1993), *A Radical Hegelian: The Political and Social Philosophy of Henry Jones* (Cardiff: University of Wales Press).

Brooks, T. (2003), "T.H. Green's Theory of Punishment", *History of Political Thought*, 24, pp. 685–701.

Brooks, T. (2004), "Is Hegel a Retributivist?", *Bulletin of the Hegel Society of Great Britain*, 49/50, pp. 113–26.

Brooks, T. (2007), "Between Natural Law and Legal Positivism: Dworkin and Hegel on Legal Theory", *Georgia State University Law Review*, 23, pp. 513–60.

Field, G. (1933), Review of *Rule and End in Morals* by John H. Muirhead, *Philosophy*, 8, pp. 229–30.

Harvey, J. (1941), "J.H. Muirhead, 1855–1940", *Mind*, 50, pp. 88–91.

Muirhead, J. (1892), Review of *The Impossibility of Social Democracy* by A. Schäffle, *International Journal of Ethics*, 3, pp. 126–8.

Henderson, J. (1989), "'The Relation of Ethics to Economics': J.S. MacKenzie's Challenge to Neoclassical Economics", *Review of Social Economy*, 47, pp. 239–65.

Hetherington, H. (1917-8), "The Conception of a Unitary Social Order", *Proceedings of the Aristotelian Society*, 18, pp. 286–316.

Hetherington, H. (1918a), "Social Institutions", in H. Hetherington and J. Muirhead (eds.), *Social Purpose: A Contribution to a Philosophy of Civil Society* (London: Allen & Unwin).

Hetherington, H. (1918b), "The Industrial System", in H. Hetherington and J. Muirhead (eds.), *Social Purpose: A Contribution to a Philosophy of Civil Society* (London: Allen & Unwin).

Hetherington, H. (1918c), "Education", in H. Hetherington and J. Muirhead (eds.), *Social Purpose: A Contribution to a Philosophy of Civil Society* (London: Allen & Unwin).

Hetherington, H. (1918d), "The State", in H. Hetherington and J. Muirhead (eds.), *Social Purpose: A Contribution to a Philosophy of Civil Society* (London: Allen & Unwin).

Hetherington, H. (1918e), "The Internal and External Relations of the State", in H. Hetherington and J. Muirhead (eds.), *Social Purpose: A Contribution to a Philosophy of Civil Society* (London: Allen & Unwin).

Hetherington, H. (1922), "Sir Henry Jones: 1852–1922", *International Journal of Ethics*, 33, pp. 169–87.

Hetherington, H. (ed.) (1924), *The Life and Letters of Sir Henry Jones: Professor of Moral Philosophy in the University of Glasgow* (London: Hodder and Stoughton).

Hetherington, H. and Muirhead, J.H. (eds.) (1918), *Social Purpose: A Contribution to a Philosophy of Civil Society* (London: Allen & Unwin).

Hutcheson, R. (1965), *Hector Hetherington 1888–1965*, *The College Courant*, vol. 18 (Glasgow: University of Glasgow).

Jones, H. (1892), Review of *The Elements of Ethics* by J.H. Muirhead, *International Journal of Ethics*, 3, p. 113–5.

Mackenzie, J. (1890), *An Introduction to Social Philosophy* (Glasgow: James Maclehose & Sons).

Mackenzie, J. (1894a), "Moral Science and the Moral Life", *International Journal of Ethics*, 4, pp. 160–73.
Mackenzie, J. (1894b) "Reply to Some Criticisms", *International Journal of Ethics*, 4, pp. 380–4.
Mackenzie, J. (1896), "Rights and Duties", *International Journal of Ethics*, 6, pp. 425–41.
Mackenzie, J. (1897), "The Relation of Philosophic Theory to Practice", *International Journal of Ethics*, 7, pp. 354–9.
Mackenzie, J. (1914), "The Meaning of Reality", *Mind*, 23, pp. 19–40.
Mackenzie, J. (1917), *Elements of Constructive Philosophy* (London: Allen & Unwin).
Mackenzie, J. (1918), *Outlines of Social Philosophy* (London: Allen & Unwin).
Mackenzie, J. (1915), *A Manual of Ethics*, 5th edn. (London: University Tutorial Press).
Mackenzie, J. (1924), "Constructive Philosophy", in J. Muirhead (ed.), *Contemporary British Philosophy: Personal Statements*, (First Series) (London: Allen & Unwin)
Mackenzie, J. (1928), *Fundamental Problems of Life: An Essay on Citizenship as Pursuit of Values* (London: Allen and Unwin).
Mackenzie, J. (1931), *Cosmic Problems: An Essay on Speculative Philosophy* (London: Macmillan).
Mackenzie, J. (1933a), Review of *The Elements of Ethics* by J.H. Muirhead, *Mind*, 42, pp. 533–4.
Mackenzie, J. (1933b), Review of *The Elements of Ethics* by J.H. Muirhead, *Philosophy*, 8, pp. 364–6.
Mackenzie, M. (ed.) (1936), *John Stuart Mackenzie* (London: Williams and Norgate).
Muirhead, J. (1893), Review of *A Manual of Ethics*, by J.S. Mackenzie, *Mind*, ns 2, pp. 395–7.
Muirhead, J. (1896), Review of *Introduction to Social Philosophy*, by J.S. Mackenzie, *International Journal of Ethics*, 6, pp. 390–2.
Muirhead, J. (1900), *Chapters from Aristotle's Ethics* (London: John Murray).
Muirhead, J. (1903), "The Problem of Conduct", *Mind*, 12, pp. 365–73.
Muirhead, J. (1908), *The Service of the State: Four Lectures on the Political Teaching of T.H. Green* (London: John Murray).
Muirhead, J. (1909), *Nine Famous Birmingham Men: Lectures Delivered in the University* (Birmingham: Cornish Brothers).
Muirhead, J. (1910), *The Elements of Ethics*, 3rd ed. (London: John Murray).
Muirhead, J (1915), *German Philosophy and the War. Oxford Pamphlets 1914–1915* (London: Oxford University Press).
Muirhead, J. (1918a), "Social Theory in the Making", in H. Hetherington and J. Muirhead (eds.), *Social Purpose: A Contribution to a Philosophy of Civil Society* (London: Allen & Unwin).
Muirhead, J. (1918b), "Citizenship and Personality", in H. Hetherington and J. Muirhead (eds.), *Social Purpose: A Contribution to a Philosophy of Civil Society* (London: Allen & Unwin).
Muirhead, J. (1918c), "Will in Society", in H. Hetherington and J. Muirhead (eds.), *Social Purpose: A Contribution to a Philosophy of Civil Society* (London: Allen & Unwin).
Muirhead, J. (1918d), "Introductory", in H. Hetherington and J. Muirhead (eds.), *Social Purpose: A Contribution to a Philosophy of Civil Society* (London: Allen & Unwin).
Muirhead, J. (ed.) (1924), *Contemporary British Philosophy: Personal Statements (First Series)* (London: George Allen & Unwin).
Muirhead, J. (ed.) (1925), *Contemporary British Philosophy: Personal Statements (Second Series)* (London: Allen & Unwin).
Muirhead, J. (1927), "How Hegel came to England", *Mind*, 36, pp. 423–47.
Muirhead, J. (1932), *Rule and End in Morals* (London: Oxford University Press).
Muirhead, J. (1936), "J.S. Mackenzie (1860–1935)", *Mind*, 45, pp. 277–8.
Muirhead, J. (1942a), *Reflections by a Journeyman in Philosophy on the Movements of Thought and Practice in His Time*, ed. J.W. Harvey (London: Allen & Unwin).
Muirhead, J. (1942b), "Some Reminiscences by the Late J.H. Muirhead", *Philosophy*, 17, pp. 334–50.
Muirhead, J. and Jones, H. (eds.) (1921), *The Life and Philosophy of Edward Caird* (Glasgow: Maclehose).

Muirhead, J. and Radhakrishnan, S. (eds.) (1936), *Contemporary Indian Philosophy* (London: Allen & Unwin).

Mukerji, N. (1914), "Idealism and the Conception of Law in Morals", *International Journal of Ethics*, 24, pp. 321–33.

Nicholson, P. (1990), *The Political Philosophy of the British Idealists: Selected Studies* (Cambridge: Cambridge University Press).

Sweet, W. (ed.) (2010), *Biographical Encyclopedia of British Idealism* (London/New York: Continuum).

Watson, J. (1916), "German Philosophy in Relation to the War", in D. Boucher (ed.), *The British Idealists* (Cambridge: Cambridge University Press), pp. 253–69.

James Connelly

Collingwood's Moral Philosophy
Character, Duty and Historical Consciousness

Introduction

This chapter examines R.G. Collingwood's conception of duty in connection with his claim that it is identical with historical consciousness, rebuts the charge that it is a disguised form of intuitionism, and argues that he developed an agent-centred ethics of character. Duty, for Collingwood, is an autonomous form of historically situated consciousness and action comprising both practical and theoretical elements. In answer to the charge that Collingwood espouses a disguised form of ethical intuitionism, I argue that a more accurate way to capture his position is as a form of particularism.

Utility, Right and Duty

In *An Autobiography*, Collingwood summarised his approach to moral philosophy:

> My notion was that one and the same action, which as action pure and simple was a 'moral' action, was also a 'political' action as action relative to a rule, and at the same time an 'economic' action as means to an end … There were, I held, no merely moral actions, no merely political actions, and no merely economic actions. Every action was moral, political and economic. But … these three characteristics, their morality, their politicality and the economicity, must be distinguished and not confused as they are, for example, by utilitarianism. (1939: 148)

Utility, right and duty differ both in degree and in kind and exhibit different levels of rationality. Collingwood understands rationality as absence of caprice and as not acting under the compulsion of desire. The main forms of practical reason are utility, right and duty. We shall survey them in that order.

Utility

To possess utility is to be useful for something, to be a means to an end. The distinguishing feature of utility is the separation of means and end, with the means sharing in the goodness of the end only in so far as it is a means to it. This very statement, for Collingwood, immediately reveals one of utility's weaknesses as an account of action. From the vantage point of utility, there can be no recognition that if goodness really resides in the end and only secondarily in the means, and if the two are held to be logically and temporally separate, the end will never be reached and thus the means will never become good. Utility takes the means to be good; it recognizes that it must be means to an end, but it cannot give an account of the goodness of the end other than by arbitrary stipulation or as a means to a further end. Its explanations are ultimately inadequate: although there is reason in it, its conception of rationality is limited.

Let us consider this further. For utility, the specific detail of both means and ends is a matter of indifference. The means must be adequate to secure the desired outcome — that is all. Utilitarian action deals with individuals, but "each is an indefinite individual, required to satisfy certain specifications, but free to vary so long as those specifications are satisfied" (Collingwood 1992: 15.72).[1] There are elements in the execution of the means which must be settled in the performance itself, and of these elements utility, *qua* utility, takes no account. The unspecified details are free to vary and may be decided capriciously: the element of caprice renders utility imperfectly rational.

Utilitarian action is also capricious because, *qua* means, it cannot prefer one end to another. It presupposes criteria (which it does not supply) by which to judge the worth of an end. Many things are useful, but they may well be useful to quite different ends, some good, some bad. By what criterion do we choose an end? Once we reflect on the fact that utility provides no reason for choosing one end rather than another, and that, in its separating means and ends, it postpones the consummation of the means, we reach beyond utility towards a conception in which the means become part of the end and the end is implicit in the means. In such a conception the end is chosen not capriciously but rationally, for the sake solely of its intrinsic value. Consider Collingwood's answer to the question of how the life of the monks in the monastery of St Elijah on Santorini might be justified:

> Social utility, you say. Nothing in the activity of one man or class or men is good unless it is useful, for its utility is what constitutes its goodness. ... this cannot be true, because it is self-contradictory. An

---

[1] References to the original published text of *The New Leviathan* are to paragraph numbers; references to the previously unpublished additional material in the 1992 edition are to page numbers.

action is useful because it leads to some other action. If this second action is desired only for its utility ... it is desired only because it will lead to a third action ... this series must end; an action must be reached which is desired not only for its utility but for its own sake ... If utility is the only goodness, if nothing is good except in so far as it is useful, there is no utility and therefore no goodness ... Sooner or later the judgement that something is good because it is useful rests on the judgement that something is good in itself. (2003: 150–1)

The assertion that utility is the only good leads to the moral bankruptcy of finding that life is not worth living, because one is always purchasing a satisfaction which never comes. The way to avoid this is to stop judging the value of actions in terms of utility, and to judge them in terms of intrinsic worth.

Right

The next form of practical reason that Collingwood considers is right. Here we choose to do something because it is right, because it conforms with a rule. A rule is a generalized purpose to do things of a certain kind on occasions of a certain kind. To act on such a rule or principle (Collingwood does not distinguish the two) is "to decide upon a general way of behaving, defined as involving some act of a specific kind if and when some occasion of a specified kind arises" (1992: 16.31–16.32). Regularian action is capricious (although to a lesser extent than utilitarian action) because:

the regularian ground is a generalization, expressly admitting of alternative realizations ... A rule only specifies *some* act of a certain kind. The application of it to a given occasion bids me to perform one, and only one, of the acts which would conform to its specification ... but the rule cannot tell me how. From the regularian point of view my choice between the alternatives is a matter of caprice.

From this, Collingwood concludes that regularian explanations "*never explain why a man does this* act; they only explain why he does *an act of this kind*" (1992: 16.6–16.63).

Rules, as Oakeshott reminds us, are always disjunctive. "They specify only an act or a conclusion of a certain general kind and they never relieve us of the necessity of choice. They never yield more than partial explanations: to understand anything as an example of the operation of a rule is to understand it very imperfectly" (1989: 54). To recognise an act as right is to recognise it as according with a rule; the act is understood not in its individuality but as an instance of a type.

The world of rules presupposes a feature of consciousness which the regularian consciousness cannot provide. Implementation of a rule requires an act of judgement which cannot be referred to a rule without infinite regress. We therefore need to consider the moral consciousness which recognizes actions as good in themselves and in which action proceeds according to the unique qualities of concrete circumstances. Utility presupposes the intrinsically good, and regularian action presupposes moral action "which is not determined according to rule, and where the process is directly from knowledge of the situation to an action appropriate to that situation, without passing through the stage of formulating a rule" (Collingwood 1939: 103). However, it should be observed that the relation between right and duty is one of determinate negation in which right is both preserved and transformed in the higher form and it is an indispensable part of all action:

> Rules are not everything, and there is something in the life of practices which is higher than rules or rightness, namely duty; but a man who makes light of rules will no more take duty seriously, or prove a vigorous and effective force in practical life, than a man who makes light of grammar will take style seriously or prove a vigorous and effective user of words whether with his tongue or with his pen. (1992: 456)

From Right to Duty

Regularian action is not self-sufficient both because it lacks determinacy and because it presupposes a form of consciousness and action which can formulate (rather than merely follow) rules and act in the absence of rules. In every concrete act there is a vital remainder which utility or regularian thought cannot account for. This remainder will be improvised: "it is necessary to act without rules ... when you find yourself in a situation that you do not recognise as belonging to any of your known types. No rule can tell you how to act. But you cannot refrain from acting. ... you must improvise as best you can" (1992: 103–4). Improvisation is an element in all actions: but sometimes it is the entire action, as for example, when:

> you can refer the situation to a known type, but are not content to do so ... because you know that action according to rules always involves a certain misfit between yourself and your situation. If you act according to rules, you are not dealing with the situation in which you stand, you are only dealing with a certain type of situation under which you class it. The type is, admittedly, a useful handle with which to grasp the situation; but all the same it comes between you and the situation it enables you to grasp. (1992: 104)

In addressing the relation between rules and the requirements of real moral situations, Jonathan Dancy likewise points out that "generalism" (that is, the rule or principle governed opposite of moral particularism) encourages a sort of "*looking away*" from the specifics of new cases, because it tends to breed rule-fetishism, in which agents refuse to see what the particular case calls for because they are anxious to adhere to rules they have relied on in the past (Bakhurst, 2000: 169; Dancy, 1993: 64).

For Collingwood, to improvise action in a manner adequate to a concrete situation and to avoid "looking away", practical insight is required. Whence comes this insight? It cannot come from rules for it is what enables us to apply the rules: it comes from historical understanding, because "what history can bring to moral and political life is a trained eye for the situation in which one has to act" (1939: 100).

Let us consider this in relation to duty by revisiting the reasons for regarding regularian action as inadequate. The first point is that rules exist only in being consciously obeyed. In this sense, obeying a rule is the same as making a rule. Regularian action as such does not recognize this: in merely following a rule, we assume that the rule is there ready-made, whereas the truth is that "all genuine rules are constantly being reshaped in their application". It is only in its application that a rule has genuine existence: "this so called application, which is also the recreation or re-affirming, of a rule, is nothing but the element of universality that is present in all volitions" (1933a: 93). An action, therefore, cannot logically be *merely* regularian: every rule-governed act is, at the same time, also a creation of the rule. Action according to rule therefore presupposes a type of action which creates the rules it obeys: this, for Collingwood is action *per se*, or absolute action, action which contains its explanation within itself. Its visible mark on the world takes the form of duty and we now consider its characteristics as dutiful action.

Duty arises through consciousness of obligation or debt: general awareness of obligation is conscience. One of its defining characteristics is that its goodness depends not only on the external aspect of the act but the intention or motive with which it was done. "As Kant has shown, my will is the source of the goodness of a dutiful act; its goodness is merely a name for the fact that I dutifully chose to do it" (Collingwood 1933a: 84). Therefore, "nothing has moral worth … except the will of a moral agent. If that is so, the moral good and moral activity, are not related as end to means: they are identical." To do good and to be good are the same (1928–9: 159). The morally good action is a dutiful action. When we do our duty we do it *because* it is our duty and what we do is historically particular and unique:

> Duty admits of no alternatives. Whatever is my duty is an *individuum omnimodo determinatum*. There is only one of it; it is not one of a set of alternatives; there is nothing that will do as well. In the first place it is my duty and nobody else's. … Secondly, any duty is a duty to do 'this' act and only 'this', not 'an act of this kind'…. Hence dutiful action, among these three kinds of rational action, is the only one that is completely rational in principle; the only one whose explanations really explain; the only one whose answer to the question; 'why did I do that action?' … answers precisely that question and not one more or less like it. (1992: 17.51–17.55)

Conscience tells us that we are under an obligation but not what the obligation is (Collingwood 1992: 17.56–17.58). Collingwood's conception of obligation is historically specific; it encompasses more than the rule-governed obligation which arises from (for example) making a promise. It is obligation arising from a specific complex of social and historical factors in which agents recognise obligation as arising from previous actions as crystallised in their present situation. An appropriate response is achieved through thinking through what the situation requires: it demands logical thought and historical insight, and the conclusion is the determination that this act and no other is our duty. There can be no conflict of duties; "conflicting duties" are conflicting hypothetical candidates for duty, or elements which need to be taken account of in determining a duty. In the end, there is only one concrete act which the agent should perform, all factors having been taken into account:

> When a man says that such and such an act is his duty, or that it is not, or wonders if it is, what does he mean by the phrase: "his duty"? A man's duty on a given occasion is the act which for him is both possible and necessary: the act which at that moment character and circumstance combine to make it inevitable, if he has a free will, that he should freely will to do. (1992: 17.8)

Duty draws together necessity and free will, character and circumstance; and it is a "complete obligation" which eliminates all caprice:

> The obligation to do my duty is an obligation involving every detail of what I am to do. Nothing is left to caprice; and for a person who means caprice when he says freedom, freedom has vanished. A person who does his duty has no option; he has got to do exactly what he does; he has no choice. The consciousness of this complete obligation—complete in the sense that it covers every detail of what is to be done and leaves no option anywhere—is a universal feature of duty. (1992: 471-2)

Duty is also a matter of moral struggle, not just the act done, but the inner meaning of the act done. It means putting our will into a certain state and acting accordingly. Strictly speaking, only this is duty; the act itself is what it is *right* to do. What makes an action right is the fact of performing a certain deed, whereas "what makes it duty is the fact of victory in the moral struggle" (1932: 92). Thus, for Collingwood,

> telling the truth is right; telling the truth out of truthfulness is morally good; here truthfulness is the name not of a feeling but a virtue: what makes the act morally good is not that we should have a desire to tell the truth, but that our will should be set on truth-telling as a thing of intrinsic value. It is not wanting to be truthful, but trying to be truthful, that gives the act moral worth. (1932: 95-6)

There is much to commend this, but it still leaves unresolved an important matter: if duty is the only form of action whose "explanations really explain", what sort of explanation does it provide? And is it really an explanation at all?

Choice and Duty[2]

G.E. Moore notoriously argued that "good" cannot be defined, but for Collingwood *all* concepts can be defined (1992: 403).[3] He defines good in general as what is consciously chosen and as that which is "desirable, meaning 'worthy to be desired'" (1992: 11.5). Goodness is present in different degrees and kinds, depending on the purpose and the standard employed. We are aware of the good through practical activity, not contemplation:

> A mere spectator has no standards. He has, at most, make-believe standards expressing the purposes which he makes believe to entertain with regard to the things he is watching ... distinguishing things as good and bad is not an activity of the purely theoretical mind. It is an activity of the practical mind. A person who calls anything good or bad is stating that it does or does not satisfy a standard arising out of the purpose which, as a practical agent, he entertains towards it. (1992: 407)

Moore forgets this when he calls "good" (like yellow) a "simple notion". Collingwood does not believe Moore to suppose that we literally see the goodness of something by looking at it, and accepts that he is speaking metaphorically to suggest there is "a simple operation of theoretical intellect, as simple as the operation of vision, by which we become aware of goodness in the things that possess goodness." But here Collingwood disagrees:

> This seems to me a monstrous falsehood. I find ... that I become aware of goodness in things that possess goodness only by engaging in some practical activity connected with them. And I cannot help suspecting that Professor Moore becomes aware of it in the same way. I should like to know how he becomes aware of goodness in, for example, a violin or a wife or an international fourteen-foot racing dinghy. For my part, I became aware of it by playing on the violin, living with the wife, or racing the dinghy. (1992: 407)

Hence he concludes that "to call a thing good is to call it a thing that some agent is conscious of choosing" (1992: 420); in other words, "good" means "chosen". Here Collingwood rejects realism in ethics as he does in epistemology, and his linking of goodness to activity is clearly akin to his insistence on the active role of the mind in all knowing. A similar position is propounded by Richard Robinson, who argues that the question what is good is a practical, not theoretical, because "calling things good is not describing the world; it is judging the world. ... we are choosing what is to be done rather than discovering what is the nature of the world. Goods exist by choice rather than by nature" (Robinson 1964: 24). The good, then:

---

[2] This discussion is indebted to Lord (2009).
[3] See also the discussion of philosophical definition in Collingwood (1933b).

is a practical question ... of action, of what to do. To wonder whether a thing is good is to wonder what to do with regard to it, as whether to pursue it, to praise it, to preserve it. To conclude that it is good is not to reach a belief as to its qualities and peculiarities, but rather to reach an attitude towards it, an evaluation of it, and a decision of how to behave with regard to it. It is to choose it. (1964: 24)

To recognise goodness, then, is to act in a certain way, not to recognise something as a mere spectator—and this is exactly Collingwood's position. Thus for Robinson:

to say that a thing is good is in fact very like deciding to pursue it, other things being equal; and therefore it is something very like a self-contradiction to say that a thing's being good is no reason why we should pursue it. But if, as Moore thought, to say that a thing is good were to describe it as possessing a certain property, then a thing's being good *would* be no reason why we should pursue it... (1964: 25)

Recognising the good is the act of an actor, not a spectator. Escaping the clutches of the spectator theory helps Collingwood here, but the problem is that, unless he can say more about the act of choice than simply that something is chosen, the spectre of intuitionism still looms. We still need more solid support for the claim that duty is completely rational action.

On Collingwood's account, duty seems to be something that just *has* to be done. But does this imply that he has painted himself into the intuitionist corner? He assures us that duty is not capricious, but this is not enough. In answering the question "how do I determine my duty?", his answer is that the agent "knows by experience both that there is such a thing [as duty] and also what kind of a thing it is" (1992: 474). Tim Lord suggests that this is unhelpfully similar to the conclusion of Prichard's intuitionist manifesto: "[i]f we do doubt whether there is really an obligation to originate A in a situation B, the remedy lies not in any process of general thinking, but in getting face to face with a particular instance of the situation B, and then directly appreciating the obligation to originate A in that situation" (Prichard 2002: 20). Lord also suggests that Collingwood's allusion to the "unanalysed individuality" (1992: 474) of the dutiful act does little to assure us that reason has much of a role to play at the level of duty. And he goes on to suggest that "despite all attempts to elude the Oxbridge intuitionist view then so prominent, Collingwood to some extent has remained its captive" (Lord, 2009: 253). He continues by pointing out that Collingwood asserted an identity between the historical consciousness and the consciousness of duty and that:

while the historian can explain why an individual agent chose a means that achieved a certain end and recognized an act that obeyed a certain rule, the historian cannot explain why this end was chosen or this rule was recognized, beyond claiming that in this individual situation, they simply were necessary. Likewise, the consciousness of duty is concerned with individual situations and with individual actions. Reason can explain why a particular means to an end should be chosen or why an act obeys a particular rule, but the ends of humans and the rules they recognize cannot be grasped by reason, beyond maintaining that they simply are chosen as necessary in completely individual situations. Collingwood is groping more than grasping here. In fact, he is faced with a fatal dilemma, and, in my view, wisely picks the correct horn to impale himself upon. He quietly adopts a veiled intuitionism and claims that at the level of duty, *no reasons can be given* for the duties one adopts. (Lord, 2009: 254; My italics)

Although Lord makes a plausible case, in my view he misstates the position by stating that Collingwood thinks that no reasons can be given for a dutiful action and is therefore wrong to assert that Collingwood's position is vulnerable to the charge of falling into intuitionism.

Intuitionism and Reason in Ethics

Intuitionism in ethics can refer to at least two different positions. The first is methodological intuitionism, which asserts that there is a plurality of first principles; the second is epistemological intuitionism, a view concerning how ethical propositions are known. Here we are concerned primarily with the second form.

For Collingwood, seeing is more than looking: the mind is always active. In his view, Prichard, Moore and others analyse perception as a direct non-inferential relation with the object and hence when they use perceptual metaphors in ethics and elsewhere they are implicitly denying the active role of the mind in ethical as much as in perceptual knowing. Hence Timmons's estimation of Prichard as the defender of "a kind of particularist moral foundationalism, according to which our knowledge of obligation and of value is grounded in our (non-inferentially) apprehending particular cases in which these properties are present" (Timmons 2003). In Prichard's own words:

> [W]e appreciate the obligation immediately or directly, the appreciation being an activity of *moral* thinking. We recognise, for instance, that this performance of a service to X, who has done us a service, just in virtue of its being the performance of a service to one who has rendered a service to the would-be agent, ought to be done by us. This apprehension is immediate, in precisely the sense in which a mathematical apprehension is immediate ... Both apprehensions are immediate in the sense that in both insight into the nature of the subject directly leads us to recognise its possession of the predicate; and it is only stating this fact from the other side to say that in both cases the fact apprehended is self-evident. (2002: 13)

It could not be clearer that moral judgement for Prichard is a matter of immediate apprehension. And it is precisely on this point that Collingwood differs. Where Prichard says "look again", Collingwood says *think again*. He explicitly states that to answer the question what our obligation might be on a given occasion, conscience is not enough. Conscience indicates that we have an obligation, but answering the question what the obligation is:

> [D]emands a process of logical thinking, over and above the intuitive or immediate process which answers the question: 'Have I got any obligations, never mind what?' If that question is answered in the affirmative, I have next to find out what it is that I am under obligation to do, asking and answering successive questions in the form: 'Is it this?' 'Is it this?' 'Is it this?' (1992: 17.58–17.59)

It might be maintained that Collingwood's position is, in a sense, a modified methodological intuitionism, in that he accepts a plurality of first principles arranged in an overlapping scale of forms as specifications of goodness. It might also be conceded that he accepts the general intuitionist claim that there is no decision procedure for weighing principles at the point of practical deliberation and action. But neither commits him to epistemological intuitionism and he is thoroughly consistent in his objection to the epistemology on which moral intuitionism is based and hence to the claim that the good is indefinable and that moral principles or facts are intuited.

Collingwood's Rejection of Realism and Intuitionism

To answer fully the charge of intuitionism we need, first, a general account of Collingwood's rejection of realism and intuitionism in knowledge and ethics and, secondly, an account of the way in which reason is expressed in duty.

Collingwood's objection to Moore's or Prichard's intuitionism in ethics is akin to his objection to epistemological realism, which is that it ignores the active power and contribution of the mind in knowing. Anyone, he says, can put themselves into a position where the realistic theory of knowledge seems true. All we have to do is to let our minds drift until we are thinking "in so casual and haphazard a way" that we are hardly thinking at all (Collingwood, 2002: 34–5). The Oxford realists, in his view,

> talked as if knowing were a simple 'intuiting' or a simple 'apprehending' of some reality. ... Moore expressed ... the same conception when he spoke of the 'transparency' of the act of knowing; so did Alexander ... when he described knowing as the simple 'compresence' of two things, one of which was a mind (Collingwood, 1939: 25).

Collingwood maintained not that the realists believed the knowing mind to be merely passive, but that they considered it to be in a simple condition, "one in which there are no complexities or diversities, nothing except just the knowing" (1939: 25). Someone who wishes to know might have to work hard to place themselves in a position from which it could be apprehended: but that was sufficient for him or her to apprehend it. The doctrine was made plausible only by choosing examples such as "this is a red rose", "my hand is resting on the table", where "familiarity with the mental operations involved has bred not so much contempt as oblivion". For Collingwood, all knowledge is characterised by active questioning, and this was "not an activity of achieving compresence with, or apprehension of, something; it was not preliminary to the act of knowing; it was one half (the other half being answering the question) of an act which in its totality was knowing (1939: 25–6).

All knowledge is active: the knower makes a contribution to knowledge over and above spectation. This is also true (as we saw above) in ethics. For Collingwood, intuitionism and realism proceed on the assumption that what is not explicit is not anything at all, whereas his whole philosophical approach and method runs counter to this. Where others see intuition or intuitive knowledge, he sees implicit reasoning. The active powers of the mind in cognition and in moral experience and judgement can of course be neglected, forgotten or overlooked, but this is a philosophical error which we should not allow to mislead us. Collingwood distinguishes between an experience and a philosophical account of that experience. First person reports, for example, may neglect features of experience discernable to the observer who may see reason where the agent sees none. On Collingwood's view, a rational account of thought and experience is always in principle possible, because "all experience is mediate." Those who take experience to be intuitive "mutilate and distort it" by overlooking the fact that. "All sorts of processes of thought have been going on" and these are overlooked when someone tries to bring their experience "within the narrow frame of the intuitive theory of knowledge" (1968: 280).

In ethics, such views are false because they imply that no reasons can be given for actions, and that choice is nothing but caprice:

> Moore has publicly described his own life's work as 'A Defence of Common Sense', and 'Common Sense' by long-established usage is the accepted name for low-grade thinking, theoretical or practical; thinking below the level of reason, below the level of science, below the level of criticism or justification: the kind of thinking which is content to think 'this is so', and when asked for a reason replies, 'this is so because it is so'. In the case of practical thinking, 'Common Sense' is caprice; and therefore it is not surprising that the arch-Realist, the self-styled defender of common sense, should assert that all choice is capricious choice. (1992: 432)

Just as the mental operations in everyday acts of perception may not be obvious (but nonetheless present), so the mental operations presupposed in seeing the good may be hidden from the casual inquirer, but nonetheless present for all that. If we consider duty and look for its implicit rationality, we find not that it contains no reasons, but rather that its reasons are unlikely to be fully expressible in abstract terms external to the complex action itself. This is why the presence of intense, subtle and detailed thought sometimes appears to be its absence: the agent is not necessarily in a position to articulate (as it were) a one-to-one scale representation of all the reasoning employed in actions. But such inability refutes the claim that the action was rational. Robinson expresses the overall point by contrasting the complexity of making a wise important choice with simple inference. He argues that the process of making a wise choice is judgement rather than induction, deduction, inference or intuition, although it might contain these: deduction, for example, might be required to assess what a particular principle implies in a given situation. But deduction is never the whole of deliberation and judgement: it cannot be, for there is at least the choice to apply this principle to this situation. Further, deduction and induction are distinct from judgement as they are "abstractive, separative, analytical, whereas judgement is concretive and synthetical". He continues by arguing:

> We judge what is best to do in this whole concrete situation. The wise man tries to see all the relevant principles and all the important consequences, and then to make a judgement on the whole. Thus an important choice has far more grounds than an inference has. In an inference you can say quite shortly what the whole of your reason is for your conclusion. But in a wise judgement it is a very long business to give your reason, because your reason ought to be nothing less than the whole of the principles relevant to your choice and the whole of the consequences of your choice, and the whole situation in which it occurs. Hence in practice people sometimes renounce the effort to give a reason for their choice. They feel that they could only say part of it, and that to represent a part of it as the reason would be to misrepresent the choice. *Hence choice often looks like intuition, that is, like something totally unreasoned.* It often looks like intuition even to the wise chooser himself, who has really reviewed a great deal of matter in making it. Good choice is all-considering; and the all-considering sometimes looks like the nothing-considering. (Robinson 1964: 41).[4]

Collingwood's argument is similar. For him "duty is its own criterion", and "the act by which we determine what our duty is, which is the same as the act by which we do it, is a completely rational choice, a choice which we make with our eyes as open as they can ever be, and nothing other than this can either justify it or condemn it" (1929: 137). There is no more a decision procedure for a good action than for the creation of a good work of art. It is a creative act which cannot be determined in advance by theory or formula. It is directly related the virtues and character of the acting agent. Von Wright expressed the point eloquently:

> [V]irtues are essentially connected with action. This connexion, however, is with act-individuals and not with act-categories. ... virtues have an essential and peculiar connexion with *particulars*. It is here

---

4   My italics. Note that Robinson's formulation implies that the agent considers means, rules or principles and the whole situation in which the action takes place. This aligns his position closely with Collingwood's.

that choice enters the picture. ... because of the lack of an essential tie between a virtue and an act-category, *the path of virtue is never laid out in advance*. It is for the man of virtue to determine where it goes in the particular case. (1964: 145)

Likewise, Collingwood, in cases where principles collide, resolves reasons for acting into the character of the acting moral agent. The proper response to a moral situation "depends upon what kind of a man you intend to be" (1992: 16.72). At this point, Collingwood's view overlaps with the virtue theorist and the particularist, both of whom would tend to agree with Dancy's contention that "the context of each decision includes the fact that it is made by an agent struggling to determine not just what to do, what kind of person *to be*" (Bakhurst 2000: 174).

Duty and Historical Consciousness

Collingwood claims that the consciousness of duty is "identical with the historical consciousness" (1992: 477). History is a universal feature of mind. It is self knowledge of mind; in studying the past we acquire (through re-enacting the thought of those we study) self-understanding and learn the sort of person we are or are able to be. Duty has a close affinity with history because we seek to act in a manner appropriate to the concrete circumstances in which we find ourselves, accepting nothing as given. In duty, we are aware of "doing an action which is an individual action"; in describing this as "the fact of conscious individuality, the fact that an agent is aware of his action or his situation as unique" (1992: 477). The consciousness of duty means "thinking of myself as an individual or unique agent, in an individual or unique situation, doing the individual or unique action which I have to do because it is the only one I can" (1992: 18.52). It is historical because "to think historically is to explore a world consisting of things other than myself, each of them an individual or unique agent, in an individual or unique situation, doing an individual or unique action which he has to do because, charactered and circumstanced as he is, he can do no other" (1992: 18.52).

In acting we forge and reveal our character; in historical understanding we discover our character and the limits of our sympathies through considering the action of those whose thought we re-enact. Our consciousness of duty is that of an agent responding to individual circumstances; our historical consciousness is the thought of others as agents responding to individual circumstances. The ideal of duty is the ideal of a fully determinate response to a concrete situation.

But there is an obvious difficulty. Whatever the defects of utility and regularian action, nonetheless any action ever undertaken is necessarily determinate: perforce it was done in *this* way and not in *that*; all of the gaps in the situation were filled in somehow or other. Now, if all actions are, as a matter of fact, determinate, what makes duty different? How can it be more or less determinate? More or less concrete? The answer lies in duty's self-conscious effort to answer adequately all that the determinate situation requires of the agent and to replace any element of irrationality or caprice with genuine reasons for acting. All actions are, then, determinate, but only in duty is this fully recognised and consciously responded to. Duty is action at full capacity, considering everything and overlooking nothing within the complex of personal, social and historical factors within which the agent is acting.

Thus, although all actions are determinate, in non-dutiful action the "gaps" are filled, but capriciously. In duty, the agent acts in awareness of the action as a complete action. The difference between duty and other forms of action lies in the will and character of the moral agent. In acting dutifully agents consciously strive to go beyond utility and right and to respond to the individual features of the situation. Collingwood remarks that, although

> every act must possess the characteristics of utility and rightness, it must also possess those of duty, and its real nature as a case of action is seen only when it is conceived as duty. Duty is thus the truth of action; it is what all action really is; it is so far as we act morally that we really act at all. Yet in acting morally we do not rid ourselves of such distinctions as that of means and end, law and the application of law ... Moral action includes all these things within itself, [and] makes of them the material out of which it builds its own world. (1929: 142)

Particularism

In the foregoing there have been suggestions made to the effect that although Collingwood's account of duty is not an intuitionist one, it shares certain features with intuitionism's cousin, particularism. However, before we assimilate Collingwood's position (even if only broadly and tentatively) to particularism, we need to say a little more about the latter. As a preliminary, it is worth remarking that, although intuitionism tends to be particularist, not all particularism is intuitionist. Assimilating Collingwood's position to particularism, then, does not mean conceding that he succumbed to the dubious attractions of intuitionism.

Collingwood would certainly agree with the particularist claim that "the deliverances of mature moral judgement cannot be captured in a set of moral rules" (Bakhurst 2000: 161). He differs in not so much rejecting moral rules and principles as assigning them to a dialectically subordinate role within a greater whole. However, his position is certainly particularist in that he would accept that the reasons that agents can give for their actions cannot be fully and abstractly specified in advance of the action itself.

A feature of particularism is contextual holism in reason and values, in which what counts as a reason in one context might not count as a reason in the same way (or at all, or even count as a reason for the opposite conclusion) in another (Dancy 2000: 130–2, 139).[5] The strong form of this claim is that *every* reason is altered with every change of context; the weak form is, in Dancy's words, that "*some* reasons are on occasions capable of being altered by a change in context" (2000: 130). Dancy goes on to say that his holism is weak in respect of modality but strong on domain, that is, he maintains that "*all* reasons are *capable* of being altered by changes in context" (2000: 130). Collingwood's general acceptance of the contextual principle in knowledge, action and language implies that he would certainly accept at least the weak version of Dancy's formulation; whether he would accept a stronger version is a moot point, not argued for here, although it cannot be ruled out.

Collingwood, I suggest, embraces a form of particularism which emerges most clearly when he is discussing the moral reasoning of self-consciously dutiful moral agents. It is important to remind ourselves that in particularist writings, intuitionist themes and assumptions often come along for the ride. As argued above, the relation between the two is not one of two-way entailment: intuitionism *sans* particularism is probably impossible, particularism *sans* intuitionism on the other hand is perfectly possible. However, the fact that they tend to live in close proximity is what gives rise to the occasional appearance of convergence between Collingwood's position and intuitionism. But this convergence is in particularism alone, and the fact that intuitionists converge upon particularism from the opposite direction, does not entail assimilation between Collingwood's position and theirs. To remind ourselves why not, and of Collingwood's objection to intuitionism, consider the following. In commenting on the work of John McDowell, Bakhurst suggests that his position is particularist in that "practical wisdom is viewed as akin to a perceptual capacity (to discern the good) which is non-codifiable in character", and suggests that Dancy follows McDowell in viewing moral competence as a "kind of perceptual capacity to respond to the specific configuration of morally relevant properties each case presents" (Bakhurst 2000: 165). As we have seen above, it is clear that Collingwood would accept that moral judgement is non-codifiable whilst firmly objecting to any claim that practical wisdom was akin to a perceptual capacity, especially where that capacity was held to be one in which an object was immediately apprehended through direct intuition of reality. If the response to Collingwood's concern was that the term "perceptual capacity" is merely a metaphor, he would still be cautious, aware that metaphors are especially likely to mislead (where literal language might not),

---

5   For more extended discussions, see Dancy (2004).

precisely because they can smuggle into their picture of the world, undercover, presuppositions drawn from the original non-metaphorical context which, if stated explicitly, would immediately become obvious and perhaps contestable.[6]

Conclusion: Duty, Character and Virtue

In the foregoing, I have sought to show that Collingwood's ethics is an agent-centred one in which, although rules play a part, they are subordinate to the character of the historically aware moral agent. In his view, the way to resolve a moral dilemma is through the self-conscious exercise of virtue in deciding "upon what kind of man you intend to be" (1922: 16.72). Duty, he writes, includes being virtuous,

> as being virtuous includes doing what is right: for in doing my duty I am being virtuous by my own free will. To deny this on the ground that, if I am not generous or brave, I cannot make myself generous by trying, is to deny that there is any such thing as duty. ... [it is] within our power to make ourselves this or that kind of person. (1933a: 111)

This serves as a criterion for distinguishing a fully moral issue (duty or obligation) from right: "[I]f we say to ourselves "I must try to do such and such an act", the issue consciously raised is one of right; if we say "I must try to be such and such a kind of person", it is a moral issue and we are conscious of an obligation" (1933a: 111). Our duty is, above all, to be virtuous, and this includes "the entire character and disposition of the agent". It is thus my duty not only to perform a particular act, but to make myself into the right kind of person to do it and, "once I am the right kind of person the right act will flow from my character with the ease of an unimpeded and virtuous action" (1933a: 115–6). In acting, an appropriately developed character enables a certain "telescoping" of moral experience into the moment of action: but there are no short cuts to developing character itself. Action forms character, which is never a finished product. Habits are always being formed and never finish the process of formation.

In the foregoing we have also seen how utility and right both presuppose duty. It has been shown that Collingwood's equation of duty with historical consciousness provides the grounds of moral judgement, with character and virtue as the bearers of the developed ability to judge within an individual moral agent. Dutiful action, on Collingwood's account, is rational and not a collapse into intuitionism — although it does share features with particularism. Duty is the assumption of complete and determinate responsibility. The dutiful agent has not only to be a good will,

---

6   Although I have here used the distinction between 'literal' and 'metaphorical', Collingwood expressed reservations about the distinction and especially about the implication that metaphorical language is somehow secondary. See Collingwood (1933b: ch. X) and Collingwood (1938, ch. XI).

willing to act in this or that way, but also to take responsibility for acting at all: and to take responsibility for acting, and acting well is also to take absolute responsibility for the reasons for acting and acting well. That is why Collingwood characterises duty as absolute and as rational; it is also why its justifying reasons cannot be captured in ready-made formulae derived from or reducible to utility or right.

References

Bakhurst, D. (2000), "Ethical Particularism in Context", in B. Hooker and M. Little (eds.), *Moral Particularism* (Oxford: Oxford University Press), pp. 157–77.
Collingwood, R.G. (1923), *"Action": Lectures on Moral Philosophy* (Bodleian Library).
Collingwood, R.G. (1928-9), "Political Action", *Proceedings of the Aristotelian Society*, 29, pp. 153–76.
Collingwood, R.G. (1929), *Lectures on Moral Philosophy* (Bodleian Library).
Collingwood, R.G. (1932), *Lectures on Moral Philosophy* (Bodleian Library).
Collingwood, R.G. (1933a), *Lectures on Moral Philosophy* (Bodleian Library).
Collingwood, R.G. (1933b), *An Essay on Philosophical Method* (Oxford: Clarendon Press).
Collingwood, R.G. (1938), *The Principles of Art* (Oxford: Clarendon Press).
Collingwood, R.G. (1939), *An Autobiography* (London: Oxford University Press).
Collingwood, R.G. (1968), "Can the New Idealism Dispense With Mysticism" (1923), in L. Rubinoff (ed.), *Faith and Reason* (Chicago: Quadrangle Books).
Collingwood, R.G. (1992), *The New Leviathan* (1942), Revised edition, ed. David Boucher (Oxford: Clarendon Press).
Collingwood, R.G. (2002), *An Essay on Metaphysics*, ed. Rex Martin (Oxford: Clarendon Press).
Collingwood, R.G. (2003), *The First Mate's Log: of a voyage to Greece in the schooner yacht "Fleur de Lys" in 1939,* ed. with an introduction, Peter Johnson (Bristol: Thoemmes).
Collingwood, R.G. (n.d.), "Utility, Right and Duty", (Bodleian Library).
Dancy, J. (1993), *Moral Reasons* (Oxford: Clarendon Press).
Dancy, J. (2000), "The Particularist's Progress", in B. Hooker and M. Little (eds.) *Moral Particularism* (Oxford: Clarendon Press), pp. 130–56.
Dancy, J. (2004), *Ethics Without Principles* (Oxford: Clarendon Press).
Hooker, B. and Little, M. (eds.) (2000), *Moral Particularism* (Oxford: Clarendon Press).
Lord, T. (2009), "R.G. Collingwood's response to Oxbridge Meta-Ethics: hierarchical moral pluralism", in J. Connelly and S. Panagakou (eds.), *Anglo-American Idealism: Thinkers and Ideas* (Oxford: Peter Laing).
Oakeshott, M. (1989), *The Voice of Liberal Learning*, ed. T. Fuller (New Haven and London: Yale University Press).
Prichard, H.A. (2002), "Does Moral Philosophy rest on a Mistake?" in J. MacAdam (ed.), *Moral Writings* (Oxford: Clarendon Press), pp. 7–20.
Robinson, R. (1964), *An Atheist's Values* (Oxford: Blackwell).
Timmons, M. (2003), review of H.A Prichard, *Moral Writings* and W.D. Ross, *The Right and the Good. Notre Dame Philosophical Reviews*, 10 July 2003, http://ndpr.nd.edu/review.cfm?id =1317.
Von Wright, G.H. (1963), *The Varieties of Goodness* (London: Routledge and Kegan Paul).

Efraim Podoksik

Without Purpose or Unity: Moral and Social Life in the Thought of Michael Oakeshott

Introduction

In April 1924, Michael Oakeshott composed an essay which he entitled "The Cambridge School of Political Science". A year earlier he had graduated from the History Faculty at Cambridge, obtaining a double first degree, which was the best result among history undergraduates of Gonville and Caius College that year. Oakeshott had stayed an additional year in the college after graduating, having won a prestigious post-graduate studentship. Yet, the success of his studies notwithstanding, or perhaps even because of it, Oakeshott developed a critical attitude towards the kind of education he had received, and used the period of his studentship to put into writing his own ideas about what was wrong with the study of politics in his faculty and especially with the study of the history of political thought — a subject which had a key role in the curriculum. "I can remember", wrote Oakeshott in the essay, "that I looked forward with some eagerness to these lectures on political science, for I cherished to know what I ought to think about our life as human beings in society, but instead of any satisfaction, however momentary, of these questionings, what stands out in my mind is rather a series of the bitterest disappointments" (2004: 47).

What was the cause of these disappointments of someone who would become one of the leading teachers of that faculty in the very near future? The matter was that Oakeshott strongly disagreed with the very principles on which the study of politics in Cambridge was based. He thought that the university had failed to delineate the proper place of "Political Science" in the sphere of knowledge. It mistook what was only secondary and unnecessary for what was primary and essential. It provided a good deal of factual material and concentrated on the study of government institutions. But the curriculum lacked any solid philosophical basis, and thus reflected a far too narrow understanding of what politics was about. In

Oakeshott's view, the proper subject matter of political science was the life of human beings in society. And he suggested that, in order to understand social life, the study of politics in the university had to be a study of moral philosophy. As he put it, "if the term Political Science is to have any valid meaning at all, it must refer to a *moral* and not a natural science, that is, our subject is more properly named Political Philosophy than anything else" (2004: 56). True political science, Oakeshott stressed, "is the study of the nature of meaning of human association and the principles that underlie it" (2004: 60).

One will notice that, by saying this, Oakeshott in fact subverted the value of political science as an autonomous discipline within its own narrow subject matter, distinct from that of other humanistic branches of knowledge. But he cared little about this; he was not concerned with the study of technicalities of political life. Rather, his approach to the study of politics was reminiscent of what had been previously known as human studies, which implied an integrated inquiry into the meaning of social life. He recommended studying the great books of ethics and authors such as Aristotle and St. Paul rather than, say, Harold Laski. Political science then was supposed to preoccupy itself with "a study of the human mind and the principles of association which its nature displays; for the problem of Unity is the central question of political science, and friendship the basis of all politics" (2004: 60).

In accordance with this view, Oakeshott called for a reassessment of the entire curriculum in politics. He recommended a division of the subject into two fields. The first was to be called "History of Political Science", where "the history of man's struggle to think rightly about his relation to his fellow creatures" would be taught (2004: 62). The syllabus would include the great thinkers of the past who exemplified the historical development of ethical and political philosophy. The second part of the curriculum would be an exercise in political theory, focusing on "the construction of a theory of the State" (2004: 64). The state was conceived by Oakeshott as the ultimate human association, being thereby the primary object of the study of political philosophy.

This division of the curriculum into two parts also signified two possible ways to approach the realm of politics. The historical part of the curriculum focused mainly on ethics and moral conduct. The theoretical part adopted the point of view of the whole, exemplified by the highest form of association, which was the state. Thus, on the one hand, the study of social life could begin with a study of man and his conduct, moral habits and intellectual perceptions. On the other hand, such a study could focus on the totality of social relations and on the association which exemplified this totality to the highest degree. Yet these two approaches were not dealing with two separate things. Rather, these were attempts to understand the same subject from two different vantage points. Moral habits and social institutions were for Oakeshott just partial aspects of the totality of social life.

Thus two assumptions lay at the heart of Oakeshott's view of politics. First, he rejected the understanding of politics in a specialised sense, regarding the separation of political science from the rest of questions about society as artificial.[1] Politics in this narrow sense, and attempts to produce "scientific" political science, bored him. At the same time, he was strongly devoted to the search for the meaning of life in society. He was attracted to the quest for an integrated worldview and to classical humanistic studies in the tradition of Montesquieu, Hegel and Dilthey. (He continued to think about society in this manner even after rejecting the possibility of the existence of a completely integrated philosophical *Weltanschauung*.)

Secondly, Oakeshott conceived moral conduct and social organisation to be the two points from which the study of political life could proceed. His approach to the study of society always combined these two aspects: a view of man and a view of association. The study of man was his "moral" philosophy and the study of association was his "social" philosophy. The term "social and moral philosophy" therefore is exceptionally appropriate for the study of Oakeshott's ideas.

These two assumptions laid out by Oakeshott in his juvenile essay provide the basis for all his subsequent moral and social philosophy, and therefore offer the framework for an analysis of his ideas. This is not to deny, however, that his thought underwent significant changes. The development of his moral and social philosophy can be roughly said to comprise three stages. In the first, Oakeshott's view of both morality and society was influenced by British Idealism and founded on two philosophical pillars: teleology and holism. In the second stage, Oakeshott rejected the teleological vision of man and society, while preserving, at least in part, his holistic quasi-Hegelian approach. Finally, in the third stage he abandoned both his holism and his teleology, thus arriving at a comprehensive moral and social philosophy significantly distinct from that of his early period.

This development was always driven by the same underlying passion to understand the meaning of the relationship of human beings in society. Yet Oakeshott significantly changed the presuppositions of what such relationship entailed. In the following sections I wish to discuss the evolution of those presuppositions in more detail.

---

1   See Worthington (1997: 727–38).

II

The first stage of Oakeshott's moral and social thought encompasses the period of the 1920s and 30s. In the early '30s Oakeshott seems to have already fully developed the postulates of his philosophy in general, articulated in *Experience and Its Modes* (1933), which represent a break with his previous philosophical convictions. Yet, with respect to moral and social philosophy, Oakeshott's thought in the '30s still shows a continuity with the ideas of his youth, as he does not immediately adjust them to the changes in his general philosophical framework.[2] Therefore, one can regard these years as one and the same period with regard to the development of his moral and social ideas.

As a young man, Oakeshott generally followed the political philosophy associated with British Idealism, especially that of Bosanquet. Furthermore, his Idealist inclinations are combined with basic Aristotelian assumptions. This double background finds its expression in the two most characteristic features of his thought of that period: teleology and holism.

The young Oakeshott regards teleology as the foundation of true philosophy. For him, philosophy is an inquiry into the meaning of things, and such meaning can only be reached in terms of understanding the purpose of each thing (1925: 20). Both moral conduct and social life have to be understood in purposive terms. The purpose of human fellowship is leading a good life, and association can be understood in terms of this purpose. Thus the state is conceived by Oakeshott as a "cultural unit" (1925: 72), and culture is regarded as the end a state sets before itself. This means that the state possesses "more than a mere unity of action; it must also have some degree of unity of purpose" (1925: 75).

The teleological understanding of the meaning of association is connected with a teleological view concerning morality and practical life. Oakeshott's view of practice may be briefly described as follows: Practice is a world of experience. It is an attempt to achieve what is satisfactory in experience. Practical experience is based on certain presuppositions. It postulates the world understood under the category of change. This experience is always an action, directed to the alteration of existence; even the activity of preservation is actually an alteration. Therefore it involves the discrepancy between what is here and now, and what is yet to be.

The "here and now" and "yet to be" are moments of two distinct worlds within the world of practical experience: the world of practical fact and the world of what "ought to be" lie within, in other words, a world of value. These two worlds within the world of practical experience have presuppositions of their own. Thus the world of "here and now" has its own explicit concepts of fact, truth and reality. This is the world of the present as such,

---

2   See Podoksik (2005).

which lacks internal stability. What is true now can be untrue later; the fact of today is a "non-fact" of tomorrow. It always presupposes a situation which is subject to change, and the achievement of a certain outcome just creates a new situation demanding an alteration.

The other world is the world of valuation. It is an independent mode of experience which cannot be reduced to "the mode of what is". In practical experience there is an attempt to reconcile "what is" and "what ought to be", but this cannot occur theoretically; the reconciliation is not between the two worlds as worlds — this would be impossible, as these are two different abstract worlds — but between two particular instances of "what is" and what is "not yet". And if the future state of things appears to possess "superior coherency", this specific action becomes a duty or obligation (Oakeshott 1933: 280 fn.).

The category of duty cannot serve as the most concrete reconciliation because "every achievement brings with it a new view of the criterion, which converts this momentary perfection into imperfection" (1933: 291). Reconciliation is achieved only in religion, which is regarded as "the form of practical activity in which this attempt is carried furthest ... it is merely practical experience at its fullest" (1933: 292). Yet, in *Experience and Its Modes*, morality is, in some sense, central to practical experience. For every action is seen as reconciling a specific "is" with a specific "ought to be". Such reconciliation is aimed at bringing about a more coherent world and, therefore, can be seen as an obligation. Though morality as a world is never achieved, what is implied in Oakeshott's argument is that every action is somehow done under the category of duty. The world of valuation presents itself as a kind of ideal purpose under which actions are performed, however futile our hope to achieve perfection may be.

Oakeshott, then, refers both to social organisation and practical life in purposive terms. Moreover, this teleological approach is integrated into a holistic framework. As mentioned above, for Oakeshott, the task of philosophy is to understand the purpose of each thing. But when such understanding is pressed towards its conclusion, it approaches the totality of experience, and therefore true philosophy presupposes an attempt to reach the whole (1925: 19).

This philosophical emphasis on totality also corresponds with the holistic view of society and the individual. Oakeshott speaks about the state as a self-sufficient moral and cultural association and cites Burke, who sees in the state a "partnership" (1925: 77). The more an association is a real unity with a common tradition, memory and purpose, the more it is a state in the true meaning of the word. Oakeshott's views in this respect recall the concept of the state delineated by Bosanquet (2001). One should point out, however, that this holistic vision of the state is not followed by illiberal conclusions. Oakeshott proceeds along familiar Idealist lines, where the perception of the state as a moral association reflecting the totality of social relations is called upon to shore up liberal political convictions. Although, or because, the state is an association with a clear moral purpose, government should not be equated with the state. In fact, its authority is self-limiting. The purpose of government is to serve the moral ends of society, but government "may not attempt that which it is unable to achieve" (1925: 160). Government is only one of the associations within the state that serve its main purpose.

Oakeshott also uses the holistic vocabulary in his approach to the practical conduct of the individual. He puts a special emphasis on the integrity of the self. The pursuit of integrity is the essence of practical conduct, for the tendency of all practical activity is towards an "integrated state of mind" (1933: 295). The attempt at reaching integrity is basically a religious quest, although rarely achievable, for "it is a rare and peculiar genius which enables a man to see clearly what belongs to his life and to follow it without reserve, unhindered by the restraint of prudence or the impediment of doubt" (1933: 295).

Furthermore, besides considering the individual and society separately, Oakeshott wishes to transcend their dualism and present them as two sides of the same unity; we see this especially in the writings preceding the publication of *Experience and Its Modes*. He rejects methodological individualism with regard to the concept of the self, claiming that the self cannot be coherently understood as a combination of an individual body and its thoughts (although this view can serve some practical purposes). The self is a thing and therefore must be self-complete. As no particular human being is self-complete, "the only true, because the only perfect, self is the universe" (1925: 130). Only the totality of experience can be absolutely self-complete and thereby possess individuality. Therefore "a self is its society" (1925: 131), "the self is the State, the State is the self" (1925: 133). No real conflict occurs between the state and the individual. "Individuality means finding our activity within a whole" (1925: 135). It is expressed in finding one's own place within society, and "only through his particular station and the faithful performance of its particular duties, can [man] take hold of this thing called 'humanity'" (1925: 140).[3]

III

Thus teleology and holism are key aspects of the philosophy of the young Oakeshott, and his further intellectual development must be understood in light of his gradual abandonment of these ideas. The second stage of his

---

[3] This is the dominant line in Oakeshott's writings of his early period. Yet, from the late 1920s onwards, there appear some intimations of a different way of thinking which put an emphasis on the subjectivity of individuality. This line, however, finds its full expression only in the later writings. For details, see Podoksik (2008a).

social and moral philosophy is found in his writings of the late 1940s and early '50s, including some of the essays published in *Rationalism in Politics* (1962). As mentioned above, the evolution of Oakeshott's general philosophy had begun already in the early '30s with his move away from the holistic assumptions of Absolute Idealism towards more pluralistic ones emphasising the independence and mutual irrelevance of different worlds of experience such as science and history.[4] Already then he had come to profess a view from which he would never depart. According to him, philosophy and practice are two distinct and mutually irrelevant worlds of experience that should never be confused. A philosophical argument can never serve as a guide to a practical life; likewise, nothing in the conduct of our lives can be relevant to the search for philosophical truth (Oakeshott 1933: 1). This claim represents a departure not only from the views of many Idealists, whose holism did not allow maintaining such a strong separation of philosophy and practice—although many Idealists had warned against the vulgar application of philosophy for the sake of practical purposes. This also meant a departure from the views of the young Oakeshott himself, who previously had not drawn such a clear distinction.

Oakeshott's abandonment of Absolute Idealism in the realm of general philosophy was not, however, immediately accompanied by similar changes in his moral and social thought. Although, in the end, his social and moral philosophy proceeded in the same direction, it took more time for this evolution to take place. During the 1930s, Oakeshott published relatively little directly connected with the questions of social life. The first significant changes in his views on this theme, then, become apparent only in the critical essays which he started to publish in the late 1940s. These essays still retain features of his old Absolute Idealist vocabulary, especially with regard to morality and society. Oakeshott seems to continue to adhere to the quest for the unity of the human self—a unity based on that or another form of synthesis between the self and society. For example, he criticises J.D. Mabbott's *The Citizen and the State* for trying to make too sharp a distinction between the individual and society (1949: 378–9). Up to the early '50s, then, Oakeshott speaks about politics and society in Hegelian or Idealist terms, describing politics as a concrete activity, and society as a partnership between the past, present and future (Oakeshott 2001: 56; see also 388). He tends to see the state neither as a government nor as a multitude of people but rather as a social whole.

Nevertheless, even when Oakeshott's works display this kind of Hegelian language, he discards an important feature of it; he attempts to overcome the teleological view of human life so characteristic of his early writings. One can see this change, for example, in his revised understanding of morality, which finds its clearest expression in "The Tower of Babel"

---

[4] See Podoksik (2005).

(1948). In that essay, Oakeshott distinguishes between two ideal types of morality: the morality of habit or custom, and reflective morality. Although Oakeshott points out that any actually existing morality is a combination of these two types, he thinks that they can be mixed in differing degrees. In some societies, the morality of habit predominates, in others, reflective morality does. Oakeshott is more sympathetic to the morality of habit, and so recommends a mixture of the two moralities in which this form prevails. Therefore he is quite pessimistic about the condition of modern moral life in which, he believes, the prevalent type is conversely reflective morality.

The morality of custom refers to acting in accordance with a certain habit of behaviour. Oakeshott equates this with language, and attributes to it a "poetic" character. Although this morality is in danger of becoming superstition, because it has no intellectual resources with which to examine itself, there is an advantage in its lack of rigidity. It springs from a natural flow of behaviour and can be learned the same way that one acquires one's native language. It does not require explicit rules, but living with people who are used to behaving in the same way. Nothing in this form of morality is fixed. As it is not formulated in rules, it is typically responsive to the nuances of particular situations. Like language, it is in a process of constant change. This morality is very volatile, presupposing a significant freedom of individual performance.

Reflective morality, on the contrary, establishes patterns of behaviour according to explicit *rules* or, alternatively, *ideals* which guide it. This form of morality avoids the danger of falling into superstition that is characteristic of the morality of habit. But it carries dangers of its own. It precludes certainty in conduct, for there is always uncertainty in questions of how a rule may be applied to a particular situation and what specific action should be performed. Furthermore, it is very rigid and has little power of self-modification. It is inherently oppressive, since it does not allow any expression of eccentricity which would be unsuited to its declared ideals. Thus, of the two forms of morality — the morality of rules and that of ideals — Oakeshott sees the major threat in the latter. The morality of rules is not so dangerous because "the rule is not represented as perfection" but, rather, constitutes "a mediation, a cushion, between the behaviour it demands on each occasion and the complete moral response to the situation" (2001: 475). By contrast, the morality of ideals cannot escape from the vision of perfection, and Oakeshott is very suspicious of claimants to moral perfectionism.

On account of this essay, Oakeshott was often accused of justifying a conservative moralistic worldview, yet this interpretation is not quite correct. It ignores the logic of an inner development of Oakeshott's position. What escapes its notice is that his attack on the morality of ideals, rather than the morality of rules, is driven not by some parochial traditionalism but by the concern to deny teleology to human conduct, putting instead an emphasis on contingency. He does not mourn the loss of a particular old system of values; rather, he is against systems of moral values as such if they become dogmatic, and especially if they display some sort of purposiveness. He prefers the morality of habit precisely because he regards it as providing more opportunities for spontaneous enjoyment.

In this respect, Oakeshott somewhat resembles Nietzsche, whom he mentions in this essay. Yet perhaps the most interesting parallel is with Ferdinand Tönnies' distinction between two kinds of human will: *Wesenwille*, the essential will that expresses a natural and spontaneous development of one's character; and *Kürwille*, the "artificial" will in which reason, or reflection, acquires a logic of its own and imposes its calculation on conduct (Tönnies 2001; Podoksik 2008a). For Tönnies, "essential" or "natural" will corresponds to the idea of community (*Gemeinschaft*), whereas "artificial", "rational", or "calculative" will corresponds to the idea of modern society *(Gesellschaft)*, based on the principles of exchange and contract.

These two types of will look very similar to Oakeshott's two types of morality. Both Tönnies and Oakeshott may sound quite traditionalist in their nostalgia engendered by the loss of the feeling of moral community, yet they value customary morality precisely for its spontaneity. For Oakeshott, only the morality of habit can create an integrated human being, whereas reflective morality creates dissonance and leads to the loss of the art of behaviour. Similar to Tönnies, for whom the modern world is characterised by alienation as the result of the domination of the calculative will, Oakeshott regards the reflective purposiveness in behaviour as harming its spontaneity. The beauty of the morality of custom is precisely that it is not purposive but poetic. A poem, according to him, is never written according to a designed plan: "what the poet says and what he wants to say are not two things, the one succeeding and embodying the other, they are the same thing; he does not know what he wants to say until he has said it" (Oakeshott 2001: 479). This feature of poetic activity must also be true of all moral activity, the ideals of which are just products "of human practical activity, to which reflective thought gives subsequent, partial and abstract expression in words" (2001: 480).

A similar repudiation of the idea of "purpose" is also found in Oakeshott's social philosophy. Far from reiterating his earlier claim that the purpose of an association must be the pursuit of a good life, he famously asserts that in political activity "men sail a boundless and bottomless sea; there is neither harbour for shelter nor floor for anchorage, neither starting-place nor appointed destination. The enterprise is to keep afloat on an even keel ..." (2001. 60). The journey therefore has no purpose, and the guide to it can be found only in the existing tradition of behaviour and its "intimations".

That the primary feature of modern social life is the replacement of political activity as an art with planned action in which everything is seen as the process of problem-solving, is the major idea of Oakeshott's famous essay, "Rationalism in Politics" (1947). The rationalist, according to Oakeshott, is characterised by the disposition to stand for independence of mind on all occasions. He believes in the authority of reason, and his aspiration is to free the mind of all traditions and prejudices, to purge it in order to undertake critical inquiry, so that as a result he will be able to achieve knowledge unhindered by superstition.

This attitude is grounded upon a certain theory of knowledge. For Oakeshott, every practical activity involves knowledge, and it is always of two sorts: "technical" and "practical". "Technical" knowledge is that which can be formulated by explicit rules capable of being deliberately learned and put into practice. The second sort of knowledge cannot be explicitly formulated. This is the knowledge of know-how, and it can be learned only by the performance of an activity itself. The fallacy of the rationalist is that he does not recognise this second sort of knowledge, and believes that all knowledge can be reduced to "technique". For him, learning any activity is merely learning a set of defined rules. Therefore, "his knowledge will never be more than half-knowledge, and consequently he will never be more than half-right" (2001: 36).

In politics, this rationalism expresses itself in the "problem-solving" approach. Rationalistic politics is the politics of the "felt need". The rationalist sees society as composed of problems, and he believes that there should always exist an optimal administrative solution for every problem, although he is sometimes aware of his own inability to find this solution. For the rationalist, politics turns into continually engaging in actions in order to "improve" society by means of a defined set of rules, i.e., an ideology or doctrine. Any tradition not fitting this doctrine is rejected as a superstition.

In modern politics, rationalism has become the prevalent approach. The reason for this development is the displacement of the old classes traditionally educated in the art of politics by new players—ones lacking practical political knowledge, whose only way of doing politics is through cribs, that is, hastily cobbled-together doctrines. Even resistance to this style of rationalism must now be dressed in rationalistic clothes. "This is, perhaps, the main significance of Hayek's *Road to Serfdom*—not the cogency of his doctrine, but the fact that it is a doctrine. A plan to resist all planning may be better than its opposite, but it belongs to the same style of politics" (2001: 26).

It is not difficult to notice that this criticism is directed at what Max Weber might call the rationality of purpose. Various critics took Oakeshott's attack on rationalism to be an attack on rationality in general, but this criticism was misplaced. He pointed a number of times to there being an alternative concept of rationality, one which does not require "purposive" thinking. In "Rational Conduct" (1950), Oakeshott criticises the tendency to take "*purpose* as the distinctive mark of 'rationality' in conduct" (2001: 102). Such a view presupposes the idea of instrumental mind, whose activity precedes an action and whose deliberation on principles, purposes and rules of behaviour governs this behaviour. Oakeshott considers this to be a false description of what conduct involves. Instead, he suggests that rationality should be seen as faithfulness to the tradition of behaviour. In other words, rationality in conduct is "acting in such a way that the coherence of the idiom of activity to which the conduct belongs is preserved and possibly enhanced" (2001: 122). Rational conduct is characterised, not by the ability to achieve a certain end, but by its contribution to the coherence of human activity as a whole. One of the problems of the mistaken view of rationality is that it breaks up activity into separate actions, thereby merely abstracting a partial aspect of conduct from the whole to which it belongs. In reality, however, "'rationality' is the certificate we give to any conduct which can maintain a place in the flow of sympathy, the coherence of activity, which composes a way of living" (2001: 130). One might attempt to compare this view of rationality with Weber's rationality of value in the sense that, for Oakeshott, rationality resides in the inner coherence of a system of conduct rather than in some external criterion. Yet one should keep in mind the important qualification that Oakeshott's understanding of coherence presupposes far less rigid and reflective conduct than what the concept of "value" would usually imply.

IV

Oakeshott's concept of rationality points to the major feature of his thought at that stage. He came to regard purposiveness and holism as two rivals. He rejected the idea of purposive conduct in order to shore up the idea of the integral human life or, to use his own term, "concrete activity". He recommended a non-purposive morality because he considered such a morality to be conducive to the emergence of an integrated personality and a self-confident society.

The writings of that period earned Oakeshott the reputation of a conservative. Early commentators, of course, ignored many subtleties of his thought yet, in general, they had a point: much of what he said did sound conservative and traditionalist. What was often not so well recognised, however, was the inner logic of the transition that his ideas had undergone. A "traditionalist", "conservative" flavour in his thought was an outcome of the combination of his holism and anti-teleological attitude.

This was not, however, the final stage in the evolution of Oakeshott's moral and social thought. As early as the middle 1950s, the focus and the mood of his writings shift significantly, as he begins to sound more conciliatory towards modern society, stressing praise for individuality rather than criticism of rationalism. This change signifies the beginning of the third stage, culminating in the publication of *On Human Conduct* (1975), wherein Oakeshott finally arrives at a comprehensive statement placing his moral and social thought in line with the rest of his philosophy.[5] Here, he casts doubt on the legacy of his earlier social and moral ideas: the Idealist concept of unity in conduct and society. Holism (as a part of his general philosophy) had, as we have seen, been rejected much earlier. Now he adjusts his view of morality and society to conform with that general position. And when teleology and holism are finally abandoned, not a great deal remains of his conservatism and traditionalism.

Oakeshott reshapes his notion of human conduct and human association. Human conduct, he holds, is a certain observable identity which can be analysed in terms of two different aspects: practices and substantive performances. Human conduct is conditioned by practices because it is an intelligible occurrence. There are two ways of understanding a perceived event.

On the one hand, it can be seen as an event which is itself a product of intelligence. On the other hand, it can be perceived as a non-intelligible occurrence. The former roughly corresponds to the world of human actions and artefacts, the latter to the world of nature. In fact, everything can be understood either as a product of intelligence or not, depending on the approach of an observer. Yet each of these two kinds of event requires a specific order of inquiry strictly separated from the other. An event which is not a product of intelligence is perceived as a part of "process", being explained in terms of cause and effect. By contrast, an event which is an outcome of intelligence is understood through "practice", a certain system of rules which gives a meaning to occurrences without determining a specific consequence. "Human conduct", being the product of intelligent agents, falls in this latter category. Thus each action can be seen in terms of its subscription to certain practices. A forensic speech, for example, subscribes to the grammar of the language in which it is uttered, to specific requirements of the relevant system of legal rules and perhaps to the presumed sentiments of the audience. Sometimes, a performer may choose a particular system of rules to which his performance will subscribe, but he cannot avoid subscribing to at least *some* rules. One cannot imagine a

---

[5] On this point, see in more detail Podoksik (2003a), especially ch. 3.

human action which is not subject to any rule—just as one cannot imagine a language without a grammar.

Yet to view a performance in terms of the practices to which it subscribes is not sufficient for a complete understanding of human conduct. For one can see an action also in terms of its substantive performances, of decisions to do *this* rather than *that*. Thus, in delivering a speech, an orator may use or decline to use *this* or *that* specific argument or to be assisted by *this* or *that* rhetorical device, so long as the argument chosen is recognised as valid within the system of the practice of forensic oratory. It is up to the agent to choose, and such a choice is never determined by practices. A choice is always made in an anticipation of a certain outcome, and the meaning of an action "is a wished-for response from other agents" (1975: 44).

Thus, since every performance consists of these two distinct aspects, there are two different ways of approaching human conduct. One is to study practices, which may lead to an articulation of a certain social theory; the other is to study substantive choices of particular human beings in a particular time and place—and history is, for Oakeshott, the best-suited discipline for an inquiry of this kind (1975: 106–7).

One can see the difference between this account of human conduct and the one presented earlier in "Rational Conduct". Previously, Oakeshott regarded instrumental conduct as an abstraction which obscures the vision of conduct as a coherent whole. Purposive conduct was just a partial aspect of the totality of human life. Yet here the distinction is not between what is partial and what is concrete, so that the partial necessarily dissolves into the whole. It is rather between two independent aspects of conduct which cannot be reduced to each other. One corresponds to general conditions which qualify actions. The other refers to the sphere of the intentions and purposes of those actions.

One might be tempted to conclude here that Oakeshott gives up the quest for understanding human conduct as concrete activity, but simply brings back a qualified appreciation of the purposive character of human life. The matter, however, is more complicated. There may be two possible ways to speak about purpose in human conduct. One is to ascribe an overall purpose to all of human life, a sort of final cause or *telos*. Oakeshott, however, claims that expressions such as "the good life" are acceptable only in so far as they do not indicate some substantive condition of things. A life can be seen as "good", but "goodness" here does not relate to the substantive aspect of actions: "'Human excellence' or 'the human good' is not a substantive purpose to be achieved … it is not a purpose which an agent might choose to pursue in preference to the satisfaction of some other want … like joining an expedition to climb Mount Everest or agreeing with another to settle in Katmandu" (1975: 61). In other words, what is often seen as a general purpose of human life is not a purpose at all, but a certain condition, qualifying conduct but not directing it to any outcome. Therefore, the idea of "the good life" refers to the sphere of practices rather than to substantive performances.

The other way to approach purpose in conduct is to break up activity into a series of individual actions, each presupposing its own particular outcome, and this is how Oakeshott deals with the aspect of substantive performances. Yet this means, not only that the sphere of intentions does not provide unity to conduct, but also that, while every particular action possesses a specific meaning, this does not make conduct in general meaningful. Indeed, Oakeshott seems to be minimising the significance of the element of purpose even here. For him, substantive action is the subject of historical inquiry; history deals with what is singular and particular and not with what is common and general. The tricky point is that, for Oakeshott, history was never an inquiry either into the subjective meaning of historical occurrences in the minds of historical actors or into the objective spirit of world events. He was always sceptical with regard to the Collingwoodian approach, according to which history was a re-enactment of past thought or experience.[6] Neither did he approve of attempts to construct a meaningful path of history as a whole — to create a kind of teleological historiography, be it a Hegelian, Whig or Spenglerian interpretation of history. For Oakeshott, true history was the history of observable events, not of meanings. But if this is so, then the analysis of substantive performances does not lead to questions about the intended outcome of an action, but rather to questions about the outcome itself, irrespective of the intention. Whether it is possible to write history in such a way is another question. What is worth noting, however, is that for Oakeshott the sphere of purposes in human conduct is the one of substantive performances, and yet, when he discusses it, he recommends a mode of inquiry which, by his own definition, avoids dealing with supposed purposes of conduct.

Furthermore, Oakeshott does not conceal his preference for the aspect of practices when looking for what makes conduct truly meaningful and valuable. Substantive actions bring uncertainty, for the reaction of other agents is never dependent on the intention of our action: "acting is making a bargain with an imperfectly imagined future" (1975: 44). Practices, on the contrary, provide a common ground for what is durable, although at the same time this durability lacks a "purpose". Oakeshott regards the aspect of human conduct which may be understood in terms of purpose as the less important one, compared with the aspect which bestows on it a kind of durability. This can be seen from his attitude concerning the concepts of "self-disclosure" and "self-enactment". The language of self-dis-

---

[6] See, for example, O'Sullivan (2003: 170–2).

closure relates to "the intercourse of agents, each concerned with procuring imagined and wished-for satisfactions ... and each seeking them in responses of another or of others", whereas, in the language of self-enactment, actions are "understood in terms of the motives in which they are performed" (1975: 70). Conduct understood as self-disclosure is a long chain of actions and wants. No outcome brings us to final satisfaction, but instead creates new wants. Actions understood only as performed in the quest for the satisfaction of wants cannot be related to a person as *one's* own, since one of the characteristics of human conduct is the ability to make judgments about the meaning of one's actions for oneself. Therefore, a life understood as mere self-disclosure would be perceived as futile, and would render the idea of personality nonsensical. Unlike self-disclosure, self-enactment qualifies the unresolved character of this condition. For when the exercise of agency is understood as a "movement about a world where achieved satisfactions breed wants", this world may be "habitable only when the energy of pursuit is prudentially mixed with *nonchaloir* in respect of the outcome" (1975: 73). And thus the integrity of conduct can be achieved only when it springs from a certain character of an agent, not from the intended outcome of an action.

Yet Oakeshott is pessimistic about the quest for the perfect integrity of human conduct. Indeed, he does not think that the language of self-enactment is capable of achieving such integrity. It is true that it qualifies the imperfect character of human condition, but this is just qualification, not a solution. It creates an "echo of durability", yet self-enactment "is itself an episodic and an inconclusive engagement, as *ondoyânt* and as full of unresolved tensions as any other" (1975: 84). This pessimism with regard to the possibility of reaching integrity in conduct goes contrary to the sentiments of the young Oakeshott. Thus in *Experience and Its Modes* practical experience was seen as an intimation of eternal youthfulness, the joy of life, an attempt to live fully and without reservations. In *On Human Conduct*, however, Oakeshott speaks about the illusion of practical affairs, and seems no longer to believe in the possibility of the full integration of practical experience.

Thus this two-fold understanding of human conduct in the terms of practices and of substantive performances helps Oakeshott to reject both unity and purposiveness. On the one hand, the separation of these two aspects, so that they cannot be reduced to one another, precludes perceiving conduct as concrete activity, as an integrated whole. On the other hand, a close identification of the sphere of substantive performances with caprices of "self-disclosure" points to Oakeshott's continuous denial of the value of purposiveness in human affairs.

This idea is accompanied by a parallel two-fold understanding of human association. According to Oakeshott, any more or less durable relationship of human agents can be understood in two different ways or "modes of association" (1975: 108). One is association in respect of the substantive element of human conduct, namely the pursuit of the satisfaction of specific wants; the other is association in respect of the formal character of human conduct, that is, in terms of practices governing these actions. These two modes are not types of actually existing associations, but represent two categorically distinct ideal characters.

An association in respect of the pursuit of wants may take different forms. One is the "intermittent, transactional association" (1975: 112), where agents are bargainers entering into a relationship with each other in order to pursue their own individual ends. A more durable association is, however, an "enterprise association", where members are joined in the pursuit of some common goal. In order to pursue this goal in contingent and always-changing circumstances, the members design a certain procedure for making managerial decisions, appoint people responsible for making such decisions, and may formulate a system of rules designed to aid the achievement of their common purpose. However, the terms of the association are not its rules but the purpose and its pursuit in contingent circumstances.

It is this last consideration that distinguishes such an association from the categorically different "moral association", which is an association in terms of its own conditions. Its rules are perceived as not having an extraneous purpose but as being the very terms of the association, irrespective of whatever goals its members may pursue. The civil association is a moral association, the peculiarity of which is that its practice is the system of the deliberately enacted and alterable law (1975: 182).

To put it briefly, the civil association is everything that the enterprise association is not. It is a non-purposive moral association in terms of its conditions, whereas the enterprise association is a purposive instrumental association in terms of the pursuit of substantive satisfactions. The requirements of its law (which Oakeshott calls *lex*) are general rules and not specific commands. They demand, not the performance of specific actions, but the subscription to their conditions in any self-chosen action. These rules are equal and general, referring not to particular persons or places, but to a certain kind of relationship.

Members are inherently free in such an association, firstly, because general rules do not specify particular actions; everyone is free to pursue any goals in his or her self-chosen actions, so long as the conditions of the association are not violated. Secondly, because these conditions are recognised only in terms of their authority, while their desirability can always be contested. This is not true for the enterprise association, in which the members are required to recognise the common purpose of such an association and to approve specific performances which supposedly promote this purpose. This freedom is contingent upon its members acknowledging this purpose and these decisions as their own and being capable of leaving the association (1975: 157–8).

Oakeshott is certainly more favourably disposed towards the civil association. Human beings are associated in it not in respect of achieving a substantive outcome but in respect of their subscription to *lex*. Within the framework of civil association they will, of course, join certain enterprise associations, but the authority of these associations will always be limited by the conditions of the civil association. Associates should always be free to withdraw from enterprise associations. But the ultimate human association (i.e., the modern state, according to Oakeshott) should be understood only as a civil association.[7]

It is remarkable that Oakeshott considers the lack of purpose as the central characteristic of civil association. Having rejected purposive morality, he also rejects a teleological understanding of society. Moreover, civil association does not provide "unity" in the strong Idealist sense of the word. It can hardly be called a fellowship. There are no friends in such an association. It is described as a relationship of strangers which does not recognise the languages of love, affection or rivalry (Oakeshott, 1975: 123). The associates are connected here only through their common adherence to the same system of civil rules. Yet it has a value of its own, for it contains the recognition of one's inherent freedom. Civil association is a framework within which the contingencies of life can be explored whatever they may be. And the modern individual needs such freedom of exploration much more than he needs or can experience the warm feeling of communal unity.[8]

Conclusion

A review of Oakeshott's moral and social philosophy shows that he makes a full reversal of his early views in which he saw the state as a purposive moral unit existing for the sake of the good life of its members. This evolution corresponds to the change in his concept of morality. With regard to both of these moments, Oakeshott's ideas evolved in the same direction. As a young man, he came under the influence of Absolute Idealism and Aristotle, those influences being combined with a strong religious conviction and some flavour of mysticism or intuitivism in his ideas. Yet he radically transformed those ideas when he came to develop his own philosophy, in which he put emphasis on the contingency of human affairs. Human life becomes for him a journey without destination, where human beings are endowed with radical freedom at the expense of social

---

[7] Though, of course, European states are ambiguous identities and were quite often perceived as enterprise associations.
[8] On Oakeshott's individualism, see, for example, Riley (1992).

certainty.[9] And this condition of contingency and radical freedom must be reflected in the mode of association of such individuals.

References

Bosanquet, B. (2001), *The Philosophical Theory of the State* (4th edn., 1923); new edn. with Introduction, notes, and related essays, ed. William Sweet and Gerald F. Gaus (South Bend, IN: St Augustine's Press).

Oakeshott, M. (1925), "A Discussion of Some Matters Preliminary to the Study of Political Philosophy", *LSE Archives*, 1/1/3.

Oakeshott, M. (1933), *Experience and Its Modes* (Cambridge: University Press).

Oakeshott, M. (1949), Review of *The State and the Citizen* by J.D. Mabbott, *Mind*, 58, pp. 378-89.

Oakeshott, M. (1975), *On Human Conduct* (Oxford: Clarendon Press).

Oakeshott, M. (2001), "Political Education", "The Tower of Babel", "Rational Conduct", and "The Political Economy of Freedom", in *Rationalism in Politics and Other Essays* (Indianapolis: Liberty Fund).

Oakeshott, M. (2004), "The Cambridge School of Political Science", in *What Is History? And Other Essays* (Exeter: Imprint Academic).

O'Sullivan, L. (2003), *Oakeshott on History* (Exeter: Imprint Academic).

Podoksik, E. (2003a), *In Defence of Modernity: Vision and Philosophy in Michael Oakeshott* (Exeter: Imprint Academic).

Podoksik, E. (2003b), "Oakeshott's Theory of Freedom as Recognized Contingency", *European Journal of Political Theory*, 2, pp. 57-77.

Podoksik, E. (2005), "How Oakeshott Became an Oakeshottean", *European Journal of Political Theory*, 4, pp. 67-88.

Podoksik, E. (2008a), "The Idealism of Young Oakeshott", in J. Connelly and S. Panagakou (eds.), *Anglo-American Idealism: Thinkers and Ideas* (Oxford: Peter Laing).

Podoksik, E. (2008b), "Overcoming the Conservative Disposition: Oakeshott vs. Tönnies", *Political Studies*, 56, pp. 857-80.

Riley, P. (1992), "Michael Oakeshott: Philosopher of Individuality", *Review of Politics*, 54, pp. 649-64.

Tönnies, F. (2001), *Community and Civil Society*, trans. J. Harris & M. Hollis (Cambridge: Cambridge University Press).

Worthington, G. (1997), "Oakeshott's Claims of Politics", *Political Studies*, 45, pp. 727-38.

---

9 On Oakeshott's idea of freedom, see Podoksik (2003b).

Elizabeth Trott

John Watson and the Foundation and Applications of Moral Philosophy

Introduction

John Watson was born in Glasgow, Scotland, on 25 February 1847, and died in Kingston, Ontario, Canada, on 26 January 1939. On his arrival in Kingston in 1875, Watson called the place a one-horse town, and when judging his new home, Queen's University, he remarked that the architect had taken seriously Aristotle's definition of a building—four walls and a roof.

From this 'station,' however, Watson's reputation grew—not only in the scholarly world, but throughout Canada. He published eight major works in philosophy and over two hundred articles and reviews. Watson was, until 1998—more than 100 years after their establishment—Canada's only Gifford lecturer. These lectures (1910–2), published in two volumes as *The Interpretation of Religious Experience*, are the fullest expression of Watson's metaphysical and epistemological views, and his social and moral thought—revealed in *The State in Peace and War* (1919), his 1876 article "Hedonism and Utilitarianism" (containing his arguments against utilitarianism), his public addresses on education, and his theories about the relation between reason and religion as a social institution—is closely connected to his metaphysics.

Watson was a well-known teacher as well. Almost every student at Queen's attended his classes, and this, coupled with the fact that Queen's regularly staffed the civil service in Ottawa, may help considerably in explaining some aspects of Canadian culture. Hilda Neatby writes: "In the fifty-two years of his active work at Queen's, Watson sent out hundreds of young men and women with a profound concern for truth and an absolute conviction of their own personal responsibility to exemplify it in their conduct by making 'true', that is, unselfish choices" (Neatby 1978: 138). Yet, in spite of teaching twenty-five hours a week, Watson balanced his academic career with other interests. He enjoyed painting in water colours; he wrote plays and poetry; he corresponded with a friend about Latin syntax, and worked at translating Anne of Green Gables into Italian. He kept notes on golf swings in the hope of improving his own. He was a curling skip, and a founder of the Queen's Lawn Bowling Club. Watson was one of the first teachers for Queen's summer courses which began at the turn of the century. He allowed his three daughters to host house parties only if their requests to do so were made in French or German. In short he was a family man, a scholar, and an active member of his community.

Watson's philosophical mission was to create a unified theory of existence, one that could accommodate various seemingly competing interests: religion and science, self-interest and civic duty, diversity and political unity, and fragmented disparate knowledge claims and the universality of truth. In pursuing this philosophical vision, he foreshadowed the public culture of accommodation and tolerance — and also the continuing tensions of national unity — that define Canada today. The 'truth' of responsible behaviour was revealed in knowing that such unselfish acts were chosen freely. Acting because one feared God's wrath was neither free nor truthful behaviour. Watson's sense of duty as freedom had obvious Kantian overtones. He extended his beliefs about duty and freedom to all areas of social concerns. In order to make sense out of our claims to freedom we must understand the self as both a social concept (dialectically embedded in the community), and an individual concept.

Watson, the Self and the Community

Watson's understanding of the community begins with an account of the self. Accepting neither F.H. Bradley's suggestion that the self is an illusion, nor Bernard Bosanquet's position that the community is the truly real, Watson argues (as did Hegel), that the individual and the community are logical counterparts. Being able to individuate features of existence, and then group them as different from other features and other groupings, is a defining ability of self-conscious minds. The individual self distinguishes itself first from non-conscious beings, *as a subject* which, no matter how many changes that subject endures, is aware of itself (for the most part), as identical. Common experiences become grouped as 'me'. This view is not quite a replica of Hume's 'bundle of perceptions'. Watson thinks that the process of 'bundling' the perceptions triggers awareness of the self as *acting*.

Now this sense of identity, of individuality, has its dialectical opposition in the world of other selves, more specifically in communities of selves, for they are the systems within which, or in terms of which, changes to the self are interpreted and made intelligible. Watson writes:

> To be conscious of myself implies that I am conscious of myself as possessing a character which distinguishes me from other modes of being.

> My individuality is for me the consciousness of what I feel, know, and will. But if I have no consciousness of what is felt, known, and willed by others, I must be incapable of distinguishing between myself from other selves. It is therefore only in relation and contrast to other selves that I become conscious of what I as an individual am. (Watson, 1908: 186).

The self acts, and becomes aware of itself, through the effects of and responses to those actions.

Feelings, desires, volitions, to be so, must be more than sensations. They are sensations in conjunction with intentions, actions, and self-consciousness. To know one's goals, ambitions, and disappointments is more than to have them or to experience them. To know them as a *kind* of experience is to locate them within a rational order that characterizes *experiences of self-conscious beings*. Watson calls this kind of knowing self-activity or self-determination. To know them as one's own, is to know them as different from the experiences of others. If one were truly an isolated individual, one would have no sense of one's own uniqueness. One's sense of self develops gradually against the background of communities and society. The self is locked in a dialectical relation with other selves; a metaphysical tension pervades one's acts of individuation.

For Watson, a community establishes its character and culture precisely from the way its members are differentiated as individuals. A community is the set of shared meanings in terms of which one acts, responds, and gradually individuates oneself. For example, members of a group may be differentiated by class, rank, sex, and age, but may share a uniform set of meanings. Members may be differentiated by skills, discourse, and beliefs, and may be suspicious of a uniform set of meanings. A community that does not provide the means for a plurality of particular individuations does not give rise to individuals. If a community produces only conformities, there is little opportunity for development and growth. The intersections and interactions of individuals will be stilted by the community's limitations on actions, in mental, spiritual, physical systems. Watson writes:

> The conception of the state as a social contract…, gives no justification for the existence of the State, since it makes society an arbitrary combination of individual wills. There is nothing to compel individuals to enter into the contract, and therefore nothing to explain why it should be made. To reduce the contract to a mere expedient for a larger amount of happiness, does not explain why a man should be under obligation to assent to the contract, if he thinks he would attain more satisfaction by individual initiative…. The theory can only explain the compulsion placed by society upon the individual by saying that the good of the greatest number is more important than the private interest of any individual. But this obviously identifies that State with the power of the majority to have its own conception of the good forcibly realized. (Watson, 1919: 194–5)

Man's nature is social, declares Watson. Government is to provide opportunities for us to realize, develop and express ourselves as *social* beings, individuals in networks of social relations not individuals as isolated and disconnected. Watson is indebted to T.H. Green when he appeals to the idea of self-realization, but resists Green's conclusion that we are all expressions of a universal mind. Developing an inner coherence in understanding our experiences and the world does move us closer to freedom, in that we can have a greater array of intersections with the world and so make more decisions that can free one from the dominance of sensations and poorly understood desires. But, for Watson, it is not one's participation in a universal consciousness (as Green proposed), but one's participation in an energetic expressive community that enables one to learn about fellow members as being the same in nature but different in their realization of their individual natures. Without the social orders for the expression of differences and the social means for accommodating them, *knowledge* — the outcome of communal efforts at problem-solving — would not develop.

Watson thought that free interaction among individuals was the basis of the development of objective knowledge. Such interactions developed perspectives on the world beyond personal points of view. Watson, while welcoming 'science' as an inevitable product of communities with maximum freedoms for individuals, was none the less wary of the determinism that Darwin's theory seemed to support. Watson asks, Does this mean that there is no freedom in the development of knowledge, that man can only know what his disposition suits him to know? Watson interprets determinism as meaning that one is *determined to hold certain beliefs*. Without shared beliefs and conflicting beliefs, the clash of which produces knowledge, the objectivity of knowledge claims will be seriously undermined.

Watson regards evolutionary theory as one kind of rational order, the applicability of which requires prudent restraint. In the orders of non-conscious beings (plants) and non-self conscious beings (other animals), evolutionary theory is tremendously revealing. But were it to encroach on the possible orders of knowledge that sustain individuals and their communities, evolutionary theory would not encourage a constant search for new solutions, because it favours only those solutions that fit its model. Acceptance of a single explanatory theory, Watson urges, will seriously undermine moral actions which require individual free choice.[1] This free choice

---

1   Knowledge arises when one understands the available orders for interpreting experience, as well as the difficulties of assigning knowledge claims to one order or another. For example, in trying to settle land claims or environmental issues with communities that bring Traditional Knowledge (as geographers refer to it) to the negotiations, what weight does this form of knowledge have in building a case when such knowledge claims do not accord with the standard methods and procedures of verification of modern-day science? To what kind of epistemological or metaphysical order does Traditional or Local knowledge belong?

gives moral behaviour its meaning. Evolution does not explain morality. Watson writes:

> Selfishness is not the way to obtain the satisfaction of the individual... [Man] is by his very nature social, and forms part of an organism in which the good of each is bound up with the good of all.... the feeling of dissatisfaction experienced by the individual when he acts contrary to the common opinion rests upon the very same consciousness of a self higher than his merely individual self. It is because he has the same consciousness of a social self as is embodied in common opinion that the individual man is dissatisfied with himself when he has sought for the satisfaction of his own separate self at the expense of others. (Watson, 1908: 148-9)

As part of a determined master plan, people would have little awareness of these mental experiences. One's individuality as a self is most apparent when one must determine the meanings (from multiple options) that will create a narrative for one's identity. These acts of determination will reveal one's conformity, or one's uneasy alliance, with the predominant community or communities that mark out one's current arena of action.

Watson and the Foundations of Morality

Consciousness is a common property which we all share. It is an awareness of the data in reality and the orders through which the data is manifested.¹ We are individuated in that we all experience different data. We are united in that the different data can be known because all data is sustained by the same ordering principles. The tensions in our lives reflect our struggles to understand the experiences of others, while holding to the principle that these experiences can be understood. One way of understanding this is to say that "There is always a tension in human affairs, a basic instability in the relation of individual to community. Were this not so morality would not arise. Morality is essentially the process of finding out not what is good for me or good for you but what is good in general" (Armour and Trott, 1981: 232). Watson thought that this was a plausible quest because, given the logical and material necessity of the existence of another to one's understanding of one's own existence, conditions need to be established that sustain both of us. What harms one person, in the long run, also harms someone else. Metaphysical theories of the self can be debated, and Watson believed that ethical questions needed some status independent of their metaphysical commitments. Two persons may support different metaphysical theories and yet both can still recognize the same dilemma as ethical.

Watson wrote no major text on ethics, but he did write one significant paper, "Hedonism and Utilitarianism" (1876). Here, Watson confronts J.S.

---

¹ Conscious beings experience their consciousness in awareness of the mental acts of ordering, classifying, revising, debating.

Mill and his theory that pleasure is the ground of ethical judgement. Utilitarianism is the theory that acts are to be judged by their consequences. For Mill, those consequences worthy of moral approbation were ones which produced pleasure.[2] Difficulties begin to arise when we try to identify the act being judged separate from the individual who performed the act, the intentions of that individual, and the measurable outcome. For example, there may be acts, the nature of which seems reprehensible, such as lying (deceiving someone about the nature of the consequences he or she is about to encounter). Such acts could not be supported as good or just acts. But such acts, when embedded in circumstances, may produce a greater aggregate of happiness. Withholding news about a person's failing health, the content of which news could have very adverse effects if received suddenly, and the impact of which content, given time, might be less severe, is an example of lying with good intentions, that is, with the hope of producing good consequences. The consequences of this act of lying has at least a chance of being good and cannot make the person's present health condition worse. But such an outcome would not be grounds for supporting lying as such, as an act to be valued. The point is that the same act can produce both pleasure and pain. How can it be judged morally worthy or unworthy solely as an act? Mill's measure of good or bad consequences was the maximizing of pleasure over pain, a pleasure he equated with happiness. Lying as a recommended act, in the long run would not produce a maximum distribution of happiness.

What causes difficulties with the hedonistic utilitarian view is that, if pleasure is the criterion for judgement, then the individual may have to choose between pleasure for oneself (e.g., lower taxes entail more expendable income for the individual who has a history of good health), or pleasure for the group of which one is a member. Higher taxes will produce more accessible health care for all, including oneself, but there will be less personal income for individual pleasures. Both consequences produce pleasure. What criteria would enable one to assess the greater pleasure when faced with that choice? Watson suggests, as the above example is intended to illustrate, that sooner or later reasons other than the appeal to pleasure must be factored in to ethical problem solving.

Watson concludes (after analyzing the concept of pleasure, as feeling or intuition), that sorting out the relation between pleasure, and the acts and objects which give rise to pleasure — which thereby affect our understanding of its potential distribution — requires the application of rational principles. In other words:

---

[2] Mill was fully aware that there could be different kinds of pleasures, and was an advocate for the pleasures of the intellect. The contentious question is whether the concept of pleasure is sufficient to provide grounds for social duties that further the good life for the community.

> We must decide how to distribute pleasure. We must decide which pleasures deserve our attention. We must decide how to balance the consequences against the nature of the act. All of this forces upon our attention the fact that the desires, goals, and so on which attract our attention are located in the context of a community of persons. We come to understand that the choices make sense within this community, and in the course of this making sense we come to understand the rational principles which give intelligibility to the process. (Armour and Trott, 1981: 266)

Thus, Watson writes:

> The choice is not, as it is usually represented to be, between the derivation of moral conceptions from Experience, or their foundation on intuition; on the contrary, it may be easily shown that these rival methods, however they pretend to differ, are at bottom beset by essentially the same imperfection. Both alike deny to Reason any share in the constitution of objects; for although Utilitarianism affects to obtain all moral distinctions from experience, while Intuitionism claims that right and wrong are given in an immediate judgment, still the former resolves experiences into a series of feelings, and the latter has no test to apply save the various convictions of individuals… Utilitarianism must be able to show, not merely that moral conceptions have grown up in time, and that the virtuous man adopts as his rule of life the good of his kind, but that an ethical system may be raised upon a purely Hedonistic basis. It has to be proved that, in the words of Bentham, 'pleasure is in itself a good; nay even setting aside immunity from pain, the only good; pain itself is an evil, and indeed, without exception, the only evil;' and that, consistently with this fundamental postulate, legal, moral and social relations can be accounted for. (Watson, 1876: 273–4)

Watson clearly thinks such an undertaking will be fraught with surveys of personal preferences, evolving taste and shoddy appeals to distribution principles dictated by those in power. There must be ways of understanding justice, rights and good that are immutable to the expressions of cultural preferences of the times. His appeal to reason as having a 'share in the constitution of objects', as essential for us to give meaning to our lives (a process that has evolved as we come to create a community of understandings, made possible by the sharing of knowledge), is intended to reveal our rationally constituted world as a place in our lives from which decisions can be made. To undo that long history of sorting out the activities and the forces that are incommensurable with and destructive of living a flourishing life in a community would be to contravene the good life that we gradually come to understand as the result of community effort. First and foremost, to act in a morally good way is to not destroy that which enables one to cope as well as one does. One's institutions, one's legal system, one's freedom to criticize and orchestrate change through channels for making change, one's recognition of the necessity of others to one's very existence, these above conditions ground one's capacity to act morally. One's pleasure seems relevant, but is not the determining criterion of moral judgements and acts.

What is interesting about Watson is that he did not think there could be one universal moral theory such as Kant's categorical imperative, or Mill's utilitarian principle, that would provide solutions to all ethical problems. Communities change as new knowledge develops and new ways of problem solving evolve. New rational orders will evolve through the interchange of ideas. The critical factor is to provide for such interchange in an atmosphere of freedom. "The moral is not what is happening now because we could not have done anything else. The moral is that we must not expect to be able to solve all our social, political, and constitutional problems instantly because we may or may not have developed the regions of experience which would provide the basis for the discovery of the rational order which we require for a solution" (Armour and Trott, 1981: 235). Balancing the rights of the individuals to seek new rational orders in conjunction with the community that supports him or her is the foundation of moral development.

Watson, the Individual and the State

We can easily anticipate Watson's social theory in relation to the body politic. The individual and society are mutually interdependent. Neither has any supremacy (not even society in the guise of the state) over the other. Society is revealed through the individuation of members. The manners in which individuals express their differences require shared arenas for action. These arenas or institutions reflect the collective character of the society. Watson thought the state to be the society understood as a political order, one that is *not* supreme, *not* visionary, *not* beyond reproach, but *nonetheless*, an order that is a necessary condition of the conscious awareness of a self *as an individual self*. There can be many rational orders in society, and many cultural expressions of individuality. Knowledge of *differences* is essential for the larger community of society to support a political order which seeks out the particular expressions of individuals and groups. "Civilization is necessarily a slow and gradual process, because it implies the response of those upon whom it is attempted to be imposed. Unless they respond, all that is secured is an external conformity, which is very different from a real assimilation of the new spirit, and is sure to be accompanied by hypocrisy and other evils" (Watson, 1919: 181).

Watson's focus on the importance of individuals having freedom to differentiate themselves from one another, and of individual communities being able to express different cultural perspectives, was in keeping with the developing federalism in Canada. The federal government was the necessary condition for individuation of communities and cultures. Its job was to make provisions for many expressions of reason. Communities, in turn, having knowledge not just of their identities, but of the identities of others, expressed this knowledge by recognizing a need for a collective moral commitment to the grounds, or conditions, that make different identities part of a society. States are measured by the opportunities they provide for multiple expressions of reason. Watson thought the best State would support multiple orders, the interaction of which would build a continuing knowledge base. He emphasizes *continuing* because experience will constantly reveal new ways of ordering ourselves. New ways of providing for our interests as new knowledge develops will have to be found. The tensions and uncertainties that surround our efforts to do so also unite us as we struggle to survive. Thus Watson resists political orders that have fixed ideological ends, such as socialism, or hierarchical class systems, or even social contract theories which, he thinks, presume ready-made individuals with conflicting interests that require reconciliation. Watson goes so far as to suggest that this latter theory supports a concept of individuals that is metaphysically suspect and immoral, immoral because it does not require a recognition of the whole as the condition of moral behaviour. Watson does not think we will all recognize the same moral rules as binding. But we must recognize the whole as necessary to our experiences. Not to do so, in the long run, is to harm oneself.

Watson's reliance on knowledge as the expression of public reason allows him to argue in the following way: Knowledge emerges from clashes of perspectives and mutual efforts at problem solving. The community is essential for the development of knowledge, and knowledge, as a result embodies the expressions of shared or universal interest. The recognition of the universality of interests is the recognition of the world from a standpoint that is not that of the personal viewpoint of the individual. For Watson, the more a perspective is shared, the more universal it becomes as it develops, the more it reflects those principles of order we value and support because we have chosen to develop them collectively, beyond our own personal perspectives. One's duty to the state is derivative upon one's recognition of its reasonableness. At times, one curtails one's agendas to make possible the pursuit of the agendas of others. But individuals and communities must also develop systems and institutions to curtail the agendas of those who, once given the mandate of acting at the level of universal or objective reason, confuse this mandate of duty with power. Political leadership is the embodiment of a duty to sustain the principles of political knowledge — knowledge of the dialectical relation of individuals and the community known as the state.

Watson clearly favours multiple layers of governing. Each level will contribute to platforms for liberty and individual flourishing; each will act as a check or balance on others. A genuine sense of community and a shared moral commitment to the State will emerge only if one truly *understands* the principles of operation of the State to be necessary conditions of one's freedoms and one's own well being. In short, reason is the constitutive ground of "objects" such as the State, or justice or the public good. Such objects do not arise from sensations, feelings, pleasures and pains.[3]

Watson's commitment to the dialectic of individual and community is evidenced in some of his comments on law, rights and property. The community, being the necessary condition of individual choices and actions, will embody moral value, not just instrumental value. The community has moral value in that it embodies common meanings that are part of its members' sense of identity. Surely, Watson reasons, one will want to preserve and protect oneself. A duty to one's community is a duty to develop oneself, to seek excellence. The larger community, that is, the people of the state, embody at the most universal level the good of the individual as well. Laws are primarily principles of order that ensure conditions for people to seek common goods. "Written laws are the definite formulation of a people's conception of what is for the good of all" (1919: 214). Watson does not think that each person will always assent to the laws. Nor does he think that the collective assent of individuals to the law gives it moral or authoritative force. Watson is mindful that the majority may not always express the general good. Presumably the general good must be rationally consistent. No state that sanctions internal contradictions in its most fundamental principles can be strong. (This is different from providing for the expression of contradictory points of view.) "The laws of a nation are therefore on the whole the expression of those objects which are of vital interest to human life, and all the institutions of society are of this nature" (1919: 214). The state is moral in as much as it provides conditions for citizens to experience mental and moral and physical well-being. But "the State cannot directly promote morality, because morality is a matter of will and motive, and though it can secure outward conformity to the law, it cannot penetrate to the inner self" (1919: 215). For Watson, in his time, legislation must address the prevention of disease, pass Factory Laws which promote the physical well-being of workers, provide conditions of existence for living a decent life, and provide education in order to maximize freedoms. Acts of moral kindness cannot be enforced, but the state can, through regulations, "make such acts possible" (1919: 217). Watson's faith in human nature's propensity to choose decency and dignity was such that he thought that education — and not the heavy hand of the law — was the route to moral goodness.

---

[3] See Watson (1876: 273): "Both [experience and intuition] alike deny to Reason any share in the constitution of objects."

Watson, Education and Rights

Freedom to act morally required education. The maximum freedom in society would be had through state-supported education of both sexes. Education must have a unity of purpose—that each citizen have a clear understanding of "the importance, and significance of the various functions discharged in the community by his fellow citizens" (Watson, 1901: 324). This mandate required a balanced education in the arts and sciences. It also required equal access to the same education, no matter what one's background or station in life. "There is evidently some radical defect in a system of education which causes the literary man to despise scientific or industrial pursuits, and the scientific business man to undervalue humane letters" (1901: 324). Watson continues: "We must not, in our zeal for industry and commerce, ignore the claims of literature, history and philosophy, any more than, in our preoccupation with the latter, we should starve the former" (1901: 326). The aim of the university, for Watson, is to produce noble, intelligent, unselfish men. And this result required the "grasp of principles", not the "remembrance of facts." Having facts in your head, Watson observed in a Sunday afternoon address, made you nothing other that a "perambulating encyclopedia", convenient, "though not nearly so convenient as a printed book, which is never sick and may be kept always at hand" (Watson, 1898: 25).

To be educated is to understand systems beyond oneself and one's personal interests. (This is what he means by unselfish.) Only if one can see beyond the self, can one grasp the significance of civic duties. One learns to see beyond the self by learning the principles of artistic, humane, scientific, and other such systems. For example, regarding nature, he writes: "The scientific man of the highest type... comes to see that there are no breaks in the continuity of its processes: that the world is not liable to be invaded by the unexpected and incalculable interference of a capricious Being, but is a rational system everywhere governed by unchanging law" (1898: 25). Watson is not suggesting that the same laws apply to all aspects of the world. He means that the laws of various systems are understood and developed by conscious experience of those systems. Our concepts of systems develop and change. (For example, we now talk about ecosystems, not human versus natural systems.) Only by grasping this developmental aspect of systemic change is a man truly educated. Yet Watson warns that understanding the rational aspect of the natural world is not enough. "But, if his education stops here, it is of a very partial and inadequate type. It is, perhaps for this reason, that men whose education has been confined to the study of nature are apt to so imperfect a comprehension of human life, and to be victims of superficial or conventional ideas in all regions beyond their special sphere" (1898: 25). Reason does not only reveal uniformities in our relations with nature, but enables us to understand the multiple relations we have in all aspects of our lives. The scientific mind, in thinking that the more we comprehend the natural world with its uniform properties, the more easily this knowledge can be applied to other systems, is simply wrong. Our experience of the world will reveal it to be an increasingly complex web of pluralities. The tensions between components of pluralities and systems as they develop and change will require on-going adaptations and innovations by everyone involved. Education must address the tensions and pluralities, and not just provide sets of facts.

Watson's commitment to universal access to education for all was in keeping with his position on individual rights. The individual could not participate in the state, nor exercise his/her rights as a citizen, unless he/she understood the complex relations between citizens as individuals, and citizens and their greater political community. One does not just grasp these complexities intuitively; one comes to understand them through the study of civilizations both past and ongoing. Rights, for Watson, are essential to the realization of the good will of a community as well as the free development of each individual. The right to an education was paramount.

Watson rejects the notion of "natural" rights as "fictitious" (Watson, 1919: 222). Rights as such represent the common moral conscience, and are representations of the moral nature of man (but not the isolated 'individual'). Legal enactments do not create rights. Legal enactments express rights that people understand as necessary to leading as free a life as possible under external conditions. The state 'enunciates' the law and secures the institutions in which rights are embodied and expressed. Watson declares that there is no right to life except as we have a position in the state. This right is not exclusive to a particular nation State. "As a man is also capable of being a member of any State, he possesses the right to free life as a human being" (1919: 230). But freedom means having the capacity and knowledge to engage in public service, that is, to be able to function within a civil society in full recognition of the same capacity of others — hence, Watson's insistence on public education.

The right to liberty is restrained by the right of others to liberty. One is free to develop one's natural talents and interests as long as one's doing so does not act as a detriment to the well-being of the whole, or the freedoms of others. "Self-development is the creation of law, and not something which could exist apart from the action of the State" (1919: 232). Watson is not suggesting that the same laws apply to all aspects of the world. He means that the laws of various systems can be understood and developed by conscious experience of them apart from the State. Watson does reserve one right for the State in its capacity as the logical other, namely, the right "to interfere with anything that prevents a large number of the citizens from acquiring property" (1919: 234). Watson thought the system of landed property in England was unjust to the working class. Land is not like capital. Owning land only benefits the owner. Capital can benefit both possessor and those who labour under it. But land possessed deprives others entirely. "The State ought therefore to exercise some control over rights of property in land" (1919: 235). Watson's point is that everyone should be able to acquire the means for making a living. He was not a socialist. But he did not think the unrestrained accumulation of property that did not contribute to the economic well-being of others could be justified as a practice that was in keeping with knowledge of the common good.

Watson's metaphysics of individual and community is the determinant of his social and moral thought. The sharing of duties and responsibilities between the individual and the state is required. Supreme authority can only be so as the reflection of the public will. The federalist state, by definition, embraces our patterns of individuation; its job is to provide for these patterns. Individuals in the state must recognize the political order which makes their lives possible. To focus on one part of the dialectic and neglect the other will harm both.

Watson never wants to lose sight of the individual. A community is necessary to the individual; each person has, however, the freedom to change groups, to disagree, to walk away. Yet without some group from which one derives one's identity one will have no sense of duty to the community or the extended society. Watson did not think you could create rights by law and have them understood as morally binding. Rights were the expression of collective reason. And yet Watson recognized that not all communities are united by reason. They are united by shared meanings, or by traditions, beliefs and myths. The state should ensure the means whereby individuals with common identities are able to express them — be that through life styles, cultural distinctiveness, art, or religion. If the political order is to also address individuals, then community rights or collective rights are suspect because they are designed to further the survival of the community, not the flourishing of individuals. The particular community cannot be considered to be an 'individual,' lest the identity expressed exacts from its members some duty to continue that expression. For Watson, growing, flourishing and developing objective orders for knowledge comes through the interactions, the clashes of beliefs and opinions, of many communities. Such knowledge does not spring from customs, traditions, rituals, and irrational beliefs. Only reason, tested by fractious individuals sharing and developing common objects of knowledge, is the ground of a political community, one that makes possible the good life for every individual.

Idealism, Reconciliation, and Rational Religion

In the Victorian culture of the late nineteenth century, the good life was popularly promoted through exhortations to revere God who, in return for a devoted and hard working life, would offer salvation. This social vision of one's due in life as a return on one's religious investment was wearing thin amongst the intelligentia, in particular Edward Caird, who schooled the young Watson in Scotland. Confronted with the harshness of the Canadian climate, Watson soon realized that it seemed faintly ridiculous to place the blame for the heat wave, or the drought, or the endless freezing winters on one's failure to make it to church. Thus the meaning of religion and its role in one's moral fortitude, one's social responsibilities, and one's personal guilt became a challenge to be met head on through philosophy. Watson began his challenge and adaptations to the conventional homilies with the examination of the relation between science and religion as sources of explanation.

In his Inaugural Address, *The Relation of Philosophy to Science* (1872), he boldly challenged the supremacy of science while seeking to ameliorate the growing dissension between science and religion. His targets were Thomas Henry Huxley and Herbert Spencer. He would follow this presentation five years later with the publication of "The World as Force", in which he attacked Spencer fearlessly (Watson, 1878: 113). The debates of the times raised serious problems for Christian philosophers. Huxley had made Darwin a household word, and promoted a materialism that predicted science as the replacement for religion. Spencer, the author of the phrase 'survival of the fittest', suggested that religion dealt with the unknowable; this suggestion generally undercut any claims that religious theories offered truths about existence. In taking on the proponents of scientific supremacy, Watson was attempting to restructure the concepts of Christian belief systems. Science and religion, he argued, could be understood as complementary rather than adversarial. Given the general social upheavals between church and state, biologists and clerics, and biblical scholars and educational theorists (after all, curricula at universities could not ignore the new scientific articulations reverberating throughout the 19th century, and still be in the business of pursuing truth and pushing back the frontiers of knowledge), we can begin to appreciate the courage and determined genius of the young Watson in his adopted home.

Watson suggested that beliefs — such as religion being mysterious or the eternal salvation of the soul being possible — should be subject to the same methodologies of analysis as the theories of evolution. Science demanded the consistencies of rational justification. Why should religion be exempt? Leslie Armour, in his "An Introduction to Watson", describes Watson's dilemma: "How then, do science and religion clash? Religion is, after all, practical as well as theoretical. Souls have always found their way to God through all the difficulties. Science, however, very often seems to clash with received opinion about how this ascent to God is to be achieved and about how God is made manifest in the world" (Armour, 1988: 9).

Watson, while respectful of the role of religion in stabilizing new communities in Canada, was not content to leave the concept of God as the final source for explanation of events and things for which science had no account (at least, yet). Sooner or later, science would provide explanations. Watson did not support any argument that reduced mind to a material component of the universe and thus threaten the need for a concept of God. The concept of God, he proposed, was required by consciousness itself. Watson began his restructuring of God, in the Inaugural Address, with an appeal (though not directly stated) to Hegelian categories. No matter what truths science offered, they were still contingent for their expression upon categories of thought, such as cause and effect, or general and particular, or relative and universal. Scientific truths were relative to particular circumstances and fixed methods of measurement. The minute they aspired to universality, they required a perspective on the world that was not relative to the observer, but encompassed the whole. Consciousness could conceive of and aspire to that perspective, and that meant that consciousness required a concept that expressed the idea of complete knowledge, or total understanding.

> Nature is undoubtedly rational, but not *to itself*; it is only in so far as it is brought within the dominion of thought that it renders up its meaning, and the whole progress of thought is a history of the discovery and the deepening of categories... To make consciousness dependent upon matter is to reason in a circle; for matter has no meaning apart from consciousness. (Watson, 1872: 18)

Matter is simply another category for ordering our experiences of the world. Watson acknowledges his debt to Kant with his appeal to categories of the mind. But he rejects Kant's noumenal world on the grounds that the unknowable contradicts the tenets of science. If we are to take seriously the methods and discoveries of science, with their principles of verification and continuing adoption of truth claims in face of new discoveries, then there can be no rational grounds for that which cannot be known. The universe is not mysterious. Our knowledge of it is merely restrained by our limited capacities. What we know now is cumulative and interdependent. Knowing that means that we can conceive of total understanding of all things—even though, trapped as we are in time, we can never achieve that state. Discovering the laws of nature is another way of reconfirming the laws of thought as the grounds and possibility of all bodies of knowledge. God as the concept which represents the wholeness of all and unity of all knowledge also represents the unity of all mankind as conscious beings. Science is one piece of the puzzle, not a replacement for the Truth. Watson's suggestion that God exists through each of our individual conscious minds removed His properties of divine transcendence. Suddenly, the propensity to account for the unexpected, the disastrous, the joys and the sorrows of life through principles of divine intervention is drastically reduced. Responsibility for oneself as well as the joys and sorrows of others rests with each of us.

This was a new concept of God, for a new world. The reconciliation of science and religion was unproblematic when rationality became the measure of truth.

Throughout his career, Watson pursued the idea that each individual consciousness participated in God's very being. His metaphysics of experience was finally worked out in his Gifford Lectures (1910-2) published in two volumes, *The Interpretation of Religious Experience*, with the first part historical, and the second part constructive. His quest to unite opposing concepts compelled him to dispense first with Kant's bifurcated world — yet, in doing so, he established himself as the North American Kant scholar for decades. *The Philosophy of Kant as Contained in Extracts from his own Writings* (1888), and *The Philosophy of Kant Explained* (1908) were used at universities across the North American continent and in Britain. The feeble ending of Kant's *Critique of Pure Reason*, with its irreconcilable antinomies, threatened the concept of God, and Watson was not about to let history self destruct. His papers on Spencer, idealism, and Kant, published in the major journals (e.g., *Mind, Journal of Speculative Philosophy, International Journal of Ethics*) brought him to the attention of those active in the American idealist movement, such as Josiah Royce.[4]

A number of Watson's pupils were training as clergy who would eventually staff the little churches that dotted that vast countryside and small clusters of towns across Canada. These newly minted proponents of God's word would be facing church attendees from a variety of denominations who, for reasons of distance, weather, seasonal agricultural demands or poor roads, gathered at the nearest church building, hoping for advice and consolation. Nature was a force to be reckoned with and the idea that God was watching over them seemed fanciful if not highly unrealistic. In his little book, *The Scotch*, John Kenneth Galbraith reminisces on his upbringing in Southwestern Ontario.

> The weather, to a similar degree, is of heavenly manufacture. Yet none of our neighbors would have dreamed of appealing to God for relief

[4] Watson was a participant in what the *New York Times* called 'the great debate', and the *New York Tribune*, 'the debate of the century'. He was invited to speak at a series of lectures for the Philosophical Union of the University of California at Berkeley, in 1895-6. The participants, Josiah Royce, Edward Mezes, Joseph Le Comte, George Holmes Howison, and Watson, defended their different interpretations of the Absolute. The lectures and the replies received daily coverage in the major newspapers of the day. Watson's pluralistic interpretations received considerable press and undoubtedly helped to sell many papers. *George Howison, Philosopher and Teacher*, by John Buckham and George M. Stratton, 1934, describes the debate carried in the papers, and includes Howison's view that Watson had won the day.

from a drought, or for dry weather for the bean harvest. Every once in a while a well meaning minister…would take note of the damage being done by a prolonged dry spell and ask for rain. His terrestrial audience, to the extent that they were listening, would attribute the request to a lack of farm experience. Certainly they did not expect it to do any good…. They did not ask God for anything they could do for themselves or, as a practical matter, for anything they couldn't do for themselves and didn't expect to get done…. I have told of a neighbor who got late to his fields because of his morning devotions. From the point of view of the community there couldn't have been a worse reason. If God made sense, he didn't want a man staying around the house when he should have been out on his land. (Galbraith, 1964: 104–5)

It was exactly this mission, to make sense of God, that informed Watson's writings. His students needed to help the settlers understand their often frightening circumstances, in which change was unpredictable. If their sufferings were simply the result of their sins, then Canada seemed sinister to the core. Watson knew he could not change the diehard Presbyterians and Calvinists who gathered to share their collective blame and beg forgiveness. But others, less stalwart in their rationality and comic cynicism, were vulnerable to the power of rhetoric. Indifference to their plight, or polemic from the pulpit that cajoled them towards more prayer, would sound ridiculous and might encourage religious skepticism. Some middle road had to be found.

Watson, had to defend a God that existed in time, through change, and without retributive powers to frighten people.

Watson's first step was to establish time as an idea of order, not an independent feature of the world or an unknowable force. It is an expression of the categories of thought, of permanence and change. Thought at all times works dialectically, and does not come endowed with self evident truths. We experience continuous succession both in our judgments about the world and in our experience of it. Conscious thought requires contradictions out of which meanings emerge. Permanence and change are two such ideas of which time is an expression. Watson pursued these arguments in his two-part paper "The Absolute and the Time-Process" (1895). His concept of time as an idea that helps capture the truth about reality as perpetual but changing (not a series of appearances) meant that God, as part of this reality, would have to be an expression of that which was permanent and yet changing. The Absolute [Watson's God] is conceivable but never completely knowable, because change is part of its very nature. To transcend the limit of time is to conceive not of actual determinate ordered events in succession, but of "the universal possibility of events" (Trott, 1996: 70), an idea which synthesizes both permanence and change. If we can conceive of the possibility of the totality of knowledge, we can conceive of a consciousness which could grasp the totality of knowledge, including the knowledge that knowledge claims change and are revised. Watson's concept of God corresponds to such a consciousness.[5]

Such a cerebral God might have some appeal to the philosophical community but, having struggled through a blizzard, with hot potatoes underfoot to ward off frozen toes, would a lecture on the Absolute, the great consciousness able to conceive of all possible states of knowledge, provide comfort and sustenance to the faithful? Metaphysics at the best of times is a hard sell. In a snowstorm or a heat wave, it might seem a tad irrelevant. Watson knew his students needed more than metaphysics. The real point of religion had to be addressed.

In Canada, in the late nineteen-hundreds, surviving very much depended on others. This interdependence became the mediating principle between the struggling individual, the infidels down the road (if that is how one thought of one's neighbours), and the God who was supposed to be in charge. The concept of God was of no use at all unless everyone could find solace. Solace was to be found in the following argument: Each person had the capacity to conceive of the universal consciousness; therefore each person had the capacity to conceive of a particular consciousness. Each person could conceive of each particular consciousness as having the same capacities of understanding as his or her own, and that included all the pains and pleasures of the human condition. Therefore, to serve God, or celebrate God, or confess to God, was a universal human capacity because doing so included knowing that all members of the community could do so as well. Now, knowing that meant knowing that others loved, lived and suffered in the same way as oneself (which, of course, God knew, too) and so the path to God, or the way to demonstrate one's love of God, was not through self directed prayer or pious demonstrations, but through aspiring to acts in the service of others and acts in the service of nature, which we come to know as essential as we grasp dialectically its indispensability to our lives. Each person through his unfailing reason carried God within. "[I]n his religious life man does not withdraw into himself, but 'lives in the world though not of it'" (Watson, 1912, II: 128). Any Protestant or Catholic who set differences aside to assist another in a barn raising stood as an example of Watson's dialectical (universal and particular, eternal and changing) God within.

Yet, as each of us is differentiated by our individual limitations, each of us will have the potential for a different expression of God. Not everyone will be duty bound; selfishness will continue to be relative, and some will resist the compulsion of a rational metaphysics of God. Through these differences, we continue to express our individuality, but as participants in consciousness we cannot plead ignorance of the needs of others. We can

---

5   For a further explanation of this rational conception of God, see Armour and Trott (1981: 289–91, 309–18) and Watson (1908: 439).

choose to ignore their needs. At best, the local preacher could remind us of that choice and remind us *publicly* within earshot of the community, urging us to set aside our personal disagreements with the beliefs of others. "It is this *expression of consciousness in the world* which constitutes God. All the expressions of God in the world constitute a natural community, the same in essence but different in expression" (Armour, 1988: 11n33).

Towards the end of Part Two of *The Interpretation of Religious Experience*, Watson introduced the idea of "the invisible church". The capacity for moral thought and actions is in each of us. The conception of supreme goodness is, simply, a conception, and yet, as such, cannot be dismissed. It is neither incoherent nor contradictory. The church, as the embodiment of all possible good, will be limited by its participation in a finite and limited world. To further its mission, it must participate in its changing world, and not remain aloof, for to do so is to increase its limitations. The church as social servant represents Watson's conception of the invisible church.

"The invisible church is not a community of slaves but of free men, and therefore men must be allowed the freedom of action, even if it leads to much evil. In no other way can a spiritual community be developed. The divine spirit cannot be imposed upon men" (Watson, 1912, II: 302). Organized religion with its symbolism and irrational propositions is to be avoided: the ceremonial too quickly "may degenerate into a dead and lifeless routine" (1912, II: 303). For Watson, all individuals have the capacity to understand their unique relationships with God and may seek ways to express their divine nature to the best of their abilities (though not all may choose to do so). Numerous hurdles could limit the opportunities for expression in Watson's Canadian world. It is small wonder that in communities scattered over the landscape, tiny gestures of help assumed such significance. Each struggling newcomer knew in his or her deepest heart that sharing a couple of eggs, or lending a team of horses, could mean the difference between life and death.

References

Armour, L. (1988), "An Introduction to John Watson", in D. Rabb (ed.), *Religion and Science in Early Canada* (Kingston, ON: Ronald P. Frye).
Armour, L. and Trott, E. (1981), *The Faces of Reason* (Waterloo: Wilfrid Laurier University Press).
Galbraith, J. (1964), *The Scotch* (Baltimore, MD: Penguin Books).
Neatby, H. (1978), *Queen's University. 1441–1917: And not to yield* (Kingston: McGill Queen's University Press).
Trott, E. (1996), "Bradley and the Canadian Connection", in J. Bradley (ed.), *Philosophy after F. H. Bradley*, (Bristol, UK: Thoemmes Press), pp. 57–72..
Watson, J. (1872), *An Inaugural Lecture, The Relation of Philosophy to Science* (Kingston: Baillie).
Watson, J. (1876), "Hedonism and Utilitarianism", *Journal of Speculative Philosophy*, 10/3.
Watson, J. (1878), "The World as Force", *The Journal of Speculative Philosophy*, 12/2.
Watson, J. (1895), "The Absolute and the Time-Process", *Philosophical Review*, 4/4; "The Absolute and the Time-Process, Part II", *Philosophical Review*, 4/5.

Watson, J. (1898), "The University and the State", *Queen's University Journal*, 27/1.
Watson, J. (1901), "The University and the Schools", *Queen's Quarterly*, 8/3.
Watson, J. (1908), *An Outline of Philosophy*, 4th edn. (Glasgow: James Maclehose & Sons); first published under the title, *Comte, Mill, and Spencer, An Outline of Philosophy* (1895).
Watson, J. (1912), *The Interpretation of Religious Experience*, Parts I, II, (Glasgow: James Maclehose & Sons).
Watson, J. (1919), *The State in Peace and War* (Glasgow: James Maclehose & Sons).

William Sweet

British Idealism and Ethical Thought in South Africa and India

British idealism has crossed borders and boundaries—not only spreading beyond the British Isles, but taking root and thriving in countries sometimes half a world away.

There have been several studies of the influence of British idealism in Canada and in Australia,[1] but it has a place as well in the intellectual histories of South Africa and India.[2] Frequently, this idealism was engaged with or brought to bear on moral and social issues and, while its direction may have become less and less homogeneous with that of the founders of the movement, its principal concerns (such as the rejection of naturalism, materialism, various forms of reductionism, and individualism, and the insistence on a greater recognition of the community and of the role of 'mind' in the understanding of social and political reality) remained fairly congruent.

The presence of British idealism, and particularly British idealist moral and social philosophy, outside of Britain is interesting for several reasons. It shows something of the development of idealism in response to various criticisms levied against it, particularly in the early 20th century. It provides an illustration of whether and how British idealist ethics could exist, and even flourish, in an environment outside of its culture of origin. And, given the multi-cultural and multi-ethnic milieu of places such as South Africa and India, it allows a consideration of why and how idealism, and idealist ethics, could have a place in a specifically pluralistic environment.

But how was British idealist ethics engaged in South Africa and India? Why was idealism as influential as it was? And does this success tell us anything about British idealism? Is British idealism simply an idealism for

---

[1] In Canada, see Armour and Trott (1981), Irving, (1951), and McKillop (1976). For idealism in Australia see, for example, Boucher (1990), Grave (1978), Miller (1929–30), and Weblin (2010). For more recent studies of idealism's impact in each of these areas, see the survey essays in Sweet (2010).

[2] And beyond. A further illustration of how idealism has crossed boundaries and has been influential is found in late 19th and early 20th century philosophy in Japan and China. See, for example, Hirai (1979) and (1982), Reitan (2000), Shigeru (1970), and Roy (1963).

the British, or is it an idealism that has a value beyond the distinctive environment of late 19th and early 20th century Britain?

What I wish to do in this chapter is, first, to briefly present some of the philosophers in South Africa and India who were influenced by British idealism and, then, to look closely at two of the best known of them—near contemporaries—R.F.A. Hoernlé and Sarvepalli Radhakrishnan. And although there were differences between the two (which is manifested in how they brought idealism to bear on issues, and in the specific character of their ethical and social thought), there are also some important similarities in their work. An examination of each's ethical thought should allow one to see in more detail how British idealist ethics was received, or was able to fit or to address concerns, outside of the culture in which it was first articulated. It should help in determining to what extent and why British idealism was influential outside of Britain—but it should also tell us something about that idealism itself.[3]

1. Idealism and Idealist Ethical Thought in South Africa

1.1. Background

Idealism came to South Africa at the very end of the 19th century, and its presence is notable in both the Afrikaner and the 'English' traditions in the country.

Within the Afrikaner intellectual tradition, the presence and place of idealism was largely a result of idealism's relation to Scottish Protestantism and Calvinism, i.e., because of the large number of Scots who came to South Africa and who eventually assimilated into the Dutch-Afrikaner community.

The University of Stellenbosch—founded as Stellenbosch College (1874) and named Victoria College in 1886—was a key educational institution during the early period of idealism in South Africa. Two influential philosophers here were Thomas Walker (1847–1916) and N.J. Brümmer (1866–1947). Walker, Professor of Mental and Moral Philosophy from 1878 until his death, was a graduate of Edinburgh (MA, 1st class, Classics, 1870), a contemporary of D.G. Ritchie[4], and in many respects a "product of British Idealism" (Duvenage 2001: 113); apart from his teaching, his philosophical work, however, was negligible.[5] Brümmer had a deeper and

---

[3] Despite the apparently rapid shift away from idealism in philosophy and political thought in Britain, it did not vanish altogether. For more on this point, see the Introduction, p. 12 above.

[4] Ritchie was at Edinburgh, 1869–74, and among Walker's professors would have been A. Campbell Fraser (logic), and Henry Calderwood (moral philosophy).

[5] In a letter to his parents of 7 March 1911, Hoernlé wrote, concerning the appointment of Brümmer to Stellenbosch: "he cannot possibly be worse than the original Professor of Philosophy whom he has now gone to assist"; in a later letter, Hoernlé writes that the Appointments Committee had preferred T.M. Forsyth for Brümmer's position, but it was overruled by the College (Nash [1985]: 82–3).

more sustained impact within philosophy and within theological spheres, serving as Professor of Moral, Social, and Political Philosophy from 1911 to 1941. South African born, he was initially influenced by the thought of Green (Nash 1997: 133) likely through Walker. But Brümmer also visited Edinburgh in 1894, where he attended classes by Andrew Seth (later Pringle-Pattison) and Henry Calderwood, and he had earlier studied theology through the University of St Andrews in Scotland.[6]

Another philosopher within the Afrikaner community who was influenced by British idealism was William Macfadyen (1865-1924).[7] Macfadyen came from Manchester and studied at Brasenose College before moving to South Africa in 1889. He was a polymath, teaching (at various times) economics, mathematics, psychology, philosophy, and law, writing on topics ranging from a study of decimal coinage to law reports, and even patenting a design for heat jacketing and screening. He taught at Rhodes University College (1906-11), Grey University College in Bloemfontein (1911-12) and the Transvaal University College in Pretoria (1912, until his death). Sympathetic to the idealism of Bradley and Bosanquet,[8] Macfadyen's primary interest was in political philosophy — which led him to take the position at Pretoria, where he became an influential teacher (and where he taught J.N. Findlay). But at Pretoria, Macfadyen left the lectures in ethics to an assistant, and produced no significant philosophical work.[9]

Finally, one should note the somewhat idiosyncratic figure of Jan C. Smuts (1870-1950). Smuts was the author of *Holism and Evolution* (1926) — it was he who coined the word 'holism' — but he never held a university teaching position, being instead a lawyer, military leader (during the Boer War and in the two world wars), politician, Minister of Justice and, twice, Prime Minister (1919-24 and 1939-48). While his philosophical work would seem to have much in common with the idealist movement in Britain, the direct influence was slight; he had difficulties with his philosophy teacher at Stellenbosch, Walker, and his own studies focussed on literature, science, and (while at Cambridge) the law. Indeed, there was no discernable engagement of Smuts's philosophical work by idealist philosophers in South Africa.[10]

At the predominantly 'English' universities, the influence of idealism was certainly stronger. T.M. Forsyth (1871-1958), who taught at Grey University College (1911-33) and, later, at Rhodes (1941-4), had been a student and, later, assistant of Andrew Seth Pringle Pattison in Edinburgh.

---

6 See "Professor N.J. Brümmer; skrijwer van "eerbied", "de afrikaner en de onzedelikheid", ens. *Die Brandwag*, 10 Desember 1918, p. 15, in Brümmer papers, University of Stellenbosch.
7 See the biographical entry in Sweet (2010).
8 See J.N. Findlay (1985) see also http://www.jnfindlay.com/findlay/biographical/index.html
9 For more biographical information, see the entry in Sweet (2010).
10 A rare exception is Forsyth (1929). A Thomistic response is Kolbe (1928).

Moreover, in his Edinburgh D.Phil. thesis, published as *English Philosophy: a study of its method and general development* (1910), Forsyth defended a view of the relation of knowledge and reality that was sympathetic to T.H. Green and F.H. Bradley. At Rhodes University College, A.R. Lord (1880–1941, a student of Edward Caird, H.H. Joachim, and J.A. Smith at Oxford), was Professor of Philosophy from 1905 until 1940. Lord's work in ethics and political philosophy was clearly in line with that of Green and Bosanquet, and he made important developments in idealist political thought[11] — but much of his work remained unpublished at his death.[12]

At the South African College at Cape Town (after 1918, the University of Cape Town), the influence of Kantian and Hegelian idealism can be seen in the teaching of Henry Freemantle (1874–1931, a graduate of Oriel College, Oxford, who taught from 1899 to 1903) and Thomas Loveday (1875–1955, of Magdalen College, Oxford, who taught from 1903 to 1908). But it is with their successors that we find the strongest influences of idealism.

R.F.A. Hoernlé (1880–1943) — who had been a student at Balliol College under Edward Caird, and who was Bernard Bosanquet's assistant at St Andrews (1905–7) — taught at the South African College from 1908 to 1911; he returned to South Africa in 1923 to take up a Professorship in Johannesburg. Hoernlé was succeeded at Cape Town by the Glasgow University-trained author of *The Ethical Theory of Hegel*, Hugh Reyburn (1886–1950, who taught philosophy from 1912 to 1920, before moving to a Professorship in Psychology).[13] A strong idealist influence is also to be found in South-African born G.H.T. Malan (1886–1959). A student of Loveday and Hoernlé, Malan also studied in Europe at Leipzig, and finished a D.Phil. thesis at Glasgow under Henry Jones and Robert Latta.[14]

---

11 See Sweet (2005).

12 Most of Lord's philosophical work has only recently been published (see Lord [2006a] and [2006b]). Lord published little in his lifetime, and some of his finished manuscripts — an essay on the passions and a book on ethics — have disappeared. But Lord had a strong interest in ethics and ethical reasoning, and had a long-standing interest in political philosophy as well. Lord does not, however, seem to have taken an active role in politics and social affairs in South Africa. At the time of his death, Lord was at work on a manuscript in ethics, but much of this work, save an introductory chapter, is not among his papers, held in the Cory Library at Rhodes University.

13 Reyburn became a leading figure in university affairs and intellectual culture in South Africa. He was the first editor (1932–6) of *The Critic*, a literary and historical quarterly, and published on a wide range of topics, from history to economics to political philosophy. But, in the late 1910s, his principal research interests turned to psychology, and he wrote virtually nothing outside of psychology for the rest of his career — except a biography of Nietzsche. See the entry on Reyburn in Sweet (2010).

14 Gabriel Hercules Malan had initially gone to Leipzig, where he completed a doctoral thesis on "Die dialektische Methode bei Hegel und den Nach-hegelianern" under Paul Barth (1858–1922) and Johannes Volkelt (1848–1930) — but was forced to leave Germany with the breakout of the first world war, and never received his degree. His Glasgow D.Phil. thesis, *An Absolute Logical Criterion* (1916), was on an entirely different topic. (I draw here on information from G.H.T. Malan materials at the University of Cape Town Library Archives, D65/151 III.2[a].) Malan

Interested not only in Hegelian logic, but in questions of law and intentionality, Malan took on responsibility for the courses in ethics and politics at Cape Town (1916-36) and, later, at the University College of the Orange Free State, Bloemfontein (1940-51). Finally, Andrew Howson Murray (1905-97), grandson of the famous South African clergyman Andrew Murray and Professor of Ethics and Political Philosophy at Cape Town (1937-70), was also strongly influenced by idealism[15] — though this idealism was mediated by his interest in Calvinist and Reformed political thought. Murray was a graduate of the University of Stellenbosch under Brümmer,[16] and won a Rhodes Scholarship to Oxford, where he completed a B.Litt. (1929) and a D.Phil. (1931) at Oriel College with a dissertation supervised by J.A. Smith.[17]

The University of Witwatersrand in Johannesburg was also a stronghold of idealism. Founded in 1922, its roots lay in the South African School of Mines and the Transvaal University College. The Glasgow and Balliol-educated John Macmurray taught there — though for only 18 months (1920-2) — to be succeeded by Hoernlé (in 1923) until 1943. Andrew Howson Murray taught there (from 1931 to 1936, where he reputedly 'revitalized' the teaching of political philosophy), as did another South African, Errol E. Harris (from 1946 to 1956). Harris was a student of A.R. Lord at Rhodes, but also of H.H. Joachim and J.A. Smith at Oxford, later becoming a leading scholar in idealist thought in the 20th century.

Idealism, then, strongly influenced the study of philosophy in both the English and Afrikaner milieus[18] — even though some, like Brümmer and, later, Murray, would distance themselves from it. Although many of the

---

resigned his post at Cape Town in 1936 due to illness, but later taught at the University College of the Orange Free State (1940-51).

15 See Conradie (1980: 409).

16 *Die plek van die Baster in die Unie van Suid-Afrika*, [The Place of the Half-caste in the Union of South Africa], a manuscript held in the University of Cape Town archives, is Murray's M.A. thesis.

17 For a short biographical entry on Murray, see the *Routledge Encyclopedia of Philosophy* entry, Sweet (2007). Murray is noteworthy for many reasons. He was one of the leading figures in philosophy in South Africa from the early 1930s until the 1970s. He had a strong interest in the political philosophies of Bosanquet and Green, and published, in 1937, a sympathetic yet critical study of the personal idealist, James Ward. Murray also had a strong sense of the public responsibilities of the intellectual — lecturing and writing for the general public, and serving on a number of governmental commissions, such as the (South African) Publications Control Board (i.e., the censorship board), the National Library Commission, and the Commission on Native Education. Murray is also known — at least in South Africa — for being one of the star prosecution witnesses during the Treason Trials of 1957, where one of the defendants was Nelson Mandela. See Kathrada (2004).

18 The influence of idealism in the non-white communities is more difficult to discern — and the existing research is such that it is premature to make any judgements here. But it is worth noting that the South African Native College (today, the University of Fort Hare) was established in 1916 by members of the United Free Church of Scotland for the education of the non-white populations — and that, in 1930, the College had, as its professor of philosophy, a young E.E. Harris.

South African philosophers published relatively little, the impact of idealism is evident in their teaching, and especially in their views on ethics and social and political philosophy. In fact, the curriculum in philosophy in South African universities emphasized idealist authors and themes from the early 20th century until well into the 1950s[19] — though this emphasis was not uncritical. Students in political philosophy and ethics would have been very familiar with Green and Bosanquet in particular, and in other subject areas, such as the philosophy of religion, students would have encountered idealism as well. (It is worth noting that most of the students preparing at Stellenbosch for the ministry in the Reformed Church in South Africa would have taken Brümmer's courses in ethics and social philosophy.) It is also worth noting that many of the South African philosophers and their students influenced by idealism, were interested not only in ethics and political philosophy, but in political practice or social action — though some were led down rather different political paths than others.

To see an example of how British idealism was specifically engaged within the South African context, and what form an idealist ethics had there, I turn now to look closely at perhaps the best known South African philosopher, R.F.A. Hoernlé.

1.2. Hoernlé and the Ethics of Liberty

R.F.A. Hoernlé was not only one of the key figures in South African philosophy who made a particular contribution to moral and social philosophy, but he was strongly influenced by British idealist thought.[20]

Hoernlé was a man of many cultures. Born in Bonn, Germany, to the famous Indologist A.F.R. Hoernlé, Hoernlé spent his early years in India (where he became fluent in Hindi), attended elementary and secondary school in Germany, and proceeded to Balliol College, Oxford, in 1899, to prepare for a career in the Indian Civil Service. Through the influence of his tutor, J.A. Smith, and of the Master of Balliol, Edward Caird, Hoernlé turned to philosophy. After graduation (BA 1903; MA 1907), as noted above he served from 1905 to 1907 as Assistant to Bernard Bosanquet in St Andrews (completing at the same time a B.Sc. at Oxford, with a thesis on "Modern Theories of the Will"). He followed this with teaching at Cape Town (1908–11), Newcastle (England) (1912–13), Harvard (1914–20), Newcastle again (in 1920–3), finally moving to Johannesburg in 1923, where he remained until his death.

---

19 Up to 1911, Bosanquet (*Essentials of Logic*) and Lotze were taught in the course on Logic and, after 1911, in the Ethics and Politics course, we find books by Muirhead, Sidgwick (both his *Methods of Ethics* and *Methods of Politics*), and Green (*Prolegomena to Ethics, Lectures on the Principles of Political Obligation*).

20 For a short biographical entry on Hoernlé, see the *Oxford Dictionary of National Biography* entry, Sweet (2006), and Sweet (2005a), reprinted in Sweet (2010).

Hoernlé's earliest work focused on theories of the mind, the self, and the will — his first articles and books provided defences of idealist metaphysics and epistemology[21] — and it was not until his return to South Africa, as Professor of Philosophy at the University of Witwatersrand, that his writing turned almost exclusively to social and political issues. There, Hoernlé taught the usual range of courses in logic and psychology — but particularly the basic courses on ethics.[22] He also came to be actively engaged in social and political ethics and in public policy,[23] and wrote scores of essays on social and political affairs.[24]

Throughout his life Hoernlé acknowledged himself as a 'Bosanquetian'[25] — and not only the broad philosophical, but the moral, social and political views he adopts are congruent with principles that one finds in Bosanquet.

Like many of the idealists in Britain, Hoernlé's focus was on practical matters — in his case, on the "race question" and education in South Africa — and on the moral response called for by the concrete situation. Like his mentor Bosanquet, Hoernlé did not provide a systematic study of moral philosophy and never wrote a book on ethics or social philosophy as such. He did write a little on moral theory — on Kant's moral philosophy[26] — and one of his last publications was a lengthy review of John Elof Boodin's *The Social Mind: Foundations of Social Philosophy* (Hoernlé 1941).[27] But even here, his objective was principally to show problems in existing theories, and not to present a theory of his own.

21 See, for example, Hoernlé (1920) and (1927).
22 In the Hoernlé papers at the University of Witwatersrand archives, one finds notes for Ethics I (on the ethics of Plato and Aristotle) — particularly, on Plato's Republic: (a) Criticism on Plato's theory of justice. (b) Details from Book 5 on the organization of the ideal state.
23 Hoernlé came to be seen as one of the leaders of the liberal movement in South Africa against segregation, and is named and praised in one of the most popular novels about the South African situation — Alan Paton's, *Cry the Beloved Country* (1948). Hoernlé was a trenchant critic of the policy of segregation from the time of the first Hertzog government in 1924 (see MacCrone [1945]).
24 A number of his important lectures or speeches on 'applied ethical' topics were published in Hoernlé (1939) and (posthumously) in Hoernlé (1945) and (1952).
25 See Hoernlé (1920: viii) and his autobiographical essay, Hoernlé (1925: 144). In addition to Hoernlé's books on idealism (see note 21 above), one might also note his 1934 essay on "The Absolute", reprinted in Hoernlé (1952).
26 See "Kant's Theory of Freedom" (1939) and "Kant's Concept of the 'Intrinsic Worth' of every 'Rational Being'" (1943), reprinted in Hoernlé (1952).
27 Hoernlé's review was rather mixed. He had "great sympathy with Boodin's plea for "ethical democracy", for "individuals with community consciousness", and for "creative goodwill", but he also writes: "I feel, none the less, bound to urge that it is very unsafe for the philosopher to descend from the plane of general principles to approval or disapproval of particular political events and actions. If Boodin had been in the shoes of the statesmen whom he criticises, would he have been able (at the time, and not with the present wisdom of after-sight) to deduce from his philosophical principles a policy which would have been better; or, if he thinks he could have conceived such a policy, would he have been able for certain to persuade his people to adopt it, let alone get the consent of other peoples and their statesmen, whose co-operation he would have needed?" (Hoernlé, 1941: 398).

Hoernlé was cautious about 'importing' theories; he did not believe that the proper approach to ethics, to social and political philosophy, or—for that matter—to public policy, could simply be to import a model from, for example, Britain. For Hoernlé, "attempts to apply [a theory], while ignoring differences between individuals belonging to different racial or cultural groups, are unrealistic and therefore doomed to failure" (MacCrone 1945: xxxiv).

Yet while Hoernlé did not give a systematic statement of his moral and social philosophy, there is a consistency in his approach. That consistency in approach reflects what Hoernlé's calls his 'synoptic method':

> Wherever I have lived, I have found in myself a desire to identify myself with the life around me, to enter into it and share it from the inside, rather than to stand outside as a mere spectator or even to reject it as foreign to myself. [...] This attitude [...] is for me one with the synoptic method of all of my philosophical thinking, which itself rests on the assumption that truth has many sides, and that to the whole truth on any subject every point of view has some contribution to make. (Hoernlé 1925: 138)

We can use this method to review Hoernlé's 'applied philosophy' and the characteristics of the ethics that underlay it.

The principal issue with which Hoernlé was concerned was how one is to respond ethically to the challenges of race relations and the requirements of equality in a multi-cultural and multi-ethnic milieu. The principle on which Hoernlé drew for a response was liberty or freedom; for Hoernlé, ethics is an "ethics of liberty" or of freedom.[28]

To understand what such an ethics of liberty is, and what it requires of us, however, involves looking at context. Hoernlé believed that the best way to understand something is to start with experience—"from the life" (Hoernlé 1920: 138)—rather than with abstract claims or principles. This is how Hoernlé approached religion—see his 1920 *Studies in Contemporary Metaphysics*[29]—and the same approach applies to moral and social philosophy. Thus, Hoernlé held, it is important "to re-examine, *in light of the experience* of a multi-racial society, like South Africa, what liberty means and how, if at all, it can be realised in that sort of society" (MacCrone 1945: xxxiv; emphasis mine).

According to Hoernlé, if we begin with experience, we see that ethics is based in community, and that morals is a "part of culture" (Hoernlé 1937:

---

28   It is interesting that among Hoernlé's first publications is his translation (with his wife, A. Winifred Hoernlé) of R. Steiner's *The Philosophy of Freedom* (1916), which was later revised as *The Philosophy of Spiritual Activity* (1922).

29   Here he argues that the study of religion should focus on experience, rather than dogmas—for to be religious is not primarily to believe in doctrines about another world, but to appreciate the value of this world.

415). Indeed, morals reflect culture, just as thinking reflects culture,[30] for it is from a people's or a community's culture that "they draw the materials [...] for a life worth living" (Hoernlé 1945: 9).[31] And culture sustains morality as well; Hoernlé writes of the importance of a supportive environment for moral action. Nevertheless, individuality is also important. Hoernlé recognizes that the claim that "every human soul is a thing of absolute value" is a key contribution to humanity — though noting that Kant's arguments here are problematic (Hoernlé 1952: 323). This concern for individuality is also expressed by Hoernlé's view that liberty is a liberty of individuals. Thus, Hoernlé writes that "one must love liberty as an ideal of universal application; as a value to the enjoyment of which all human beings have an indefeasible right, *simply because they are human*" (Hoernlé 1939: xi, emphasis mine).[32] And, of course, individuality is important because morality is inseparable from agency, and requires individuals who have the capability to "will".[33]

Some see claim a conflict here, between an ethics rooted in community and one which reflects the apparently inherent value of the human person, and between an ethics that is part of culture, and one which recognizes that there are values which lead us beyond existing cultural norms. There are three points that Hoernlé could make in response.

First, there is no fundamental conflict or antagonism between the individual and the community. The individual is a being in a culture and in a community — i.e., a social being, determined in large part by its culture. Hoernlé writes: "individuals live their lives as members of social groups..." (Hoernlé 1945: 9) and are unintelligible apart from them; in an early essay, "The Analysis of Volition", he calls into question whether one can "stop short at the distinction of individual minds or selves and take it as his ultimate basis", or instead must be led to a "social mind" (Hoernlé: 1912-3: 188). Indeed, Hoernlé notes a view rooted in his reading of Kant's theory of morality — that there is a reciprocal obligation on society to "the cooperative realisation of the fullness of rational personality in every one of its members" (Hoernlé 1952: 323). There is, then, no opposition between the individual and the community.

Second, even though individuality is rooted in and supported by society, this does not mean that Hoernlé thought the individual wholly subordinate to society. And even though ethics is sustained by culture, he did not hold that a cultural relativism or subjectivism is true. To begin with, if

---

30 See, for example, Hoernlé's comments on the development of Afrikaans and the Afrikaner culture, in "On the Concept of the Soul of a People" (1933), reprinted in Hoernlé (1945: 13).

31 This is Hoernlé's 1939 essay, "A Theory of Liberty", which appears as part of Hoernlé (1939). It was revised by Hoernlé later for separate publication, and appears in Hoernlé (1945). I use this latter version here.

32 See also MacCrone (1945: xxxii).

33 See Hoernlé (1952: 323), but also his early views on volition, in Hoernlé (1912-3).

one were to ask what it is to be moral, and how people should engage social problems, Hoernlé's response would not be simply to follow convention. A philosopher—particularly, a good idealist philosopher—will start from existing practice and experience, but this is not the end of the matter. Responding morally may call the individual to go beyond the parameters of a particular culture. Moreover, values are not purely culturally determined. Hoernlé holds that values are "of the essence of" Reality (1952: 53),[34] and that a principle of coherence applies to values. People seek coherence in their values and, as values become more and more coherent, they become more and more stable and, therefore, true—"the truth of value judgements lies in their stability" (1952: 52). Indeed, cultures as a whole not only "work through" existing values, but also come into contact with and interact with the values of other cultures—living cultures are not closed—and there is an impetus for them to respond in a positive way to such contact. Thus, Hoernlé holds that experience leads us beyond relativism or subjectivism; "experience, taken as a whole, gives us clues which, rightly interpreted, lead to the perception of … a graded order of varied appearances [in the universe]" (1920: v). Hoernlé insists that this is "not an a priori assumption, but a conclusion slowly gathered from the business of philosophizing" (1920: v). Society is not, therefore, fundamental or the norm for individuality.

Third, according to Hoernlé, liberty is something that exists only in a society—and so, again, there is no conflict between the individual and the community. On Hoernlé's view, liberty is "the socially permitted, or authorized, exercise of one's power to do; it is a power to do, as a socially recognized and guaranteed right" (Hoernlé, 1945: 1). Now, at first glance, at least, this seems troubling, since it appears to eviscerate individual liberty—and, by extension, individuality—as values. But Hoernlé's point is, I would suggest, that it is just a fact that liberty has always been demanded and secured in a social context; that it needs to "exist concretely as liberties; as a system of rights… or permitted patterns of conduct" (1945: 1), and that it can never be absolute (1945: 3). Nevertheless, Hoernlé also recognises that human values and excellences need to be "realised in individual human beings" (1945: 9). The value of individuals is not denied.

Liberty, then, is something *individuals* have (Hoernlé 1939: 113; see 1945: 4), and a society is measured by the liberty and the quality of life of the individuals within it (Hoernlé 1945: 4). But this does not entail an individualism, or a right to determine one's own good in one's own way, which society must unquestioningly respect. Yet neither is liberty or the value of the individual something that is left to the opinions (of a majority) in a society. For Hoernlé, the liberty and the quality of life of individuals is something objective. He writes: "the ground for the defence of social

---

34 This is from his undated, posthumously published essay "Fact and Value," in Hoernlé (1952).

restrictions is identical with the ground for the challenge of them, viz., the quality of the human lives which such restrictions promote or hinder. And by quality I mean spiritual, moral, cultural quality" (1945: 3).

Hoernlé's ethics of liberty, therefore, contains a 'thick' account of the individual as a social being and as a being that aspires to spiritual, moral, and intellectual values which, as we have seen, he holds to be "of the essence of" Reality (Hoernlé 1952: 53). And at the root of Hoernlé's account of liberty there is not just an account of human nature, but also a notion of a common good that brings the 'social' and the 'individual' together. Hoernlé writes of "an aspiration towards an order of society in which every human being, and every group of human beings, has the opportunity to live *a life worth living*, according to the pattern and standards of culture within its reach" (Hoernlé 1945: 115, emphasis mine), and it is only because there is a common good that liberty is possible. It is this "life worth living" that is the common good.

Can anything more be said specifically about this common good?

This common good is found in community — even (at least, at one stage) on a national basis — but it is more than a good agreed to by the majority or even by all. It reflects, as noted above, a range of moral, spiritual, and intellectual values whose realisation depends in varying degrees on that community. This good — a "life worth living" — has, moreover, a rational character;[35] Hoernlé agrees that "reason, as embodied in rational beings has absolute value" (Hoernlé 1952: 323). This good is also 'open.' This is, perhaps, in part a consequence of Hoernlé's 'synoptic method', described above — "that truth has many sides, and that to the whole truth on any subject every point of view has some contribution to make" (Hoernlé 1925: 138). But, moreover, Hoernlé looks at the world around him and sees that the common good in a society or culture is never complete; the values in a society are always in the process of becoming more coherent (Hoernlé 1952: 42; see p. 298 above), and there is always new experience to be had and new value to be encountered. Hoernlé also writes of the importance of "a mind alive, receptive, attentive to as many sides of human experience as possible" (Hoernlé 1925: 140). What all this suggests is that "a life worth living" must be open to new experience — including, for example, knowledge of other cultures and traditions. But even though this common good cannot be defined in advance, it nevertheless provides an objective basis for the value of liberty.

This common good is pluralistic — by which I mean that it allows for a range of instantiations of the good — a range of 'lives worth living' (see Hoernlé 1939: 130-1). This is in part a consequence of the "openness" of the common good, but also of the value of individuals and of the value of

---

35   See, for example, his remark that "Our passions constantly becloud our vision of the common good" (Hoernlé [1923: 18]).

culture in itself. We see an illustration of this when Hoernlé speaks of the importance of what we would call today an 'education in diversity' for all — that Native peoples and the South African Whites should understand and appreciate and value the *diversity* of the nation (e.g., in terms of occupation, education, tribalization, etc. [Hoernlé 1945: 112] [36]). This is also a product of 'the liberal spirit'; he writes, "the liberal spirit... shows itself as respect for social groups other than one's own, for cultures other than one's own, for sentiments and traditions other than one's own" (1945: 9).

Hoernlé would insist, however, that this pluralism not be exaggerated. "Native interests [are] an integral part of the interests of South Africa as a whole" (1945: 113), and ultimately cannot be separated from them. Focus should be on a broad or national, rather than a sectional or ethnic, interest. Hoernlé is also rather suspicious of attempts to exaggerate the differences among cultures (seeing this in arguments for what would be called apartheid). He writes: "many of the claims which are made in the name of the soul of a people are ... unfounded in fact and false" (1945: 32). And this is consistent with the synoptic method — that the recognition of diversity is not for its own sake, but because it has a contribution to make to a more comprehensive and inclusive understanding of reality (MacCrone 1945: xvi).

Substantively, then, Hoernlé's ethics of liberty rests on a common good that is "a life worth living" — i.e., human flourishing. Hoernlé does not, admittedly, say specifically what 'human flourishing' is. All one can (and perhaps need) say is that it involves the development of human potential and what this broadly entails. In his 1919 essay, "Bernard Bosanquet's Philosophy of the State",[37] Hoernlé writes that the idealist theory of freedom — and this we may take to be his own theory as well — looks "to what human nature demands for its own realisation" (Hoernlé 1919: 628),[38] and not to mere subjective preference — and in *South African Native Policy and the Liberal Spirit*, he lists a number of "the elements of a life which a man ought to be 'free' ... to realise" (Hoernlé 1939: 113), such as health, housing, citizenship, culture, and the like. Hoernlé would also note the importance of such institutions, as language, science, art, state, and church, which are "rooted in human nature but through human nature in the universe" (Hoernlé 1919: 631). Hoernlé would say, then, that an idealist ethics offers a comprehensive approach to reality, reflects human nature, is open,

---

36   This comes from Hoernlé's 1937 address, "On the Future of the Native Peoples in South Africa."

37   Hoernlé (1919), reprinted in *Idealism as a Philosophy* (Hoernlé 1927).

38   Here, he goes on to quote Bosanquet's *The Philosophical Theory of the State* that "If ... you start with a human being as he is in fact, and try to devise what will furnish him with an outlet and a stable purpose capable of doing justice to his capacities — a satisfying object of life — you will be driven on by the necessity of the facts at least as far as the State, and perhaps further." (Hoernlé 1919: 628).

is objective, and has a clear teleological character. One might even say — as Hoernlé himself suggests — that it has a metaphysical character.

Hoernlé seems open to the idea of (what Bosanquet called) a "nisus" in reality towards coherence. But does this teleological character entail that moral progress or social change is evolutionary and inevitable? No, but neither is it something contingent. Clearly there is room for moral struggle — and for moral failure — in the world. One can certainly, as it were, fail to be "adequate to the situation".

Hoernlé does not develop the metaphysical background to his view in his late social and political writings. Neither does he explicitly ground his ethics or his social philosophy in anything like a theory of the Absolute. (Of course, the explicit introduction of such a metaphysical notion would likely only have complicated matters with his audiences.) But it is clear that there is some kind of "social mind" underlying his ethics and social philosophy.[39] Hoernlé notes that any collective body — and, to be sure, any international body — "must be rooted in a deep will to sustain it, and this will must be a will of the constituent states running through the rank and file of their citizens" (Hoernlé 1919: 624).[40] But whatever this "will" or this 'Absolute' may be, it does not lie outside of experience or 'external' to the world; even though Hoernlé's moral philosophy reflects a metaphysics, it is resolutely immanentist.

Hoernlé does not explicitly present his views as an ethics of self-realisation. Still, he clearly has an expansive view of the self that is characteristic of idealist theories of self-realisation and self-transcendence.[41] Moreover, his emphasis on the importance of the flourishing of the individual, that people are to have "lives worth living by rational human beings" (Hoernlé 1939: 113), that they therefore have a right to liberties, and that these liberties be for "the whole man", "for man as a whole", also point in this direction.[42] It is plausible, then, to see Hoernlé's view as one of self-realisation.

For Hoernlé, self-realisation is possible only if there is an appropriate social context. Recall that it is from our culture that we "draw the materials [...] for a life worth living" (Hoernlé 1945: 9). And in any case, how far one can progress is determined by the cultural resources available; "the excel-

---

39 See his review of Boodin (Hoernlé [1941]).
40 See Hoernlé (1927: 624).
41 This is certainly suggested in Hoernlé (1927: 252). See also Hoernlé (1912–3); (1927: 258); (1945: 9).
42 In addition to the texts cited here, in an early letter to R.M. MacIver (of 12 April 1912) Hoernlé discusses the distinction between the "real" will and the "actual" will, insisting that we need a notion like the real will in order for the notion of obligation ("ought") to be even possible; see MacIver (1969: 244–5).
    In "Bernard Bosanquet's Philosophy of the State," Hoernlé also follows Bosanquet when he writes that "With this spirit of his community the individual learns, in his own unique way, to identify himself; he grows into one of the organs through which it lives on and develops itself" (Hoernlé [1919: 630]).

lence of their [i.e., the individuals'] lives *is relative* [emphasis mine], therefore, to the culture (in the widest sense) of their group" (1945: 9). Moreover, Hoernlé would hold that, to the extent to which reference to the (common) good of human flourishing is too abstract or vague, this self-realisation may be achieved through the performance of the 'stations and duties' which individuals have within a culture — though this, too, may be somewhat vague, Hoernlé writes (Hoernlé 1927: 282). Still, here the principle is — Hoernlé reminds his readers of Royce's similar view — to "work loyally in your groove, for it is your obvious channel of service to the common good, and think chiefly of how much more you can do than you are doing" (Hoernlé 1919: 629).

Such a view may lead some to hold that there is a very strong moral — and, by extension, social and political — conservatism here. But Hoernlé's position on the source of ethical obligation is much more nuanced than it may appear. We should note that 'culture' is not synonymous with 'the community' or 'the state,' and what one is morally obliged to do because of one's 'station' within a culture may be other, or more, than what the state expects. Culture may justify or even require, in other words, what community forbids.

Hoernlé's social and political philosophy is similarly nuanced. Hoernlé notes, by his own example, the importance of the law-abiding citizen and carrying out the duties of one's station (Hoernlé 1945: 115), even with regard to morally questionable laws. Moreover, as we have seen, Hoernlé writes that *political* liberties themselves are always determined within a social context; liberty is not something that has been, or can be, demanded in the abstract, and as such (1945: 5). Indeed, no liberty is absolute; Hoernlé writes: "There is no such thing as freedom of conscience, if by this phrase is meant that society should guarantee to every one of its members the power to disobey any law of which his conscience disapproves" (Hoernlé 1939: 116). Nor are European-style political liberties necessarily relevant to, or able to support, with regard to context, an ethics of liberty. When efforts are made to bring "European civilization, 'White' culture" (Hoernlé 1945: 16) to bear on traditional ways of living, the result may be not the liberation, but the destruction of a culture. By way of illustration — though he is convinced that all human beings need to be considered when we engage in moral action — Hoernlé is suspicious of theories of pure equality (Hoernlé 1939: 129–30).

But, again, when we look more closely at Hoernlé's arguments, we see that he goes beyond a conservative understanding of one's station and its duties. He consistently notes the importance of working for "the liberal spirit" (1939: 116), that "the spirit of liberty is ineradicable and cannot be denied" (1939: 185), and that there is no going back. Moreover, this 'life worth living' is for Hoernlé, then, a good for all individuals — and it provides a basis for "a theory of liberty [...] for man as a whole" (Hoernlé 1939: 112; Hoernlé 1945: 3). For example, as pluralistic, this good—this 'life'—must allow for a participation of all in public and political affairs; "in all practical matters ... each interest has a right to be considered a factor in the problem to be solved" (Hoernlé 1925: 138-9). Hoernlé's ethics of liberty, then, is consistent with a theory of "my station", and it has a clear political implication—there is no *a priori* moral justification for restricting active participation in politics to certain races (see Hoernlé 1945: 115ff). Thus, Hoernlé's questions concerning the appropriateness of cultural interaction—"Are we destroying a soul or giving one [...] Should we call a halt? Should we undo the work we have done, so far as that is possible? Should we withdraw from contact with them and leave them to recapture, as far as may be, their ancestral ways?" (1945: 16-7)—are purely rhetorical. Hoernlé suspected—correctly—that "White South Africa" would resist "genuine co-operation and community of purpose" with non-Whites (Hoernlé 1939: 185). And so he noted "the great victories of the liberal spirit have been gained when those to whom liberty has been denied, have successfully achieved it for themselves" (see 1939: 185)—and foresaw—again, correctly—that radical change would require Africans "taking fate in their own hands" (Skinner [2005: 248]; see Hoernlé [1939: 185-6]). His ethics of liberty could serve to justify what the political liberties of his time did not.

1.3. Conclusion

Like several of the South African philosophers of the late 19th and early 20th centuries, Hoernlé does not provide a fully developed and explicit statement of his moral, social, or even political philosophy. Yet he had much to say about such matters, and was interested and actively engaged in applied, practical ethical, social, and political issues. A student of some of the leading British idealists who wrote on moral and social philosophy, Hoernlé focuses on practical concerns, and held that, in order to engage concrete moral and social issues, the idealist does not just take things "as they seem" but goes to things "as they are". While Hoernlé does not describe his views, in his later political and social writings, as reflecting a distinctively idealist account, and while he does not explicitly draw on a theory of the Absolute, such views clearly underlie his remarks.

Hoernlé's ethics of liberty understands 'liberty' in a broad, positive sense, and not as a power 'in the abstract' to do whatever one wills. The aim of this liberty is to allow individuals to lead "a life worth living", and such a life requires an openness to difference and a pluralism in the conceptions of what such a life would be like. But Hoernlé's approach is far from individualistic. Hoernlé recognises the importance of culture and of the "social mind"—what Bosanquet called the "general will" in ethics and in understanding the nature of individuality, and he insisted that the social rootedness of the individual and the existence of a common good indicated a relation of the individual to the community that avoided the extremes of individualism. This social rootedness, in turn, reflects what some have called a "social ontology" of the individual, the community, and the state. Thus, metaphysics grounds values and provides a basis for an objective morality.

Hoernlé's view, then, recognises the presence of "the underlying pattern of reality which alone can serve as the basis of any final solution of the practical, political problems of a multi-racial society such as in South Africa" (MacCrone 1945: xxxiii). He holds that there is a tendency towards a coherence in culture and values, that is characteristic of what he called "the liberal spirit" and of his "ethics of liberty". These principles of Hoernlé's idealism, then, provided a basis for his liberalism. In this way, Hoernlé's 'British idealism' could be seen as responding to problems and addressing concerns outside of its context of origin. And his moral, social, and political philosophy provided a rallying point for liberal political opinion in South Africa.

But Hoernlé was also sufficiently "practical" to recognise the challenges to realising such an interracial liberty in the concrete context of South Africa; so "practical", perhaps, that by deferring to institutions and to "practicalities", his views have sometimes been regarded, in retrospect, as providing a basis for a conservatism. Hoernlé himself came to despair about the chances of effecting change, given the dominance of the South African European culture and context. Still, he had no doubt of the progressive possibilities of the liberal spirit, and he seems to have been right in his prediction that it would take a radical effort to effect real change in the South African context.

2. Idealism and Idealist Ethical Thought in India

2.1 Background

Much like in South Africa, idealism came to India in the late 19th and early 20th centuries. It flourished principally through the work done in the colleges; the oldest universities in India—Bombay, Madras, and Calcutta (all established in 1857)—were primarily examination bodies until the early 20th century, and instruction took place in the various affiliated colleges, which had existed (in many cases) for some decades before the establishment of the universities.[43] The colleges in India were staffed by both

---

43 From the late 17th century until 1858, India was divided into the 'Presidencies': Bombay (covering the west and the north of the subcontinent, including today's Pakistan), the Bengal (which covered the north east, as well as what are now Bangladesh and Burma) and Madras (the southern portion of today's India). Each Presidency had at least one government affiliated college.

locally-educated philosophers and Europeans—the Europeans generally having been sent to India through the Indian Educational Service (IES) but also, and frequently, by religious bodies such as the Scottish Free Church.[44] Indeed, a number of the leading colleges were founded by, or in affiliation with, the Scottish church, and it was often in these institutions that the presence of British idealist philosophy was strongest. (While the teaching of philosophy in these institutions was initially informed by Christian missionary zeal, over time, there was more of an effort made to engage positively Indian thought.)

Some of the more notable philosophers influenced by British idealism are to be found at Allahabad, Mysore, Baroda, Pondicherry, and Amalner,[45] but there was a particularly strong presence of idealist thought in colleges in Bombay, Madras, and Calcutta.

In Bombay, two institutions in which idealism was rather marked were Wilson College (established in 1832, under the aegis of the Scottish Free Church) and The Elphinstone College (established in 1856).

At Wilson College, professors such as J.R. Cuthbert (who taught from 1906 to 1920) and John McKenzie (who taught 1908–21, and served as Principal until 1944), were influential teachers,[46] and McKenzie was the author of the controversial *Hindu Ethics* (1922).[47] Among the Indian philosophers on the faculty who were drawn to the British idealist tradition, we have Pestonji Ardesir Wadia (1878-1970), Ganesh Narayan Lawande[48], and more recently Sheryar Ookerjee (b. 1925, who taught from 1949 to 1985).

At Elphinstone College, idealism had a place in the courses of Michael Macmillan (1853–1925, who taught philosophy, 1878–91), W.H. Sharp (1865–1917, who taught 1894–1900 and 1906–7, in the interval serving at the Deccan College as Principal), Robert Marrs (1884–1951, who served there from 1909 to 1916), and, later, Jehangir Nasserwanji Chubb (1910–2001). The most thoroughgoing representative of idealism at the College, however, is likely J.C.P. d'Andrade (1888–1949) who taught there

---

44 A notable exception is Alban Widgery, who taught at Baroda from 1915 to 1922, and for 6 months in 1926. For more on Widgery see Widgery (1961), and Sweet (2010).

45 At the University of Allahabad, we have A.C. Mukerji (1890-1968); at the Indian Institute of Philosophy at Amalner, we have G.K. Malkani (1892–1977); at the University of Mysore, we have A.R. Wadia (1888–1971); and Aurobindo Ghose (1872–1950) established a philosophical/religious community at Pondicherry. These thinkers were, however, often products of these three major centres. Wadia was educated at Wilson College (Bombay) and in Britain, Malkani at Bombay and in Britain, and Mukerji was a student of Haldar's at Calcutta. Aurobindo entered King's College, Cambridge, in 1890, obtaining a first class in Part 1 of the Classical Tripos in 1892.

46 Cuthbert was a graduate of Edinburgh (MA, 1902) and McKenzie a graduate of Aberdeen (MA, 1904).

47 See the response and review by A.R. Wadia (1924).

48 Lawande (BA, MA [1937] Bombay), taught at Wilson College for several years, beginning in 1940. His early work was in philosophy (see Lawande 1938-9, and 1943), but he left Wilson College as the result of a serious dispute. He later became Professor of Economics at S.B. Garda College in Gujarat.

from 1913 until 1943. D'Andrade, whose major work was collected in a posthumously published volume entitled *The Philosophy of Life* (1952), espoused a strong idealism influenced by Bradley, and had a significant impact on a number of students and colleagues.

Madras was an important home for idealist philosophy as well. In Madras, the three premier colleges of the late 19th and early 20th centuries were Presidency College,[49] Pachiyappa's College, and the Madras Christian College (MCC) — but it was at the latter that idealism had its strongest presence.

Most of the professors at the MCC were graduates of the Scottish universities — particularly Aberdeen and Edinburgh — and many had been students of idealists such as Robert Adamson at Aberdeen, and James Seth and Andrew Seth Pringle-Pattison at Edinburgh.[50] William Skinner, William Meston, A.G. Hogg, and Alfred James Mackenzie, along with John Bangaru Raju[51], formed a core of philosophers whose impact on succeeding generations was noteworthy. Of these men, Hogg (1875–1954) is today perhaps the best-known. Hogg had been a student of Pringle-Pattison, and served at MCC as Professor of Philosophy from 1905 to 1928 (and, after 1928, as Principal).[52] Ordained only relatively late in life, Hogg saw his vocation as more philosophical than religious, and it is plausible to say that it was the 'openness' of his idealism that led him to try to start to bridge western and Indian philosophical traditions. Hogg has a place in the history of Christian theology as a result of his efforts in Hindu-Christian dialogue (see Hogg 1947), but in philosophy his fame is related to his role as the influential teacher of Sarvepalli Radhakrishnan (1888–1975), who later became not only one of the leading figures in Indian philosophy of the 20th century, but a major intellectual force in the country, and, towards the end of his life, its President.

---

49 There was a presence of idealist thought at Presidency College, though it did not have a significant place overall. Radhakrishnan's first academic position was at the College — he taught there for 10 years until the age of 30, and for some years one of his colleagues was another scholar, slightly older than Radhakrishnan, Potaraju Narasimham. Narasimham briefly corresponded with F.H. Bradley, and was the author of two articles in *Mind*, on Vedantic Idealism (Narasimham 1912; under the pseudonym of Homo Leone) and Narasimham 1915); see the references to his correspondence with Bradley in Bradley (1999, vol. 5: 151-3; 162). Narasimham also gave the Miller Lectures at University of Madras (1939-40).

50 At Edinburgh, they would have studied under Alexander Campbell Fraser and, after 1891, Andrew Seth Pringle Pattison; at Aberdeen, they would have studied under Alexander Bain in Logic or, in Moral Philosophy, with John Fyfe (1876-94), Robert Adamson (1893-95), W.R. Sorley (1895-1900), Robert Latta (1900-2) and J.B. Baillie (1902-24).

51 Skinner graduated from Aberdeen (MA 1880) as did Meston (MA 1890; BD Edinburgh, 1895); Hogg graduated from Edinburgh (MA 1897), as did Mackenzie (MA 1913). John Bangaru Raju, one of the very first native-born philosophers at MCC, graduated from Madras (BSc, MA).

52 For biographical information, see the entry in Sweet (2010) and Sharpe (1997). Hogg arrived at MCC as Acting Professor of History (1903-4) before moving to Philosophy. He later became Acting Principal (1928-30) and Principal (1930-8).

At Calcutta, the place of British idealism was relatively strong. In the late 19th century, at the Presidency College, one finds traces of German idealism in P.K. Ray[53] (who was said to have been a friend of R.B. Haldane), A.F.R. Hoernlé (the father of R.F.A. Hoernlé) and C.R. Wilson, and one of the most famous students of the College was the future philosopher Krishna Chandra Bhattacharyya (1875-1949). But it was at "The Scottish Churches College" (the successor to "The General Assembly's Institution" and Duff College, both established by Scottish churches) and — once it became a teaching institution — at the University of Calcutta, that idealism had an especially important presence.

At the General Assembly's Institution and the Scottish Churches College, through the classes of William Hastie (1842-1903), Henry Stephen (1847-1927), and W.S. Urquhart (1877-1964),[54] students were introduced to the classics of western philosophy principally through Kant and Hegel but also, to a lesser extent, other idealist authors. (Among their students were Brajendra Nath Seal (1864-1938), Hiralal Haldar (1865-1942), Narendranath Dutta [Swami Vivekananda] (1863-1902), Abhay Charan De [Swami Abhay Caranaravinda Bhaktivedanta], founder of the International Society for Krishna Consciousness (1896-1977), and Haridas Bhattacharyya (1891-1956).) Hastie — today known as the translator of *Kant's Principles of Politics, Including His Essay on Perpetual Peace* — stayed in India for what was a rather brief and tumultuous period (1878-83). Nevertheless, during that time he taught Seal and Dutta, and Haldar later remarked that Hastie's influence continued after he left. Stephen was strongly influenced by Hegel, though his interests were more literary than philosophical, and he ended his career at the University of Calcutta as a Professor of English. Urquhart, who had also studied at Aberdeen under W. Ritchie Sorley, taught in the Scottish colleges in Calcutta from 1902. Urquhart's interests were influenced by his 'missionary' activity — he wrote an early work criticizing Hindu ethics, *Pantheism and the Value of Life* (1919) — though he gradually came to engage Indian thought more positively (e.g., in his *The Vedanta and Modern Thought*, 1928), where he notes several parallels between 'western' and Vedantic thought.

Once it came to take on a teaching function, the University of Calcutta also became a centre for idealism in India. Two of its best known professors — both holders of the King George V Chair of Mental and Moral Sci-

---

53 Prasanna Kumar Ray (1849-1932) studied at Dacca College (from which he received a Gilchrist Scholarship in 1870), the University of London (BSc 1874, 2nd cl Honours; DSc 1876) and Edinburgh (DSc Mental Philosophy, 1876), joined the Indian Educational Service in 1877, and was Assistant Professor of Physical Science at Patna College, Professor of Logic and Philosophy at Dacca College, and Professor of Philosophy at Presidency College starting in 1888 (and Principal in 1902, 1903 and 1905).

54 Hastie studied at Edinburgh (MA 1867, BD 1869), Stephen at Aberdeen (MA 1870), and Urquhart at Aberdeen (MA 1897) as well.

ence there—B.N. Seal[55] and K.C. Bhattacharyya, are generally associated with idealism, though it is fair to say that the influence on both was more from Kant than from Hegel and that the place of the British idealists was minimal. It was, rather, two other holders of the King George V Chair, Hiralal Haldar and Sarvepalli Radhakrishnan, who are remembered for promoting an idealism exhibiting characteristics of the British form.

When British idealism began to have a distinctive impact is difficult to say. Author of *Neo-Hegelianism* (1927), as well as of a number of articles engaging the work of the British idealists, Haldar noted that "The philosophical movement known as Neo-Hegelianism was in my student days gathering strength in Great Britain and I was one of the very few, not improbably the only one, who then felt its power in India" (Haldar 1952: 316). Nevertheless, by the time of Radhakrishnan's arrival in Calcutta in 1920, British idealist philosophy had an established place, and the University produced a number of students (such as P.T. Raju[56]) who came to have an important role in engaging British idealism from the perspective of the Indian traditions.

Students of the history of philosophy in the 20th century have remarked on this contact between British philosophy—particularly, British idealism—and Indian thought. And for at least the first half of that century, the texts of major British idealists appear on the syllabi and on the examinations of the colleges and universities. Though there was no focus on any particular idealist, by the 1910s—and well into the 1940s—T.H. Green's *Prolegomena to Ethics* appears annually on the list of required or recommended texts in ethics, along with the ethics 'textbooks' of James Seth (*A Study of Ethical Principles*, 1894, and several subsequent editions), and J.S. Mackenzie (*A Manual of Ethics*, 1893, and subsequent editions). Bradley's *Appearance and Reality* appears on reading lists at Calcutta (by 1911), but not until 1933 at Bombay (where it was, nevertheless, one of the 'set texts' in the 1930s and 40s). We find work by Bosanquet on logic on the list of texts at Calcutta and Madras by 1914, on into the 1930s (though, interestingly, not at Bombay), but there is little mention of Bosanquet's other work, except his political philosophy—and there, principally only at Bombay. Green's principal study in political philosophy, the *Lectures on the Principles of Political Obligation*, is sometimes included as required or recommended reading, as well (by the 1920s) as the "natural theology" of

---

55 Seal spent most of his life as a teacher of English and a school Principal but, in 1913, he was appointed to the newly-established King George V Chair of Philosophy at University of Calcutta (which he held until his first retirement in 1921).

56 Raju was a student of A.C. Mukerji at Allahabad (BA 1928), and moved to the University of Calcutta, where he studied with Radhakrishnan and Hiralal Haldar, and from which he received his MA in 1930 and his PhD in 1935. For more biographical information, see the entry in Sweet (2010).

A.S. Pringle-Pattison, James Ward, C.C.J. Webb, and Josiah Royce. But one very rarely finds mention of J.M.E. McTaggart except, briefly, at Madras.[57]

During this period, there was no other Western 'philosophical school' or tradition that was as frequently represented on syllabi as British idealism. This indicates an impact of this idealism, through much of the first half of the 20th century, on the generations of future leaders of India who passed through classes in philosophy, psychology, and ethics. It is an influence which, in a limited degree, continues even to this day.[58]

One feature that may help to explain the place of British idealism in India is that idealism — in the broad sense — was not an 'imported' theory; idealism had — in the tradition of Advaita Vedanta — a long history in India (though the central character of Advaita in the early and mid 20th century is plausibly due to its relation to British idealism).[59] And there were, arguably, a number of similarities between the two — in terms of questions if not answers — that facilitated the interaction of them. For example, like many of the British idealists, the work by Indian idealist philosophers on ethics, values, and political philosophy was often connected with broader, metaphysical claims about the nature of the self and its relation to larger 'wholes' (e.g., the community or the Absolute).

Idealism in India was, of course, developed in different ways by philosophers such as K.C. Bhattacharrya, Haldar, Malkani, D'Andrade, Mukerji, and others. Some made little effort to directly engage Indian traditions or philosophies, others made no explicit effort to identify their relation to such work, while others still used the vocabulary or approach of western philosophy to bring western and Indian philosophy into contact. Nevertheless, in general, a significant number of Indian philosophers engaged the insights and arguments of British idealism, particularly in the areas of metaphysics and of moral and social philosophy, and brought them to bear on their reading, interpretation, and articulation of classical Indian thought, as well as on practical social and political issues, such as religion and caste.

A fruitful example of the constructive 'engagement' of British idealism with Indian thought is in the work of Sarvepalli Radhakrishnan. To see how this idealism was encountered, and how it was brought to bear on ethics, I turn now to look closely at Radhakrishnan's early writings.

---

57 See the university calendars at Madras, Bombay, and Calcutta, from 1900–50.
58 Mackenzie's book on ethics long continued as a text on syllabi at some Indian universities. One also sees reference to the work of idealists, especially Green, in more recent studies, e.g., Balasubramanian (1969).
59 For example, N.S.S. Raman notes that "one has lost sight of the fact that non-metaphysical Hinduism forms the core of popular Hinduism"; see Raman (2001: 11).

2.2. Radhakrishnan and the duty of universal spiritual emancipation

Educated primarily in Christian schools in India, Radhakrishnan studied at the Madras Christian College from 1905 to 1909 under Skinner, Meston, and Hogg. He taught in India—at Presidency College, Madras (1907–17), the University of Mysore (1918–21), and the University of Calcutta (intermittently, from 1921–41)—and in England, at Oxford (1929–30, and 1936–9)—and was, later in life, Vice Chancellor at Andhra (1931–6) and at Benares (1939–48), and Vice-President (1952–62) and President (1962–7) of India.[60]

Radhakrishnan's work exemplifies the pursuit of scholarly dialogue on ethics, religion, politics, and culture across cultural and philosophical traditions. He is well-known for his promotion of "comparative philosophy"—a term coined by B.N. Seal[61]—which held that there were common or shared grounds from which different philosophical traditions could understand one another, and arrive at some kind of "integrative" outlook (Raju 1992: 300)[62]—a view which, for some time, strongly influenced education in the humanities in India. But Radhakrishnan also defended an idealist ethics, social philosophy, and metaphysics (presented at length in his 1929 Hibbert lectures, *An Idealist View of Life* [1932])—taking a position sometimes referred to as "spiritual humanism" (Sharma 1965).

Radhakrishnan was not a direct student of any of the British idealist philosophers, but he was nevertheless significantly influenced by them.

Radhakrishnan's studies for the bachelors and masters degrees in Mental and Moral Science at Madras followed a syllabus in which the major British idealists figured prominently.[63] T.H. Green's *Prolegomena to Ethics* and W.R. Boyce Gibson's *A Philosophical Introduction to Ethics* (subtitled, "An Advocacy of the Spiritual Principle in Ethics from the Point of View of Personal Idealism",[64] and a set text for the MA in 1908, in which Green's ethics played a dominant part), had an important place. Among the other

---

60   For a short biographical entry on Radhakrishnan, see Sweet (2005), reprinted in Sweet (2010).
61   See Halbfass (1988: 307). Radhakrishnan himself, however, also notes the influence of the famous comparativist, Paul Deussen. See also P.T. Raju (1985: 539).
62   Other British and Indian philosophers interested in "comparative philosophy" were Alban Widgery and P.T. Raju. The objective of comparative philosophy is, however, somewhat ambiguous. Is it simply to bring philosophical traditions into contact? into dialogue? Is it simply to compare concepts or arguments or traditions? Or is the "comparative activity" more substantive; is it to achieve some "integrative" outlook based on assumptions about "a common platform" from which philosophical reflection is to begin, namely certain common interests and aspirations of humanity (Raju, 1992: 293ff)?
63   I refer here to the syllabi and the examination papers in the Madras University Calendars for 1906–7, 1907–8, and 1908–9.
64   W.R. [William Ralph] Boyce Gibson (1869–1935), often regarded as a personalistic idealist, was author of *Philosophical Introduction to Ethics; an advocacy of the spiritual principle in ethics, from the point of view of personal idealism* (1904). He had studied at Queen's College, Oxford (2nd cl. math mod, 1889; 2nd cl. math, 1892), but also at Jena, Paris, and Glasgow, and was much influenced by the ideas of Rudolf Eucken [see Boyce Gibson's *Rudolf Eucken's philosophy of life* (1906)].

standard texts at the time and into the 1930s were Bosanquet's *Essentials of Logic* and his *Logic,* James Seth's *A Study of Ethical Principles,* and J.S. Mackenzie's *A Manual of Ethics.* J.M.E. McTaggart's *Studies In Hegelian Cosmology* (a set text for 1907), A.E. Taylor's *Elements of Metaphysics,* and Henry Sidgwick's *Ethics of Green, Spencer, and Martineau* (another set text for 1907) were among the texts to be read. F.H. Bradley's *Appearance and Reality* was supplementary reading by the early 1910s, but became a standard by 1927.

Moreover, as noted earlier, many of the teachers at the Madras Christian College had been students of some of the leading British idealist philosophers, and Radhakrishnan studied under the supervision of Hogg,[65] who had been a student of A.S. Pringle-Pattison. (Radhakrishnan's respect for Hogg — and for his teachers at MCC — was acknowledged throughout his life, and it was reciprocated.) Radhakrishnan's MA thesis, and much of his early work, engaged the writings of contemporary idealists, and his *The Reign of Religion* (1920), which collects a number of his early essays, responds not only to Bergson, Russell, and James, but primarily to the personalistic idealism of Hastings Rashdall, James Ward, and G.H. Howison. Radhakrishnan identified his own view as 'absolute idealism.'

It is also relevant to note that it was through British idealists, such as J.H. Muirhead, R.B. Haldane, and J.S. Mackenzie, that Radhakrishnan's views were introduced to a wider audience. A fortuitous remark by Mackenzie helped Radhakrishnan in securing the King George V Chair at Calcutta (Gopal 1989: 56), it was through Haldane that Radhakrishnan gave his first lectures outside of India, and Muirhead commissioned — and supported — a number of Radhakrishnan's publications.[66] The close connection between British idealism and Radhakrishnan was remarked on in 1921 by E.L. Hinman, then President of the American Philosophical Association, who saw Bosanquet and Radhakrishnan as two representative idealists (see Hinman 1921).

There were, of course, other influences on Radhakrishnan's thought aside from that of British idealism. Radhakrishnan studied Hinduism and Jainism at university and in his early career, and Rabindranath Tagore and Vivekananda were also subjects of Radhakrishnan's early essays — though it is interesting that these men, too, were both influenced by western thought.

Radhakrishnan wrote on a wide range of topics throughout his career, but the theme for which he is best known — and indeed the area of his earliest work — is ethics, in the expansive sense that we might call 'the philosophy of life.'

---

65 For a discussion, see Kalapati (2002).
66 See Gopal (1989: 41, 55, 59, 69, 73). See also Radhakrishnan (1952: 10).

What led to Radhakrishnan's first publications was the critique of Hindu ethics, principally by Hogg, which occurred in Hogg's exchange with the Indian philosopher Subrahmanya Sastri and in Hogg's lectures to the MA class on ethics at the Madras Christian College. (Hogg's early views were later separately published as *Karma and Redemption* [1909].) Hogg challenged Hinduism first, for not having a genuine ethical view and, second, because it was "quietistic" (see Radhakrishnan 1914a: 183).

Radhakrishnan responded to these and related criticisms in a number of studies published between 1908 and 1914[67] — which were later developed at length in *The Hindu View of Life* (1927) and *The Idealist View of Life* (1932). But his initial attempt to directly address these issues is in his MA thesis, *The Ethics of the Vedanta and Its Metaphysical Presuppositions* (published in 1908);[68] Radhakrishnan later wrote that, despite its limitations, "that little essay indicates the general trend of my thought" (Radhakrishnan 1937: 20). In that study and in several articles that appeared soon thereafter, Radhakrishnan takes the view that not only does Hinduism contain a genuine ethics, but it also provides a basis for active moral engagement in the world. The strategy and target of this early work clearly — and perhaps not surprisingly — bears the influence and vocabulary of western Idealism.

In response to the first charge of Hogg — a charge also made by other idealist-influenced European philosophers in India, such as John McKenzie and W.S. Urquhart[69] — Radhakrishnan argues that Hinduism in fact does provide an account of the metaphysical foundations and underpinnings of ethical life. Radhakrishnan acknowledges that "It is true, the Vedanta does not contain an articulate code of morality derived from an acknowledged ethical ideal" (Radhakrishnan 1914a: 168), but this does not mean that it has no principles whatever. According to Radhakrishnan, one can find a Kantian morality of duty for duty's sake in Vedantin ethics (Radhakrishnan 1908a: 75[70]; Radhakrishnan 1911: 474; Radhakrishnan 1914a: 177, Radhakrishnan 1932), though there is more to Hindu Vedanta than that. An idealist ethics in the Hindu tradition gives us real freedom, Radhakrishnan would say, not just a Kantian "empty and unreal" freedom (Radhakrishnan 1908a: 23–4; Radhakrishnan 1911: 470).

---

67 See, for example, Radhakrishnan (1908a), (1914a), (1914b), (1911). For the background on this, see Radhakrishnan (1937). See also Radhakrishnan (1920), (1961), and (1932).

68 Though Radhakrishnan received a second class in his MA in January 1909 [see University of Madras Calendar, 1910: 165], Hogg wrote of Radhakrishnan: "The thesis which he prepared in the second year of his study for this degree shows a remarkable understanding of the main aspects of the philosophical problem, a capacity for handling easily a complex argument besides more than the average mastery of good English."

69 See McKenzie's *Hindu Ethics* (1922), and Urquhart's *Pantheism and the Value of Life* (1919; based on his D.Phil. thesis at Aberdeen).

70 Radhakrishnan writes, for example, "Thus according to both '*Vedanta*' and kant [sic] the highest type of morality consists in doing duty for duty's sake without any personal attachment or hope of a reward" (Radhakrishnan, 1908a: 75; see also 1911: 473–4).

Moreover, Radhakrishnan holds that in Hindu ethics there is a connection between metaphysics and a principle of value, and an "inseparability of the highest value from the truly real" (Radhakrishnan 1932: 16); this is something that one finds in many of the British idealists as well. And, finally, Radhakrishnan insists that his Hindu ethics blends a recognition of the importance of the will and activity of the individual moral agent with an emphasis on the community and the Absolute. Hinduism, then, provides a genuine, idealist ethics.

Although Radhakrishnan holds that ethics has a metaphysical foundation — what this means needs to be explained — it must focus on practice not theory (see Radhakrishnan 1908a: 59; Radhakrishnan 1914a: 172, 174) (i.e., practice, in the sense of activity which aims at religion or spiritual emancipation) — and he writes that "in a very real sense practice *precedes* theory" (Radhakrishnan 1927: 77, emphasis mine). Radhakrishnan says that, like Tagore, he is not especially interested in dogma or abstract doctrine; this is, again, interestingly, also the philosophical view of Hogg and indeed many of the British idealists, concerning religion. And this point, properly understood, addresses the concern about a Hindu (idealist, Vedantin) ethics being quietistic.

What Radhakrishnan means here is that the search for and achievement of spiritual emancipation is a fundamentally moral activity. As he argues in *The Hindu View of Life*, Indian thought reflects a way of life that involves engagement in the world. He writes, in "The Ethics of the Vedanta" (1914): "In the world here and now, the individual inspired by the vision beatific must do his level best to make his small corner of the world happier, nobler, and better" (Radhakrishnan 1914a: 174).[71] The model of the ethical individual is of "the warrior fighting with righteous indignation the battle against the forces of evil and wickedness" (Radhakrishnan 1914a: 174; see 1908a: 91). Morality, then, focuses, not simply on identifying and following certain ethical principles, but on being "adequate to the situation" (Bosanquet 1919: 146).

Radhakrishnan offers an idealist ethics. He writes: "an idealist view finds that the universe has meaning, has value. Ideal values are the dynamic force, the driving power of the universe" (Radhakrishnan 1932: 15). His Hindu Vedantin ethics is "idealist" because, in contrast to the mechanistic and materialist approach of the sciences, it recognises "the supremacy of spirit" in human beings, by which they may have the "immediate intuition of [their] unity with the eternal" (Radhakrishnan 1952a: 484), and by which "an ultimate connection of value and reality is maintained" (Radhakrishnan 1932: 16). "The spiritual status is the essential dignity of man and the origin of his freedom" (Radhakrishnan, 1952a:

---

[71] There is a parallel here with B.N. Seal, who saw 'the Absolute' as something that is pursued as quest rather than dogma; see Seal (1936).

484). It is easy to see from this how Radhakrishnan comes to the view that "the moral spirit ... in the main is identical with the religious" (Radhakrishnan 1914a: 173). As he says later, in "My Search for Truth", "the aim of religion is to attain a knowledge or a vision of God and the aim of ethics is to remake human life into the mould of the unseen" (Radhakrishnan 1937: 21).

What exactly, then, are the metaphysical underpinnings of Radhakrishnan's ethics? What, specifically, is the connection between metaphysics and a principle of value? To begin with, for Radhakrishnan, ethics, the community, and 'the whole' are fundamental to the community. In his 1914 essay on "The Ethics of the Vedanta", Radhakrishnan writes: "moral life is an organism in which every part contributes to the life of the whole. Every rule is justified by its relation to the other rules and its place in the system of morality" (Radhakrishnan 1914a: 178). This 'whole', however, cannot be reduced to any particular community; Radhakrishnan adds: "The finite world is not the absolutely real, for it demands something else on which it depends" (Radhakrishnan 1914b: 441). Thus, on Radhakrishnan's view, the foundation of values is in the Absolute (Radhakrishnan, 1914a: 178)[72] — which, following the Indian tradition, he calls 'Brahman.' What makes a good act good, or a moral act moral, then, is ultimately its relation to the Absolute. (And Radhakrishnan would add that this is characteristic properly only of an absolute idealism — but not a personalistic idealism, which he regards as inconsistent and incomplete (Radhakrishnan, 1920 and 1918).

Yet Radhakrishnan would insist that individuality, too, is essential to ethics. Like Green and Bosanquet, for example, Radhakrishnan holds that an action is good "on account of its inner will", not because of its consequences (Radhakrishnan 1914a: 173; see 1908a: 26); "we must *do* the right whether the right is *done* or not" (see Radhakrishnan 1914a: 182). Radhakrishnan also recognizes that ethics is an individual task, and that individual responsibility is key, insisting that "Personal responsibility is given its due importance" (1914a: 180). Furthermore, virtue is "a function or exercise of the [individual] will" (1914a: 173), and character is "self-created" (1914a: 181). In fact, Radhakrishnan would argue that the Hindu tradition takes personal responsibility more seriously than western traditions; the doctrine of karma shows that there is "a principle governing the universe", by which one's life has a "spiritual continuity" with one's earlier life (Radhakrishnan 1914a: 180), and experiences the effects of it.

---

72 Radhakrishnan writes, for example, that "there can only be one Absolute in morality as in metaphysics" (1914a: 178).

But this recognition of the nature and value of individuality, Radhakrishnan would insist, is not inconsistent with the fundamental character of the community or with absolutism.

To begin with, Radhakrishnan sees no contradiction between the Absolute and individuality. In a familiar idealist idiom, he writes that: "Just as the general exists in the particular, so the Absolute exists in the finite" (Radhakrishnan 1914b: 450), and "the Absolute is not merely the negation of the finite, but is its explanation" (1914b: 450). This, Radhakrishnan would hold, is a consequence of the spiritual nature of human beings and of reality. Moreover, there is a drive within the finite individual to go beyond its finitude; "Man is a part of God aspiring to be the whole" (Radhakrishnan 1914a: 169). This is, Radhakrishnan believes, characteristic of our efforts as "self-creators"; "There is in the self of man, at the very centre of his being, something deeper than the intellect, which is akin to the Supreme" (Radhakrishnan 1932: 103). By emphasising the relation to the absolute, however, "we are not ... abolishing our individuality but transforming it into a conscious term of the universal being, an utterance of the transcendent divine" (Radhakrishnan 1940: 37). Radhakrishnan sees this feature of the individual echoed in the Hindu dictum *Tat tvam asi*—That thou art—i.e., that the individual self (Atman) is the Absolute (Brahman); this is not very far, if at all, from Bosanquet's remark: "[i]f I possessed myself entirely, I should be the Absolute" (Bosanquet 1918: 85).

To show the compatibility of individuality with the community and the Absolute, Radhakrishnan would also remind his audience of the social character of the individual—that individuals are fundamentally social beings. He writes, for example, that "Individuality is attained not through an escape from limitations but through the willing acceptance of obligations" (Radhakrishnan 1940: 68). Given Radhakrishnan's "metaphysical monism" (Radhakrishnan 1914a: 168–9), the relation to society may appear to be much stronger than one finds it in many other idealists; for Radhakrishnan, individuals are only 'modifications' of Brahman (the sole reality) (Radhakrishnan 1914a: 168). But Radhakrishnan does not suggest "the individual [is] to be absorbed in the society" (Radhakrishnan 1914a: 177; see 1908a: 61). Rather, he sees a Vedantin idealism as simply "press[ing] home the organic nature of society which would do justice to both individual independence and social solidarity" (Radhakrishnan 1914a: 177).

Such a metaphysical account of the relation of the individual to the Absolute does not undermine, Radhakrishnan believes, our individuality or our relations with others and with the world. There is, Radhakrishnan maintains, no ultimate separation between the Absolute (Brahman) and the world. Brahman "is not apart from the world, —it is the world" (Radhakrishnan 1914b: 437), the finite world itself is "a real modification of Brahman" (1914b: 444). What this also reminds us, Radhakrishnan holds, is that "The world *is* the spirit" (1914b: 439), and that individuals are ultimately "spirit" as well.

In short, then, for Radhakrishnan Hinduism has an ethics—an ethics that is founded on a theory of the Absolute—and what unites the community and the individual, and provides unity to moral life is, for Radhakrishnan, not (merely) a temporal "common good", but this Absolute.

In his early writings, Radhakrishnan provides an extensive account of the "moral life" and of idealistic ethics in general. Because this Absolute is not separate from or independent of the world of finite beings and their actions, Radhakrishnan's ethics is—although it may sound paradoxical—immanentist. This is the position of Absolute idealism (see Radhakrishnan 1920: 139-40), and it is also, Radhakrishnan maintains, that of the Vedas; the notion of there being a transcendent reality, and that "this world" is "unreal" or "Maya", is—Radhakrishnan claims—a later addition to Hinduism (Radhakrishnan 1914b: 434). Even the law of karma and the occurrence of an afterlife are principles that Radhakrishnan would regard as characteristic of "this world". Thus, there is no question of morality being dependent upon some force or principle external to or independent of the world.

Moreover, for Radhakrishnan, the moral life is "a life of reason" (Radhakrishnan 1914a: 169). And while Radhakrishnan does not say, unambiguously, what reason is[73]—he has a rather broad understanding of the word—how such a life is "rational" can be seen in several ways.

To begin with, Radhakrishnan holds that ethical life is rational in that human beings have "to throw off the yoke of the passions and rise to rational freedom" (Radhakrishnan [1911: 468]; see 1908a: 25). Now, this 'rational freedom' does not exclude feeling, emotion or intuition. Indeed, Radhakrishnan notes that "Intuitive knowledge [which provides us with knowledge of the Absolute] is not non-rational; it is only non-conceptual" (Radhakrishnan 1932: 153). Besides, feelings and reason can act together; for example, Radhakrishnan writes that "Reason makes us act on a feeling of the unity of the whole human race" (Radhakrishnan 1914a: 170). But Radhakrishnan does insist that feelings, desires, and emotions be "regulated" (Radhakrishnan 1914a: 171), in the sense that "demands of the lower self... have to be subordinated" to those of one's 'higher self' (Radhakrishnan 1911: 472). 'Rational freedom' is to be understood as what Radhakrishnan calls "integral experience" (Radhakrishnan 1932: 147).

There is a second way in which one can see the moral life as rational; moral activity involves "the realisation of reason in the world"

---

73 Robert W. Browning identifies at least 3 different senses of reason, though it tends to be identified with capacities used in science. See Browning (1952: 238ff).

(Radhakrishnan 1914a: 179). Ethical life is rational, then, so far as it aims at coherence in ethical belief and ethical practice. Radhakrishnan writes that "Our whole moral life must be a rational unity" (Radhakrishnan 1914a: 179). As we have seen above, this involves one's "lower self" being subordinated to the demands of reason or what we may call our "higher self", resulting in a deeper, genuine unity of the person, but also in a deeper unity of the person with the community and, ultimately, the Absolute.

Third, Radhakrishnan holds that the moral life is rational because all of reality is rational — understanding that this is not to imply that (conceptual) thought is "constitutive of reality" (Radhakrishnan 1932: 151).[74] And so the moral life involves acting in a way in which one brings to fruition the 'reason' that is already present in the world. Thus any measure of international order is based on reason. This reflects Radhakrishnan's view that a consistently rational approach leads "inevitably" to Absolute Idealism (Radhakrishnan 1920: vii).[75]

The moral life that Radhakrishnan describes is not only rational, but one that aims at human flourishing. And so Radhakrishnan's ethics may, in a way, be said to be one of "self-realisation" (Radhakrishnan 1914a: 175) — a realisation of and by the self that involves growth and development — though one needs to be careful about how this is supported.

Radhakrishnan writes of there being a cosmic and thus a human evolution — though not in a purely naturalistic sense; this looks very close to Bosanquet's notion of a "nisus towards a whole" (Bosanquet 1912: xx). There are driving forces in the world — these are "ideal values" — and in human beings their end or telos is flourishing — what Hinduism calls Anand or Eternal Bliss. There is, then, a drive to realise one's self — i.e., what Indian philosophy calls Atman — but in a way that is consistent with ultimate reality (Brahman). On Radhakrishnan's view, the presence of this drive shows that humanity has a "destiny that is not limited to the sensible world" (Radhakrishnan 1932: 15). Thus, for Radhakrishnan, there is a teleological character to the moral life — but this is because there is a teleological character to humanity, and, indeed, to all of reality.

It is important to recognise that, for Radhakrishnan, self-realisation is not just focussed on individual selves. The self-realisation that Radhakrishnan describes is not simply the realisation of an isolated self but (as many British idealists also held) of a community of selves — and of a 'universal' self. It is the self-realisation of humanity as a whole. Self-realisation, then, is a "universal spiritual emancipation" — what

---

[74] Radhakrishnan writes: "Reality becomes thought incarnate, the idea made flesh. It is an all-inclusive rational experience or mind. The world process is a fragment of a rational process, an unfinished syllogism…" Radhakrishnan (1932: 152).

[75] See also Suda (1966: 329): "In other words, the conclusion at which Radhakrishnan arrives in this volume is that on rational grounds Absolute Idealism is inevitable."

Radhakrishnan calls the "*brahmaloka*" or the "Kingdom of God"[76] — which is also another expression of a principle of unity. (Some parallels could be drawn here with Bradley's move from an ethics of individual self-realisation to that of an "ideal morality".)

While this process of self-realisation follows and reflects rational principles, Radhakrishnan sees it as leading one to religious consciousness. The aim of ethics and the moral life, then, ultimately leads to the aim of religion and to religious consciousness. It is the moral life — and the Absolute that unifies it — which enable a person "to make his whole nature divine" (Radhakrishnan 1914a: 169). But this process, Radhakrishnan would insist, remains resolutely rational. There is no conflict between reason and religion. Indeed, in a later essay, Radhakrishnan writes that "Religion must establish itself as a rational way of being" and that "religion must express itself in reasonable thought" (Radhakrishnan 1937: 20).

Self-realisation — this universal spiritual emancipation or *brahmaloka* — not only involves others but, he writes, "consists in *living for* others" (Radhakrishnan 1914a: 175, emphasis mine) — and thus implies an obligation of service to others; Radhakrishnan would say that this is part of one's *dharma* or duty. Self-realisation, then, serves as the ground for the "ideal" of "social service" (1914a: 176). This principle of universal spiritual emancipation also reflects, Radhakrishnan would say, a recognition of the fundamental equality of human beings, for "social service" involves serving *all* members of society; Radhakrishnan writes that every individual is one's coequal (1914a: 169) and is to be treated as an end and not as a means (see 1914a: 176).

But how is this obligation of service to others to be carried out? Radhakrishnan is well aware that we live in contexts that limit possibilities to what we can do — to serve and, if necessary, to sacrifice (1914a: 181). Yet serve others we must; "The ideal of unselfish service of humanity is the only absolute moral rule which ought never to be broken" (1914a: 178). Service to others, then, requires attempting to carry out, as far as one can, the duties determined by the "highest ideals" and the common good (see 1914a: 177) but, concretely (and more importantly), it also involves carrying out one's "particular duties" — i.e., performing one's 'station and its duties' (1914a: 176). For, Radhakrishnan writes, "Every man has a certain station to occupy and a certain function to fulfill in the social economy" (1914a: 176), and that it is "by every man performing his assigned task" that "the kingdom of God may be planted on earth" (1914a: 170).[77]

---

76 I am indebted for this interpretation here to Sullivan (2000).
77 This can explain in some way how Radhakrishnan long retained the notion of caste — as paradoxical as it may seem — as something based on "social needs and individual actions" (Radhakrishnan [1948: 129]). Radhakrishnan also holds, interestingly, that the Upanisads promote universal brotherhood, as distinct from the Vedas which promote caste (Radhakrishnan [1908a: 7, 51]; see [1908c: 29]).

Self-realisation, i.e., working towards universal spiritual emancipation, involves fulfilling these duties—which promote the development of virtues but may also involve self-sacrifice (Radhakrishnan 1908a: 61; 1914a: 173). Still, this is far from the usual standard of social service; when called for and when possible, it may involve going beyond the requirements of one's 'station.'

Interestingly, self-realisation and spiritual emancipation require openness. Paradoxically, perhaps—given the description of the absolutist character of Radhakrishnan's ethics and of his idealist philosophy as a whole—ethical life and the moral end must be *open* to new experience and new knowledge; "an idealist view of life is not expressed in any one pattern" (Radhakrishnan 1932: 16). Its key feature, to paraphrase B.N. Seal, is quest rather than dogma.

Although Radhakrishnan's idealist ethics is 'open' in this way and although he insists on room for "the individual's private judgement" (Radhakrishnan 1914a: 176), it is objective. According to Radhakrishnan, Vedantin morality reflects "an objective system of right" (1914a: 176). "It is many-coloured and its forms are varied; yet underneath all the variations and oppositions there are certain common fundamental assumptions that show them all to be products of the same spirit" (Radhakrishnan 1932: 16). This should not be surprising because, for Radhakrishnan, there is a 'right' view of the world. Recall that the foundation of values is not individual choice or desire or preference, but human nature (i.e., the kinds of beings human beings are) and, ultimately, in the Absolute. And Radhakrishnan insists that we know this. "Knowledge", he writes, "is an organic part of the spiritual good of humanity" (Radhakrishnan 1914a: 172) and it "enables us to take a right view of things and our place in the world" (1914a: 172). It "enables us to see the oneness of things […] gives us the power to recognize the brotherhood of all, and points out the necessity of merging the individual will in the collective will" (1914a: 172).

This ethics, Radhakrishnan argues, bears not only on the religious and spiritual, but also on the political; Radhakrishnan turned explicitly to these issues in the early 1930s and thereafter. In a short essay, Radhakrishnan writes that "religion includes faith in human brotherhood, and politics is the most effective means of rendering it into visible form. Politics is but applied religion" (Kabir 1952: 706). And so ethics and social and political philosophy must recognise what human beings are—'spiritual' individuals who, while 'discrete,' are also integrally connected with one another and with the whole of reality. Given Radhakrishnan's views on self-realisation, then, it is clear that all human beings need freedom to

---

There are very few mentions of caste in his earliest work—and none in Radhakrishnan (1908b), (1910b), (1916b), and related texts—and he seems rather ambivalent about the matter. While he defends the notion of caste in *The Hindu View of Life* (1927), he seems to reject it by 1947 and the time of *Religion and Society*. For an extensive discussion, see Wadia (1952: 766ff).

develop. And, given his notion of universal spiritual emancipation, this freedom must be a freedom of all. Because of this need for freedom, Radhakrishnan concludes that "in this imperfect world, democratic government is the most satisfactory" (Radhakrishnan 1944: 40). For Radhakrishnan, democracy balances individual freedom and social responsibility. It recognises the value of the individual and that all individuals are fundamentally and ultimately equal, but also that individuals are essentially social (see Wadia [1952: 775–6]).

Radhakrishnan's insistence on the duty of universal spiritual emancipation reflects this principle of human equality. And for this duty to be fulfilled, there needs to be a broad system of positive right. Radhakrishnan admired Marxism for its egalitarianism, but rejected its "atheistic conception of ultimate reality, its naturalistic view of man and its disregard of the sacredness of personality" (Radhakrishnan 1948: 25). Individuals are 'spiritual' as well as physical or material. Thus, Radhakrishnan's ethics favours a politics that is social democratic—and open to religion and the spiritual—but not Marxist.

Radhakrishnan's ethics are rooted in and depend on a metaphysics, and in his early writings he worked out the presuppositions of such a metaphysics, making, however, few references to social and political events in India. Nevertheless, Radhakrishnan's ethics offered a challenge to many dominant views. It drew on principles congruent with British idealism, reaffirmed the strength of the Hindu tradition, but also came to challenge existing practice in India.

2.3 Conclusion

A number of philosophers in India in the first half of the 20th century engaged—and sometimes adopted—an idealist view that was broadly that of the British idealists. The place of British idealism in modern Indian philosophy should not, of course, be exaggerated. Few scholars embraced it wholeheartedly. Nevertheless, many of them did make use of it, a prime example being Sarvepalli Radhakrishnan. Radhakrishnan's idealist ethics was expressed through his interpretation and defence of Hindu Vedantin ethics—a defence given initially in response to critics of Hinduism who had been influenced by personalistic idealism. But his was a contested interpretation. Radhakrishnan's reading of Hinduism (especially, of the Vedas) placed it close to Absolute Idealism, and for this and other reasons it was challenged by Hindu scholars.

There are several parallels of Radhakrishnan's ethics with the ethics of some of the British idealists; Radhakrishnan himself recognises the influences here. As he says in an autobiographical essay, "among the Western thinkers, the writings of Plato, Plotinus and Kant, and those of Bradley and Bergson influenced me a great deal" (Radhakrishnan 1952b: 10). And in his earliest work in ethics, there are numerous references to Kant and Hegel, but also to contemporary personalistic idealists. In *The Ethics of the Vedanta and its Metaphysical Presuppositions*, for example, there are 20 references to Kant, 14 to Hegel, but also 12 to the American personalistic idealist George Holmes Howison[78] (specifically, to his *The Limits of Evolution*).[79] Radhakrishnan's preferred view, as noted above, is that of absolute idealism, and he finds several similarities between it and classical Indian thought.

For example, the idealist emphasis on action in this world — found in Green, Bosanquet, Henry Jones, and others — is reflected in Radhakrishnan's Vedantin ethics, which aims at building the kingdom of God on earth as well as at universal spiritual emancipation. Radhakrishnan also defends the view that human beings are, importantly, both 'spiritual' and social beings — that they are members of a moral community — and that self-realisation and fulfillment are possible only through service to others. Such views appear, as well, in Green's *Prolegomena to Ethics*, particularly in Book III, a text on which — when Radhakrishnan was a student at Madras — philosophy students were examined. Furthermore, Radhakrishnan emphasises that the ethical life, and one's effort to realise one's true self, are connected to the nature of ultimate reality. For the Vedantin Hindu, this is the search to realise Atman as Brahman; for a philosopher like Bosanquet — and indeed for many of the idealists — this is the realisation of the individual in the Absolute. Radhakrishnan's ethics of the Vedanta, then, is clearly an idealist ethics that reflects, and rests on, a theory of the Absolute, and that makes an "ultimate connection of value and reality" (Radhakrishnan 1932: 16) — a connection which Radhakrishnan sees in both the western and the Indian traditions. Ethical life, therefore, is not fundamentally distinct from religion. But such religion is not one of doctrine or dogma, and it is also not otherworldly. Radhakrishnan writes, in *The Hindu View of Life*, of "the unity of religion not in a common creed but in a common quest" (Radhakrishnan 1961: 42). Radhakrishnan later extended this notion of a quest for universal spiritual emancipation, and brought it to bear on his social and political thought.

Yet despite these similarities with British idealist thought, Radhakrishnan insists that "I cannot say that I am a follower of any" philosopher, that his "thought does not comply with any fixed traditional pattern", and that his views "proceeded from [his] own experience" (Radhakrishnan 1952a: 10). Some scholars have agreed. C.E.M. Joad, in his *Counter Attack from the East* (1933), saw in Radhakrishnan "a new synthesis of thought expressing

---

78   George Holmes Howison (1834–1917) was author of *The Limits of Evolution* (1901; 2d ed. rev. and enl., 1905). For general information on Howison, see Buckham and Stratton (1934).

79   There are, interestingly, few references to contemporary British Idealists in this work — e.g., none to Pringle Pattison (Hogg's teacher), Green or Bosanquet, only two to Caird, and just one to Bradley, McTaggart, Watson, Spencer, and Sidgwick. One has, of course, to take account of the fact that Radhakrishnan was very parsimonious in his references to contemporary scholars.

itself in religion, politics, and civilization" (Gopal 1989: 103).[80] And it is evident that Radhakrishnan's ethics is neither a straightforward development of 'European' idealist ethics nor a mere recapitulation and defence of Vedanta ethics. It is, as he says, the result of an attempt to think through the problems of ethics and values, drawing on both Western and Indian thought.

Still, it is noteworthy that Radhakrishnan was able to bring western and Indian idealism into contact on many points of ethical theory. He does not do so, however, through practical issues; indeed, although Radhakrishnan's moral and social philosophy has strong practical concerns, his work on ethics — especially his early writings — does not focus, for example, on social problems. Rather, he concentrates on the source of ethics and ethical principle — on the metaphysics of the Vedanta and of absolute idealism — and, only secondarily, explores their implications for practical questions. From what we have seen, these theoretical concepts and principles in idealism offered both a means to bring Radhakrishnan's Hinduism into contact with the philosophical views of his teachers, and a way to help develop and articulate his own ethics and philosophy.

Radhakrishnan's early education gave him a firm grounding in western idealism, and as he turned to the Indian tradition to engage western views, he was able to develop his own version of Vedantic idealism. His writings, then, exhibit the influence of western thought, but also draw on the Indian traditions in order to defend a broad version of absolute idealism.

Thus, it is plausible to see Radhakrishnan as not only building on, but continuing, the British idealist traditions. By this emphasis on ethics as social and based in the community and yet, at the same time, attentive to the value of the self; by this recognition and acknowledgement of the value of diversity, and yet the necessity of bringing the social and the individual together through a common good and an Absolute; by calling for self-realisation, and yet recognising that this realisation involves and includes all of humanity, Radhakrishnan continues a project that was not far from that of his teachers and of his teachers' teachers. Radhakrishnan offers an idealist ethics that exhibits a respect for the individual and its spiritual nature, but also for the community and for underlying metaphysical principles. Yet Radhakrishnan's own views were being developed at a time when idealism in Britain was under significant attack and so, in part, constitute a reply to these challenges.

One should take care not to exaggerate the influence of European, particularly British, idealism on Radhakrishnan's work, given that his views are rooted in and draw on India's own idealist traditions. Nevertheless there was such an influence, and given his own example of bringing western and Indian thought together through a "comparative philosophy", it is

---

80 See Joad (1933: 56 and 116).

not surprising that British idealism had a legacy that outlasted that which it had in Britain.

3. Concluding Remarks

This chapter deals with the moral, social and — by extension — political philosophy of British idealism as introduced far beyond its 'home' — in South Africa and India. This 'migration' is particularly interesting for a number of reasons: it shows how British idealism responded and adapted to the challenges raised against it in the early 20th century, in an environment that was multicultural and pluralistic; it reveals the practical contributions of British idealism to ethics and political philosophy; and — by virtue of its flourishing outside of its place of origin — it provides some insight into the nature of that idealism as well.

In the preceding pages, I have focused on two of the best known 'products' of this British idealism — R.F.A. Hoernlé and Sarvepalli Radhakrishnan — leading philosophers, in their own right. Both Hoernlé and Radhakrishnan present us with an ethics that is based on, or influenced by, British idealism.

Radhakrishnan and Hoernlé called themselves idealists, indeed, absolute idealists, and there are important similarities in their views. Both were metaphysicians, and saw a relation between reality and value. Both were to be actively engaged in public affairs. Both saw idealism as based in experience, but as requiring one to move beyond appearances. And both brought that idealism to bear on current issues and, in the process, articulated an ethics and a social and political philosophy.

Nevertheless, the ways in which British idealism engaged philosophy in South Africa and India differed. Hoernlé brought it to bear on ethical and social questions of race, education, and participation in the politics and the economy of a multi-ethnic and multicultural state. But in so doing, not only advantages but limitations came to the fore. Radhakrishnan's writings illustrate a different kind of encounter. For Radhakrishnan, British idealism and British idealist ethics provided not only an opportunity to address issues in contemporary ethics, but also a stimulus and a vocabulary to address criticisms of Indian philosophy. As a consequence, Radhakrishnan was able to provide both an apologetic for Indian thought — that arguably made it more intelligible to both an Indian and a non-Indian audience — but also an example of what he came to call a "comparative philosophy". In both cases, British idealism was seen as providing resources to respond to problems, and it met with a measure of success.

In South Africa, idealism was — so to speak — imported, though it was imported into an intellectual culture that was largely western European in origin, and had strong affinities with Scottish Presbyterianism and Calvinism, and this clearly facilitated its reception. The challenge, however, was that it encountered a very different social and political reality than what one found in Britain; South Africa was a multiethnic and multicultural nation. Idealists like Hoernlé recognized that this 'reality' did not allow an automatic borrowing of ideas from Europe—or, more precisely, that any one who wished to borrow such had to take account of the fact that their expression would need to be different in order to fit a reality quite unlike the one in which these ideas were first articulated, and that the practical implications might be different, too.

What Hoernlé held was required for in that situation is what I have called an "ethics of liberty." To address the challenges of a multi-racial society, he drew on an (idealistic) ethics and social philosophy that was 'open'—which acknowledged the existence and value of plurality and diversity—while, at the same time, rested on something objective—what he called "underlying patterns of reality." Indeed, we see efforts to meet these challenges not only in Hoernlé but in other philosophers influenced by idealism, such as A.R. Lord and Andrew Murray—though not always with the same progressive character.

British idealist ethics could have a place in South Africa because it fit the dominant European culture, but also the pluralistic context. It addressed questions about diversity and openness while emphasizing unity and community.

The presence of British Idealism in India was different, in that idealism—in the broad sense—was not an imported theory; it had, in the tradition of Advaita Vedanta, a long history and it could engage local (i.e., Indian) thought more directly. Yet it, too, had its challenges. At the time, Advaita Vedanta was far from the leading of the six orthodox (*Astika*) schools of Indian philosophy; indeed, the importance of Advaita Vedanta in early 20th century India is arguably due to its affinities with some schools of European Idealism. Nevertheless, what was sought from British idealism was a way of defending the value of Indian thought from western critique, but also a way of expressing that thought in a modern idiom that made it accessible to Indians and non-Indians alike, challenging the increasing presence of naturalism and rationalism in the culture, addressing new ideas and allowing new interpretations of classical Indian philosophy, enabling a better understanding of Indian ethics in the modern world, and providing a way in which Indian philosophers might have a place in the broader philosophical community.

The consequence was that in Radhakrishnan's work—and in that of his contemporaries and successors—western thought was brought into contact with Indian thought in a fruitful way.[81] What Radhakrishnan was able

---

81 As just one example of this, consider the 1936 volume *Contemporary Indian Philosophy*, co-edited by Muirhead and Radhakrishnan, in which half of the contributors were sympathetic to idealism.

to show was that within Indian thought one finds ideas that are at least on a par with, if not serve to develop, corresponding insights within European idealist traditions—and that while Indian thought needed "to incorporate elements from Western thought" (Raju 1952: 523), the reverse was true as well. And we see similar views in other philosophers influenced by British idealism—such as A.C. Mukerji, N.C. Mukerji, G.K. Malkani, and P.T. Raju.

What Radhakrishnan focused on were issues related to moral and social philosophy—and he offered an ethics that emphasised the duty to "universal spiritual emancipation". The goal of such an ethics was not just the emancipation of the individual; it was rooted in, and oriented towards, humanity as spiritual beings and as members of a spiritual community. Such an ethics of duty—of duty to the community—required a fulfillment of the obligations of one's station—and, of course, for Radhakrishnan, there is no contradiction between "emancipation" and doing one's duty. But such an emancipation also requires responding appropriately to novelty and new cultural contact, and being open to different cultures and traditions, which could be expressed in different "patterns of life". And still, Radhakrishnan would insist, it is an objectivist ethics, based on an account of human nature and, ultimately, the Absolute. Radhakrishnan's ethics—sometimes called a "spiritual humanism"—is, then, an idealist ethics, but it is neither a mere interpretation of Vedantin ethics nor an application or extension of European ethics, and it reflects themes characteristic of both.

There are, of course, historical and sociological reasons—the cultural conditions at the time, the dominance of western European thought, the colonial systems of education and administration, the character and kind of religious affiliation of educational institutions, and the like[82]—that also bear on how idealism could take hold and, in varying ways, succeed or flourish in India and South Africa. But this success may also say something about the character of British idealism, and particularly its moral and social philosophy.

In Britain, the idealists called for change, but a constructive change. They sought individual and collective transformation and recognised the importance of acting in the here and now—i.e., they offered a view that was able to engage difference in a practical, yet principled (teleological), way, and was attentive to the particulars of an ethical situation without seeing every situation as sui generis and so tending to relativism.

British idealism also recognised the importance of local practices, traditions and cultures, institutions, and the social character of the individual, and sought not to negate them but to draw on them in the articulation of its applied moral, social, and political thought. Hoernlé, for example, notes

---

[82] See, for example, Gilbert (1972) and (1973); Shah (1973); Bhagavan (2001) and (2003); Ashby and Anderson (1966); Dickinson (1971).

that his synoptic approach starts with a willingness to enter into the local environment—into the life around oneself—and "share it from the inside, rather than to stand outside as a mere spectator or even to reject it as foreign" (Hoernlé 1925: 138), and philosophers as diverse as Bosanquet and Henry Jones insisted that philosophy begins with experience—that it begins with "the world of fact." But they also held that the world is "full of contradiction" which "point beyond themselves" (Bosanquet 2003: 151) to ideas, principles, and order that is already implicit or present in an inchoate way within that world.

That idealism was, arguably, also 'open' to religious and cultural difference; it allowed different ways of expressing the spiritual dimension of individuals and cultures, held that various traditions could make a genuine contribution to the whole (i.e., no account is a priori excluded), and was certainly more open to difference and diversity than other models available at that time (e.g., utilitarianism)—while, at the same time, providing a principle of philosophical unity and of political community where the rights and needs of individuals were set in balance with one's duties and the common good, and contributing to a legitimizing discourse for challenging 'monolithic' views of international culture.

Finally, British idealism had a strong practical character; it encouraged dialogue within other cultures, and provided a means of engaging other cultures—which Hoernlé employed in his synoptic view, and Radhakrishnan in his 'comparative' approach to philosophy and comparative philosophy.

Idealism, as an influential school of thought, lasted longer in India and South Africa than in Britain—well into the 1950s—and, outside of universities, perhaps longer still. Its decline in influence in India and South Africa may, indeed, have been inevitable, but there is no evidence that it was for any of the reasons often given for explaining how idealism came to lose its hold in Britain.[83] But its ability to respond to local concerns, and to

---

83   There are many reasons that have been given for the decline of the influence of idealism in Britain. Some were broadly "political"; L.T. Hobhouse and others saw "idealism" as reflecting principles that led to war and, specifically, to the First World War (see Hobhouse 1918) and, as Leslie Paul notes, "[p]erhaps, too, the collapse of idealism as a great school of philosophy in England was not unconnected with the First World War. This threw a fierce light on German scholarship" (See Paul [1953: 267]). The association of idealists like Bosanquet with social conservatism (e.g., views on the poor laws) and, by extension, with the status quo, led to many of them—implausibly, given their political views, being accused of political conservatism. See Hobson (1909: 197). Hobhouse (1918: 24), MacIver, and Russell—and, more recently, John Morrow (1984: 108) who describes their work as more "illiberal" than that of Green. According to Stefan Collini, until the 1920s, "[a]n attack on the neo-Hegelian theory of the state became almost a rite de passage for the budding social scientist" (see Collini, (1978: 27, n. 27).

There were 'philosophical' reasons as well. Paul also notes "[a]bout the time of Bosanquet, the Absolute finally blew up. Perhaps there is a parallel to be found in the reaction of the fourteenth century to the debates of the schoolmen: as then, speculation was exhausted. No further progress seemed possible along this road…" (Paul, 1953: 266). Some hold that the rigor of early 20th century Cambridge and Oxford analysts, such as Moore, Russell, Wittgenstein,

flourish, is suggestive. For this invites the prospect that, should one today have an interest in a universal or a global or a cross cultural ethics, or even in a fruitful dialogue concerning ethics across cultures, one might turn to idealism as a starting point.

References

Armour, Leslie and Elizabeth Trott (1981), *The Faces of Reason: Philosophy in English Canada, 1850–1950* (Waterloo, ON: Wilfrid Laurier University Press).
Ashby, Eric and Mary Anderson (1966), *Universities: British, Indian, African; a study in the ecology of higher education* (London, Weidenfeld & Nicolson).
Balasubramanian, R. (1969), "From Green to Gandhi: A Study of their views on War, the role of the Individual and the way to peace", *Bulletin of the Institute of Traditional Cultures, Madras* (January-June 1969).
Bhagavan, Manu (2001), "Demystifying the 'Ideal Progressive': Resistance Through Mimicked Modernity in Princely Baroda, 1900–1913", *Modern Asian Studies*, 35, pp. 385–409.
Bhagavan, Manu (2003), *Sovereign Spheres: Princes, Education, and Empire in Colonial India* (Oxford University Press).
Bosanquet, Bernard (1912), *The Principle of Individuality and Value* (London: Macmillan).
Bosanquet, Bernard (1918), "Do Finite Individuals Possess a Substantive or Adjectival Mode of Being?", *Proceedings of the Aristotelian Society*, 18 (1917-8), pp. 479–506; reprinted in H. Wildon Carr (ed.) *Life and Finite Individuality* [*Proceedings of the Aristotelian Society*, supp. vol. 1], pp. 75–102; 179–94.
Bosanquet, Bernard (1919), *Some Suggestions in Ethics*, 2nd ed. (London: Macmillan).
Bosanquet, Bernard (2001), *The Philosophical Theory of the State and Related Essays* (1899; 4th ed. 1923), ed. William Sweet and Gerald F. Gaus (South Bend, IN: St Augustine's Press).
Bosanquet, Bernard (2003), "Idealism in Social Work" (1899), reprinted in William Sweet (ed.), *Essays in Philosophy and Social Policy 1883–1922* (Bristol: Thoemmes Press), vol. 3, pp. 149–60.
Boucher, David (1990), "Practical Hegelianism: Henry Jones's Lecture Tour of Australia", *Journal of the History of Ideas*, 51, pp. 423–52.
Bradley, F.H. (1999), *The Collected Works of F.H. Bradley*, ed. C.A. Keene and W.J. Mander (Bristol: Thoemmes).
Browning, Robert W. (1952), "Reason and Types of Intuition in Radhakrishnan's Philosophy", in Paul Arthur Schilpp (ed.), *The Philosophy of Sarvepalli Radhakrishnan* (New York: Tudor), pp. 173–277.
Buckham, John Wright and George Malcolm Stratton (1934), *George Holmes Howison: philosopher and teacher; a selection from his writings, with a biographical sketch* (Berkeley: University of California Press).
Collini, Stefan (1978), "Sociology and Idealism in Britain: 1880–1920", *Archives européennes de sociologie*, 19, pp. 3–50.
Conradie, Anna-Louize (1980), "Republic of South Africa", in John R. Burr (ed.), *Handbook of World Philosophy: Contemporary Developments Since 1945* (Westport, CT: Greenwood Press).
D'Andrade, J.C.P. (1952), *The Philosophy of Life* (Bombay: Orient Longmans).
Dickinson, Richard. D.N. (1971), *The Christian College in Developing India: A Sociological Inquiry* (Bombay and London: Oxford University Press).

and Ayer, exposed the vagueness and ambiguity of British idealism—though the contemporary fascination with the work of Bradley and McTaggart belies this.

Some have simply pointed to the fact that many of the leading figures in idealism (Bosanquet, Bradley—but also R.B. Haldane, H.W.J. Hetherington, J.B. Baillie, and, to an extent, Henry Jones) spent relatively little time in teaching, and, of those who did, many of their students did not pursue university careers, but left the academy to engage in practical work. Three of the major idealists—Bosanquet, Bradley, and McTaggart all died within 3 years of one another in the mid 1920s.

Duvenage, Pieter (2001), "Is There a South African Philosophical Tradition?", *APA Newsletter on International Cooperation*, 1, pp. 112-7.
Findlay, J.N. (1985), "My Life", in R.S. Cohen, R.M. Martin, and M. Westphal (eds.) *Studies in the Philosophy of J. N. Findlay* (Albany, NY: SUNY Press); see also http://www.jnfindlay.com/ findlay/biographical/index.html
Forsyth, T.M. (1929), "The Significance of Holism", *South African Journal of Science*, 26, pp. 945-8.
Gibson, W.R. [William Ralph] Boyce (1904), *Philosophical Introduction to Ethics; an advocacy of the spiritual principle in ethics, from the point of view of personal idealism* (London: S. Sonnenschein).
Gilbert, Irene (1972), "The Indian Academic Profession: The Origins of a Transition of Subordination", *Minerva*, 10, pp. 384-411.
Gilbert, Irene (1973), "Tradition, Adaptation, and Initiative", *Minerva*, 11, pp. 140-7.
Gopal, Sarvepalli (1989), *Radhakrishnan: A Biography* (New Delhi: Oxford University Press).
Grave, S.A. (1978), *The History of Philosophy in Australia* (St. Lucia, Qld: University of Queensland Press).
Halbfass, Wilhelm (1988), *India and Europe: an essay in understanding* (Albany, NY: State University of New York Press).
Haldar, Hiralal (1927), *Neo-Hegelianism* (London: Heath Cranton).
Haldar, Hiralal (1936), "Realistic Idealism", in S. Radhakrishnan and J.H. Muirhead (eds.), *Contemporary Indian Philosophy* (London: Allen and Unwin), pp. 313-31.
Hinman, E.L. (1921), "Modern Idealism and the Logos Teaching " [APA Presidential address], *Philosophical Review*, 30, pp. 333-51.
Hirai, Atsuko (1979), "Self-realisation and Common Good: T.H. Green in Meiji Ethical Thought", *Journal of Japanese Studies*, 5, pp. 107-36.
Hirai, Atsuko (1982), "Thomas Hill Green in Modern East Asia, with special reference to the thought of Mao Tse-tung", in Graciela de la Lama (ed.), *El Colegio de Mexico, 30th International Congress of Human Sciences in Asia and North Africa [1976]*, vol. 4 China (Mexico: El Colegio de Mexico), pp. 145-63.
Hobhouse, L.T. (1918), *The Metaphysical Theory of the State* (London: Allen & Unwin; New York: Macmillan).
Hobson, J.A. (1909), *The Crisis of Liberalism: New Issues of Democracy* (London: King)
Hoernlé, R.F.A. (1912-13), "The Analysis of Volition", *Proceedings of the Aristotelian Society*, 12, pp. 156-189.
Hoernlé, R.F.A. (1916), tr. (with A. Winifred Hoernlé), R. Steiner, *The Philosophy of Freedom: a modern philosophy of life developed by scientific methods* (London & New York: Putnam's); rev. under title *The Philosophy of Spiritual Activity*, 1922.
Hoernlé, R.F.A. (1919), "Bernard Bosanquet's Philosophy of the State", *Political Science Quarterly*, 34, pp. 609-31.
Hoernlé, R.F.A. (1920), *Studies in Contemporary Metaphysics* (New York: Harcourt, Brace and Howe).
Hoernlé, R.F.A. (1923), *Matter, Life, Mind, and God: Five Lectures on Contemporary Tendencies of Thought* (New York: Harcourt, Brace).
Hoernlé, R.F.A. (1925), "On the Way to a Synoptic Philosophy", in J.H. Muirhead (ed.), *Contemporary British Philosophy*, Second Series (London: The Macmillian company), pp. 129-156.
Hoernlé, R.F.A. (1927), *Idealism as a Philosophy* (New York: George H. Doran).
Hoernlé, R.F.A. (1937), "Differences in culture and morals", in E.G. Nalherbe [with the assistance of J.J.G. Carson and J.D. Rheinallt Jones] (eds.), *Educational adaptations in a changing society: report of the South African Education Conference, held in Cape Town and Johannesburg in July 1934 under the auspices of the New Education Fellowship*, (Cape Town: Juta), ch. XV, pp. 413-16.
Hoernlé, R.F.A. (1939), *South African Native Policy and the Liberal Spirit* (Cape Town: University of Cape Town).
Hoernlé, R.F.A. (1941), "Review of John Elof Boodin, *The Social Mind: Foundations of Social Philosophy*", *Mind*, 50, pp. 393-401.

Hoernlé, R.F.A. (1945), *Race and Reason*, (ed.) I. D. MacCrone (Johannesburg: Witwatersrand University Press).
Hoernlé, R.F.A. (1952), *Studies in Philosophy*, (ed.) Daniel S. Robinson (London: G. Allen & Unwin).
Hogg, A.G. (1947), *The Christian Message to the Hindu* [Duff Missionary Lectures, 1945] (London: SCM Press).
Howison, George Holmes (1905), *The Limits of Evolution: and other essays illustrating the metaphysical theory of personal idealism* (London: Macmillan, 1901; 2d ed. rev. and enl.).
Irving, John A. (1951), "Philosophical Trends in Canada between 1850 and 1950", *Philosophy and Phenomenological Research*, 12, pp. 224–45.
Joad, C.E.M. (1933), *Counter Attack from the East: The Philosophy of Radhakrishnan* (London: Allen and Unwin).
Kabir, Humayun (1952), "Radhakrishnan's Political Philosophy", in Paul Arthur Schilpp (ed.), *The Philosophy of Sarvepalli Radhakrishnan* (New York: Tudor), pp. 357–75.
Kalapati Joshua (2002), "Radhakrishnan, A.G. Hogg, and Hindu-Christian Apologetics", *Philosophy, Culture, and Traditions*, 1, pp. 11–26.
Kolbe, Frederick C. (1928), *A Catholic View of Holism* (London, Macmillan).
Kathrada, Ahmad M. (2004), *Memoirs* (Johannesburg: Zebra Press).
Lawande, G.N. (1938–39), "A Defence of Political Idealism", *Journal of the University of Bombay*, 7, pp. 168–187.
Lawande, G.N. (1943), *The Problem of Universals, a Metaphysical Essay* (Bombay: New Book Company).
Lord, Arthur Ritchie (2006a) *Foundational Problems in Philosophy*, (eds.) Errol E. Harris and William Sweet (Lewiston, NY: Mellen Press).
Lord, Arthur Ritchie (2006b), *The History of Philosophy from Descartes to Hegel*, (eds.) Errol E. Harris and William Sweet (Lewiston, NY: Mellen Press).
MacCrone, I.D. (1945), "Introduction", *Race and reason. Being mainly a selection of contributions to the race problem in South Africa*, ed. with a memoir by I.D. MacCrone (Johannesburg: Witwatersrand University Press, Africa).
MacIver, R.M. (1969), *Politics and Society*, (ed.) David Spitz (New York: Atherton Press).
Mackenzie, J.S. (1894), *A Manual of Ethics* (Glasgow: Maclehose).
McKenzie, John (1922), *Hindu ethics: a historical and critical essay* (London: H. Milford, Oxford University Press).
McKillop, Alexander Brian (1976), *A Disciplined Intelligence: Intellectual Inquiry and the Moral Imperative in Anglo-Canadian Thought, 1850–1890* (Kingston: Microfilm Books).
Malan, Gabriel Hercules (1916), *An Absolute Logical Criterion*. Thesis (D.Phil.), Glasgow University.
Miller, E. M. (1929–30), "The Beginnings of Philosophy in Australia and the Work of Henry Laurie", Part 1, *Australasian Association of Psychology and Philosophy*, Vol VII, pp. 241–51; Part 2, Vol VIII, pp. 1–22.
Morrow, John (1984), "Liberalism and British Idealist Political Philosophy: A Reassessment", *History of Political Thought*, 5, pp. 91–108.
Murray, Andrew Howson (1924), *Die plek van die Baster in die Unie van Suid-Afrika*, [The Place of the Half-caste in the Union of South Africa], University of Cape Town archives.
Narasimham, Potaraju (1912) [under the pseudonym of Homo Leone], "The Vedantic Absolute", *Mind*, 21, pp. 62–78.
Narasimham, Potaraju (1915),"The Vedantic Good", *Mind*, 24, pp. 37–59.
Narasimham, Potaraju (1941), "The Individual in Progress" and "The Quest After Perfection" [Miller Lectures at University of Madras (1939–40)], *Journal of Madras University*, 12, Pt. 1, pp. 1–32.
Nash, Andrew (1985), *Colonialism and Philosophy: RF Alfred Hoernlé in South Africa, 1908–11*, MA thesis (Political Science), University of Stellenbosch.
Nash, Andrew (1997), "How Kierkegaard came to Stellenbosch : the transformation of the Stellenbosch philosophical tradition, 1947–1950", *South African Journal of Philosophy*, 16, pp. 129–39.
Paul, Leslie (1953), *The English Philosophers* (London: Faber and Faber).

Radhakrishnan, Sarvepalli (1908a), *The Ethics of the Vedanta and Its Metaphysical Presuppositions* [MA thesis] (Madras: The Guardian Press).
Radhakrishnan, Sarvepalli (1908b), "Karma and Free Will", *Modern Review*, 3, pp. 424–8.
Radhakrishnan, Sarvepalli (1908c), "Indian Philosophy: the Vedas and the Six Systems", *The Madras Christian College Magazine*, 3 (New Series), pp. 22–35.
Radhakrishnan, Sarvepalli (1910a), "Egoism and Altruism: The Vedanta Solution", *East and West* (Bombay), 9, pp. 626–30.
Radhakrishnan, Sarvepalli (1910b), "'Nature' and 'Convention' in Greek Ethics", *Calcutta Review*, 130, pp. 9–23.
Radhakrishnan, Sarvepalli (1911), "The Ethics of the Bhagavadgita and Kant", *The International Journal of Ethics*, 21, pp. 465–75.
Radhakrishnan, Sarvepalli (1914a), "The Ethics of the Vedanta", *The International Journal of Ethics*, 24, pp. 168–83.
Radhakrishnan, Sarvepalli (1914b), "The Vedanta Philosophy and the Doctrine of Maya", *The International Journal of Ethics*, 24, pp. 431–51.
Radhakrishnan, Sarvepalli (1916a), "Religion and Life", *The International Journal of Ethics*, 27, pp. 91–106.
Radhakrishnan, Sarvepalli (1916b), "The Vedantic Approach to Reality", *The Monist*, 26, pp. 200–31.
Radhakrishnan, Sarvepalli (1918), "James Ward's Pluralistic Theism", *The Indian Philosophical Review*, 2, pp. 97–118; pp. 210–32.
Radhakrishnan, Sarvepalli (1920), *The Reign of Religion in Contemporary Philosophy* (London: Macmillan).
Radhakrishnan, Sarvepalli (1932), *An Idealist View of Life* (London: Allen and Unwin).
Radhakrishnan, Sarvepalli (1937), "My Search For Truth", in Vergilius Ferm (ed.), *Religion in Transition* (London: George Allen & Unwin), pp. 11–59.
Radhakrishnan, Sarvepalli (1940), *Eastern Religions and Western Thought* (2nd ed, New York: Oxford University Press).
Radhakrishnan, Sarvepalli (1944), *Education, Politics and War* (International Book Service).
Radhakrishnan, Sarvepalli (1948), *Religion and Society*, 2nd ed. (London: George Allen & Unwin).
Radhakrishnan, Sarvepalli (1952a), "The Spirit in Man", in S. Radhakrishnan and J.H. Muirhead (eds.), *Contemporary Indian Philosophy*, 2nd ed. (London: Allen and Unwin), pp. 465–505.
Radhakrishnan, Sarvepalli (1952b), "The Religion of the Spirit and the World's Need (Fragments of a Confession)", in Paul Arthur Schilpp (ed.), *The Philosophy of Sarvepalli Radhakrishnan* (New York: Tudor), pp. 3–82.
Radhakrishnan, Sarvepalli (1961), *The Hindu View of Life* (1927; Upton Lectures at Manchester College, 1926) (London: George Allen & Unwin).
Raman, N.S.S. (2001), "Reincarnation and Personal Immortality: The Circle and the End of History in Hinduism" in Peter Koslowski (ed.), *Progress, Apocalypse, and Completion of History and Life After Death of the Human Person in the World Religions* (Dordrecht: Kluwer).
Raju, P.T. (1942), "Indian Philosophy: A Survey (1917–42)", in R.N. Dandekar (ed.), *Progress of Indic Studies 1917–42* (Poona: The Bhandarkar Oriental Research Institute).
Raju, P.T. (1952), "The Inward Absolute and the Activism of the Finite Self", in Paul Arthur Schilpp (ed.), *The Philosophy of Sarvepalli Radhakrishnan* (New York: Tudor), pp. 509–35.
Raju, P.T. (1985), *Structural Depths of Indian Thought* (Albany, NY: State University of New York Press).
Raju, P.T. (1992), *Introduction to Comparative Philosophy* (New Delhi: Motilal Banarsidass).
Reitan, Richard (2000), "The Emergence of Ethics as an Academic Discipline in 1880s Japan", paper delivered at the Asian Studies Conference, 2000.
Roy, A. T. (1963), "Confucianism and Social Change", *The Chung Chi Journal* [Chinese University of Hong Kong], 3, pp. 88–104.
Seal, B.N. (1936), *The Quest Eternal* (London; New York: H. Milford, Oxford University Press).
Seth, James (1894), *A Study of Ethical Principles* (Edinburgh/London: Blackwood).
Shah, A.B. (1973), "The Indian Academic Profession", *Minerva*, 11, pp. 137–9.
Sharma, I.C. (1965), *Ethical Philosophies of India* (New York: Harper Torchbooks).

Sharpe, Eric J. (1997), *Alfred George Hogg 1875–1954: an intellectual biography* (Madras: Christian Literature Society).
Shigeru, Yukiyasu (1970), "The Backgrounds of the Birth of Green's Prolegomena to Ethics", *The Bulletin of the Okayama College of Science* [Okayama University of Science], 6, pp. 13–27.
Skinner, R. (2005), "Christian Reconstruction, Secular Politics: Michael Scott and the Campaign for Right and Justice, 1943–1945", in S. Dubow and A. Jeeves (eds), *South Africa's 1940s: Worlds of Possibilities* (Cape Town: Double Storey), pp. 246–66.
Smuts, Jan Christiaan (1926), *Holism and Evolution* (London: The Macmillan Company; 3rd ed., 1936).
Suda, Jyoti Prasad (1966), *Main Currents of Social & Political Thought in Modern India: v. 3 The socialist, democratic and communal traditions* (Meerut: Jai Prakash Nath).
Sullivan, Kevin (2000), "Radhakrishnan's Concept of Universal Liberation", in William Sweet (ed.), *Idealism, Metaphysics, and Community* (Aldershot, UK: Ashgate), pp. 189–203.
Sweet, William (2005a), "A.R. Lord and Later British Idealist Political Philosophy", *British Journal of Politics & International Relations*, 7, pp. 48–66.
Sweet, William (2005b), "R.F.A. Hoernlé", *Dictionary of Twentieth Century British Philosophers*, ed. Stuart Brown, (Bristol, UK: Thoemmes Press), vol. 1, pp. 434–8; reprinted in Sweet (2010).
Sweet, William (2006), "R.F.A. Hoernlé" and "A.F.R. Hoernlé", *Dictionary of National Biography* (Oxford: Oxford University Press).
Sweet, William (2007a), "R.F.A. Hoernlé", in Edward Craig (ed.), *Routledge Encyclopedia of Philosophy*, (London: Routledge) www.rep.routledge.com/
Sweet, William (2007b), "Andrew Howson Murray", in Edward Craig (ed.), *Routledge Encyclopedia of Philosophy* (London: Routledge) www.rep.routledge.com/
Sweet, William (ed.) (2010), *Biographical Encyclopedia of British Idealism* (London: Continuum).
Urquhart, W.S. (1919), *Pantheism and the Value of Life, With Special Reference to Indian Philosophy* [based on D.Phil. thesis, Aberdeen] (London: Epworth Press).
Urquhart, W.S. (1928), *The Vedanta and Modern Thought* (London: Oxford University Press).
Wadia, A.R. (1924), "Review of McKenzie's *Hindu Ethics*", *The Indian Review*, pp. 359ff.
Wadia, A.R. (1952), "The Social Philosophy of Radhakrishnan", in Paul Arthur Schilpp (ed.), *The Philosophy of Sarvepalli Radhakrishnan* (New York: Tudor), pp 755–85.
Weblin, Mark (2010), "Idealism in Australia and New Zealand", in William Sweet (ed.), *Biographical Encyclopedia of British Idealism* (London: Continuum).
Widgery, Alban (1961), *A Philosopher's Pilgrimage* (London: George Allen & Unwin).

Archival Materials

N.J. Brümmer papers, University of Stellenbosch library, Stellenbosch, South Africa.
R.F.A. Hoernlé papers, University of Witwatersrand archives, Johannesberg, South Africa.
Arthur Ritchie Lord papers, Cory Library, Rhodes University, Grahamstown, South Africa.
G.H.T. Malan materials, University of Cape Town Library Archives, Cape Town, South Africa.
University of Bombay, examination papers, 1905; 1926.
University of Bombay, calendar, 1912–3; 1916–7; 1920–1; 1921–2; 1922–3; 1925–6; 1926–7, 1932, 1937.
University of Calcutta, calendar, 1864–5; 1884–5; 1893; 1899; 1900; 1902; 1911; 1913; 1915; 1918; 1920; 1926; 1930; 1935; 1940.
University of Madras, calendar, 1880-1; 1884-5; 1889–90; 1901-2; 1906-7; 1907-8; 1908-9; 1910; 1912; 1913; 1915; 1916; 1919; 1923; 1927-8; 1933-4; 1939-40; 1951-2.

Index

Absolute: 2, 3, 8, 15, 17, 20, 22, 59, 105, 120, 143, 154, 161, 166, 184-186, 190-192, 195, 200-201, 285-286, 288, 295, 301, 303, 309, 313-319, 321-322, 325, 328
Alexander, S.: 242
Apperception 188-189
Aristotelian 4, 17, 32, 33, 40-45, 74, 87, 183-184, 188, 254
Aristotle 2, 5-6. 29, 31-32, 41-45, 48-50, 53, 66-67, 73, 87, 97, 121-122, 166, 187, 213, 231, 252, 267, 269, 295
Arnold, M. 96, 217
art 68, 141
associationism: 3
associationist: 24, 79
atomism 92, 205
atomistic: 35, 87, 117, 129-130, 176, 179, 181, 192, 215

Bain, A. 3, 90, 102-103, 306
beauty 8, 97, 99, 113, 122-124, 126-127, 130, 133, 141, 259
Bentham 3, 24, 66, 79, 90, 138, 275
Bergson 162, 210, 311, 321
Berkeley 3, 64, 210, 284
Berlin (University) 59
Biology 69, 73, 77, 140, 190
Boodin, J. E. 295, 301, 329
Bosanquet 2, 3, 7-9, 13, 16, 18, 21-23, 25-30, 82, 84-85, 87, 108, 110-135, 180, 183-186, 191-192, 194, 196, 207-208, 211, 254-255, 268, 270, 291-295, 300-301, 303, 308, 311, 313-315, 317, 321, 326-328
Boucher, D. 8-9, 28-29, 65, 71, 84, 121, 134, 138, 140-141, 150-151, 176, 210, 217-218, 224, 230, 232, 249, 289, 327
Bradley, A. C. 49
Bradley, F.H. 1, 2-9, 16, 21-23, 25, 28-30, 34, 39-40, 62, -64, 84, 87-111, 113, 116, 122, 134-135, 161, 205, 207-208, 211, 287, 291-292, 306, 321, 327
Bradley, James 27-28, 91, 109-110, 208, 287

Broad, C.D. 168, 173-174

Caesar 168, 171
Caird, E. 3-5, 8, 15, 18, 21, 23-24, 26, 29, 42, 51-55, 57-65, 115, 134, 137, 140, 209-211, 217, 224, 231, 282, 292, 294, 321
Cambridge 13, 153-154, 165, 173, 224, 251, 291, 305, 327
Cambridge Platonists: 3
Canada 2, 14-15, 269, 270, 276, 283-286, 289
Cause 263
Character 4, 7-9, 12-13, 17-18, 19, 20-22, 24, 27, 33, 43-44, 48, 50, 83, 97, 102, 104, 105, 112, 115-116, 128, 133, 138, 143-149, 172, 184, 188-190, 193, 197, 199, 233, 238, 245, 247-248, 259, 265, 270-271, 276, 314-315, 326
Charity Organisation Society (COS) 24, 112
Child 91, 102-103, 107, 126, 145-146, 148-150
Children: 102-103, 107, 114, 137, 143, 146, 210, 221
China 289
Christian 105, 113-115, 119, 127, 132, 166, 175-178, 205, 282, 305-306, 310,
Christianity 56, 114-116, 120, 122, 127, 187, 195, 313
Church 24, 282, 284, 287, 293-294, 300, 305
Citizen 38, 45, 52, 66, 69-70, 73, 75, 78-80, 82-84, 131, 197, 215-216, 220-221, 257, 278-280, 301-302
Citizenry 216
Citizenship 32, 34, 44-47, 66, 84, 115, 128, 131, 133, 194, 300
class 76, 98, 126, 129, 139, 161, 234, 271, 277, 281
coherence 5, 8, 11, 18-19, 21, 72, 74, 79, 82, 106, 112, 117, 119, 122, 134, 261, 272, 298, 301, 304, 317
Coleridge, S. 4, 29, 142, 178

Collingwood, R.G. 3, 12-13, 22, 26, 29-30, 110, 135, 217, 233-243, 245-249
Collini, S. 27, 147, 326
Community 4, 7, 9-12, 14-20, 23-24, 27, 32-33, 35, 37-40, 44-46, 49, 65-66, 74-76, 78, 81, 84, 90-92, 94-95, 98, 105, 121, 125, 128, 133, 149, 154, 156, 166, 172, 194, 196, 204, 215, 222, 228, 259, 270-281, 285-287, 289-291, 296-299, 301-305, 309, 313-317, 321-322, 324-325
Communitarian 31-32, 35-36, 39, 44-45
compulsion 78, 82, 125, 233, 271, 286
Comte, A. 4-5, 51, 53-58, 64, 284, 288
concrete universal 6, 18, 92, 184, 194, 206
Correspondence 155, 162
Creative 97, 195, 220-221, 244, 295
Croce, B. 122-123
Crossley, D. 1, 29, 87, 91-92, 100, 106-109
Cudworth..154, 165-166, 173
Cunningham G.W. 14

Dancy, J. 237, 247, 249
Darwin 21, 65-66, 74, 84, 140, 145-146, 150-151, 282
democracy 194, 202-203, 211, 295, 320, 328
Dewey 28
duty / duties 6, 8, 11-13, 17-19, 22, 24-25, 27, 29, 36, 52, 60, 62, 75-76, 78. 84, 87, 90, 92-99, 107, 113, 115, 128-129, 131-133, 139-140, 145, 148, 183, 194, 202-203, 210-211, 216, 221-223, 226-228, 233, 236-249, 255-256, 270, 274, 277-279, 281, 287, 290, 302, 310, 312, 318-321, 325
Dworkin 214, 222, 230

Emmet, D. 12
equality 16, 33, 67, 71, 80-81, 84, 172-173, 196, 296, 302, 318, 320
eudaimonism 10, 187
evolution 3, 7, 15, 21, 52-53, 58, 61, 63-70, 74, 80, 83, 94, 107, 119-120, 126, 140, 143-147, 176, 183, 187, 253, 257, 261, 267, 273, 282, 317, 321

family 24, 49, 58, 88, 92, 121, 126, 194, 197, 215, 276
feeling 18, 56, 58-59, 61, 90-92, 100-103, 106, 114, 117, 155, 187, 200, 221-222, 238, 259, 267, 273-274, 316
freedom 8, 10, 15, 19, 24, 46, 60, 66, 73, 80-82, 103-104, 118-119, 126, 130-131, 142-143, 149, 160, 172, 177, 181, 187-189, 191, 197-200, 202, 204, 206, 220, 238, 258, 266-267, 270, 272, 275-276. 279, 281, 287, 295-296, 300, 302, 312-313, 316, 320
function 7, 23, 46-47, 56, 62, 76, 78, 88, 92, 101, 114, 117, 126, 130, 169, 179, 214, 219, 280, 307, 314, 318

Gaus, G. 28, 34, 49, 83-84, 123, 125, 134-135, 208, 268, 327
general will 8, 37, 179, 194, 303
Gentile 122-123
Gifford (lectures)..51_53, 58, 111-112, 137, 186, 192, 269, 284
Ginsberg, M. 27
Green, T.H. 1, 3-7, 10-11, 23-25, 28-50, 65-67, 83-84, 87, 115,125, 134-135, 137, 140, 180, 183, 209-211, 213-215, 217-218,231, 270, 282,291, 298, 294, 309, 311, 314, 321, 326-328
Group 47, 121,271, 274, 281, 299, 308

Haldane, R.B. 24, 150-151, 211, 307, 311, 327
Haldar, H. 307-309, 328
Harris, E. 12, 29, 50, 217, 268, 293, 329
Hart, H.L.A. None
Hedonic 21, 79, 80
Hedonism/ Hedonist/Hedonistic:4, 15, 19, 21, 47, 90, 100-103, 105-107, 187, 189, 269, 273-275
Hegel, G.W.F. 1, 4, 8, 17-18, 21, 23, 28-29, 31-32, 51, 58-59, 63-66, 74,84, 122, 124, 137-139, 150, 154,166-167, 178, 180, 183, 190, 198, 200-201, 205, 209, 217,220-221, 224, 230-231, 253, 270, 292, 307-308, 321, 329
Hegelian 21, 23,27, 30, 32, 36, 40-41, 44, 53-54, 57, 63-64, 71, 83-84,87, 90, 100, 105, 112-113, 140, 142, 144, 150, 161, 173, 177, 180. 182, 185, 191, 205, 207, 228, 230, 253, 257, 264, 283, 292-293, 311, 326
Hetherington 11-12, 29, 209-210, 213, 215, 218-224, 226, 230-231,
Hill, J. 2, 29
Hindrance: 25
History 2, 12-13, 22, 24, 27, 41, 53, 67, 69, 77, 83, 90, 93-94, 120, 125, 142, 164, 166, 168, 176-177, 180, 190, 192, 194, 201, 237, 245, 251-252, 257, 263-264, 274-275, 279, 284, 292, 306, 308-309, 330
Hobbes, T. 42, 61, 63, 206
Hobhouse, L.T. 27, 33, 47, 50, 135, 139, 211, 326, 328
Hobson, J. 27, 326, 328
Hoernlé, R.F.A. 14, 16, 290, 294-304, 307, 323,326, 328-329, 331
Holism 14, 29, 50, 92-93, 107, 247, 253-254, 256-257, 261-262, 291
Hume, D. 3, 63, 270
Huxley, T. 67, 126, 150, 282

Identity 183, 191, 270, 273, 314
India 2, 12, 14, 16, 289-290, 294, 304-305, 307-312, 320, 323-326
Induction 244
Intuition 94, 243-244, 247, 274-275, 278, 319, 322, 327

Inference 71, 191, 244

James, William 23, 27, 30, 114, 134, 176, 201
Japan 23, 289
Jesus 61, 120, 127, 143, 149–150
Joachim, H. 292–293
Joad, C.E.M. 12, 217, 322, 329
Jones, (Sir) H. 3, 7–9, 24, 137–144. 147–151, 164, 209–212, 218–219, 224, 230–231, 292, 321, 326–328,
Jowett, B. 3–4, 6, 52
Justification 34, 69, 105, 127, 229, 243, 271, 282, 303
Justice 23–24, 32–34, 38, 41, 44, 46–49, 59, 98, 138, 183, 187, 196–197, 207, 215, 217, 222, 228, 275, 291, 295, 300, 315

Kant, I. 2, 4, 10, 23, 30–31, 35–41, 43–44, 49–52, 63–64, 66–67, 92, 138, 177–178, 182, 188–189, 193, 198–202, 209, 217, 226, 237, 283–284, 307–308, 312, 321, 330
Kingdom of God 8, 18, 28, 111, 112–114, 127–129, 133, 173, 318, 321

Labour Party 139
Laissez faire 83
Laski, H. 27, 252
Library/ies: 87, 165, 210, 292–293
Locke, J. 51, 67, 74, 166, 271
Logic 1, 51, 57, 63, 77, 90, 111–112, 130, 176–177, 180, 198, 206, 213, 258–259, 261, 290, 293–295, 306–308, 311
Love 9, 34, 42, 56–57, 93, 97, 127–129, 132, 143, 153, 155–159, 165–167, 171–172, 185, 196, 267, 286, 297
Lord, A.R. 3, 14, 18, 24, 29, 239, 241, 292–293, 324, 329, 331
Lord, T. 240, 241, 249
Lotze, H. 139, 150, 178, 184, 199, 294

Mabbott, J.D. 257, 268,
Maturity 129
MacIntyre, A. 50, 108, 110
MacIver, R.M. 27, 301, 326, 392
Mackenzie, J. 2–3, 11–12, 29, 74, 84, 89, 108, 110, 209–213, 216, 218–219, 223–231, 306, 308, 311, 329
Mander, W. 29, 135, 333
Manser, A. 30, 109, 110
Marx, K. 59–60, 64, 140, 194, 207–208
Martineau, J. 139, 178, 186, 201–202, 311
McTaggart, J.M.E. 3, 5, 9, 13, 21, 110, 153–174, 176, 211, 224, 309, 311, 321, 327
Metz, R 138, 151, 176
Mill, J. 3, 24, 50, 53–55, 64, 79, 87, 90–91, 98, 102, 109–110, 198, 274, 288
Milne, A.J.M. 1, 90, 110
Morefield, J. 30, 69, 83–84
Moore, G.E. 29, 154, 173, 211, 239–243, 327

Monster 213
Morality (ideal) 6, 62, 88, 98–100, 105, 107, 318
Morrow, John 50, 154, 255, 326, 329
Muirhead, J.H. 1–3, 7, 11–12, 21–22, 28, 30, 87, 108, 110, 134, 209–219, 223–226, 229–232, 294, 311, 325, 328, 330
Murder 216

nation state 280
Nettleship, R.M. 3, 49, 135, 210
Nicholson, P. 29–30, 35, 48, 50, 65, 84, 87, 100, 105, 110, 121, 205, 209, 232
Nisus 8, 21, 138, 301, 317

Oakeshott 12–14, 21, 29, 235, 249, 251–268
obligation 18, 22, 24, 29, 38, 40–41, 45–47, 50, 67, 78, 81, 129, 132, 148, 151, 200, 202–204, 213, 221, 223, 227, 237–238, 240–242, 248, 255, 271, 294, 297, 301–302, 308, 315, 318, 325
organism 8, 69–70, 76–78, 83, 88–90, 94–95, 99, 105–106, 110, 126, 132, 144–145, 148
organicism / organicist 6, 65–66, 68–69, 76–78, 84, 92, 179

Particularism 12, 26, 189, 233, 236, 246–248
Perfectionism 1, 258
Plato 1, 2, 6, 30, 52. 66–67, 69, 76, 79, 85, 121–124, 127, 134, 168, 187, 203, 295, 321
Platonic 17, 71, 79, 83, 105, 110, 113, 127, 189, 190
Platonism 190
Pleasure 18–19, 21–22, 42. 48, 79, 91, 100–104, 106, 155, 166, 203, 215–216, 274–276, 278, 386
Pluralism/ist 14–17, 28, 31, 184, 257, 284, 289, 299–300, 303, 323–324
Plurality 198, 201, 241–242, 271, 280, 324
Postulates 140, 142, 199, 254
Poverty 68, 149, 185, 220
Pragmatism 23, 176
Prichard, H.A. 1, 29, 240–242, 249
Pringle-Pattison, A. Seth 3, 9–10, 52, 110, 114, 139–140, 175–178, 181–187, 189–190, 192, 195–197, 201, 205, 207–208, 291, 306, 309, 311
Process 4, 6, 8, 18, 21, 23, 40–41. 51–54, 57, 62–63, 68–69, 72–73, 76, 83, 91, 93, 95, 100, 103, 112, 121, 123–126, 128, 130–133, 140–141, 143–145, 148, 160–161, 182–183, 186, 195, 223, 226, 236, 240, 242–244, 248, 258, 266, 262, 270, 273, 275–276, 279, 285, 299, 317–318, 323
Profitability 225
Progress 6, 55, 67–69, 74, 79–80, 83, 116, 132, 138, 194, 219, 221–222, 283, 301, 327
Property 7, 45, 75, 81, 126, 158–161, 207, 212, 215–216, 240, 273, 278, 281

Prudential 75
psychology 5-6, 12, 63, 79, 89, 100, 102, 106, 120, 199, 213, 291-292, 295, 309, 329
punishment 46, 48, 78, 107-108, 114, 228-229

Rashdall, H. 10, 114, 176, 187, 311
Rawls, J. 34, 50,
real will 8, 118, 121, 126, 128-130, 132, 301
realism 140, 181, 184, 189, 193, 239, 242-243
realist 154, 242-243
rebellion 197, 217, 224
recognition 13-14, 17, 19, 27, 35, 38, 40, 47, 67, 70, 74-75, 84, 106, 117-118, 121, 127, 198, 202, 211, 216, 234, 267, 275, 277, 280, 289, 300, 313, 315, 318, 328
relations 6, 8-9, 20, 24, 27, 34-35, 39-40, 43, 45, 62, 68, 70, 75, 90-91, 96, 124, 129, 144, 147-148, 153, 158-161, 165, 169, 171-172, 177, 179, 195, 212, 214-215, 220, 222, 225, 252, 256, 272, 275, 279-280, 296, 315
relativism 63, 93, 96, 107, 297-298, 325
religion 4-9, 15, 23, 28, 51-53, 56-64, 77, 88, 100, 105-107, 111-123, 126-128, 130, 132-133, 140-142, 165, 176-177, 183, 201-202, 214, 225, 269-270, 281-284, 286, 287, 294, 296, 309-311, 313-314, 318-322
Rescher, N. 12, 218
Rights 1, 22, 24, 27, 31-32, 35, 38, 40-41, 44-49, 66, 74-76, 80-81, 128-129, 153-154, 179-180, 192, 197, 203, 210, 212, 214, 222-223, 225-228, 275-276, 287, 280-281, 298, 326
Ritchie, D.G. 3, 6-7, 10, 14, 21, 30, 44, 50, 65-85, 137, 176, 290, 307, 329, 331
Robinson 64, 239-240, 244, 249, 329
Ross, W. 17, 28, 30, 87, 110, 249
Rousseau, J-J 74, 179, 202-203
Royce, J. 14, 284, 309
Rule 8, 13, 18, 25-26, 37, 44, 44-45, 84, 93-94, 107, 154, 163-164, 168, 187, 196, 199, 211, 233, 235-238, 240-241, 244, 246-248, 258, 260-262, 266-267, 275, 277, 314-318
Russell, B. 154, 157, 169, 173, 210-211, 311, 326-327

Sabine, G. 87, 110
Salvation 122, 125, 127, 130-131, 133, 282
Schelling 78, 183, 185, 190, 198, 201, 208
Science 6, 10-11, 23, 41, 54-57, 62-63, 67, 70, 72-74, 78, 97-98, 140-142, 177, 198, 212-214, 226, 242-243, 252, 257, 270, 272, 29, 282-284, 291, 300, 302, 307, 313, 316
Science (ethical) 226
Science (moral) 310
Scruton, R. 33, 50, 205
self-realisation / self-realization 4-8, 10-11,15-19, 23, 26, 32-34, 38, 43-44, 46, 48-49, 62, 65-66, 69, 76, 78, 80, 82, 84, 87-89, 93-94, 96-97, 99, 104, 107, 112-113, 115-117, 119, 121, 123, 126-133, 147, 187-188, 192-193, 226, 272, 301-302, 317, 322
Seth (Andrew) - see Pringle-Pattison
Seth (James) 2, 10, 12, 30, 176-177, 182, 187-190, 193-194, 196-201, 203, 205, 207-208, 306, 308, 311, 330
University Settlement House 24
Sittlichkeit 100
Slave / Slavery 142, 227, 287
Smith, J.A. 134, 159, 164, 292-294
Smith, Quentin, 167, 174
social contract 74, 203, 271, 277
social ontology 41, 84, 304
socialism 7, 69, 139, 144-145, 193-194, 207, 277
soul 112, 119, 121, 123-124, 126-127, 130, 142, 147, 177, 184-187, 189-190, 198, 201, 203, 282, 297, 300, 303
Spencer, H. 3, 30, 50, 67-68, 74, 138-140, 144-146, 149-151, 224, 282, 288, 311, 321,
Spinoza 166, 200
Sprigge, T.L.S. 12, 23, 30, 105, 110, 114, 135, 218
St. Paul 120, 125, 127, 252
Stout, G. F. 229
station 6, 8, 22, 25, 87-88, 91-99, 107, 113, 128-129, 131, 133, 256, 269, 279, 302-303, 318-319, 325
stupidity 138-139
Supernatural 18, 54-55, 113-114, 120, 124, 198
Sweet, W. 1, 7, 16, 23, 28-30, 65, 76, 82, 84-85, 89, 106, 110-111, 114-115, 125, 128, 133-135, 165, 176, 192, 208, 210, 224, 232, 268, 289, 291-294, 305-306, 308, 310, 327, 329, 331
Synoptic 16, 55, 296, 299-300, 326, 328

Taylor, Charles 31-32, 45-46, 50, 176, 311
teleological 8, 12, 14, 19-20, 23, 36, 94, 104, 253-255, 257, 261, 264, 267, 301, 317, 325
teleology 4-7, 14, 19, 23, 65, 107, 253-254, 256, 258, 262
Thomas, G. 1, 30
Tide 90
Time 9, 59, 154-155, 157, 161, 168-171, 182, 184, 192, 201, 214, 283, 285
Transcendence 123, 143, 196, 204, 206, 284, 301
Transcendence (Self) 8, 26, 112-113, 116-117, 121, 126, 128-130, 301
Tyler, C. 1, 4, 36, 192, 208

Unemployment 53
Unity 2, 8-10, 13, 16, 18-19, 58-59, 61, 66, 70-73, 87-88, 91, 104, 115, 122, 127, 130,

132–133, 139–144, 147–148, 155, 183,
187–189, 193, 195, 201, 204, 219, 251–252,
254–257, 262, 264–265, 267, 270, 279, 283,
313, 316–318, 321, 324, 326
Utilitarianism 1, 6, 15, 24–25, 47, 63, 66–67,
79–80, 82, 175, 179, 187, 203, 215, 233, 269,
273, 275, 287, 332

Vincent, A. 23, 28, 30, 71, 76, 85, 88, 105,
110, 141, 147, 150–151,176, 218, 230

Wallace, W. 3, 64
Walsh 1, 19, 23, 30, 63–64
war 24, 137, 140, 153, 173, 204, 217, 222, 269,
291–292, 326
Ward, J. 9, 286, 299, 317
Watson, J. 2, 14–15, 21, 23, 30, 137, 217, 232,
269–288, 321
Webb, S and B 27
Webb, C.C.J. 3, 10, 114, 135, 176, 187,
194–196, 208, 309
Webb (don't know) 27, 182, 192, 201–205
Wilson, C.R. 307
Wilson College 305